ICS

RUSSIAN THINKERS

ISAIAH BERLIN was born in Riga, now capital of Latvia, in 1909. When he was six, his family moved to Russia; there in 1917, in Petrograd, he witnessed both Revolutions – Social Democratic and Bolshevik. In 1921 his family came to England, and he was educated at St Paul's School and Corpus Christi College, Oxford. At Oxford he was a Fellow of All Souls, a Fellow of New College, Professor of Social and Political Theory and founding President of Wolfson College. He died in 1997.

Berlin's most acclaimed contributions to Russian studies are to be found in this volume. His superb translations of Turgenev's *First Love* and *A Month in the Country* are also available in Penguin Classics. Among his many other publications are *Karl Marx* (1939; 4th ed. 1978), *Concepts and Categories* (1978), *Against the Current* (1979), *Personal Impressions* (1980; 2nd ed. 1998), *The Crooked Timber of Humanity* (1990), *The Sense of Reality* (1996), *The Proper Study of Mankind* (1997), *The Roots of Romanticism* (1999), *The Power of Ideas* (2000), *Three Critics of the Enlightenment* (2000), *Freedom and Its Betrayal* (2002), *Liberty* (2002), *The Soviet Mind* (2004) and *Political Ideas in the Romantic Age* (2006). *Russian Thinkers* was first published as a collection in 1978, and was the initial inspiration for Tom Stoppard's trilogy of plays *The Coast of Utopia* (2002).

HENRY HARDY, in addition to co-editing this volume, has edited fourteen other books by Berlin (including all but the first of those listed above), and *The Proper Study of Mankind* (co-edited with Roger Hausheer), an anthology drawn from previous volumes. From 1977 to 1990 he was an editor at Oxford University Press. He is now a Fellow of Wolfson College, Oxford, where he is working on an edition of Berlin's letters whose first volume appeared in 2004.

AILEEN KELLY, introducer and co-editor of this volume, received her D.Phil. in Russian Studies from Oxford and is now a Reader in Slavonic Studies at Cambridge University and a Fellow of King's College. She is the author of *Mikhail Bakunin: A Study in the*

Psychology and Politics of Utopianism (1982), *Toward Another Shore: Russian Thinkers between Necessity and Chance* (1998) and *Views from the Other Shore: Essays on Herzen, Chekhov, and Bakhtin* (1999).

For further information about Isaiah Berlin visit
http://berlin.wolf.ox.ac.uk/

2008

10/2 —   xxiii — 92 Introduction —

10/16 —   93 — 169

10/30 —   170 — 272

11/13 —   273 — 352

11/27 — ~~Holiday~~

ISAIAH BERLIN

Russian Thinkers

Edited by HENRY HARDY *and* AILEEN KELLY
With an Introduction by AILEEN KELLY

SECOND EDITION

Revised by HENRY HARDY
Glossary by JASON FERRELL

PENGUIN BOOKS

PENGUIN CLASSICS

Published by the Penguin Group
Penguin Books Ltd, 80 Strand, London WC2R ORL, England
Penguin Group (USA) Inc., 375 Hudson Street, New York, New York 10014, USA
Penguin Group (Canada), 90 Eglinton Avenue East, Suite 700, Toronto, Ontario, Canada M4P 2Y3
(a division of Pearson Penguin Canada Inc.)
Penguin Ireland, 25 St Stephen's Green, Dublin 2, Ireland
(a division of Penguin Books Ltd)
Penguin Group (Australia), 250 Camberwell Road, Camberwell, Victoria 3124, Australia
(a division of Pearson Australia Group Pty Ltd)
Penguin Books India Pvt Ltd, 11 Community Centre, Panchsheel Park, New Delhi – 110 017, India
Penguin Group (NZ), 67 Apollo Drive, Rosedale, North Shore 0632, New Zealand
(a division of Pearson New Zealand Ltd)
Penguin Books (South Africa) (Pty) Ltd, 24 Sturdee Avenue, Rosebank, Johannesburg 2196, South Africa

Penguin Books Ltd, Registered Offices: 80 Strand, London WC2R ORL, England

www.penguin.com

First published in Great Britain by The Hogarth Press Ltd 1978
First published in the United States of America by The Viking Press 1978
Published in Pelican Books 1979
Reprinted in Penguin Books 1994
This completely revised and reset edition published 2008

1

Copyright Isaiah Berlin 1948, 1951, 1953, 1955, 1956; © Isaiah Berlin 1960, 1961, 1972, 1978
'Herzen and Bakunin on Individual Liberty' copyright President and Fellows of Harvard College 1955
This selection and editorial matter © Henry Hardy 1978, 2008
Introduction © Aileen Kelly 1978, 1998
Glossary of Names © The Isaiah Berlin Literary Trust 2008
All rights reserved

Set in 10.25/12.25 pt PostScript Adobe Sabon
Typeset by Rowland Phototypesetting Ltd, Bury St Edmunds, Suffolk
Printed in England by Clays Ltd, St Ives plc

Посвящается Дереку Оффорду и Татьяне Поздняковой
sine quibus non

Contents

Author's preface

The essays collected in this volume, the first of four,[1] were written, or delivered as lectures, on various occasions over almost thirty years, and therefore possess less unity of theme than if they had been conceived in relation to one another. I am naturally most grateful to the editor of these collected papers, Dr Henry Hardy, for his conviction that they are worth exhuming, and for the meticulous and unremitting care with which he has seen to it that some of their blemishes, in particular inaccuracies, inconsistencies and obscurities, have been, so far as possible, eliminated. Naturally, I continue to be solely responsible for the shortcomings that remain.

I owe a great debt also to Dr Aileen Kelly for furnishing this volume with an introduction: in particular, for her deep and sympathetic understanding of the issues discussed and of my treatment of them. I am also most grateful to her for the great trouble to which, in the midst of her own work, she has gone in checking and, on occasion, emending, vague references and excessively free translations. Her steady advocacy has almost persuaded me that the preparation of this volume may have been worthy of so much intelligent and devoted labour. I can only hope that the result will prove to have justified the expenditure of her own and Dr Hardy's time and energy.

A number of these essays began life as lectures for general audiences, not read from a prepared text. The published versions were based on transcripts of the spoken words, as well as the notes for them, and, as I am well aware, they bear the marks of their origin in both their style and their structure.

1   [See xi below, note 2.]

The original texts remain substantially unaltered: no attempt has been made to revise them in the light of anything published subsequently on the history of Russian ideas in the nineteenth century, since nothing, so far as I know, has appeared in this (somewhat sparsely cultivated) field to cast serious doubt on the central theses of these essays. I may, however, be mistaken about this; if so, I should like to assure the reader that this is due to ignorance on my part rather than unshakeable confidence in the validity of my own opinions.

Indeed, the entire burden of these collected essays, so far as they can be said to display any single tendency, is distrust of all claims to the possession of incorrigible knowledge about issues of fact or principle in any sphere of human behaviour.

ISAIAH BERLIN

July 1977

Editorial preface

Henry Hardy

[. . .] a cumbrous editorial apparatus apparently, if hopelessly, designed to embalm the most effervescent of all contemporary historians [. . .] Nicholas Richardson[1]

This is one of four volumes in which, between the mid-1970s and 1980, I brought together, and prepared for reissue, the majority of the more substantial published essays by Isaiah Berlin that had not hitherto been made available in a collected form.[2] His many writings had previously been scattered, often in obscure places, most were out of print, and only half a dozen essays had previously been collected and reissued.[3] By making much more of his work readily accessible than before, these volumes revealed a quantity, a range and a depth of writing that surprised many readers, and their author's reputation was, as he himself generously recognised, markedly enhanced.

Since then I have edited twelve further volumes by Berlin, including a number that draw on previously unpublished material; some

1   Reviewing the first edition of *Russian Thinkers* in *New Society*, 19 January 1978, 142.
2   This volume was first published in London and New York in 1978. The other volumes are *Concepts and Categories: Philosophical Essays* (London, 1978; New York, 1979), *Against the Current: Essays in the History of Ideas* (London, 1979; New York, 1980) and *Personal Impressions* (London, 1980; New York, 1981; 2nd, enlarged, ed., London, 1998; Princeton, 2001).
3   *Four Essays on Liberty* (Oxford, 1969; New York, 1970), now incorporated in *Liberty* (Oxford and New York, 2002), and *Vico and Herder: Two Studies in the History of Ideas* (London and New York, 1976), now incorporated in *Three Critics of the Enlightenment* (London and Princeton, 2000). Other collections have appeared only in translation.

of these, mentioned below, have points of contact with the present volume. More of Berlin's *Nachlass* is posted in *The Isaiah Berlin Virtual Library* (the website of the Isaiah Berlin Literary Trust),[1] and here too items on Russian themes will be found.

Russian Thinkers comprises ten essays on nineteenth-century Russian literature and thought. Their previous publication details are as follows:

'Russia and 1848': *Slavonic Review* 26 (1948)

'The Hedgehog and the Fox': in a shorter form, as 'Lev Tolstoy's Historical Scepticism', *Oxford Slavonic Papers* 2 (1951); reprinted with additions under its present title (London, 1953: Weidenfeld and Nicolson; New York, 1953: Simon and Schuster)

'Herzen and Bakunin on Individual Liberty': in Ernest J. Simmons (ed.), *Continuity and Change in Russian and Soviet Thought* (Cambridge, Massachusetts, 1955: Harvard University Press)

'A Remarkable Decade', the Northcliffe Lectures for 1954, delivered at University College London, and broadcast later that year on the Third Programme of the BBC: as 'A Marvellous Decade' in *Encounter* 4 No 6 (June 1955), 5 No 11 (November 1955), 5 No 12 (December 1955) and 6 No 5 (May 1956)

'Russian Populism': as the introduction to Franco Venturi, *Roots of Revolution* (London, 1960: Weidenfeld and Nicolson; New York, 1960: Knopf); in *Encounter* 15 No 1 (July 1960)

'Tolstoy and Enlightenment', the PEN Hermon Ould Memorial Lecture for 1960: in *Encounter* 16 No 2 (February 1961); in *Mightier than the Sword* (London, 1964: Macmillan)

'Fathers and Children: Turgenev and the Liberal Predicament', the Romanes Lecture for 1970: Oxford, 1972: Clarendon Press; reprinted with corrections 1973; *New York Review of Books* (18 October, 1 and 15 November, 1973); as the introduction to Ivan Turgenev, *Fathers and Sons*, translated by Rosemary Edmonds (Harmondsworth, 1975: Penguin)

---

1   At <http://berlin.wolf.ox.ac.uk/>: see Catalogues, Unpublished work. This website also includes a continuously updated bibliography of Berlin's works.

I am grateful to the publishers concerned for allowing me to reprint these essays. A few passages – chiefly translations – were revised by Berlin for this volume: his versions, which characteristically refine their originals without misrepresenting their substance, were occasionally too free even by this unpedantic criterion. In addition, some overlaps between passages quoted in more than one essay were reduced by excision or substitution. Otherwise, apart from necessary corrections, and the addition of missing references in the footnoted essays, the texts were reprinted in the first edition of this book essentially in their original form. In particular, overlapping treatments of the same topics in what were originally independent essays, and remarks in the present tense about events current at the time of writing, were not altered. Moreover, 'A Remarkable Decade', 'Russian Populism' and 'Tolstoy and Enlightenment' were left without references, as they had originally appeared, partly because we were unable to find the sources of all the quotations they contain.

The same policy has been followed in this edition,[1] with one important exception. Since 1978, the sources of many more (though not quite all) of the unreferenced quotations have been tracked down, by myself and others. The resetting of the book for Penguin Classics has created the welcome opportunity for me to add this information, so that all the essays are now treated consistently. I shall be grateful to be told of any remaining sources that I have not yet unearthed,[2] though my guess is that some at any rate of the remaining unsourced 'quotations' are in fact closer to paraphrase, and in some cases, following Berlin's own practice for the first edition, I have removed quotation marks where the relationship of his renderings to his source is somewhat approximate.

Some critics have argued against adding footnotes to essays originally published without. I have quoted the opinion of Nicholas Richardson at the head of this preface; in another context Stefan Collini referred to 'a slightly bastardised state of [Berlin's] essays', observing that the provision of references 'threaten[s] to

1 So that references to the Soviet Union have been left in the present tense.
2 My email address is <henry.hardy@wolfson.ox.ac.uk>. I shall post any new information on the website mentioned above (xii, note 1).

domesticate what had been personal and stylish into appearing merely conventional and industrious'.[1] I have responded to these criticisms in Berlin's *The Roots of Romanticism*.[2] The main contrary consideration is that Berlin himself was thoroughly in favour of footnotes, deploying them himself in four of the essays included here; he would most probably have included them throughout if he had kept a more careful record of his sources for the essays that started life as lectures not destined for publication. Having spent more time than I care to remember looking for these sources, I also wish to spare others the need to repeat the process. So I make no apology for adding references throughout this edition, and only regret that this was not done thirty years ago. The references will enable scholars to follow Berlin's intellectual path in more detail, and they have also enabled me to eliminate numerous errors, both in the text and in the notes – Berlin's mention in his preface of 'vague references and excessively free translations' being something of an understatement.

I have also sought to make this edition a little more user-friendly in other ways. I have added in the notes, for the benefit of readers without the relevant languages, details of English translations of the works quoted from, and translations of a number of French passages that had previously been left untranslated. Jason Ferrell has generously compiled a glossary of names, modelled on the one

1   Reviewing *The Proper Study of Mankind* in *The Times Literary Supplement*, 22 August 1997, 3.
2   London and Princeton, 1999: see 148–50 there, and also my remarks on Berlin's ventriloquistic practice of 'semi-quotation' (ibid., xiv–xv). There are several striking examples in *Russian Thinkers* of resonant semi-quotations with which, if only because they have achieved an independent currency of their own, I am loath to tamper, and I have for the most part confined myself to providing more literal translations in the notes. A semi-quotation (at best) from Herzen in another volume, *The Power of Ideas* (see xv below), 10, 'Where is the song before it is sung?', also used by Berlin in his own voice in *Freedom and Its Betrayal* (London, 2002), 60, has now been immortalised in the title of a novel by Justin Cartwright based on the relationship between Berlin and Adam von Trott, *The Song Before It Is Sung* (London, 2007). In the first play of Tom Stoppard's trilogy *The Coast of Utopia* (see xvi below) this becomes 'Where is the song when it's been sung?': *Shipwreck* (London, 2002), 100. What Herzen wrote (see 224 below) was 'What is the purpose of the song the singer sings?' – a question different from either of these.

by Helen Rappaport in *The Soviet Mind*[1] (and incorporating some of her material), which provides basic background information on (principally Russian) figures mentioned by Berlin who may not be familiar to all his readers. And in one or two cases my explorations, or those of others, yielded additional information that it seemed helpful to pass on to readers: this is printed within square brackets in the notes to make its editorial authorship clear.

Those who know the author's work in this field will notice that three important items are missing. Two of these are his introductions to translations of Herzen's works mentioned in the list of abbreviations and conventions (xx–xxii below). These were excluded because they both overlap to some extent with the two essays on Herzen in this volume. The introduction to *From the Other Shore* and *The Russian People and Socialism* has now been included in a collection of Berlin's shorter essays, *The Power of Ideas* (London and Princeton, 2000); the introduction to *My Past and Thoughts* is in *Against the Current*. The third piece is 'Artistic Commitment: A Russian Legacy', which was not available in 1978, but has now appeared in Berlin's *The Sense of Reality: Studies in Ideas and Their History* (London, 1996; New York, 1997), a collection mainly comprising previously unpublished essays.

Berlin's special affinity with Turgenev, vividly displayed in 'Fathers and Children', is also reflected in three translations he made of Turgenev's work – a novella, a play and an autobiographical story. The translations of the novella, *First Love*, and the play, *A Month in the Country*, are also available in Penguin Classics. The story, 'A Fire at Sea', was published with an introduction by Berlin as 'An Episode in the Life of Ivan Turgenev' in the *London Magazine* in July 1957, and reissued with the novella as *First Love* and *A Fire at Sea* (London, 1982: Hogarth Press; New York, 1983: Viking).

Readers may also like to know of other pieces in, or related to, this area which do not appear here. There are three radio talks, 'The Man Who Became a Myth' (Belinsky), 'The Father of Russian Marxism' (Plekhanov) and 'The Role of the Intelligentsia', all

1   See xvi below.

included in *The Power of Ideas.* There are several essays on Soviet
Russia, collected as *The Soviet Mind: Russian Culture under Com-
munism* (Washington, 2004: Brookings Institution Press), which
also includes a bibliography of Berlin's other writings on Russia.
'Meetings with Russian Writers in 1945 and 1956', mainly about
Anna Akhmatova and Boris Pasternak, is to be found in *Personal
Impressions*; a shortened version of this essay, entitled 'Conver-
sations with Akhmatova and Pasternak', is one of the essays in *The
Soviet Mind*, and also appears in *The Proper Study of Mankind*
(London, 1997; New York, 1998), an anthology of essays drawn
from the preceding collections.

Another recent episode in the history of Berlin's writings on
Russia should also be mentioned here. Tom Stoppard's trilogy of
plays on the Russian intelligentsia, *The Coast of Utopia*, premiered
at the National Theatre in London in 2002, at the Lincoln Center
in New York in 2006–7, and at the Russian Academic Youth
Theatre in Moscow in 2007, 'was inspired', in Stoppard's words,
'by reading Isaiah Berlin's *Russian Thinkers*, and becoming fascinated by some of the people he wrote about'; indeed, he is 'the
presiding spirit of the trilogy'.[1] Certainly Berlin's 'complex vision',
to borrow the title of Aileen Kelly's illuminating introduction,[2]
palpably informs the world portrayed in these remarkable plays.

I have many debts of gratitude, and can mention only the
weightiest here. I begin with the first edition. First and foremost,
the great bulk of the detailed editorial work was undertaken by Dr
Aileen Kelly, without whose specialist knowledge of the Russian
language and of nineteenth-century Russian culture my task would
have been impossible. During an unusually busy time she devoted

1   The first remark is from an interview with Brendan Lemon posted at the time
     of writing on the Lincoln Center Theater website; the second is from 'The
     Presiding Spirit of Isaiah Berlin', *Lincoln Center Theater Review*, Fall/Winter
     2006 (issue 43, 5; also available on the same website). In the acknowledge-
     ments he includes in the published plays, Stoppard describes *Russian Thinkers*
     as 'the book which was my entry to the world of *The Coast of Utopia*',
     adding that Berlin is one of the authors 'without whom I could not have
     written these plays'.
2   Reprinted here in the revised version included in her collection *Toward
     Another Shore: Russian Thinkers between Necessity and Chance* (New Haven
     and London, 1998).

many hours to the search for answers to my queries, and my obligation and gratitude to her remain very great. Isaiah Berlin himself was unfailingly courteous, good-humoured and informative in response both to my persistent general advocacy of the revival of his work, which he regarded with considerable, and mounting, scepticism, and to my often over-meticulous probings into points of detail. Lesley Chamberlain gave valuable help with 'Herzen and Bakunin on Individual Liberty'. Pat Utechin, Isaiah Berlin's last and longest-serving secretary, was an indispensable source of aid and encouragement at all stages.

Turning to the revised edition, I should like first to extend my exceedingly grateful thanks to Derek Offord for spending an enormous amount of time, over a long period, tracing quotations and checking their accuracy, with saintly patience and generosity. It is no exaggeration to say that without him I could not have prepared this edition in its present form. I am also greatly indebted to the expert knowledge (and ready willingness to help) of Tatiana Pozdnyakova, who miraculously tracked down almost all the passages despaired of by others (helped on occasion by Konstantin Glebovich Isupov), as well as arranging for the illustrations in 'Fathers and Children' to be scanned by the Russian National Library in St Petersburg. The dedication of these two scholars, far beyond any conceivable call of duty, is reflected in the dedication of the book, whose editorial element depends so substantially on their help.

Marshall Shatz has most kindly and uncomplainingly assisted me with many problems, especially those involving Bakunin; Andrew Drozd, Jaap Engelsman, Richard Freeborn, Steffen Gross, Robin Hessman, Aileen Kelly, Marina Khmelnitskaya, Marina Kozyreva, Nikolai Sergeyevich Matveyev, Helen Rappaport, Judy Skelton, Roman Davidovich Timenchik, Patrick Waddington and Andrei Zorin have also come to my aid, some of them more than once. I was rescued, too, on several occasions by Nick Hearn, Richard Ramage, Lisa-Maria Spierin and their colleagues in the Slavonic section of the Taylorian Institution Library in Oxford. Indeed, my rusty and in any event somewhat rudimentary knowledge of Russian has made me specially dependent on others in revising this volume, which is in this sense a collective enterprise,

unjustly credited on the title page to only four of those who
have contributed to it. Nevertheless, the responsibility for any
remaining editorial deficiencies is of course mine alone.

H.H.

Wolfson College, Oxford
October 2007

Note on the cover photograph

Portraits of several of the thinkers discussed in this book are among those hanging behind the readers in the Herzen Library in Nice[1] who appear in the cover photograph. Those in the detail on the front cover include (numbering from left to right):

First row: 2 Petr Kropotkin; 3 Alexander Herzen; 4 Mikhail Bakunin
Second row: 1 Vladimir Solov'ev; 2 Anton Chekhov; 3 Nikolay Ogarev; 4 Ivan Turgenev; 5 Petr Lavrov
Third Row: 1 Maksim Kovalevsky; 2 Nikolay Chernyshevsky

Some of the newspapers and journals in the photograph can also be identified. Again from left to right:

Being read: *Russkie vedomosti* ('The Russian Gazette'), *Utro Rossii* ('The Russian Morning'), *Russkoe delo* ('The Russian Cause')
On the table (where two identifiable items are in a similar left–right position, the one nearer the readers is listed first): *Iskry* ('Sparks' – also on the wall), *Otkliki zhizni* ('Echoes of Life'), *Prizyv* ('Summons'), *Niva* ('The Field'), *Lukomor'e* ('The Cove'), *Ezhegodnik [?]* ('[?] Yearbook'), *Russkie zapiski* ('Russian Notes'), *Solntse Rossii* ('Sun of Russia'), *Severnye zapiski* ('Northern Notes')

---

1   Formally 'Chital'naya-biblioteka v Nitstse imeni A. I. Gertsena' ('Reading-Room–library in Nice named after A. I. Herzen').

Abbreviations and conventions

> [T]he trail of the passing editor.
> J. R. R. Tolkien and E. V. Gordon[1]

[ ]   Editorial addition

[. . .] Editorial ellipsis

. . .   Ellipsis used by quoted author

B   V. G. Belinsky, *Polnoe sobranie sochinenii* (Moscow, 1953–9)

C   N. G. Chernyshevsky, *Polnoe sobranie sochinenii* (Moscow, 1947–53)

D   *Polnoe sobranie sochinenii F. M. Dostoevskogo v XVIII tomakh* (Moscow, 2003–6)

E   *Tolstoy on Education: Tolstoy's Educational Writings 1861–62*, ed. Alan Pinch and Michael Armstrong, trans. Alan Pinch (London, 1982)

F   Alexander Herzen, *From the Other Shore*, trans. Moura Budberg, and *The Russian People and Socialism*, trans. Richard Wollheim, with an introduction by Isaiah Berlin (London, 1956)

FC   *Fathers and Children* (followed by the chapter number, and the page in vol. 8 of S: thus FC 7, 226 = *Fathers and Children*, chapter 7, S viii 226)

H   A. I. Gertsen [Herzen], *Sobranie sochinenii v tridsati tomakh* (Moscow, 1954–66)

---

1   *Sir Gawain and the Green Knight*, ed. J. R. R. Tolkien and E. V. Gordon (Oxford, 1925), Preface, v: 'a litter of italics, asterisks, and brackets, the trail of the passing editor'.

L   Alexander Herzen, *Letters from France and Italy, 1847–1851*, ed. and trans. Judith E. Zimmerman (Pittsburgh and London, 1995)

M   Alexander Herzen, *My Past and Thoughts*, trans. Constance Garnett, with an introduction by Isaiah Berlin, 4 vols (London and New York, 1968)

O   Michel Bakounine, *Œuvres* (Paris, 1895–1913)

OC *Œuvres complètes de J. de Maistre* (Lyon/Paris, 1884–7)

P   I. S. Turgenev, *Polnoe sobranie sochinenii i pisem* (Moscow/Leningrad, 1960–8), *Pis'ma*

S   I. S. Turgenev, *Polnoe sobranie sochinenii i pisem* (Moscow/Leningrad, 1960–8), *Sochineniya*

SPD Joseph de Maistre, *St Petersburg Dialogues*, trans. Richard A. Lebrun (Montreal etc., 1993)

T   L. N. Tolstoy, *Polnoe sobranie sochinenii* (Moscow/Leningrad, 1928–64)

W   Leo Tolstoy, *War and Peace*, trans. Louise and Aylmer Maude (London, 1942: Macmillan); because the Maudes' subdivisions of the text vary from edition to edition of their translation, and also differ from those in T, references to W are given by page alone

The two separate abbreviations for Turgenev's writings (S for works and P for letters) are required because in the edition cited the volumes of works and the volumes of letters are numbered in two separate sequences, whereas the editions of the writings of other authors use a single sequence. References to most multi-volume editions are by volume and page in this form: iv 476. Volumes divided into separately bound parts are cited thus: xviii/2. Page references are given as plain numerals, without the prefix 'p.' or 'pp.'. Dates of letters written in Russia are given according to the pre-Revolutionary Julian calendar: for the Gregorian dates used in the West add 12 days.

As in the original edition, Russian is transliterated according to the system used in *Oxford Slavonic Papers*: see J. S. G. Simmons, *Russian Bibliography: Libraries and Archives* (Twickenham, 1973), 60. Exceptions are made for a few names familiar in different English versions, e.g. Alexander, Gogol, (Tsar) Nicholas,

Peter the Great (not Aleksandr, Gogol', Nikolay, Petr the Great); and the use of '-y' for final '-ий' and '-й' in proper names is not extended to titles of published works.

Introduction

A COMPLEX VISION

Aileen Kelly

> Do not look for solutions in this book – there are none; in general modern man has no solutions.
>
> Alexander Herzen, *From the Other Shore*[1]

In an attempt to explain Russian Bolshevism to Lady Ottoline Morrell, Bertrand Russell once remarked that, appalling though it was, it seemed the right sort of government for Russia: 'If you ask yourself how Dostoevsky's characters should be governed, you will understand.'[2]

In the eyes of many Western liberals, the Soviet tyranny was the inescapable outcome of the ideas and actions of Dostoevsky's 'possessed': the Russian radical intelligentsia. In the degree of their alienation from their society and of their impact on it, the Russian intelligentsia of the nineteenth century were a phenomenon almost *sui generis*. Their ideological leaders were a small group with the cohesiveness and sense of mission of a religious sect. In their fervent moral opposition to the existing order, their single-minded preoccupation with ideas, and their faith in reason and science, they paved the way for the Russian Revolution and thereby achieved major historical significance. But they are too often treated by English and American historians with a mixture of condescension and moral revulsion – because the theories to which they were so fervently attached were not their own but borrowed from the West and often misunderstood and misapplied, and because in their fanatical passion for extreme ideologies they are

---

1 H vi 7; F 3. For abbreviations used in the notes see xx–xxi above.
2 *The Autobiography of Bertrand Russell*, vol. 2 (London, 1968), 122.

held to have rushed, like Dostoevsky's devils, to blind self-destruction, dragging their country, and then much of the rest of the world, after them. The Russian Revolution and its aftermath have strengthened the belief, deeply entrenched in the Anglo-Saxon outlook, that a passionate interest in ideas is a symptom of mental and moral disorder.

One powerful liberal voice never failed to dissent from this view of the Russian intelligentsia. Isaiah Berlin is one of the most widely admired political thinkers of the second half of the twentieth century, the proponent of what John Gray describes as a 'stoical and tragic liberalism' of unavoidable conflict between competing values, which injected new life into the liberal intellectual tradition.[1] His writings are penetrated with the conviction that liberal values are best defended by those who best understand the power of ideas, in particular the intellectual and moral attractions of what he has called the great despotic visions of the right and left. One of his distinctive contributions to English intellectual life was as a counterforce to its parochial indifference to intellectual movements in Europe. In a succession of dazzling studies he carried the personalities and ideas of some of the most original thinkers of the post-Renaissance world to a wide audience, and in the essays brought together in this book he achieved the same for the phenomenon of the Russian intelligentsia.

Berlin's approach to Russian thought was directed by his interest in how ideas are 'lived through' as solutions to moral problems. Avoiding the common tendency to pronounce on Russian solutions with the wisdom of historical hindsight, he focused instead on the dilemmas they were conceived to resolve. Though his essays on Russian subjects stand by themselves, with no need of philosophical annotation or cross-reference, they are also a substantial contribution to the central theme of all his writings on intellectual history, and their originality can best be appreciated if they are approached within this wider framework.

Berlin's writings are centrally concerned with what he sees as one of the most fundamental of the open issues on which moral conduct depends: Are all absolute values ultimately compatible

1   John Gray, *Isaiah Berlin* (London, 1995), 1.

with one another, or is there no single final solution to the problem of how to live, no one objective and universal human ideal? In the essays on liberty that encapsulate his thinking on this issue, he explores the historical and psychological roots and consequences of monist and pluralist visions of the world. He argues that the great totalitarian structures built on Hegelian and Marxist foundations are not a terrible aberration but rather a logical development of the central assumption shared by the main currents of Western political thought: that a fundamental unity, deriving from a single universal purpose, underlies all phenomena. This can be discovered, according to some, through scientific enquiry or, according to others, through religious revelation or metaphysical speculation. When discovered, it will provide a definitive answer to the question of how one should live.

Although the most extreme forms of this faith, with their dehumanising visions of individuals as instruments of abstract historical forces, have led to criminal perversions of political practice, Berlin emphasises that the faith itself cannot be dismissed as the product of sick minds. It is the basis of all traditional morality and is rooted in a 'deep and incurable metaphysical need'[1] that arises from humanity's sense of an inner split and its yearning for a mythical lost wholeness. This craving for absolutes is often the expression of an urge to shed the burden of responsibility for one's fate by transferring it to a 'vast amoral, impersonal, monolithic whole – nature, or history, or class, or race, or the "harsh realities of our time", or the irresistible evolution of the social structure – that will absorb and integrate us into its limitless, indifferent, neutral texture, which it is senseless to evaluate or criticise, and against which we fight to our certain doom'.[2]

Berlin believes that precisely because monistic visions of reality answer fundamental human needs, truly consistent pluralism is rarely found in history. In the sense in which he uses the word, *pluralism* is not to be confused with that which is commonly defined as a liberal outlook – according to which all extreme positions are distortions of true values and the key to social

---

1   'Two Concepts of Liberty', in *Liberty* (see xi above, note 3), 217.
2   'Historical Inevitability', ibid. 164.

harmony and a moral life lies in moderation and the golden mean.
True pluralism, as Berlin understands it, is much more tough-
minded and intellectually bold: it rejects the view that all conflicts
of values can be finally resolved by synthesis and that all desirable
goals may be reconciled. It recognises that human nature generates
values which, though equally sacred, equally ultimate, exclude
one another, without there being any possibility of establishing an
objective hierarchical relation among them. Moral conduct may
therefore involve making agonising choices, without the help of
universal criteria, between incompatible but equally desirable
values.

This permanent possibility of moral uncertainty is, in Berlin's
view, the price that must be paid for recognition of the true
nature of one's freedom: the individual's right to self-direction, as
opposed to direction by State or Church or Party, is plainly of
supreme importance if one holds that the diversity of human goals
and aspirations cannot be evaluated by any universal criterion or
subordinated to some transcendent purpose. But he maintains
that although this belief is implicit in some humanist and liberal
attitudes, the consequences of consistent pluralism are so painful
and disturbing, and so radically undermine some of the central
and uncritically accepted assumptions of the Western intellectual
tradition, that they are seldom fully articulated. In seminal essays
on Giambattista Vico, Niccolò Machiavelli and Johann Gottfried
von Herder, and in 'Historical Inevitability', Berlin has shown that
those few thinkers who spelled out the consequences of pluralism
have been consistently misunderstood and their originality under-
valued.

In *Four Essays on Liberty*[1] he suggests that pluralist visions of
the world are often the product of historical claustrophobia, during periods of intellectual and social stagnation, when a sense of
the intolerable cramping of human faculties by the demand for
conformity generates a demand for 'more light',[2] an extension of
the areas of individual responsibility and spontaneous action. But
as the dominance of monistic doctrines throughout history shows,

1   London, 1969 [now incorporated in 'Five Essays on Liberty', in *Liberty* (see
     xi above, note 3)].
2   'John Stuart Mill and the Ends of Life', *Liberty* 243.

people are much more prone to agoraphobia: at moments of historical crisis, when the need for choice generates fears and neuroses, they eagerly trade the doubts and agonies of moral responsibility for determinist visions, conservative or radical, that give them 'the peace of imprisonment, a contented security, a sense of having at last found one's proper place in the cosmos'.[1] Berlin points out that the craving for certainties has never been stronger than in the twentieth century; and his essays on liberty are a powerful warning of the need to discern, through a deepening of moral perceptions – a 'complex vision'[2] of the world – the cardinal fallacies on which such certainties rest.

Like many other liberals, Berlin believes that such a deepening of perceptions can be gained through a study of the intellectual background to the Russian Revolution. But his conclusions are very different from theirs. With the subtle moral sense that led him to radically new insights into European thinkers, he refutes the common view that the Russian intelligentsia were, to a man, fanatical monists: their historical predicament strongly predisposed them to both types of vision of the world, the monist and the pluralist – the fascination of the intelligentsia derives from the fact that the most sensitive among them suffered simultaneously, and equally acutely, from historical claustrophobia and agoraphobia, so that they were at once strongly attracted to messianic ideologies and morally repelled by them. The result, as he reveals, was a remarkably concentrated self-searching that in many cases produced prophetic insights into the great problems of our time.

The causes of that extreme Russian agoraphobia which generated a succession of millenarian political doctrines are well known: in the political reaction following the failure of the Decembrist rising of 1825 the Westernised intellectual élite became deeply alienated from their backward society. With no practical outlet for their energies, they channelled their social idealism into a religiously dedicated search for truth. In the historiosophical systems of German idealist philosophy, then at the height of its

1   'Historical Inevitability', ibid. 160.
2   Introduction, ibid. 20.

influence in Europe, they sought a unitary vision that would make sense of the moral and social chaos around them and anchor them in reality.

This yearning for absolutes was one source of that notorious consistency which, as Berlin observes, was the most striking characteristic of Russian thinkers – their habit of taking ideas and concepts to their most extreme, even absurd, conclusions: to stop before the ultimate consequences of one's reasoning was seen as moral cowardice, insufficient commitment to the truth. But there was a second, conflicting motivation behind this consistency. Among the Westernised minority, imbued through their education and reading with both Enlightenment and romantic ideals of liberty and human dignity, the primitive and crushing despotism of Nicholas I produced a claustrophobia that had no parallel in the more advanced countries of Europe, and was expressed in a radical questioning of traditionally accepted authorities and dogmas – religious, political and social. As Berlin shows in his essay 'Russia and 1848', the failure of the European revolutions in 1848 accelerated this process by increasing the intelligentsia's distrust of Western liberal and radical ideologues and their social nostrums. The tensions and the insights generated by an iconoclasm that was driven by the thirst for faith are the central theme of Berlin's essays on Russian thinkers.

In a series of vivid portraits of individual thinkers, he presents the most outstanding members of the intelligentsia as continually torn between their suspicion of absolutes and their longing to discover some monolithic truth that would once and for all resolve the problems of moral conduct. Some succumbed to the latter urge: Mikhail Bakunin began his political career with a famous denunciation of the tyranny of dogmas over individuals and ended it by demanding total adherence to his dogma of the wisdom of the simple peasant; and many of the young 'nihilist' iconoclasts of the 1860s accepted without question the tenets of a crude materialism. In other thinkers the battle was more serious and sustained. The literary critic Vissarion Belinsky is often cited as the arch example of the intelligentsia's fanatical attachment to the principle of logical consistency: from Hegelian principles he deduced that the despotism of Nicholas I was to be accepted as a necessary stage in the march of History. But as Berlin shows in a moving study of Belinsky, after a tormenting inner struggle he surrendered to the promptings of his conscience, fervently denouncing Hegel's doctrine of progress as a Moloch to whom living human beings were sacrificed. In their search for an ideal that would withstand their destructive critique, many other Russian intellectuals were led to question the great metaphysical systems that ruled over nineteenth-century European thought as well as some of the most cherished assumptions of progressive ideologies. In an essay on the populist tradition that dominated Russian radical thought in the nineteenth century, Berlin observes that this movement was far ahead of its time in pointing to the dehumanising implications of contemporary liberal and radical theories of progress, which placed such faith in quantification, centralisation, and the rationalisation of productive processes.

Most Russian thinkers regarded their destructive criticism as a mere preliminary, the clearing of the ground for some great ideological construction; Berlin sees it as highly relevant to our time, when only a consistent pluralism can protect human freedom from the depredations of the systematisers. Such a pluralism, he has pointed out, was fully articulated in the ideas of a thinker whose originality had hitherto been largely overlooked: Alexander Herzen.

The founder of Russian populism, Herzen was known in the West mainly as a Russian radical with a Utopian faith in an archaic form of socialism. In two essays on Herzen, and in introductions to his greatest works, *From the Other Shore* and *My Past and Thoughts*,[1] Berlin established him firmly as one of Russia's 'three moral preachers of genius',[2] the author of profound reflections on liberty.

Herzen had begun his intellectual career with a search for an ideal; he found it in an advanced form of socialism that he believed existed in embryo in the Russian peasant commune. But he argued that neither his nor any other ideal could be a universal solution

1   Included in Berlin's *The Power of Ideas* and *Against the Current* respectively: for details see above, xv and xi, note 2.
2   95 below.

to the problems of social existence: the search for such a solution was incompatible with respect for human liberty. He accused the revolutionaries of his time of being conservatives in their reluctance to confront the common source of all forms of political oppression: the tyranny of abstractions over individuals. Herzen's attacks on all deterministic philosophies of progress, Berlin argues, showed a prescient understanding that 'one of the greatest of sins that any human being can perpetrate is to seek to transfer moral responsibility from his own shoulders to those of an unpredictable future order',[1] to sanctify monstrous crimes by faith in some remote Utopia.

Berlin depicts Herzen's predicament as a very modern one. Herzen was torn between the conflicting values of equality and excellence; he recognised the injustice of élites but valued the intellectual and moral freedom and the aesthetic distinction of true aristocracy. But while refusing, unlike other leading ideologists of the Russian left, to sacrifice excellence to equality, he understood, with John Stuart Mill, something that has become much clearer in our day: that the common mean between these values, represented by 'mass societies', is not the best of both worlds but more frequently, in Mill's words, an aesthetically and ethically repellent 'collective mediocrity',[2] the submergence of the individual in the mass. In a language as vivid as Herzen's own, Berlin has conveyed to the English-speaking reader the originality of Herzen's belief that there are no general solutions to individual and specific problems, only temporary expedients that must be based on an acute sense of the uniqueness of each historical situation and on a responsiveness to the needs and demands of diverse individuals and peoples.

Berlin's exploration of the self-searching of Russian thinkers includes studies of two writers – Tolstoy and Turgenev – that remove the widespread misconception that in pre-Revolutionary Russia literature and radical thought formed two distinct and

---

1   225 below.
2   *On Liberty*, chapter 3, *Collected Works of John Stuart Mill*, ed. J. M. Robson and others (Toronto/London, 1963–91), xviii 268 [misquoted as 'conglomerated mediocrity' by Herzen in 'Kontsy i nachala' (1863), first letter, H xvi 141].

mutually hostile traditions. Tolstoy's and Dostoevsky's well-known aversion to the intelligentsia has been frequently quoted to emphasise the gulf between Russia's great writers, who were concerned with exploring human spiritual depths, and its radical thinkers, perceived as obsessed with the external forms of social existence. Berlin maintains that the art of Tolstoy and Turgenev can be understood only as a product of the same moral conflict as that experienced by the radical intelligentsia. In his study of Tolstoy's view of history, 'The Hedgehog and the Fox', and in his essay on Tolstoy and the Enlightenment, he interprets the relation between Tolstoy's artistic vision and his moral preaching as a titanic struggle between monist and pluralist visions of reality. Tolstoy's lethal nihilism demolished the pretensions of all theories, dogmas and systems to explain, order or predict the complex and contradictory phenomena of history and social existence, but the driving force of this attack was a passionate longing to discover a single unitary truth, encompassing all existence and impregnable to attack. He was thus constantly in contradiction with himself, perceiving reality in its multiplicity but believing only in 'one vast, unitary whole'.[1] In his art he expressed an unsurpassed feeling for the irreducible variety of phenomena, but in his moral preaching he advocated simplification, reduction to one single level, that of the Russian peasant or the simple Christian ethic. In some of the most psychologically delicate and revealing passages ever written on Tolstoy, Berlin suggests that his tragedy was that his sense of reality was too strong to be compatible with any of the narrow ideals he set up; the conclusions articulated in Herzen's writings were demonstrated in Tolstoy's inability, despite the most desperate attempts, to harmonise opposing but equally valid goals and attitudes. Yet his failure to resolve his inner contradictions gives Tolstoy a moral stature apparent even to those most mystified or repelled by the content of his preaching.

Few writers would seem to have less in common than Tolstoy, the fanatical seeker after truth, and Turgenev, a master of lyrical prose, the author of 'nostalgic idylls of country life'.[2] But in his essay on Turgenev, Berlin shows that although by temperament

1   57 below.   2   300 below.

he was a liberal, repelled by dogmatic narrowness and opposed to extreme solutions, he had been deeply influenced in his youth by the moral commitment of his radical contemporaries and their opposition to the brutality of the Russian autocracy. He fully accepted his friend Belinsky's belief that the artist cannot remain a neutral observer in the battle between justice and injustice but must dedicate himself, like all decent people, to the search to establish and proclaim the truth. The effect of this was to turn Turgenev's liberalism into something quite distinct from the European liberalism of that time, much less confident and optimistic, but more modern. In his novels, which chronicled the development of the intelligentsia, he examined the controversies of the middle years of the nineteenth century between Russian radicals and conservatives, moderates and extremists, exploring with great scrupulousness and moral perception the strengths and weaknesses of individuals and groups and of the doctrines by which they lived. Berlin stresses that the originality of Turgenev's liberalism lay in the conviction he shared with Herzen (even though he thought that Herzen's populism was his last illusion), as against Tolstoy and the revolutionaries (even though he admired their single-mindedness), that no final solution to the central problems of society was possible. In an age when liberals and radicals alike were complacent in their faith in the inevitability of progress, when political choices seemed mapped out in advance by inexorable historical forces – the laws governing economic markets or the conflict of social classes – which could be made to assume responsibility for their results, Turgenev perceived the hollowness of the certainties invoked by liberals to justify the injustices of the existing order or by radicals to justify its merciless destruction. He thus anticipated the predicament of the radical humanist in the twentieth century, which one of the most morally sensitive political thinkers of our time, Leszek Kolakowski, has described as a continual agony of choice between the demands of *Sollen* and *Sein*, value and fact:

> The same question recurs repeatedly in different versions: How can we prevent the alternatives of *Sollen–Sein* from becoming polarisations of Utopianism–opportunism, romanticism–conservatism,

purposeless madness versus collaboration with crime masquerading as sobriety? How can we avoid the fatal choice between the Scylla of duty, crying its arbitrary slogans, and the Charybdis of compliance with the existing world, which transforms itself into voluntary approval of its most dreadful products? How to avoid this choice, given the postulate – which we consider essential – that we are never able to measure truly and accurately the limits of what we call 'historical necessity'? And that we are, consequently, never able to decide with certainty which concrete fact of social life is a component of historical destiny and what potentials are concealed in existing reality.[1]

Kolakowski's formulation of this dilemma that faced the twentieth century is surely valid. Yet Turgenev, a thinker of a very different type, faced it more than a century ago. Before proponents of one-sided visions, conservative or Utopian, possessed the technological equipment for experiments on limitless human material, it was less difficult to defend the view that one or other extreme vision, or even a middle course, was the whole answer. Isaiah Berlin has demonstrated that, at a time when both liberals and the ideologists of the left were still confident of the sufficiency of their systems, Turgenev had attained a more complex vision and had embodied it in his art.

Among the three central figures in these essays, there is no doubt where Berlin's greatest sympathies lie. As he shows us, for all Tolstoy's moral grandeur, his blindness at those moments when he relinquishes the humane vision of his art for a domineering dogmatism is repellent. And Turgenev, for all the clarity of his vision, his intelligence and his sense of reality, lacked the courage and moral commitment he so admired in the radical intelligentsia: his vacillation between alternatives was too often a state of agreeable melancholy, ultimately dispassionate and detached.

It is Herzen who emerges as the hero of *Russian Thinkers*. Although Berlin concedes that there was substance in Turgenev's assertion that Herzen never succeeded in ridding himself of one

1   Leszek Kolakowski, 'Responsibility and History', in his *Marxism and Beyond*, trans. Jane Zielonko Peel (London, 1969), 163.

illusion – his faith in the peasant 'sheepskin coat'[1] – for him this does not detract from a view of liberty that was both profound and prophetic in its perception that 'one of the deepest of modern disasters is to be caught up in abstractions instead of realities'.[2] Berlin concluded his inaugural lecture as Professor of Social and Political Theory at Oxford with a quotation from an author whom he did not identify: 'To realise the relative validity of one's convictions and yet stand for them unflinchingly is what distinguishes a civilised man from a barbarian.'[3] Herzen, who had the subtle vision of a Turgenev along with a self-sacrificing commitment to the truth that was the equal of Tolstoy's, was in this sense both brave and civilised. He possessed to a great degree that consistent pluralism of outlook which for Berlin is the essence of political wisdom.

It is often said of the Russians that their national peculiarity consists in expressing in an extreme fashion certain universal characteristics of the human condition; and for many the historical significance of the Russian intelligentsia consists in the fact that they embodied the human thirst for absolutes in a pathologically exaggerated form. Berlin's essays present us with a very different and much more complex interpretation of the intelligentsia's 'universality', showing that for a variety of historical reasons they embodied not one but at least two fundamental, and opposed, human urges. The urge to assert the autonomy of the self through revolt against necessity continually clashed with their demand for certainties, leading them to acute insights into moral, social and aesthetic problems that in this century have come to be regarded as of central importance. That this aspect of their thought has aroused so little attention in the West is due in some measure to the glaring intellectual defects of the thought of most leaders of the intelligentsia. The repetitiousness, the incoherence, the proliferation of half-digested ideas from foreign sources in the writings of men like Belinsky, together with the political disasters for which they are held responsible, have led many Western scholars to echo

1   309 below.   2   225 below.
3   Joseph A. Schumpeter, *Capitalism, Socialism and Democracy* (London, 1943), 243.

the Russian thinker Petr Chaadaev's famous pronouncement that Russia exists only to teach the world some great lesson – apparently, that its example should be avoided at all costs. But with an acute instinct for quality, and with no trace of the condescension that is the frequent concomitant of historical hindsight, Berlin has discerned behind the formal shortcomings of the intelligentsia's writings a moral passion worthy of attention and respect, a vindication of the belief he preached to his English audience over many years: enthusiasm for ideas is not a failing or a vice; on the contrary, the ability to think through political and social ideals in order to predict their ultimate consequences is the best safeguard we have against the tyranny of ideological systems.

As Berlin points out in *Four Essays on Liberty*, no philosopher has ever succeeded in proving or refuting the determinist proposition that subjective attitudes do not influence historical events. But his studies of how Russian thinkers 'lived' their beliefs, testing them in daily moral struggle, argue more powerfully than any logical demonstration in support of the message that penetrates all Isaiah Berlin's writings: that human beings are morally free and are (more often, at least, than the determinists would concede) able to influence events for good or ill through their freely held convictions and ideals.

RUSSIA AND 1848
(1948)

The year 1848 is not usually considered to be a landmark in Russian history. The revolutions of that year, which seemed to Herzen like a life-giving storm on a sultry day, did not reach the Russian Empire. The drastic changes of policy on the part of the imperial government after the suppression of the Decembrist rising in 1825 seemed all too effective: literary storms like the Chaadaev affair in 1836, the loose student talk for which Herzen and his friends were punished, even minor peasant disorders in the early 1840s in remote provincial districts, were easily disposed of; in 1848 itself not a ripple disturbed the peace of the vast and still expanding Empire. The gigantic straitjacket of bureaucratic and military control which, if not devised, was reinforced and pulled tighter by Nicholas I, appeared, despite frequent cases of stupidity or corruption, to be conspicuously successful. There was nowhere any sign of effective independent thought or action.

Eighteen years earlier, in 1830, the news from Paris had put new life into Russian radicals; French Utopian socialism made a deep impression on Russian social thought; the Polish rebellion became the rallying point of democrats everywhere, very much as did the republic in the Spanish civil war a century later. But the rebellion was crushed, and all embers of the great conflagration, at any rate so far as open expression was concerned, were by 1848 virtually stamped out – in St Petersburg no less than in Warsaw. To observers in Western Europe, sympathetic and hostile alike, the autocracy seemed unshakeable. Nevertheless the year 1848 is a turning-point in the development of Russia as of Europe, not only because of the decisive part played in subsequent Russian history by revolutionary socialism, heralded by the Manifesto composed by Marx and Engels to celebrate its birth; but more immediately because of the effect which the failure of the European revolution was destined to have upon Russian public opinion, and in particular upon the Russian revolutionary movement. At the time, however, this could scarcely have been foreseen: well might a sober political observer – a Granovsky or Koshelev – feel gloomy about the possibility of even moderate reforms; revolution seemed too remote to contemplate.

It seems unlikely that anyone in the 1840s, even among the bolder spirits, except perhaps Bakunin and one or two members of the Petrashevsky circle, counted on the possibility of an immediate revolution in Russia. The revolutions that broke out in Italy, France, Prussia and the Austrian Empire had been made by more or less organised political parties, openly opposed to the existing regimes. These were composed of, or acted in coalition with, radical or socialist intellectuals, were led by prominent democrats identified with recognised political and social doctrines and sects, and found support among the liberal bourgeoisie, or from frustrated national movements at various stages of development and animated by different ideals. They tended also to draw a good deal of strength from disaffected workers and peasants. None of these elements was articulate or organised in Russia in any sense resembling the situation in the West. Parallels between Russian and Western European development are always liable to be superficial and misleading, but if a comparison is to be drawn at all the eighteenth century in Europe offers a closer analogy. The opposition of Russian liberals and radicals which, after the severe repressions following the Decembrist rising, began to grow bolder and more articulate in the middle 1830s and early 1840s, resembled the guerrilla warfare against the Church and absolute monarchy conducted by the Encyclopedists in France or by the leaders of the German *Aufklärung*, far more than the mass organisations and popular movements in Western Europe of the nineteenth century. The Russian liberals and radicals of the 1830s and 1840s, whether they confined themselves to philosophical or aesthetic issues, like the circle gathered round Stankevich, or concerned themselves with political and social issues, like Herzen and Ogarev, remained isolated *lumières*, a small and highly self-

conscious intellectual élite; they met and argued and influenced
each other in the drawing-rooms and salons of Moscow or
St Petersburg, but they had no popular support, no widely
extended political or social framework either in the form of political parties or even in the kind of unofficial but widespread middle-
class opposition which had preceded the great French Revolution.
The scattered Russian intellectuals of this period had no middle
class to lean upon, nor could they look for help from the peasantry.
'The people feel the need of potatoes, but none whatever of a
constitution – that is desired only by educated townspeople who
are quite powerless,' wrote Belinsky to his friend Pavel Annenkov
in 1847.[1] And this was echoed thirteen years later by Chernyshevsky in a characteristic hyperbole: 'There is no European country
in which the vast majority of the people is not absolutely indifferent to the rights which are the object of desire and concern to the
liberals.'[2] While this was scarcely true of most of Western Europe,
then or earlier, it reflected the backward state of Russia accurately
enough. Until the economic development of the Russian Empire
created industrial and labour problems, and with them a middle
class and a proletariat of the Western type, the democratic revolution remained a dream: and when such conditions finally materi-
alised, as they did with increasing tempo in the last decades of the
nineteenth century, the revolution did not lag far behind. The
'Russian 1848' occurred in that country in 1905, by which time
the middle class in the West was no longer revolutionary or even
militantly reformist; and this time-lag of half a century was itself
a powerful factor in causing the final cleavage between liberal and
authoritarian socialism in 1917, and the fatal divergence of paths
between Russia and Europe which followed. Perhaps F. I. Dan
was right in supposing that this was the parting of the ways which
Herzen had in mind when, addressing Edgar Quinet, he declared,
'You [will go] *by way of the proletariat towards socialism; we by
way of socialism to freedom.*'[3] The difference in the degree of

1   Letter to P. V. Annenkov, written in Berlin, 29 September 1847, B xii 402.
2   'Bor'ba partii vo Frantsii pri Lyudovike XVIII i Karle X' (1858), C v 217.
3   *Kolokol* No 210 (15 December 1865), 1720. See F. I. Dan, *Proiskhozhdenie
     bol'shevizma: k istorii demokraticheskikh i sotsialisticheskikh idei v Rossii
     posle osvobozhdeniya krest'yan* (New York, 1946), 38–9.

political maturity between Russia and the West at this period is
vividly described in the introduction to *Letters from France and
Italy* which Herzen composed in his Putney exile. His topic is the
revolution of 1848 in Western Europe:

The liberals, those political Protestants, became in their turn the
most fearful conservatives; behind the altered charters and consti-
tutions they have discovered the spectre of socialism and have grown
pale with terror; nor is this surprising for they [. . .] have something
to lose, something to be afraid of. But we [Russians] are not in that
position at all. Our attitude to all public affairs is much simpler and
more naive.

The liberals are afraid of losing their liberty – we have none; they
are nervous of interference by governments in the industrial sphere –
with us the government interferes with everything anyhow; they are
afraid of losing their personal rights – we have yet to acquire them.

The extreme contradictions of our still disordered existence, the
lack of stability in all our legal and constitutional notions, on the
one hand makes possible the most unlimited despotism, serfdom
and military settlements, and on the other creates conditions in
which such revolutionary steps as those of Peter I and Alexander II
are less difficult. A man who lives in furnished rooms finds it far
easier to move than one who has acquired a house of his own.

Europe is sinking because it cannot rid itself of its cargo – that
infinity of treasures accumulated in distant and perilous expeditions.
In our case, all this is artificial ballast; out with it and overboard,
and then full sail into the open sea!

We are entering history full of strength and energy at precisely the
moment when all political parties are becoming faded anachronisms,
and everyone is pointing, some hopefully, others with despair, at the
approaching thunder-cloud of economic revolution. And so we, too,
when we look at our neighbours, begin to feel frightened of the coming
storm, and like them, think it best to say nothing about this peril [. . .]

But you have no need to fear these terrors; calm yourselves, for
on our estate there is a lightning conductor – *communal ownership
of the land!*[1]

1   Introduction to the 1858 edition, H v 13–14; L 9–10.

In other words, the total absence of elementary rights and liberties, the seven dark years which followed 1848, so far from inducing despair or apathy, brought home to more than one Russian thinker the sense of complete antithesis between his country and the relatively liberal institutions of Europe which, paradoxically enough, was made the basis for subsequent Russian optimism. From it sprang the strongest hope of a uniquely happy and glorious future, destined for Russia alone.

Herzen's analysis of the facts was quite correct. There was no Russian bourgeoisie to speak of: the journalist Polevoy and the highly articulate literary tea merchant Botkin, friend of Belinsky and Turgenev, and indeed Belinsky himself, were notable exceptions – social conditions for drastic liberal reforms, let alone revolution, did not exist. Yet this very fact, which was so bitterly lamented by liberals like Kavelin and even Belinsky, brought its own remarkable compensation. In Europe an international revolution had broken out and failed, and its failure created among idealistic democrats and socialists a bitter sense of disillusion and despair. In some cases it led to cynical detachment, or else a tendency to seek comfort either in apathetic resignation, or in religion, or in the ranks of political reaction; very much as the failure of the revolution of 1905 in Russia produced the call to repentance and spiritual values of the *Vekhi* group. In Russia, Katkov did become a conservative nationalist, Dostoevsky turned to orthodoxy, Botkin turned his back upon radicalism, Bakunin signed a disingenuous 'confession'; but in general the very fact that Russia had suffered no revolution, and no corresponding degree of disenchantment, led to a development very different from that of Western Europe. The important fact was that the passion for reform – the revolutionary fervour and the belief in the feasibility of change by means of public pressure, agitation, and, as some thought, conspiracy – did not weaken. On the contrary, it grew stronger. But the argument for a political revolution, when its failure in the West was so glaring, clearly became less convincing. The discontented and rebellious Russian intellectuals of the next thirty years turned their attention to the peculiarities of their own internal situation; and then, from ready-made solutions, imported from the West and capable only of being artificially

grafted on to the recalcitrant growth provided by their own
countrymen, to the creation of new doctrines and modes of action
adapted carefully to the peculiar problems posed by Russia alone.
They were prepared to learn and more than learn – to become the
most devoted and assiduous disciples of the most advanced thinkers
of Western Europe, but the teachings of Hegel and the German
materialists, of Mill, Spencer and Comte, were henceforth to be
transformed to fit specifically Russian needs. Bazarov, in Turgenev's *Fathers and Children*, for all his militant positivism and
materialism and respect for the West, has far deeper roots in Russian
soil, not without a certain self-conscious pride, than the men of the
1840s with their genuinely cosmopolitan ideal: than, for example,
the imaginary Rudin, or indeed the supposed original of Rudin –
Bakunin himself, for all his pan-Slavism and Germanophobia.

The measures taken by the government to prevent the 'revolutionary disease' from infecting the Russian Empire did no doubt
play a decisive part in preventing the possibility of revolutionary
outbreaks: but the important consequence of this 'moral quaran-
tine' was to weaken the influence of Western liberalism; it forced
Russian intellectuals in upon themselves and made it more difficult
than before to escape from the painful issues before them into a
kind of vague search for panaceas from the West. There followed
a sharp settling of internal moral and political accounts: as hope
receded of marching in step with Western liberalism, the Russian
progressive movement tended to become increasingly inward-
looking and uncompromising. The most crucial and striking fact
is that there was no inner collapse on the part of the progressives,
and both revolutionary and reformist opinion, though it grew
more nationalist, often took on a grimmer tone. It favoured
self-consciously harsh, anti-aesthetic, exaggeratedly materialistic,
crude, utilitarian forms, and continued to be self-confident and
optimistic, inspired by the later writings of Belinsky rather than by
Herzen. There is not, even at the lowest point – during the 'seven-
year-long night' after 1848 – that flatness and apathy which is so
noticeable in France and Germany during these years. But this was
bought at the price of a deep schism within the intelligentsia. The
new men, Chernyshevsky and the left-wing populists, are divided
by a much wider gap from the liberals, whether of the West or of

their own country, than any of their predecessors. In the years of
repression, 1848–56, lines of demarcation grew much more real;
frontiers between the Slavophils and the Westerners, which had
hitherto been easily crossed and re-crossed, became dividing walls;
the framework of friendship and mutual respect between the two
camps – the Janus with two faces but one heart[1] – which had made
it possible for radicals like Belinsky and Herzen to argue furiously
but in an atmosphere of deep regard, in some cases even of affection, with Katkov or Khomyakov or the Aksakov brothers, no
longer existed. When Herzen and Chicherin met in London in
1859, Herzen saw in him not an opponent but an enemy, and with
reason. There was an even more painful process of polarisation in
the radical camp itself. The quarrel between the moderates of
Kolokol (the *Bell*) and the St Petersburg radicals in the 1860s grew
bitter. Despite the continued existence of a common enemy –
the imperial police State – the old solidarity was fatally broken.
Chernyshevsky's meeting with Herzen in London was a stiff,
awkward and almost formal affair. The gulf between what became
the left- and the right-wing oppositions grew steadily wider; and
this despite the fact that the left wing regarded Western ideals far
more critically than before, and like the right looked for salvation
to native institutions and a specifically Russian solution, losing
faith in universal remedies, compounded out of liberal or socialist
doctrines imported from the West.

Thus it came about that, when at last direct Western influence
had again reasserted itself in the form of the orthodox Marxism
of the Russian social democrats of the 1890s, the revolutionary
intelligentsia was unbroken by the collapse of liberal hopes in
Europe in 1849–51. Its beliefs and principles were preserved from
contamination by the very hostility of the regime, and remained
free from the danger, prevalent among their old allies in the West,
of growing soft and blurred as a result of too much successful
compromise, mingled with disillusion. Consequently, during the
time of almost universal *malaise* among socialists, the Russian
left-wing movement retained its ideals and its fighting spirit. It

1   'Konstantin Sergeevich Aksakov' (1861), H xv 9–10. See also H ix 170; M ii
     549.

had broken with liberalism out of strength and not out of despair. It had created and nurtured its own tough-minded, radical, agrarian tradition, and it was an army ready to march. Some of the factors responsible for this trend – the independent development of Russian radicalism as it was born in the storms of 1848–9 – may be worth recalling.

Tsar Nicholas I remained all his life obsessed by the Decembrist rising. He saw himself as the ruler appointed by Providence to save his people from the horrors of atheism, liberalism and revolution; and being an absolute autocrat in fact as well as in name, he made it the first aim of his government to eliminate every form of political heterodoxy or opposition. Nevertheless, even the severest censorship, the sharpest political police, will tend to relax its attention to some degree after twenty years of relative quiet; in this case the long peace had been disturbed only by the Polish rebellion, with no signs of serious internal conspiracy anywhere, and no greater dangers to the regime than a few small and localised peasant disorders, two or three groups of radical-minded university students, a handful of Westernising professors and writers, with here and there an odd defender of the Roman Church like Chaadaev, or an actual convert to Rome like the eccentric ex-professor of Greek, the Redemptorist Father Pecherin. As a result of this, in the middle 1840s the liberal journals, such as *Otechest-vennye zapiski* (*Notes of the Fatherland*) or *Sovremennik* (the *Contemporary*), took courage and began to print, not indeed articles in open opposition to the government – with the existing censorship and under the sharp eye of General Dubel't of the political police, this was out of the question – but articles ostensibly concerned with conditions in Western Europe or in the Ottoman Empire, and written in an apparently dispassionate manner; but containing, for those who could read between the lines, vague hints and concealed allusions critical of the existing regime. The centre of attraction to all progressive spirits was, of course, Paris, the home of all that was most advanced and freedom-loving in the world, the home of socialists and Utopians, of Leroux and Cabet, of George Sand and Proudhon – the centre of a revolutionary art and literature, which in the course of time were bound to lead humanity towards freedom and happiness.

Saltykov-Shchedrin, who belonged to a typical liberal circle of the 40s, says in a famous passage of his memoirs:

> In Russia, everything seemed finished, sealed with five seals and consigned to the Post Office for delivery to an addressee whom it was beforehand decided not to find; in France, everything seemed to be beginning [. . .]
>
> [Our French] sympathies became particularly intense towards 1848. With unconcealed excitement we watched all the *peripeteias* of the drama provided by the last years of Louis-Philippe's reign. With passionate enthusiasm we read *The History of Ten Years* by Louis Blanc. [. . .] Louis-Philippe and Guizot, Duchatel and Thiers – these men were almost personal enemies, perhaps more dangerous than even L. V. Dubel't.[1]

The Russian censorship had evidently not at this period reached its maximum severity; the censors were themselves at times inclined towards a timid kind of right-wing liberalism; in any case they were often no match for the ingenuity and, above all, unending persistence of the 'disloyal' historians and journalists, and inevitably they let through a certain amount of 'dangerous thought'. Those zealous watchdogs of autocracy, the editors Bulgarin and Grech, who acted as virtual agents of the political police, often denounced such oversights in private reports to their masters. But the Minister of Education, Count Uvarov, author of the celebrated patriotic triple watchword 'Orthodoxy, autocracy and the national way of life', who could scarcely be accused of liberal leanings, was nevertheless anxious not to acquire the reputation of a bigoted reactionary, and turned a blind eye to the less blatant manifestations of independent writing. By Western standards, the censorship was exceptionally severe; Belinsky's letters, for example, make quite plain the extent to which the censors managed to mutilate his articles; nevertheless, liberal journals contrived to survive in St Petersburg, and that in itself, to those who remembered the years immediately following 1825 and knew the temper

1 'Za rubezhom' (1881), in M. E. Saltykov-Shchedrin, *Sobranie sochinenii* (Moscow, 1965–77), xiv 112–13.

of the Emperor, was remarkable enough. The limits of freedom were, of course, exceedingly narrow; the most arresting Russian social document of this period, apart from the writings of the émigrés, was Belinsky's open letter to Gogol denouncing his book *Selected Extracts from a Correspondence with Friends*, and that remained unpublished in Russia in its full version until 1917. And no wonder, for it was an exceptionally eloquent and savage onslaught on the regime, inveighing violently against the Church, the social system and the arbitrary authority of the Emperor and his officials, and accusing Gogol of traducing the cause of liberty and civilisation as well as the character and the needs of his enslaved and helpless country. This celebrated philippic, written in 1847, was secretly circulated in manuscript far beyond the confines of Moscow or St Petersburg. Indeed, it was largely for reading this letter aloud at a private gathering of disaffected persons that Dostoevsky was condemned to death and so nearly executed two years later. In 1843, subversive French doctrines were, so Annenkov tells us, openly discussed in the capital: the police official Liprandi found forbidden Western texts openly displayed in the bookshops. In the year 1847, Herzen, Belinsky and Turgenev met Bakunin and other Russian political émigrés in Paris – their new moral and political experiences found some echo in the radical Russian press; this year marks the highest point of relative toleration on the part of the censorship. The revolution of 1848 put an end to all this for some years to come.

The story is familiar and may be found in Shil'der.[1] Upon receipt of the news of the abdication of Louis-Philippe and the declaration of a republic in France, the Emperor Nicholas, feeling that his worst forebodings about the instability of European regimes were about to be fulfilled, decided to take immediate action. According to Grimm's (almost certainly apocryphal) account, as soon as he heard the disastrous news from Paris, he drove to the palace of his son, the future Tsar Alexander II, where an eve-of-Lent ball

1   N. K. Shil'der, 'Imperator Nikolai I v 1848 i 1849 godakh', *Imperator Nikolay Pervyi, ego zhizn' i tsarstvovanie* (St Petersburg, 1903), second supplementary volume, *Primechaniya i prilozheniya ko vtoromu tomu* ('Notes and Supplements to Volume 2'), 619–39, at 619–20.

was in progress. Bursting into the ballroom, he stopped the dancers with an imperious gesture, cried 'Gentlemen, saddle your horses, a republic has been proclaimed in France!' and with a group of courtiers swept out of the room. Whether or not this dramatic episode ever occurred – Shil'der does not believe it – it conveys the general atmosphere accurately enough. Prince Petr Volkonsky at about this time told V. I. Panaev that the Tsar seemed bent on declaring a preventive war in Europe and was stopped only by lack of money. As it was, large reinforcements were sent to guard the 'western provinces', i.e. Poland. That unhappy country, broken not only by the savage repression of the rebellion of 1831, but by the measures taken after the Galician peasant rising in 1846, did not stir. But Polish liberty was being acclaimed, and Russian autocracy denounced, as a matter of course, at every liberal banquet in Paris and elsewhere; and, although this awoke no echo in Warsaw, then under the heel of Paskevich, the Tsar suspected treason everywhere. Indeed, one of the principal reasons why such importance was attached to the capture of Bakunin was the Tsar's belief that he was in close touch with Polish émigrés – which was true – and that they were plotting a new Polish mutiny in which Bakunin was involved – which was false – although Bakunin's extravagant public utterances may have lent some colour to such a supposition. Bakunin at the time of his imprisonment seems to have been entirely unaware of this obsession on the part of the Tsar, and therefore ignorant throughout of what was expected of him. He failed to include the non-existent Polish plot in his otherwise imaginative and altogether too accommodating confession. Soon after the outbreak in Berlin, the Tsar published a manifesto, in which he declared that the wave of mutiny and chaos had fortunately not reached the impregnable frontiers of the Russian Empire; that he would do everything in his power to stop this spreading of the political plague, and that he felt certain that all his loyal subjects would, at such a moment, rally to him in order to avert the danger to the throne and to the Church. The Chancellor, Count Nessel'rode, caused an inspired commentary on the Tsar's manifesto to appear in the *Journal de St Pétersbourg*, seeking to mitigate its bellicose tone. Whatever the effect on Europe, in Russia the commentary seems to have deceived no one:

it was known that Nicholas had drafted the manifesto with his own hand, and had read it to Baron Korf with tears in his eyes. Korf too was apparently almost reduced to tears and at once destroyed as unworthy the draft which he had been commissioned to prepare. The heir apparent, Alexander, when he read the manifesto to a meeting of guards officers, was overcome by emotion; Prince Orlov, the head of the gendarmerie, was no less deeply moved.[1] The document stimulated a genuine surge of patriotic feeling, although this does not appear to have lasted long. The Tsar's policy corresponded to some degree with popular feeling, at any rate among the upper and official classes. In 1849, Russian armies, commanded by Paskevich, crushed the revolution in Hungary; Russian influence played a major part in the suppression of the revolution in the other provinces of the Austrian Empire and in Prussia; the power of Russia in Europe, and the terror and hatred which it inspired in the breast of every liberal and constitutionalist beyond its borders, reached their zenith. Russia was to the democrats of this period very much what the fascist powers were in our own time: the arch-enemy of freedom and enlightenment, the reservoir of darkness, cruelty and oppression, the land most frequently, most violently denounced by its own exiled sons, the sinister power, served by innumerable spies and informers, whose hidden hand was discovered in every political development unfavourable to the growth of national or individual liberty in Europe. This wave of liberal indignation confirmed Nicholas in his conviction that, by his example, no less than by his exertions, he had saved Europe from moral and political ruin: his duty had at all times been plain to him; he carried it out methodically and ruthlessly, unmoved by either flattery or abuse.

The effect of the revolution on internal affairs in Russia was immediate and powerful. All plans for agrarian reform, and in particular all proposals for the alleviation of the condition of the serfs, both private and State-owned, not to speak of plans for their liberation to which the Emperor had at one time given much sympathetic consideration, were abruptly dropped. For many years it had been a commonplace, and not in liberal circles alone,

1   ibid. 626–9; my account of this episode is based on Shil'der's.

that agricultural slavery was an economic as well as a social evil. Count Kiselev, whom Nicholas trusted and had invited to be his 'Agrarian Chief of Staff', held this view strongly, and even the landowners and the reactionary bureaucrats who did their best to put difficulties in the path of positive reform had not, for some years, thought it profitable to question the evil of the system itself. Now, however, the lead given by Gogol in his unfortunate *Selected Extracts from a Correspondence with Friends* was followed in one or two government-approved school textbooks which went further than the most extreme Slavophils, and began to represent serfdom as divinely sanctioned, and resting on the same unshakeable foundation as other patriarchal Russian institutions – as sacred in its own way as the divine right of the Tsar himself. Projected reforms of local government were likewise discontinued. The 'hydra of revolution'[1] was threatening the Empire, and internal enemies, as so often in the history of Russia, were therefore to be handled with exemplary severity. The first step taken was connected with censorship.

The steady stream of secret denunciation which issued from Bulgarin and Grech at last had its effect. Baron Korf and Prince Menshikov almost simultaneously, it appears, compiled memoranda giving instances of the laxity of the censorship and the dangerous liberal tone to be found in the periodical press. The Emperor declared himself shocked and indignant that this had not been detected earlier. A committee under Menshikov was immediately set up with instructions to look into the activities of the censors and tighten up existing regulations. This committee summoned the editors of *Sovremennik* and of *Otechestvennye zapiski* and reproved them strongly for general unsoundness. The latter changed its tone, and its editor-publisher Kraevsky produced in 1849 a *bien pensant* article denouncing Western Europe and all its works, and offering the government a degree of sycophantic adulation at that time unknown even in Russia, and scarcely to be found in Bulgarin's subservient *Severnaya pchela* (the *Northern Bee*). As for *Sovremennik*, its most effective contributor, Belinsky, whom nothing could corrupt or silence, had died early

1   Tolstoy, *War and Peace*, vol. 1, part 1, chapter 1, T ix 5; W 4.

in 1848.[1] Herzen and Bakunin were in Paris, Granovsky was too mild and too unhappy to protest. Of major literary figures in Russia Nekrasov was left almost alone to continue the fight; by displaying his extraordinary agility and skill in dealing with officials, and by lying low for a good many months, he managed to survive and even publish, and so formed the living link between the proscribed radicals of the 1840s and the new and more fanatical generation, tried and hardened by persecution, which carried on the struggle in the 1850s and 1860s.

The Menshikov Committee was duly superseded by a secret committee (the Emperor was in the habit of submitting critical issues to secret committees, which often worked at cross purposes in ignorance of each other's existence) headed by Buturlin, and later by Annenkov – commonly known as the 'Second of April Committee'. Its duty was not that of pre-censorship (which continued to be performed by censors under the direction of the Ministry of Education) but of scrutinising matter already published, with instructions to report any trace of unsoundness to the Emperor himself, who undertook to execute the necessary punitive measures. This committee was linked with the political police through the ubiquitous Dubel't. It worked with blind and relentless zeal, ignoring all other departments and institutions, and at one point, in an excess of enthusiasm, actually denounced a satirical poem approved by the Tsar himself.[2] By going with a fine comb through every word published in the none too numerous periodical press, it succeeded in virtually stifling all forms of political and social criticism – indeed everything but the conventional expressions of unlimited loyalty to the autocracy and the Orthodox Church.

This proved too much even for Uvarov, and, on the plea of

1   There is a story still to be found in the latest Soviet lives of the great critic that at the time of his death a warrant had gone out for his arrest, and it is true that Dubel't later said that he regretted his death, as otherwise 'We would have rotted him in a fortress': M. K. Lemke, *Nikolaevskie zhandarmy i literatura 1826–1855 godov*, 2nd ed. (St Petersburg, 1909), 190. But Lemke has conclusively shown that no such warrant had ever been signed and that the invitation to Belinsky to visit Dubel't, which had largely inspired the story, was due mainly to a desire of the Third Department to get a specimen of his handwriting in order to compare it with that of a subversive anonymous letter circulating at the time (ibid. 187–90).

2   Shil'der, op. cit. (10 above, note 1), 638–9.

ill-health, he resigned from the Ministry of Education. His successor was an obscure nobleman – Prince Shirinsky-Shikhmatov,[1] who had submitted a memorandum to the Tsar, pointing out that one of the mainsprings of disaffection was undoubtedly the freedom of philosophical speculation permitted in the Russian universities. The Emperor accepted this thesis and appointed him to his post with express instructions to reform university teaching by introducing stricter observance of the precepts of the Orthodox faith, and in particular by the elimination of philosophical or other dangerous leanings. This medieval mandate was carried out in the spirit and the letter and led to a 'purge' of education which exceeded even the notorious 'purification' of the University of Kazan ten years earlier by Magnitsky. 1848 to 1855 is the darkest hour in the night of Russian obscurantism in the nineteenth century. Even the craven and sycophantic Grech, torn by anxiety to please the authorities, whose letters from Paris in 1848 denounce the mildest liberal measures of the Second Republic with a degree of scorn hardly equalled by Benkendorf himself – even this poor creature in his autobiography,[2] written in the 1850s, complains with something approaching bitterness about the stupidities of the new double censorship. Perhaps the most vivid description of this literary 'White Terror' is the well-known passage in the memoirs of the populist writer Gleb Uspensky.

> One could not move, one could not even dream; it was dangerous to give any sign of thought – of the fact that you were not afraid; on the contrary, you were required to show that you were scared, trembling, even when there was no real ground for it – that is what those years have created in the Russian masses. Perpetual fear [. . .] was then in the air, and crushed the public consciousness and robbed it of all desire or capacity for thought [. . .] There was not a single point of light on the horizon – 'You are lost,' cried heaven and earth, air and water, man and beast – and everything shuddered and fled from disaster into the first available rabbit-hole.[3]

1   'Shikhmatov is Shakhmat [checkmate] to all education' was a popular pun in St Petersburg.
2   N. I. Grech, *Zapiski o moei zhizni* (St Petersburg, 1886).
3   *Sochineniya Gleba Uspenskogo* (St Petersburg, 1889), i 175–6.

Uspensky's account is borne out by other evidence, perhaps most vividly by the behaviour of Chaadaev. In 1848, this remarkable man, no longer a certified lunatic, was still living in Moscow. The *Teleskop* debacle of 1836 had spread his fame. He seemed unbroken by his misfortune. His pride, his originality, and his independence, the charm and brilliance of his conversation, but above all his reputation as a martyr in the cause of intellectual liberty, attracted and fascinated even his political opponents. His salon was visited by both Russian and eminent foreign visitors, who testify that until the blow fell in 1848, he continued to express his pro-Western sympathies with an uncompromising and (considering the political atmosphere) astonishing degree of freedom. The more extreme members of the Slavophil brotherhood, especially the poet Yazykov,[1] attacked him from time to time, and on one occasion virtually denounced him to the political police. But his prestige and popularity were still so great that the Third Department did not touch him, and he continued to receive a variety of distinguished personalities, both Russian and foreign, in his weekly salon. In 1847 he expressed himself strongly against Gogol's *Selected Extracts from a Correspondence with Friends*, and in a letter to Alexander Turgenev damned it as a symptom of megalomania on the part of that unhappy genius. Chaadaev was not a liberal, still less a revolutionary: he was, if anything, a romantic conservative, an admirer of the Roman Church and the Western tradition, and an aristocratic opponent of the Slavophil obsession with Eastern Orthodoxy and Byzantium; he was a figure of the right, not the left, but he was an avowed and fearless critic of the regime. He was admired above all for his individualism, his unbreakable will, his incorruptible purity and strength of character, and his proud refusal to bend to authority. In 1849, this paladin of Western civilisation suddenly wrote to Khomyakov that Europe was in chaos, and in deep need of Russian help, and spoke with much enthusiasm of the Emperor's bold initiative in crushing the Hungarian revolution. While this might have been put down to the horror of popular risings felt by many intellectuals at this time, this is not the end of the story. In 1851, Herzen published a

1   See the account in M. K. Lemke, op. cit. (14 above, note 1), 451.

book abroad containing a passionate encomium of Chaadaev.[1] As soon as he heard of it, Chaadaev wrote to the head of the political police, saying that he had learnt with annoyance and indignation that he had been praised by so notorious a miscreant, and followed this with sentiments of the most abject loyalty to the Tsar as an instrument of the divine will sent to restore order in Europe. To his nephew and confidant, who asked him why he had displayed such unnecessary meanness, he merely observed that, after all, 'one must save one's skin'.[2] This act of apparently cynical self-abasement on the part of the proudest and most liberty-loving man in Russia of his time is tragic evidence of the effect of protracted repression upon those members of the older generation of aristocratic rebels who, by some miracle, had escaped Siberia or the gallows.

This was the atmosphere in which the famous Petrashevsky case was tried. Its main interest consists in the fact that it is the only serious conspiracy under the direct influence of Western ideas to be found in Russia at that time. When Herzen heard the news, it was 'like the olive branch, which the dove brought to Noah's Ark' – the first glimmering of hope after the flood.[3] A good deal has been written about this case by those involved in it – among them Dostoevsky, who was sent to Siberia for complicity in it. Dostoevsky, who in later years detested every form of radicalism and socialism (and indeed secularism in general) plainly tried to minimise his own part in it, and perpetrated a celebrated caricature of revolutionary conspiracy in *The Possessed*. Baron Korf, one of the committee of inquiry into the Petrashevsky affair, later said that the plot was not as serious or as widespread as had been alleged – that it was mainly 'a conspiracy of ideas'.[4] In the light of later evidence, and in particular of the publication by the Soviet government of three volumes of documents,[5] this verdict may be

1   *Du développement des idées révolutionnaires en Russie* (Paris, 1851). See H vii 91–3/221–3.

2   M. Zhikharev, 'Petr Yakovlevich Chaadaev iz vospominanii sovremennika', *Vestnik Evropy*, 1871 No 5, 9–54, at 51.

3   'Byloe i dumy' (1852–68), part 5, 'Russkie teni', 'II: Engel'sony' (1865), H x 335; 'C. Russian Shadows', '2. The Engelsons', M ii 969.

4   'Iz zapisok barona (vposledstvii grafa) M. A. Korfa', *Russkaya starina* 1900 No 5 (May), 279.

5   *Delo petrashevtsev* (Moscow/Leningrad, 1937–51).

doubted. There is, of course, a sense in which there was no formal conspiracy. All that had happened was that a certain number of disaffected young men gathered together at regular intervals in two or three houses and discussed the possibility of reform. It is also true that in spite of the devotion of Butashevich-Petrashevsky himself to the ideas of Fourier (the story that he set up a small phalanstery on his estate for his peasants, who set fire to it almost immediately as an invention of the devil, is unsupported by evidence) these groups were not united by any clear body of principles accepted by them all: so, for instance, Mombelli went no further than the desire to create mutual aid institutions, not so much for the workers or peasants as for members of the middle class like himself; Akhsharumov, Evropeus, Pleshcheev were Christian Socialists; A. P. Milyukov's only crime was apparently to have translated Lamennais. Balasoglo was a kindly and impressionable young man, oppressed by the horrors of the Russian social order – no more and no less than, for example, Gogol himself – who desired reform and improvement on mildly populist lines similar to the ideas of the more romantic Slavophils, and indeed not too unlike the neo-medievalist nostalgia of such English writers as Cobbett or William Morris. Indeed, Petrashevsky's encyclopedic dictionary, which contained 'subversive' articles disguised as scientific information, resembles nothing so much as Cobbett's famous grammar. Nevertheless, these groups differed from the casual gatherings of such radical men of letters as Panaev, Korsh, Nekrasov and even Belinsky. Some, at any rate, of the participants met for the specific purpose of considering concrete ideas of how to foment a rebellion against the existing regime.

These ideas may have been impracticable, and may have contained in them much that was fantastic, drawn from the French Utopians and other 'unscientific' sources, but their purpose was not the reform but the overthrow of the regime, and the establishment of a revolutionary government. Dostoevsky's descriptions in *A Writer's Diary* and elsewhere make it clear that Speshnev, for example, was by temperament and intention a genuine revolutionary agitator, who believed in conspiracy at least as seriously as Bakunin (who disliked him) and attended these discussion groups with a practical purpose. The portrait of him as Stavrogin in

The Possessed strongly stresses this aspect. Similarly, Durov and Grigor'ev and one or two others certainly seem to have believed that the revolution might break out at any moment; while they realised the impossibility of organising a mass movement, they put their faith, like Weitling and the groups of German Communist workers, and perhaps Blanqui at this period, in the organisation of small cells of trained revolutionaries, a professional élite which could act efficiently and ruthlessly and seize the leadership when the hour struck – when the oppressed elements would rise and crush the knock-kneed army of courtiers and bureaucrats that alone stood between the Russian people and its freedom. No doubt much of this was idle talk, since nothing remotely resembling a revolutionary situation existed in Russia at this time. Nevertheless, the intentions of these men were as concrete and as violent as those of Babeuf and his friends, and, in the conditions of a tightly controlled autocracy, the only possible means of practical conspiracy. Speshnev was quite definitely a communist, influenced not merely by Dézamy but perhaps also by the early works of Marx – for example, the anti-Proudhonist *Misère de la philosophie*. Balasoglo states in his evidence[1] that one of the things which attracted him to Petrashevsky's discussion group was that, on the whole, it avoided liberal patter and aimless discussion and concerned itself with concrete issues, and conducted statistical studies with a view to direct action. Dostoevsky's contemptuous references to the tendency of his fellow conspirators *poliberal'-nichat'* – to play at being liberal – look mainly like an attempt to whitewash himself. In fact, the principal attraction of this circle for Dostoevsky probably consisted precisely in that which had also attracted Balasoglo – namely, that the atmosphere was serious and intense, not amiably liberal, gay, informal and intimate, and given to literary and intellectual gossip, like the lively evenings given by the Panaevs, Sologub or Herzen, at which he seems to have been snubbed and had suffered acutely. Petrashevsky was a remorselessly earnest man, and the groups, both his own and the subsidiary, even more secret groups which sprang from it – as well as allied 'circles', for example that to which Chernyshevsky

1   ibid. ii 93.

belonged as a university student – meant business. The conspiracy was broken up in April 1849, and the *Petrashevtsy* were tried and sent into exile.

Between 1849 and the death of Nicholas I in the last months of the Crimean War, there is not a glimmering of liberal thought. Gogol died an unrepentant reactionary, but Turgenev, who ventured to praise him as a satirical genius in an obituary article, was promptly arrested for it. Bakunin was in prison, Herzen lived abroad, Belinsky was dead, Granovsky was silent, depressed and developing Slavophil sympathies. The centenary of Moscow University in 1855 proved a dismal affair. The Slavophils themselves, although they rejected the liberal revolution and all its works, and continued a ceaseless campaign against Western influences, felt the heavy hand of official repression; the Aksakov brothers, Khomyakov, Koshelev and Samarin fell under official suspicion much as Ivan Kireevsky had done in the previous decade. The secret police and the special committees considered all ideas to be dangerous as such, particularly that of a nationalism which took up the cause of the oppressed Slav nationalities of the Austrian Empire, and by implication thereby placed itself in opposition to the dynastic principle and to multi-racial empires. The battle between the government and the various opposition parties was not an ideological war, like the long conflict fought out in the 1870s and 1880s between the left and the right, between liberals, early populists and socialists on one side, and such reactionary nationalists as, for instance, Strakhov, Dostoevsky, Maikov, and above all Katkov and Leont'ev, on the other. During 1848–55, the government, and the party (as it was called) of 'official patriotism', appeared to be hostile to thought as such, and therefore made no attempt to obtain intellectual supporters; when volunteers offered themselves, they were accepted somewhat disdainfully, made use of, and occasionally rewarded. If Nicholas I made no conscious effort to fight ideas with ideas, it was because he disliked all thought and speculation as such; he distrusted his own bureaucracy so deeply, perhaps because he felt that it presupposed the minimum of intellectual activity required by any form of rational organisation.

'To those who lived through it, it seemed that this dark tunnel was destined to lead nowhere,' wrote Herzen in the 1860s. 'Never-theless, the effect of these years was by no means wholly negative.'[1] And this is acute and true. The revolution of 1848, by its failure, by discrediting the revolutionary intelligentsia of Europe which had been put down so easily by the forces of law and order, was followed by a mood of profound disillusionment, by a distrust of the very idea of progress, of the possibility of the peaceful attain-ment of liberty and equality by means of persuasion or indeed any civilised means open to men of liberal convictions. Herzen himself never wholly recovered from this collapse of his hopes and ideas. Bakunin was disoriented by it; the older generation of liberal intellectuals in Moscow and St Petersburg scattered, some to drift into the conservative camp, others to seek comfort in non-political fields. But the principal effect which the failure of 1848 had had on the stronger natures among the younger Russian radicals was to convince them firmly that no real accommodation with the Tsar's government was possible – with the result that during the Crimean War a good many of the leading intellectuals were close to being defeatist: nor was this by any means confined to the radicals and revolutionaries. Koshelev in his memoirs, published in Berlin in the 1880s,[2] declares that he and some of his friends – nationalists and Slavophils – thought that a defeat would serve Russia's best interests, and dwells on public indifference to the outcome of the war – an admission far more shocking at the time of its publication, during the full tide of pan-Slav agitation, than the facts themselves can have been during the Crimean War.

The Tsar's uncompromising line precipitated a moral crisis which finally divided the tough core of the opposition from the opportunists: it caused the former to turn in more narrowly upon themselves. This applied to both camps. Whether they were Slavo-phils and rejected the West like the Aksakovs and Samarin, or materialists, atheists and champions of Western scientific ideas like Chernyshevsky, Dobrolyubov and Pisarev, they became increasingly absorbed in the specific national and social problems of Russia and, in particular, in the problem of the peasant – his

---

1 [Perhaps a paraphrase of 'Kontsy i nachala', 6th and 7th letters (1862), H xvi 176, 191–2.]

2 *Zapiski Aleksandra Ivanovicha Kosheleva* (Berlin, 1884), 81–4.

ignorance, his misery, the forms of his social life, their historical origins, their economic future. The liberals of the 1840s may have been stirred to genuine compassion or indignation by the plight of the peasantry: the institution of serfdom had long been an acute public problem and indeed a great and recognised evil. Yet, excited as they were by the latest social and philosophical ideas which reached them from the West, they felt no inclination to spend their time upon detailed and tedious researches into the actual condition of the peasantry, upon the multitude of unexplored social and economic data which had been so superficially described by Custine, or later in greater detail by Haxthausen. Turgenev had done something to awaken interest in the day-to-day *byt*[1] of the peasants by the realism of his *A Sportsman's Sketches*. Grigorovich had moved both Belinsky and Dostoevsky by his tragic but, to a later taste, lifeless and overwrought descriptions of peasants in *The Village*, and in *Anton Goremyka*, published in 1847. But these were ripples on the surface. During the period of enforced insulation after 1849, with Europe in the arms of reaction, and only Herzen's plaintive voice faintly audible from afar, those socially conscious Russian intellectuals who had survived the turmoil directed their sharp and fearless analytical apparatus upon the actual conditions in which the vast majority of their countrymen were living. Russia, which a decade or two earlier was in considerable danger of becoming a permanent intellectual dependency of Berlin or of Paris, was forced by this insulation to develop a native social and political outlook of her own.

A sharp change in tone is now noticeable; the harsh, materialistic and 'nihilistic' criticism of the 1860s and 1870s is due not merely to the change in economic and social conditions, and the consequent emergence of a new class and a new tone in Russia as in Europe, but in at least equal measure to the prison walls within which Nicholas I had enclosed the lives of his thinking subjects. This led to a sharp break with the polite civilisation and the nonpolitical interests of the past, to a general toughening of fibre and exacerbation of political and social differences. The gulf between the right and the left – between the disciples of Dostoevsky and

1   Approximately, 'way of life'.

Katkov and the followers of Chernyshevsky or Bakunin – all typical radical intellectuals in 1848 – had grown very wide and deep. In due course there emerged a vast and growing army of practical revolutionaries, conscious – all too conscious – of the specifically Russian character of their problems, seeking specifically Russian solutions. They were forced away from the general current of European development (with which, in any case, their history seemed to have so little in common) by the bankruptcy in Europe of the libertarian movement of 1848: they drew strength from the very harshness of the discipline which the failure in the West had indirectly imposed upon them. Henceforth the Russian radicals accepted the view that ideas and agitation wholly unsupported by material force were necessarily doomed to impotence; and they adopted this truth and abandoned sentimental liberalism without being forced to pay for their liberation with that bitter, personal disillusionment and acute frustration which proved too much for a good many idealistic radicals in the West. The Russian radicals learnt this lesson by means of precept and example, indirectly as it were, without the destruction of their inner resources. The experience obtained by both sides in the struggle during these dark years was a decisive factor in shaping the uncompromising character of the later revolutionary movement in Russia.

THE HEDGEHOG AND THE FOX

An Essay on Tolstoy's View of History

(1951)

To the memory of Jasper Ridley

A queer combination of the brain of an English chemist with
the soul of an Indian Buddhist.   E. M. de Vogüé[1]

I

There is a line among the fragments of the Greek poet Archilochus
which says: 'The fox knows many things, but the hedgehog knows
one big thing.'[2] Scholars have differed about the correct interpretation of these dark words, which may mean no more than that
the fox, for all his cunning, is defeated by the hedgehog's one
defence. But, taken figuratively, the words can be made to yield a
sense in which they mark one of the deepest differences which
divide writers and thinkers, and, it may be, human beings in
general. For there exists a great chasm between those, on one side,
who relate everything to a single central vision, one system, less
or more coherent or articulate, in terms of which they understand,
think and feel – a single, universal, organising principle in terms
of which alone all that they are and say has significance – and, on
the other side, those who pursue many ends, often unrelated and
even contradictory, connected, if at all, only in some *de facto* way,
for some psychological or physiological cause, related to no moral
or aesthetic principle. These last lead lives, perform acts and enter-
tain ideas that are centrifugal rather than centripetal; their thought

1   *Le Roman russe* (Paris, 1886), 282.
2   'πόλλ' οἶδ' ἀλώπηξ, ἀλλ' ἐχῖνος ἓν μέγα.' Archilochus fragment 201 in M. L.
    West (ed.), *Iambi et elegi graeci ante Alexandrum cantati*, vol. 1, 2nd ed.
    (Oxford, 1989), 78.

is scattered or diffused, moving on many levels, seizing upon the essence of a vast variety of experiences and objects for what they are in themselves, without, consciously or unconsciously, seeking to fit them into, or exclude them from, any one unchanging, all-embracing, sometimes self-contradictory and incomplete, at times fanatical, unitary inner vision. The first kind of intellectual and artistic personality belongs to the hedgehogs, the second to the foxes; and without insisting on a rigid classification, we may, without too much fear of contradiction, say that, in this sense, Dante belongs to the first category, Shakespeare to the second; Plato, Lucretius, Pascal, Hegel, Dostoevsky, Nietzsche, Ibsen, Proust are, in varying degrees, hedgehogs; Herodotus, Aristotle, Montaigne, Erasmus, Molière, Goethe, Pushkin, Balzac, Joyce are foxes.

Of course, like all oversimple classifications of this type, the dichotomy becomes, if pressed, artificial, scholastic and ultimately absurd. But if it is not an aid to serious criticism, neither should it be rejected as being merely superficial or frivolous; like all distinctions which embody any degree of truth, it offers a point of view from which to look and compare, a starting-point for genuine investigation. Thus we have no doubt about the violence of the contrast between Pushkin and Dostoevsky; and Dostoevsky's celebrated speech about Pushkin has, for all its eloquence and depth of feeling, seldom been considered by any perceptive reader to cast light on the genius of Pushkin, but rather on that of Dostoevsky himself, precisely because it perversely represents Pushkin – an arch-fox, the greatest in the nineteenth century – as being similar to Dostoevsky, who is nothing if not a hedgehog; and thereby transforms, indeed distorts, Pushkin into a dedicated prophet, a bearer of a single, universal message which was indeed the centre of Dostoevsky's own universe, but exceedingly remote from the many varied provinces of Pushkin's protean genius. Indeed, it would not be absurd to say that Russian literature is spanned by these gigantic figures – at one pole Pushkin, at the other Dostoevsky; and that the characteristics of other Russian writers can, by those who find it useful or enjoyable to ask that kind of question, to some degree be determined in relation to these great opposites. To ask of Gogol, Turgenev, Chekhov, Blok how they stand in relation to Pushkin and to Dostoevsky leads – or, at

any rate, has led – to fruitful and illuminating criticism. But when
we come to Count Lev Nikolaevich Tolstoy, and ask this of him
– ask whether he belongs to the first category or the second,
whether he is a monist or a pluralist, whether his vision is of one
or of many, whether he is of a single substance or compounded of
heterogeneous elements – there is no clear or immediate answer.
The question does not, somehow, seem wholly appropriate; it
seems to breed more darkness than it dispels. Yet it is not lack of
information that makes us pause: Tolstoy has told us more about
himself and his views and attitudes than any other Russian, more,
almost, than any other European, writer; nor can his art be called
obscure in any normal sense: his universe has no dark corners, his
stories are luminous with the light of day; he has explained them
and himself, and argued about them and the methods by which
they are constructed, more articulately and with greater force and
sanity and lucidity than any other writer. Is he a fox or a hedgehog?
What are we to say? Why is the answer so curiously difficult to
find? Does he resemble Shakespeare or Pushkin more than Dante
or Dostoevsky? Or is he wholly unlike either, and is the question
therefore unanswerable because it is absurd? What is the mysterious obstacle with which our enquiry seems faced?

I do not propose in this essay to formulate a reply to this
question, since this would involve nothing less than a critical
examination of the art and thought of Tolstoy as a whole. I shall
confine myself to suggesting that the difficulty may be, at least in
part, due to the fact that Tolstoy was himself not unaware of the
problem, and did his best to falsify the answer. The hypothesis I
wish to offer is that Tolstoy was by nature a fox, but believed in
being a hedgehog; that his gifts and achievement are one thing,
and his beliefs, and consequently his interpretation of his own
achievement, another; and that consequently his ideals have led
him, and those whom his genius for persuasion has taken in, into
a systematic misinterpretation of what he and others were doing
or should be doing. No one can complain that he has left his
readers in any doubt as to what he thought about this topic: his
views on this subject permeate all his discursive writings – diaries,
recorded *obiter dicta*, autobiographical essays and stories, social
and religious tracts, literary criticism, letters to private and public

correspondents. But the conflict between what he was and what he believed emerges nowhere so clearly as in his view of history, to which some of his most brilliant and most paradoxical pages are devoted. This essay is an attempt to deal with his historical doctrines, and to consider both his motives for holding the views he holds and some of their probable sources. In short, it is an attempt to take Tolstoy's attitude to history as seriously as he himself meant his readers to take it, although for a somewhat different reason – for the light it casts on a single man of genius rather than on the fate of all mankind.

II

Tolstoy's philosophy of history has, on the whole, not obtained the attention which it deserves, whether as an intrinsically interesting view or as an occurrence in the history of ideas, or even as an element in the development of Tolstoy himself.[1] Those who have treated Tolstoy primarily as a novelist have at times looked upon the historical and philosophical passages scattered through *War and Peace* as so much perverse interruption of the narrative, as a regrettable liability to irrelevant digression characteristic of this great, but excessively opinionated, writer, a lop-sided, home-made metaphysic of small or no intrinsic interest, deeply inartistic and thoroughly foreign to the purpose and structure of the work of art as a whole. Turgenev, who found Tolstoy's personality and art antipathetic, although in later years he freely and generously acknowledged his genius as a writer, led the attack. In letters to Pavel Annenkov,[2] Turgenev speaks of Tolstoy's 'charlatanism', of his historical disquisitions as 'farcical', as 'trickery' which takes in the unwary, injected by an 'autodidact' into his work as an

---

1   For the purpose of this essay I propose to confine myself almost entirely to the explicit philosophy of history contained in *War and Peace*, and to ignore, for example, *Sevastopol Sketches*, *The Cossacks*, the fragments of the unpublished novel on the Decembrists, and Tolstoy's own scattered reflections on this subject except in so far as they bear on views expressed in *War and Peace*.

2   Letters of 14 February and 13 April 1868: P vii 64, 122.

inadequate substitute for genuine knowledge. He hastens to add
that Tolstoy does, of course, make up for this by his marvellous
artistic genius; and then accuses him of inventing 'a system which
seems to solve everything very simply; as, for example, historical
fatalism; he mounts his hobby-horse and is off! Only when he
touches earth does he, like Antaeus, recover his true strength.'[1]
The same note is sounded in the celebrated and touching invo-
cation sent by Turgenev from his death-bed to his old friend and
enemy, begging him to cast away his prophet's mantle and return
to his true vocation – that of 'the great writer of the Russian
land'.[2] Flaubert, despite his 'shouts of admiration' over passages
of *War and Peace*, is equally horrified: 'il se répète et il philosophise',[3] he writes in a letter to Turgenev, who had sent him the
French version of the masterpiece then almost unknown outside
Russia. In the same strain Belinsky's intimate friend and corres-
pondent, the philosophical tea-merchant Vasily Botkin, who was
well disposed to Tolstoy, writes to the poet Afanasy Fet that
literary specialists

> find that the intellectual element of the novel is very weak, the
> philosophy of history is trivial and superficial, the denial of the
> decisive influence of individual personalities on events is nothing
> but a lot of mystical subtlety, but apart from this the artistic gift of
> the author is beyond dispute – yesterday I gave a dinner and Tyut-
> chev was here, and I am repeating what everybody said.[4]

Contemporary historians and military specialists, at least one of
whom had himself fought in 1812, indignantly complained of
inaccuracies of fact;[5] and since then damning evidence has been
adduced of falsification of historical detail by the author of *War*

1   ibid.
2   Letter to Tolstoy of 29 June 1883, P xiii 180.
3   'He repeats himself and he philosophises.' Letter of 21 January 1880, Gustave
     Flaubert, *Lettres inédites à Tourguéneff*, ed. Gérard Gailly (Monaco, 1946),
     218 ['cris d'admiration' ibid.].
4   A. A. Fet, *Moi vospominaniya* (Moscow, 1890), part 2, 175.
5   See the severe strictures of A. Vitmer, a very respectable military historian,
     in his *1812 god v 'Voine i mire': po povodu istoricheskikh ukazanii IV toma
     'Voiny i mira' grafa L. N. Tolstogo* (St Petersburg, 1869), and the tones of

and Peace,[1] done apparently with deliberate intent, in full knowledge of the available original sources and in the known absence
of any counter-evidence – falsification perpetrated, it seems, in the
interests not so much of an artistic as of an 'ideological' purpose.

This consensus of historical and aesthetic criticism seems to
have set the tone for nearly all later appraisals of the 'ideological'
content of *War and Peace*. Shelgunov at least honoured it with a
direct attack for its social quietism, which he called 'the philosophy
of the swamp';[2] others for the most part either politely ignored it,
or treated it as a characteristic aberration which they put down to
a combination of the well-known Russian tendency to preach (and
thereby ruin works of art) with the half-baked infatuation with
general ideas characteristic of young intellectuals in countries
remote from centres of civilisation. 'It is fortunate for us that the
author is a better artist than thinker,' said the critic Nikolay
Akhsharumov,[3] and for more than three-quarters of a century this
sentiment has been echoed by most of the critics of Tolstoy, both
Russian and foreign, both pre-Revolutionary and Soviet, both
'reactionary' and 'progressive', by most of those who look on him
primarily as a writer and an artist, and of those to whom he is a
prophet and a teacher, or a martyr, or a social influence, or a

---

mounting indignation in the contemporary critical notices of S. Navalikhin
('Izyashchnyi romanist i ego izyashchnye kritiki', *Delo* 1868 No 6, 'Sovre-
mennoe obozrenie', 1–28), A. S. Norov (' "Voina i mir" (1805–1812) s
istoricheskoi tochki zreniya i po vospominaniyam sovremennikov (po povodu
sochineniya grafa L. N. Tolstogo: "Voina i mir")', *Voennyi sbornik* 1868 No
11, 189–246) and A. P. Pyatkovsky ('Istoricheskaya epokha v romane gr.
L. N. Tolstogo', *Nedelya* 1868: No 22, cols 698–704: No 23, cols 713–17:
No 26, cols 817–28). The first served in the campaign of 1812 and, despite
some errors of fact, makes criticisms of substance. The last two are, as literary
critics, almost worthless, but they seem to have taken the trouble to verify
some of the relevant facts.

1   See Viktor Shklovsky, *Mater'yal i stil' v romane L'va Tolstogo 'Voina i mir'*
    (Moscow, 1928), *passim*, but particularly chapters 7 and 8. See also 47
    below.

2   N. V. Shelgunov, 'Filosofiya zastoya' (review of *War and Peace*), *Delo* 1870
    No 1, 'Sovremennoe obozrenie', 1–29.

3   [More literally: 'Fortunately, the author [. . .] is a poet and an artist ten
    thousand times more than a philosopher.'] N. D. Akhsharumov, *Voina i mir,
    sochinenie grafa L. N. Tolstogo, chasti 1–4: razbor* (St Petersburg, 1868), 40.

sociological or psychological 'case'. Tolstoy's theory of history is
of equally little interest to Vogüé and Merezhkovsky, to Stefan
Zweig and Percy Lubbock, to Biryukov and E. J. Simmons, not to
speak of lesser men. Historians of Russian thought[1] tend to label
this aspect of Tolstoy as 'fatalism', and move on to the more
interesting historical theories of Leont'ev or Danilevsky. Critics
endowed with more caution or humility do not go as far as this,
but treat the 'philosophy' with nervous respect; even Derrick Leon,
who treats Tolstoy's views of this period with greater care than
the majority of his biographers, after giving a painstaking account
of Tolstoy's reflections on the forces which dominate history,
particularly of the second section of the long epilogue which
follows the end of the narrative portion of *War and Peace*, proceeds to follow Aylmer Maude in making no attempt either to
assess the theory or to relate it to the rest of Tolstoy's life or
thought; and even so much as this is almost unique.[2] Those, again,
who are mainly interested in Tolstoy as a prophet and a teacher
concentrate on the later doctrines of the master, held after his
conversion, when he had ceased to regard himself primarily as a
writer and had established himself as a teacher of mankind, an

1   e.g. Professors Il'in, Yakovenko, Zenkovsky and others. [When invited to
     identify the specific works in question, IB replied that their omission was
     deliberate. B. V. Yakovenko did not hold a professorship.]

2   Honourable exceptions to this are provided by the writings of the Russian
     writers N. I. Kareev and B. M. Eikhenbaum, as well as those of the French
     scholars E. Haumant and Albert Sorel. Of monographs devoted to this subject
     I know of only two of any worth. The first, 'Filosofiya istorii L. N. Tolstogo',
     by V. N. Pertsev, in '*Voina i mir*': *sbornik*, ed. V. P. Obninsky and T. I.
     Polner (Moscow, 1912), 129–53, after taking Tolstoy mildly to task for
     obscurities, exaggerations and inconsistencies, swiftly retreats into innocuous
     generalities. The other, 'Filosofiya istorii v romane L. N. Tolstogo, "Voina i
     mir"', by M. M. Rubinshtein, in *Russkaya mysl'*, July 1911, [section 2,] 78–
     103, is much more laboured, but in the end seems to me to establish nothing
     at all. Very different is Arnold Bennett's judgement, of which I learnt since
     writing this: 'The last part of the Epilogue is full of good ideas the johnny
     can't work out. And of course, in the phrase of critics, would have been
     better left out. So it would; only Tolstoy couldn't leave it out. It was what he
     wrote the book for.' *The Journals of Arnold Bennett*, ed. Newman Flower
     (London etc., 1932–3), ii (1911–21) 62. As for the inevitable efforts to relate
     Tolstoy's historical views to those of various latter-day Marxists – Kautsky,
     Lenin, Stalin etc. – they belong to the curiosities of politics or theology rather
     than to those of literature.

object of veneration and pilgrimage. Tolstoy's life is normally represented as falling into two distinct parts: first comes the author of immortal masterpieces, later the prophet of personal and social regeneration; first the aristocratic writer, the difficult, somewhat unapproachable, troubled novelist of genius, then the sage – dogmatic, perverse, exaggerated, but wielding a vast influence, particularly in his own country – a world institution of unique importance. From time to time attempts are made to trace his later period to its roots in his earlier phase, which is felt to be full of presentiments of the later life of self-renunciation; it is this later period which is regarded as important; there are philosophical, theological, ethical, psychological, political, economic studies of the later Tolstoy in all his aspects.

And yet there is surely a paradox here. Tolstoy's interest in history and the problem of historical truth was passionate, almost obsessive, both before and during the writing of *War and Peace.* No one who reads his journals and letters, or indeed *War and Peace* itself, can doubt that the author himself, at any rate, regarded this problem as the heart of the entire matter – the central issue round which the novel is built. 'Charlatanism', 'superficiality', 'intellectual feebleness' – surely Tolstoy is the last writer to whom these epithets seem applicable: bias, perversity, arrogance, perhaps; self-deception, lack of restraint, possibly; moral or spiritual inadequacy – of this he was better aware than his enemies; but failure of intellect, lack of critical power, a tendency to emptiness, liability to ride off on some patently absurd, superficial doctrine to the detriment of realistic description or analysis of life, infatuation with some fashionable theory which Botkin or Fet can easily see through, although Tolstoy, alas, cannot – these charges seem grotesquely unplausible. No man in his senses, during this century at any rate, would ever dream of denying Tolstoy's intellectual power, his appalling capacity to penetrate any conventional disguise, that corrosive scepticism in virtue of which Prince Vyazemsky tarred *War and Peace* with the brush of *netovshchina* (negativism)[1] – an early version of that nihilism which Vogüé and Albert Sorel later

1   P. A. Vyazemsky, 'Vospominaniya o 1812 god', *Russkii arkhiv* 7 (1869), columns 181–92, 01–016, esp. 185–7.

quite naturally attribute to him. Something is surely amiss here: Tolstoy's violently unhistorical and indeed anti-historical rejection of all efforts to explain or justify human action or character in terms of social or individual growth, or 'roots' in the past; this side by side with an absorbed and lifelong interest in history, leading to artistic and philosophical results which provoked such queerly disparaging comments from ordinarily sane and sympathetic critics – surely there is something here which deserves attention.

III

Tolstoy's interest in history began early in his life. It seems to have arisen not from interest in the past as such, but from the desire to penetrate to first causes, to understand how and why things happen as they do and not otherwise, from discontent with those current explanations which do not explain, and leave the mind dissatisfied, from a tendency to doubt and place under suspicion and, if need be, reject whatever does not fully answer the question, to go to the root of every matter, at whatever cost. This remained Tolstoy's attitude throughout his entire life, and is scarcely a symptom either of 'trickery' or of 'superficiality'. With it went an incurable love of the concrete, the empirical, the verifiable, and an instinctive distrust of the abstract, the impalpable, the super-natural – in short an early tendency to a scientific and positivist approach, unfriendly to romanticism, abstract formulations, metaphysics. Always and in every situation he looked for 'hard' facts – for what could be grasped and verified by the normal intellect, uncorrupted by intricate theories divorced from tangible realities, or by other-worldly mysteries, theological, poetical and metaphysical alike. He was tormented by the ultimate problems which face young men in every generation – about good and evil, the origin and purpose of the universe and its inhabitants, the causes of all that happens; but the answers provided by theologians and metaphysicians struck him as absurd, if only because of the words in which they were formulated – words which bore no apparent reference to the everyday world of ordinary common sense to which he clung obstinately, even before he became aware of what he was doing, as being alone real. History, only history, only the sum of the concrete events in time and space – the sum of the actual experience of actual men and women in their relation to one another and to an actual three-dimensional, empirically experienced, physical environment – this alone contained the truth, the material out of which genuine answers – answers needing for their apprehension no special sense or faculties which normal human beings did not possess – might be constructed.

This, of course, was the spirit of empirical enquiry which animated the great anti-theological and anti-metaphysical thinkers of the eighteenth century, and Tolstoy's realism and inability to be taken in by shadows made him their natural disciple before he had learnt of their doctrines. Like M. Jourdain, he spoke prose long before he knew it, and remained an enemy of transcendentalism from the beginning to the end of his life. He grew up during the heyday of the Hegelian philosophy, which sought to explain all things in terms of historical development, but conceived this process as being ultimately not susceptible to the methods of empirical investigation. The historicism of his time doubtless influenced the young Tolstoy as it did all enquiring persons of his time; but the metaphysical content he rejected instinctively, and in one of his letters he described Hegel's writings as unintelligible gibberish interspersed with platitudes. History alone – the sum of empirically discoverable data – held the key to the mystery of why what happened happened as it did and not otherwise; and only history, consequently, could throw light on the fundamental ethical problems which obsessed him as they did every Russian thinker in the nineteenth century. What is to be done? How should one live? Why are we here? What must we be and do? The study of historical connections and the demand for empirical answers to these *proklyatye voprosy*[1] became fused into one in Tolstoy's mind, as his early diaries and letters show very vividly.

1   'Accursed questions' – a phrase which became a cliché in nineteenth-century Russia for those central moral and social issues of which every honest man, in particular every writer, must sooner or later become aware, and then be faced with the choice of either entering the struggle or turning his back upon his fellow men, conscious of his responsibility for what he was doing. [Although 'voprosy' was widely used by the 1830s to refer to these issues, it

In his early diaries we find references to his attempts to compare Catherine the Great's *Nakaz*[1] with the passages in Montesquieu on which she professed to have founded it.[2] He reads Hume and Thiers[3] as well as Rousseau, Sterne and Dickens.[4] He is obsessed by the thought that philosophical principles can be understood only in their concrete expression in history.[5] 'To write the genuine history of present-day Europe: there is an aim for the whole of one's life.'[6] Or again: 'The leaves of a tree delight us more than the roots',[7] with the implication that this is nevertheless a superficial view of the world. But side by side with this there is the beginning of an acute sense of disappointment, a feeling that history, as it is written by historians, makes claims which it cannot satisfy, because like metaphysical philosophy it pretends to be something it is not – namely a science capable of arriving at conclusions which are certain. Since men cannot solve philosophical questions by the principles of reason they try to do so historically. But history is 'one of the most backward of sciences – a science which has lost its proper aim'. The reason for this is that history will not, because it cannot, solve the great questions which have tormented men in every generation. In the course of seeking to answer these questions men accumulate a knowledge of facts as they succeed each other in time: but this is a mere by-product,

seems that the specific phrase 'proklyatye voprosy' was coined in 1858 by Mikhail L. Mikhailov when he used it to render 'die verdammten Fragen' in his translation of Heine's poem 'Zum Lazarus' (1853/4): see 'Stikhotvoreniya Geine', *Sovremennik* 1858 No 3, 125; and *Heinrich Heines Sämtliche Werke*, ed. Oskar Walzel (Leipzig, 1911–20), iii 225. Alternatively, Mikhailov may have been capitalising on the fact that an existing Russian expression fitted Heine's words like a glove, but I have not yet seen an earlier published use of it. H.H.]

1   Instructions to her legislative experts.
2   T xlvi 4–28 (18–26 March 1847).
3   ibid. 97, 113, 114, 117, 123–4, 127 (20 March to 27 June 1852).
4   ibid. – Rousseau: 126, 127, 130, 132–4, 167, 176 (24 June 1852 to 28 September 1853), 249 ('Journal of daily tasks', 3 March 1847); Sterne: 82 (10 August 1851), 110 (14 April 1852); Dickens: 140 (1 September 1852).
5   ibid. 123 (11 June 1852).
6   ibid. 141–2 (22 September 1852).
7   'Filosoficheskie zamechaniya na rechi Zh. Zh. Russo' (1847), T i 222, where the next two quotations also appear.

a kind of 'side issue' which – and this is a mistake – is studied as an end in itself. Again, 'history will never reveal to us what connections there are, and at what times, between science, art and morality, between good and evil, religion and the civic virtues. What it *will* tell us (and that incorrectly) is where the Huns came from, where they lived, who laid the foundations of their power, etc.' According to his friend Nazar'ev, Tolstoy said to him in the winter of 1846: 'History [. . .] is nothing but a collection of fables and useless trifles, cluttered up with a mass of unnecessary figures and proper names. The death of Igor, the snake which bit Oleg – what is all this but old wives' tales? Who wants to know that Ivan's second marriage, to Temryuk's daughter, occurred on 21 August 1562, whereas his fourth, to Anna Alekseevna Koltovskaya, occurred in 1572 [. . .]?'[1]

History does not reveal causes; it presents only a blank succession of unexplained events. 'Everything is forced into a standard mould invented by the historian. Tsar Ivan the Terrible, on whom Professor Ivanov is lecturing at the moment, after 1560 suddenly becomes transformed from a wise and virtuous man into a mad and cruel tyrant. How? Why? – You mustn't even ask . . .'.[2] And half a century later, in 1908, he declares to Gusev: 'History would be an excellent thing if only it were true.'[3] The proposition that history could (and should) be made scientific is a commonplace in the nineteenth century; but the number of those who interpreted the term 'science' as meaning natural science, and then asked themselves whether history could be transformed into a science in this specific sense, is not great. The most uncompromising policy was that of Auguste Comte, who, following his master Saint-Simon, tried to turn history into sociology, with what fantastic consequences we need not here relate. Karl Marx was perhaps, of all thinkers, the man who took this programme most seriously; and made the bravest, if one of the least successful, attempts to discover general laws which govern historical evolution, conceived on the then alluring analogy of biology and anatomy, so

1   V. N. Nazar'ev, 'Lyudi bylogo vremeni', *L. N. Tolstoi v vospominaniyakh sovremennikov* (Moscow, 1955), i 52.
2   ibid. 52–3.
3   N. N. Gusev, *Dva goda s L. N. Tolstym* etc. (Moscow, 1973), 188.

triumphantly transformed by Darwin's new evolutionary theories. Like Marx (of whom at the time of writing *War and Peace* he apparently knew nothing), Tolstoy saw clearly that if history was a science, it must be possible to discover and formulate a set of true laws of history which, in conjunction with the data of empirical observation, would make prediction of the future (and 'retrodiction' of the past) as feasible as it had become in, say, geology or astronomy. But he saw more clearly than Marx and his followers that this had, in fact, not been achieved, and said so with his usual dogmatic candour, and reinforced his thesis with arguments designed to show that the prospect of achieving this goal was non-existent; and clinched the matter by observing that the fulfilment of this scientific hope would end human life as we knew it: 'If we allow that human life can be ruled by reason, the possibility of life [i.e. as a spontaneous activity involving consciousness of free will] is destroyed.'[1]

But what oppressed Tolstoy was not merely the 'unscientific' nature of history – that no matter how scrupulous the technique of historical research might be, no dependable laws could be discovered of the kind required even by the most undeveloped natural sciences. He further thought that he could not justify to himself the apparently arbitrary selection of material, and the no less arbitrary distribution of emphasis, to which all historical writing seemed to be doomed. He complains that while the factors which determine the life of mankind are very various, historians select from them only some single aspect, say the political or the economic, and represent it as primary, as the efficient cause of social change; but then, what of religion, what of 'spiritual' factors, and the many other aspects – a literally countless multiplicity – with which all events are endowed? How can we escape the conclusion that the histories which exist represent what Tolstoy declares to be 'perhaps only 0.001 per cent of the elements which actually constitute the real history of peoples'? History, as it is normally written, usually represents 'political' – public – events as the most important, while spiritual – 'inner' – events are largely forgotten; yet prima facie it is they – the 'inner' events – that

1   *War and Peace*, epilogue, part 1, chapter 1 (end), T xii 238; W 1248.

are the most real, the most immediate experience of human beings; they, and only they, are what life, in the last analysis, is made of; hence the routine political historians are talking shallow nonsense.

Throughout the 1850s Tolstoy was obsessed by the desire to write a historical novel, one of his principal aims being to contrast the 'real' texture of life, both of individuals and of communities, with the 'unreal' picture presented by historians. Again and again in the pages of *War and Peace* we get a sharp juxtaposition of 'reality' – what 'really' occurred – with the distorting medium through which it will later be presented in the official accounts offered to the public, and indeed be recollected by the actors themselves – the original memories having now been touched up by their own treacherous (inevitably treacherous because automatically rationalising and formalising) minds. Tolstoy is perpetually placing the heroes of *War and Peace* in situations where this becomes particularly evident.

Nikolay Rostov at the battle of Austerlitz sees the great soldier Prince Bagration riding up with his suite towards the village of Schöngrabern, whence the enemy is advancing; neither he nor his staff, nor the officers who gallop up to him with messages, nor anyone else, is, or can be, aware of what exactly is happening, nor where, nor why; nor is the chaos of the battle in any way made clearer either in fact or in the minds of the Russian officers by the appearance of Bagration. Nevertheless his arrival puts heart into his subordinates; his courage, his calm, his mere presence create the illusion of which he is himself the first victim, namely, that what is happening is somehow connected with *his* skill, *his* plans, that it is *his* authority that is in some way directing the course of the battle; and this, in its turn, has a marked effect on the general morale around him. The dispatches which will duly be written later will inevitably ascribe every act and event on the Russian side to him and his dispositions; the credit or discredit, the victory or the defeat, will belong to him, although it is clear to everyone that he will have had less to do with the conduct and outcome of the battle than the humble, unknown soldiers who do at least perform whatever actual fighting is done, that is, shoot at each other, wound, kill, advance, retreat and so on.

Prince Andrey, too, knows this, most clearly at Borodino, where he is mortally wounded. He begins to understand the truth earlier, during the period when he is making efforts to meet the 'important' persons who seem to be guiding the destinies of Russia; he then gradually becomes convinced that Alexander's principal adviser, the famous reformer Speransky, and his friends, and indeed Alexander himself, are systematically deluding themselves when they suppose their activities, their words, memoranda, rescripts, resolutions, laws and so forth, to be the motive factors which cause historical change and determine the destinies of men and nations; whereas in fact they are nothing: only so much self-important milling in the void. And so Tolstoy arrives at one of his celebrated paradoxes: the higher soldiers or statesmen are in the pyramid of authority, the farther they must be from its base, which consists of those ordinary men and women whose lives are the actual stuff of history; and, consequently, the smaller the effect of the words and acts of such remote personages, despite all their theoretical authority, upon that history.

In a famous passage dealing with the state of Moscow in 1812 Tolstoy observes that from the heroic achievements of Russia after the burning of Moscow one might infer that its inhabitants were absorbed entirely in acts of self-sacrifice – in saving their country or in lamenting its destruction, in heroism, martyrdom, despair – but that in fact this was not so. People were preoccupied by personal interests. Those who went about their ordinary business without feeling heroic emotions or thinking that they were actors upon the well-lighted stage of history were the most useful to their country and community, while those who tried to grasp the general course of events and wanted to take part in history, those who performed acts of incredible self-sacrifice or heroism, and participated in great events, were the most useless. Worst of all, in Tolstoy's eyes, were those unceasing talkers who accused one another of the kind of thing 'for which no one could in fact have been responsible'; and this because 'nowhere is the commandment not to taste of the fruit of the tree of knowledge so clearly written as in the course of history. Only unconscious activity bears fruit, and the individual who plays a part in historical events never understands their significance. If he attempts to understand them, he is struck with sterility.'[1] To try to 'understand' anything by rational means is to make sure of failure. Pierre Bezukhov wanders about, 'lost' on the battlefield of Borodino, and looks for something which he imagines as a kind of set piece; a battle as depicted by the historians or the painters. But he finds only the ordinary confusion of individual human beings haphazardly attending to this or that human want.[2] That, at any rate, is concrete, uncontaminated by theories and abstractions; and Pierre is therefore closer to the truth about the course of events – at least as seen by men – than those who believe them to obey a discoverable set of laws or rules. Pierre sees only a succession of 'accidents' whose origins and consequences are, by and large, untraceable and unpredictable; only loosely strung groups of events forming an ever-varying pattern, following no discernible order. Any claim to perceive patterns susceptible to 'scientific' formulae must be mendacious.

Tolstoy's bitterest taunts, his most corrosive irony, are reserved for those who pose as official specialists in managing human affairs, in this case the Western military theorists, a General Pfuel, or Generals Bennigsen and Paulucci, who are all shown talking equal nonsense at the Council of Drissa, whether they defend a given strategic or tactical theory or oppose it; these men must be impostors, since no theories can possibly fit the immense variety of possible human behaviour, the vast multiplicity of minute, undiscoverable causes and effects which form that interplay of men and nature which history purports to record. Those who affect to be able to contract this infinite multiplicity within their 'scientific' laws must be either deliberate charlatans or blind leaders of the blind. The harshest judgement is accordingly reserved for the master theorist himself, the great Napoleon, who acts upon, and has hypnotised others into believing, the assumption that he understands and controls events by his superior intellect, or by flashes of intuition, or by otherwise succeeding in answering correctly the problems posed by history. The greater

1   ibid. vol. 4, part 1, chapter 4 (beginning), T xii 14; W 1039–40.
2   On the connection of this with Stendhal's *La Chartreuse de Parme* see *Paul Boyer (1864–1949) chez Tolstoï: Entretiens à Iasnaïa Poliana* (Paris, 1950), 40.

the claim the greater the lie: Napoleon is consequently the most pitiable, the most contemptible of all the actors in the great tragedy.

This, then, is the great illusion which Tolstoy sets himself to expose: that individuals can, by the use of their own resources, understand and control the course of events. Those who believe this turn out to be dreadfully mistaken. And side by side with these public faces – these hollow men, half self-deluded, half aware of being fraudulent, talking, writing desperately and aimlessly in order to keep up appearances and avoid the bleak truths – side by side with all this elaborate machinery for concealing the spectacle of human impotence and irrelevance and blindness lies the real world, the stream of life which men understand, the attending to the ordinary details of daily existence. When Tolstoy contrasts this real life – the actual, everyday, 'live' experience of individuals – with the panoramic view conjured up by historians, it is clear to him which is real, and which is a coherent, sometimes elegantly contrived, but always fictitious construction. Utterly unlike her as he is in almost every other respect, Tolstoy is, perhaps, the first to propound the celebrated accusation which Virginia Woolf half a century later levelled against the public prophets of her own generation – Shaw and Wells and Arnold Bennett – as blind materialists who did not begin to understand what it is that life truly consists of, who mistook its outer accidents, the unimportant aspects which lie outside the individual soul – the so-called social, economic, political realities – for that which alone is genuine, the individual experience, the specific relation of individuals to one another, the colours, smells, tastes, sounds and movements, the jealousies, loves, hatreds, passions, the rare flashes of insight, the transforming moments, the ordinary day-to-day succession of private data which constitute all there is – which are reality.

What, then, is the historian's task? To describe the ultimate data of subjective experience – the personal lives lived by men, the 'thoughts, knowledge, poetry, music, love, friendship, hates, passions'[1] of which, for Tolstoy, 'real' life is compounded, and only that? That was the task to which Turgenev was perpetually

---

1   *War and Peace*, vol. 2, part 3, chapter 1, T x 151; W 453.

calling Tolstoy – him and all writers, but him in particular, because therein lay his true genius, his destiny as a great Russian writer; and this he rejected with violent indignation even during his middle years, before the final religious phase. For this was not to give the answer to the question of what there is, and why and how it comes to be and passes away, but to turn one's back upon it altogether, and stifle one's desire to discover how men live in society, and how they are affected by one another and by their environment, and to what end. This kind of artistic purism – preached in his day by Flaubert – this kind of preoccupation with the analysis and description of the experience and the relationships and problems and inner lives of individuals (later advocated and practised by Gide and the writers he influenced, both in France and in England) struck him as both trivial and false. He had no doubt about his own superlative skill in this very art, or that it was precisely this for which he was admired; and he condemned it absolutely.

In a letter written while he was working on *War and Peace* he said with bitterness that he had no doubt that what the public would like best would be his scenes of social and personal life, his ladies and his gentlemen, with their petty intrigues and entertaining conversations and marvellously described small idiosyncrasies.[1] But these are the trivial 'flowers' of life, not the 'roots'. Tolstoy's purpose is the discovery of the truth, and therefore he must know what history consists of, and recreate only that. History is plainly not a science, and sociology, which pretends that it is, is a fraud; no genuine laws of history have been discovered, and the concepts in current use – 'cause', 'accident', 'genius' – explain nothing: they are merely thin disguises for ignorance. Why do the events the totality of which we call history occur as they do? Some historians attribute events to the acts of individuals, but this is no answer: for they do not explain how these acts 'cause' the events they are alleged to 'cause' or 'originate'.

1   Cf. the profession of faith in his celebrated – and militantly moralistic – introduction to an edition of Maupassant, whose genius, despite everything, he admires: 'Predislovie k sochineniyam Gyui de Mopassana' (1893–4), T xxx 3–24. He thinks much more poorly of Bernard Shaw, whose social rhetoric he calls stale and platitudinous (diary entry for 31 January 1908, T lvi 97–8).

There is a passage of savage irony intended by Tolstoy to parody the average school histories of his time, sufficiently typical to be worth reproducing in full:

Louis XIV was a very proud and self-confident man. He had such and such mistresses, and such and such ministers, and he governed France badly. The heirs of Louis XIV were also weak men, and also governed France badly. They also had such and such favourites and such and such mistresses. Besides which, certain persons were at this time writing books. By the end of the eighteenth century there gathered in Paris two dozen or so persons who started saying that all men were free and equal. Because of this in the whole of France people began to slaughter and drown each other. These people killed the king and a good many others. At this time there was a man of genius in France – Napoleon. He conquered everyone everywhere, i.e. killed a great many people because he was a great genius; and, for some reason, he went off to kill Africans, and killed them so well, and was so clever and cunning, that, having arrived in France, he ordered everyone to obey him, which they did. Having made himself Emperor he again went to kill masses of people in Italy, Austria and Prussia. And there too he killed a great many. Now in Russia there was the Emperor Alexander, who decided to re-establish order in Europe, and therefore fought wars with Napoleon. But in the year '07 he suddenly made friends with him, and in the year '11 quarrelled with him again, and they both again began to kill a great many people. And Napoleon brought six hundred thousand men to Russia and conquered Moscow. But then he suddenly ran away from Moscow, and then the Emperor Alexander, aided by the advice of Stein and others, united Europe to raise an army against the disturber of her peace. All Napoleon's allies suddenly became his enemies; and this army marched against Napoleon, who had gathered new forces. The allies conquered Napoleon, entered Paris, forced Napoleon to renounce the throne, and sent him to the island of Elba, without, however, depriving him of the title of Emperor, and showing him all respect, in spite of the fact that five years before, and a year after, everyone considered him a brigand and beyond the law. Thereupon Louis XVIII, who until then had been an object of mere ridicule to both Frenchmen and the allies, began to reign. As for Napoleon, after shedding tears before the Old Guard, he gave up his throne, and went into exile. Then astute statesmen and diplomats, in particular Talleyrand, who had managed to sit down before anyone else in the famous armchair[1] and thereby to extend the frontiers of France, talked in Vienna, and by means of such talk made peoples happy or unhappy. Suddenly the diplomats and monarchs almost came to blows. They were almost ready to order their troops once again to kill each other; but at this moment Napoleon arrived in France with a battalion, and the French, who hated him, all immediately submitted to him. But this annoyed the allied monarchs very much and they again went to war with the French. And the genius Napoleon was defeated and taken to the island of St Helena, having suddenly been discovered to be an outlaw. Whereupon the exile, parted from his dear ones and his beloved France, died a slow death on a rock, and bequeathed his great deeds to posterity. As for Europe, a reaction occurred there, and all the princes began to treat their peoples badly once again.

Tolstoy continues:

The new history is like a deaf man replying to questions which nobody puts to him [. . .] the primary question [. . .] is, what power is it that moves the destinies of peoples? [. . .] History seems to presuppose that this power can be taken for granted, and is familiar to everyone, but, in spite of every wish to admit that this power is familiar to us, anyone who has read a great many historical works cannot help doubting whether this power, which different historians understand in different ways, is in fact so completely familiar to everyone.[2]

He goes on to say that political historians who write in this way explain nothing: they merely attribute events to the 'power' which important individuals are said to exercise over others, but do not tell us what the term 'power' means; and yet this is the heart of the problem. The problem of historical movement is directly

---

1   Empire chairs of a certain shape are to this day called 'Talleyrand armchairs' in Russia.

2   *War and Peace*, epilogue, part 2, chapter 1, T xii 298–300; W 1307–9.

connected with the 'power' exercised by some men over others: but
what is 'power'? How does one acquire it? Can it be transferred
by one man to another? Surely it is not merely physical strength
that is meant? Nor moral strength? Did Napoleon possess either
of these?

General, as opposed to national, historians seem to Tolstoy
merely to extend this category without elucidating it: instead of
one country or nation, many are introduced, but the spectacle of
the interplay of mysterious 'forces' makes it no clearer why some
men or nations obey others, why wars are made, victories won,
why innocent men who believe that murder is wicked kill one
another with enthusiasm and pride, and are glorified for so doing;
why great movements of human masses occur, sometimes from
east to west, sometimes the other way. Tolstoy is particularly
irritated by references to the dominant influence of great men or
of ideas. Great men, we are told, are typical of the movements of
their age: hence study of their characters 'explains' such movements. Do the characters of Diderot or Beaumarchais 'explain' the
advance of the West upon the East? Do the letters of Ivan the
Terrible to Prince Kurbsky 'explain' Russian expansion westward?
But historians of culture do no better, for they merely add as an
extra factor something called the 'force' of ideas or of books,
although we still have no notion of what is meant by words like
'force'. But why should Napoleon, or Mme de Staël or Baron Stein
or Tsar Alexander, or all of these, plus the *Contrat social*, 'cause'
Frenchmen to behead or to drown each other? Why is this called
'explanation'? As for the importance which historians of culture
attach to ideas, doubtless all men are liable to exaggerate the
importance of their own wares: ideas are the commodity in which
intellectuals deal – to a cobbler there's nothing like leather – the
professors merely tend to magnify their personal activities into the
central 'force' that rules the world. Tolstoy adds that an even
deeper darkness is cast upon this subject by political theorists,
moralists, metaphysicians. The celebrated notion of the social
contract, for example, which some liberals peddle, speaks of the
'vesting' of the wills, in other words the power, of many men in
one individual or group of individuals; but what kind of act is this
'vesting'? It may have a legal or ethical significance, it may be

relevant to what should be considered as permitted or forbidden, to the world of rights and duties, or of the good and the bad, but as a factual explanation of how a sovereign accumulates enough 'power' – as if it were a commodity – which enables him to effect this or that result, it means nothing. It declares that the conferring of power makes powerful; but this tautology is too unilluminating. What is 'power' and what is 'conferring'? And who confers it and how is such conferring done?[1] The process seems very different from whatever it is that is discussed by the physical sciences. Conferring is an act, but an unintelligible one; conferring power, acquiring it, using it are not at all like eating or drinking or thinking or walking. We remain in the dark: *obscurum per obscurius*.

After demolishing the jurists and moralists and political philosophers – among them his beloved Rousseau – Tolstoy applies himself to demolishing the liberal theory of history according to which everything may turn upon what may seem an insignificant accident. Hence the pages in which he obstinately tries to prove that Napoleon knew as little of what actually went on during the battle of Borodino as the lowliest of his soldiers; and that therefore his cold on the eve of it, of which so much was made by the historians, could have made no appreciable difference. With great force he argues that only those orders or decisions issued by the commanders now seem particularly crucial (and are concentrated upon by historians) which happened to coincide with what later actually occurred; whereas a great many other exactly similar, perfectly good orders and decisions, which seemed no less crucial and vital to those who were issuing them at the time, are forgotten because, having been foiled by unfavourable turns of events, they were not, because they could not be, carried out, and for this reason now seem historically unimportant.

After disposing of the heroic theory of history, Tolstoy turns

---

1   One of Tolstoy's Russian critics, M. M. Rubinshtein, referred to above (30 note 2), 80 ff., says that every science employs *some* unanalysed concepts, to explain which is the business of other sciences; and that 'power' happens to be the unexplained central concept of history. But Tolstoy's point is that no other science can 'explain' it, since it is, as used by historians, a meaningless term, not a concept but nothing at all – *vox nihili*.

with even greater savagery upon scientific sociology, which claims
to have discovered laws of history, but cannot possibly have found
any, because the number of causes upon which events turn is too
great for human knowledge or calculation. We know too few
facts, and we select them at random and in accordance with our
subjective inclinations. No doubt if we were omniscient we might
be able, like Laplace's ideal observer, to plot the course of every
drop of which the stream of history consists, but we are, of course,
pathetically ignorant, and the areas of our knowledge are incred-
ibly small compared to what is uncharted and (Tolstoy vehemently
insists on this) unchartable. Freedom of the will is an illusion
which cannot be shaken off, but, as great philosophers have said,
it is an illusion nevertheless, and it derives solely from ignorance
of true causes. The more we know about the circumstances of an
act, the farther away from us the act is in time, the more difficult
it is to think away its consequences; the more solidly embedded a
fact is in the actual world in which we live, the less we can imagine
how things might have turned out if something different had
happened. For by now it seems inevitable: to think otherwise
would upset too much of our world order. The more closely we
relate an act to its context, the less free the actor seems to be, the
less responsible for his act, and the less disposed we are to hold
him accountable or blameworthy. The fact that we shall never
identify all the causes, relate all human acts to the circumstances
which condition them, does not imply that they are free, only that
we shall never know how they are necessitated.

Tolstoy's central thesis – in some respects not unlike the theory
of the inevitable 'self-deception' of the bourgeoisie held by his
contemporary Karl Marx, save that what Marx reserves for a
class, Tolstoy sees in almost all mankind – is that there is a natural
law whereby the lives of human beings no less than that of nature
are determined; but that men, unable to face this inexorable process, seek to represent it as a succession of free choices, to fix
responsibility for what occurs upon persons endowed by them
with heroic virtues or heroic vices, and called by them 'great men'.
What are great men? They are ordinary human beings who are
ignorant and vain enough to accept responsibility for the life of
society, individuals who would rather take the blame for all the

cruelties, injustices, disasters justified in their name than recognise their own insignificance and impotence in the cosmic flow which pursues its course irrespective of their wills and ideals. This is the central point of those passages (in which Tolstoy excelled) in which the actual course of events is described, side by side with the absurd, egocentric explanations which persons blown up with the sense of their own importance necessarily give to them; as well as of the wonderful descriptions of moments of illumination in which the truth about the human condition dawns upon those who have the humility to recognise their own unimportance and irrelevance. This is the purpose, too, of those philosophical passages where, in language more ferocious than Spinoza's, but with intentions similar to his, the errors of the pseudo-sciences are exposed.

There is a particularly vivid simile[1] in which the great man is likened to the ram whom the shepherd is fattening for slaughter. Because the ram duly grows fatter, and perhaps is used as a bell-wether for the rest of the flock, he may easily imagine that he is the leader of the flock, and that the other sheep go where they go solely in obedience to his will. He thinks this and the flock may think it too. Nevertheless the purpose of his selection is not the role he believes himself to play, but slaughter – a purpose conceived by beings whose aims neither he nor the other sheep can fathom. For Tolstoy Napoleon is just such a ram, and so to some degree is Alexander, and indeed all the great men of history. Indeed, as an acute literary historian has pointed out,[2] Tolstoy sometimes seems almost deliberately to ignore the historical evidence and more than once consciously distorts the facts in order to bolster up his favourite thesis.

The character of Kutuzov is a case in point. Such heroes as Pierre Bezukhov or Karataev are at least imaginary, and Tolstoy had an undisputed right to endow them with all the attributes he admired – humility, freedom from bureaucratic or scientific or other rationalistic kinds of blindness. But Kutuzov was a real

1   *War and Peace*, epilogue, part 1, chapter 2, T xii 239; W 1249.
2   See V. B. Shklovsky, op. cit. (29 above, note 1), chapters 7 and 8, and also K. Pokrovsky, 'Istochniki romana "Voina i mir"', in Obninsky and Polner, op. cit. (30 above, note 2), 113–28.

person, and it is all the more instructive to observe the steps
by which Tolstoy transforms him from the sly, elderly, feeble
voluptuary, the corrupt and somewhat sycophantic courtier of the
early drafts of *War and Peace*, which were based on authentic
sources, into the unforgettable symbol of the Russian people in all
its simplicity and intuitive wisdom. By the time we reach the
celebrated passage – one of the most moving in literature – in
which Tolstoy describes the moment when the old man is woken
in his camp at Fili to be told that the French army is retreating,
we have left the facts behind us, and are in an imaginary realm, a
historical and emotional atmosphere for which the evidence is
flimsy, but which is artistically indispensable to Tolstoy's design.
The final apotheosis of Kutuzov is totally unhistorical, for all
Tolstoy's repeated professions of his undeviating devotion to the
sacred cause of the truth.

   In *War and Peace* Tolstoy treats facts cavalierly when it suits
him, because he is above all obsessed by his thesis – the contrast
between the universal and all-important but delusive experience
of free will, the feeling of responsibility, the values of private life
generally, on the one hand; and on the other the reality of inexorable historical determinism, not, indeed, experienced directly, but
known to be true on irrefutable theoretical grounds. This corresponds in its turn to a tormenting inner conflict, one of many, in
Tolstoy himself, between the two systems of value, the public and
the private. On the one hand, if those feelings and immediate
experiences upon which the ordinary values of private individuals
and historians alike ultimately rest are nothing but a vast illusion,
this must, in the name of the truth, be ruthlessly demonstrated,
and the values and the explanations which derive from the illusion
exposed and discredited. And in a sense Tolstoy does try to do
this, particularly when he is philosophising, as in the great public
scenes of the novel itself, the battle pieces, the descriptions of the
movements of peoples, the metaphysical disquisitions. But, on
the other hand, he also does the exact opposite of this when he
contrasts with this panorama of public life the superior value of
personal experience, when he contrasts the concrete and multi-
coloured reality of individual lives with the pale abstractions of
scientists or historians, particularly the latter, 'from Gibbon to

Buckle',[1] whom he denounces so harshly for mistaking their own empty categories for real facts. And yet the primacy of these private experiences and relationships and virtues presupposes that vision of life, with its sense of personal responsibility, and belief in freedom and the possibility of spontaneous action, to which the best pages of *War and Peace* are devoted, and which is the very illusion to be exorcised if the truth is to be faced.

This terrible dilemma is never finally resolved. Sometimes, as in the explanation of his intentions which he published before the final part of *War and Peace* had appeared,[2] Tolstoy vacillates. The individual is 'in some sense' free when he alone is involved: thus, in raising his arm, he is free within physical limits. But once he is involved in relationships with others, he is no longer free, he is part of the inexorable stream. Freedom is real, but it is confined to trivial acts. At other times even this feeble ray of hope is extinguished: Tolstoy declares that he cannot admit even small exceptions to the universal law; causal determinism is either wholly pervasive or it is nothing, and chaos reigns. Men's acts may seem free of the social nexus, but they are not free, they cannot be free, they are part of it. Science cannot destroy the consciousness of freedom, without which there is no morality and no art, but it can refute it. 'Power' and 'accident' are but names for ignorance of the causal chains, but the chains exist whether we feel them or not. Fortunately we do not; for if we felt their weight, we could scarcely act at all; the loss of the illusion would paralyse the life which is lived on the basis of our happy ignorance. But all is well: for we never shall discover all the causal chains that operate: the number of such causes is infinitely great, the causes themselves infinitely small; historians select an absurdly small portion of them and attribute everything to this arbitrarily chosen tiny section. How would an ideal historical science operate? By using a kind of calculus whereby this 'differential', the infinitesimals – the infinitely small human and non-human actions and events – would be integrated, and in this way the continuum of history would no longer be distorted by being broken up into

1   *War and Peace*, epilogue, part 2, chapter 1, T xii 297; W 490.
2   'Neskol'ko slov po povodu knigi: "Voina i mir"' (1868), T xvi 5–16.

arbitrary segments.[1] Tolstoy expresses this notion of calculation by infinitesimals with great lucidity, and with his habitual simple, vivid, precise use of words. Henri Bergson, who made his name with his theory of reality as a flux fragmented artificially by the natural sciences, and thereby distorted and robbed of continuity and life, developed a very similar point at infinitely greater length, less clearly, less plausibly, and with an unnecessary parade of terminology.

It is not a mystical or an intuitionist view of life. Our ignorance of how things happen is due not to some inherent inaccessibility of the first causes, only to their multiplicity, the smallness of the ultimate units, and our own inability to see and hear and remember and record and co-ordinate enough of the available material. Omniscience is in principle possible even to empirical beings, but, of course, in practice unattainable. This alone, and nothing deeper or more interesting, is the source of human megalomania, of all our absurd delusions. Since we are not, in fact, free, but could not live without the conviction that we are, what are we to do? Tolstoy arrives at no clear conclusion, only at the view, in some respects like Burke's, that it is better to realise that we understand what goes on as we do in fact understand it – much as spontaneous, normal, simple people, uncorrupted by theories, not blinded by the dust raised by the scientific authorities, do, in fact, understand life – than to seek to subvert such common-sense beliefs, which at least have the merit of having been tested by long experience, in favour of pseudo-sciences, which, being founded on absurdly inadequate data, are only a snare and a delusion. That is his case against all forms of optimistic rationalism, the natural sciences, liberal theories of progress, German military expertise, French sociology, confident social engineering of all kinds. And this is his reason for inventing a Kutuzov who followed his simple, Russian, untutored instinct, and despised or ignored the German, French and Italian experts; and for raising him to the status of a national hero, which, partly as a result of Tolstoy's portrait, he has retained ever since.

In 1868, immediately on the appearance of the last part of *War*

1   *War and Peace*, vol. 3, part 3, chapter 1, T xi 264–7; W 909–11.

and Peace, Akhsharumov observed that Tolstoy's figures were real and not mere pawns in the hands of an unintelligible destiny;[1] the author's theory, on the other hand, was ingenious but irrelevant. This remained the general view of Russian and, for the most part, foreign literary critics too. The Russian left-wing intellectuals attacked Tolstoy for 'social indifferentism', for disparagement of all noble social impulses as a compound of ignorance and foolish monomania, and an 'aristocratic' cynicism about life as a marsh which cannot be reclaimed; Flaubert and Turgenev, as we have seen, thought the tendency to philosophise unfortunate in itself; the only critic who took the doctrine seriously and tried to provide a rational refutation was the historian Kareev.[2] Patiently and mildly he pointed out that, fascinating as the contrast between the reality of personal life and the life of the social anthill may be, Tolstoy's conclusions did not follow. True, man is at once an atom living its own conscious life 'for itself', and at the same time the unconscious agent of some historical trend, a relatively insignificant element in the vast whole composed of a very large number of such elements. *War and Peace*, Kareev tells us, is 'a historical poem on the philosophical theme of the duality of human life'[3] – and Tolstoy was perfectly right to protest that history is not made to happen by the combination of such obscure entities as the 'power' or 'mental activity' assumed by naive historians; indeed he was, in Kareev's view, at his best when he denounced the tendency of metaphysically minded writers to attribute causal efficacy to, or idealise, such abstract entities as 'heroes', 'historic forces', 'moral forces', 'nationalism', 'reason' and so on, whereby they simultaneously committed the two deadly sins of inventing non-existent entities to explain concrete events and of giving free reign to personal, or national, or class, or metaphysical bias.

So far so good, and Tolstoy is judged to have shown deeper insight – 'greater realism' – than most historians. He was right

1   op. cit. (29 above, note 3), 34, 40.
2   N. I. Kareev, 'Istoricheskaya filosofiya v "Voine i mire"', *Vestnik Evropy* 22 No 4 (July–August 1887), 227–69.
3   ibid. 230; cf. *War and Peace*, vol. 3, part 1, chapter 1, T xi 16; W 665 ('There are two sides to the life of every man [. . .]').

also in demanding that the infinitesimals of history be integrated. But then he himself had done just that by creating the individuals of his novel, who are not trivial precisely to the degree to which, in their characters and actions, they 'summate' countless others, who between them do 'move history'. This *is* the integrating of infinitesimals, not, of course, by scientific, but by 'artistic-psychological' means. Tolstoy was right to abhor abstractions, but this had led him too far, so that he ended by denying not merely that history was a natural science like chemistry – which was correct – but that it was a science at all, an activity with its own proper concepts and generalisations; which, if true, would abolish all history as such. Tolstoy was right to say that the impersonal 'forces' and 'purposes' of the older historians were myths, and dangerously misleading myths, but unless we were allowed to ask what made this or that group of individuals – who, in the end, of course, alone were real – behave thus and thus, without needing first to provide separate psychological analyses of each member of the group and then to 'integrate' them all, we could not think about history or society at all. Yet we did do this, and profitably, and to deny that we could discover a good deal by social observation, historical inference and similar means was, for Kareev, tantamount to denying that we had criteria for distinguishing between historical truth and falsehood which were less or more reliable – and that was surely mere prejudice, fanatical obscurantism.

Kareev declares that it is men, doubtless, who make social forms, but these forms – the ways in which men live – in their turn affect those born into them; individual wills may not be all-powerful, but neither are they totally impotent, and some are more effective than others. Napoleon may not be a demigod, but neither is he a mere epiphenomenon of a process which would have occurred unaltered without him; the 'important people' are less important than they themselves or the more foolish historians may suppose, but neither are they shadows; individuals, besides their intimate inner lives, which alone seem real to Tolstoy, have social purposes, and some among them have strong wills too, and these sometimes transform the lives of communities. Tolstoy's notion of inexorable laws which work themselves out whatever men may think or wish is itself an oppressive myth; laws are only statistical probabilities, at any rate in the social sciences, not hideous and inexorable 'forces' – a concept the darkness of which, Kareev points out, Tolstoy himself in other contexts exposed with such brilliance and malice, when his opponent seemed to him too naïve or too clever or in the grip of some grotesque metaphysic. But to say that unless men make history they are themselves, particularly the 'great' among them, mere 'labels', because history makes itself, and only the unconscious life of the social hive, the human anthill, has genuine significance or value and 'reality' – what is this but a wholly unhistorical and dogmatic ethical scepticism? Why should we accept it when empirical evidence points elsewhere?

Kareev's objections are very reasonable, the most sensible and clearly formulated of all that ever were urged against Tolstoy's view of history. But in a sense he missed the point. Tolstoy was not primarily engaged in exposing the fallacies of histories based on this or that metaphysical schematism, or those which sought to explain too much in terms of some one chosen element particularly dear to the author (all of which Kareev approves), or in refuting the possibility of an empirical science of sociology (which Kareev thinks unreasonable of him) in order to set up some rival theory of his own. Tolstoy's concern with history derives from a deeper source than abstract interest in historical method or philosophical objections to given types of historical practice. It seems to spring from something more personal, a bitter inner conflict between his actual experience and his beliefs, between his vision of life and his theory of what it, and he himself, ought to be if the vision was to be bearable at all; between the immediate data, which he was too honest and too intelligent to ignore, and the need for an interpretation of them which did not lead to the childish absurdities of all previous views. For the one conviction to which his temperament and his intellect kept him faithful all his life was that all previous attempts at a rational theodicy – to explain how and why what occurred occurred as and when it did, and why it was bad or good that it should or should not do so – all such efforts were grotesque absurdities, shoddy deceptions which one sharp, honest word was sufficient to blow away.

The Russian critic Boris Eikhenbaum, who has written the best critical work on Tolstoy in any language, in the course of it develops the thesis that what oppressed Tolstoy most was his lack of positive convictions; and that the famous passage in *Anna Karenina* in which Levin's brother tells him that he – Levin – had no positive beliefs, that even communism, with its artificial 'geometrical' symmetry, is better than total scepticism of his – Levin's – kind, in fact refers to Lev Nikolaevich himself, and to the attacks on him by his brother Nikolay Nikolaevich.[1] Whether or not the passage is literally autobiographical – and there is little in Tolstoy's writing that, in one way or another, is not – Eikhenbaum's theory seems, in general, valid. Tolstoy was by nature not a visionary; he saw the manifold objects and situations on earth in their full multiplicity; he grasped their individual essences, and what divided them from what they were not, with a clarity to which there is no parallel. Any comforting theory which attempted to collect, relate, 'synthesise', reveal hidden substrata and concealed inner connections, which, though not apparent to the naked eye, nevertheless guaranteed the unity of all things, the fact that they were 'ultimately' parts one of another with no loose ends – the ideal of the seamless whole – all such doctrines he exploded contemptuously and without difficulty. His genius lay in the perception of specific properties, the almost inexpressible individual quality in virtue of which the given object is uniquely different from all others. Nevertheless he longed for a universal explanatory principle; that is, the perception of resemblances or common origins, or single purpose, or unity in the apparent variety of the mutually exclusive bits and pieces which composed the furniture of the world.[2] Like all very penetrating, very imaginative, very clear-sighted analysts who dissect or pulverise in order to reach the indestructible core, and justify their own annihilating activities (from which they cannot abstain in any case) by the belief that such a core exists, he continued to kill his rivals' rickety

1   B. M. Eikhenbaum, *Lev Tolstoy* (Leningrad, 1928–60), i 123–4.

2   Here the paradox appears once more; for the 'infinitesimals', whose integration is the task of the ideal historian, must be reasonably uniform to make this operation possible; yet the sense of 'reality' consists in the sense of their unique differences.

constructions with cold contempt, as being unworthy of intelligent men, always hoping that the desperately-sought-for 'real' unity would presently emerge from the destruction of the shams and frauds – the knock-kneed army of eighteenth- and nineteenth-century philosophies of history. And the more obsessive the suspicion that perhaps the quest was vain, that no core and no unifying principle would ever be discovered, the more ferocious the measures to drive this thought away by increasingly merciless and ingenious executions and more and more false claimants to the title of the truth. As Tolstoy moved away from literature to polemical writing this tendency became increasingly prominent: the irritated awareness at the back of his mind that no final solution was ever, in principle, to be found, caused Tolstoy to attack the bogus solutions all the more savagely for the false comfort they offered – and for being an insult to the intelligence.[1] Tolstoy's purely intellectual genius for this kind of lethal activity was very great and exceptional, and all his life he looked for some edifice strong enough to resist his engines of destruction and his mines and battering-rams; he wished to be stopped by an immovable obstacle, he wished his violent projectiles to be resisted by impregnable fortifications. The eminent reasonableness and tentative methods of Kareev, his mild academic remonstrance, were altogether too unlike the final impenetrable, irreducible, solid bedrock of truth on which alone that secure interpretation of life could be built which all his life he wished to find.

The thin, 'positive' doctrine of historical change in *War and Peace* is all that remains of this despairing search, and it is the immense superiority of Tolstoy's offensive over his defensive weapons that has always made his philosophy of history – the theory of the minute particles, requiring integration – seem so threadbare and artificial to the average, reasonably critical, moderately sensitive reader of the novel. Hence the tendency of most of

---

1   In our day French existentialists, for similar psychological reasons, have struck out against all explanations as such because they are a mere drug to still serious questions, short-lived palliatives for wounds which are unbearable but must be borne, above all not denied or 'explained'; for all explaining is explaining away, and that is a denial of the given – the existent – the brute facts.

those who have written about *War and Peace*, both immediately
on its appearance and in later years, to maintain Akhsharumov's
thesis that Tolstoy's genius lay in his quality as a writer, a creator
of a world more real than life itself; while the theoretical disquisitions, even though Tolstoy himself may have looked upon them
as the most important ingredient in the book, in fact threw no
light upon either the character or the value of the work itself, or
on the creative process by which it was achieved. This anticipated
the approach of those psychological critics who maintain that the
author himself often scarcely knows the sources of his own activity: that the springs of his genius are invisible to him, the process
itself largely unconscious, and his own overt purpose a mere
rationalisation in his own mind of the true, but scarcely conscious,
motives and methods involved in the act of creation, and consequently often a mere hindrance to those dispassionate students of
art and literature who are engaged upon the 'scientific' – naturalistic – analysis of its origins and evolution.

   Whatever we may think of the general validity of such an outlook, it is something of a historical irony that Tolstoy should have
been treated in this fashion; for it is virtually his own way with
the academic historians at whom he mocks with such Voltairean
irony. And yet there is much poetic justice in it: for the unequal
ratio of critical to constructive elements in his own philosophising
seems due to the fact that his sense of reality (a reality which
resides in individual persons and their relationships alone) served
to explode all the large theories which ignored its findings, but
proved insufficient by itself to provide the basis of a more satisfactory general account of the facts. And there is no evidence that
Tolstoy himself ever conceived it possible that this was the root of
the 'duality', the failure to reconcile the two lives lived by man.

   The unresolved conflict between Tolstoy's belief that the attributes of personal life alone are real and his doctrine that analysis
of them is insufficient to explain the course of history (that is, the
behaviour of societies) is paralleled, at a profounder and more
personal level, by the conflict between, on the one hand, his own
gifts both as a writer and as a man and, on the other, his ideals –
that which he sometimes believed himself to be, and at all times
profoundly believed in, and wished to be.

If we may recall once again our division of artists into foxes and hedgehogs: Tolstoy perceived reality in its multiplicity, as a collection of separate entities round and into which he saw with a clarity and penetration scarcely ever equalled, but he believed only in one vast, unitary whole. No author who has ever lived has shown such powers of insight into the variety of life – the differences, the contrasts, the collisions of persons and things and situations, each apprehended in its absolute uniqueness and conveyed with a degree of directness and a precision of concrete imagery to be found in no other writer. No one has ever excelled Tolstoy in expressing the specific flavour, the exact quality of a feeling – the degree of its 'oscillation', the ebb and flow, the minute movements (which Turgenev mocked as a mere trick on his part) – the inner and outer texture and 'feel' of a look, a thought, a pang of sentiment, no less than of a specific situation, of an entire period, of the lives of individuals, families, communities, entire nations. The celebrated lifelikeness of every object and every person in his world derives from this astonishing capacity of presenting every ingredient of it in its fullest individual essence, in all its many dimensions, as it were: never as a mere datum, however vivid, within some stream of consciousness, with blurred edges, an outline, a shadow, an impressionistic representation; nor yet calling for, and dependent on, some process of reasoning in the mind of the reader; but always as a solid object, seen simultaneously from near and far, in natural, unaltering daylight, from all possible angles of vision, set in an absolutely specific context in time and space – an event fully present to the senses or the imagination in all its facets, with every nuance sharply and firmly articulated.

Yet what he believed in was the opposite. He advocated a single embracing vision; he preached not variety but simplicity, not many levels of consciousness but reduction to some single level – in *War and Peace*, to the standard of the good man, the single, spontaneous, open soul: as later to that of the peasants, or of a simple Christian ethic divorced from any complex theology or metaphysic; some simple, quasi-utilitarian criterion, whereby everything is interrelated directly, and all the items can be assessed in terms of one another by some simple measuring-rod. Tolstoy's genius lies in a capacity for marvellously accurate reproduction of the irreproducible, the almost miraculous evocation of the full, untranslatable individuality of the individual, which induces in the reader an acute awareness of the presence of the object itself, and not of a mere description of it, employing for this purpose metaphors which fix the quality of a particular experience as such, and avoiding those general terms which relate it to similar instances by ignoring individual differences – the 'oscillations' of feeling – in favour of what is common to them all. But then this same writer pleads for, indeed preaches with great fury, particularly in his last, religious phase, the exact opposite: the necessity of expelling everything that does not submit to some very general, very simple standard: say, what peasants like or dislike, or what the Gospels declare to be good.

This violent contradiction between the data of experience, from which he could not liberate himself, and which, of course, all his life he knew alone to be real, and his deeply metaphysical belief in the existence of a system to which they *must* belong, whether they appear to do so or not, this conflict between instinctive judgement and theoretical conviction – between his gifts and his opinions – mirrors the unresolved conflict between the reality of the moral life, with its sense of responsibility, joys, sorrows, sense of guilt and sense of achievement – all of which is nevertheless illusion – and the laws which govern everything, although we cannot know more than a negligible portion of them – so that all scientists and historians who say that they do know them and are guided by them are lying and deceiving – but which nevertheless alone are real. Beside Tolstoy, Gogol and Dostoevsky, whose abnormality is so often contrasted with Tolstoy's 'sanity', are well-integrated personalities, with a coherent outlook and a single vision. Yet out of this violent conflict grew *War and Peace*: its marvellous solidity should not blind us to the deep cleavage which yawns open whenever Tolstoy remembers, or rather reminds himself – fails to forget – what he is doing, and why.

IV

Theories are seldom born in the void. The question of the roots of Tolstoy's vision of history is therefore a reasonable one. Everything that Tolstoy writes on history has the stamp of his own original personality, a first-hand quality denied to most writers on abstract topics. On these subjects he wrote as an amateur, not as a professional; but let it be remembered that he belonged to the world of great affairs: he was a member of the ruling class of his country and his time, and knew and understood it completely; he lived in an environment exceptionally crowded with theories and ideas, he examined a great deal of material for *War and Peace* (though, as several Russian scholars have shown,[1] not as much as is sometimes supposed), he travelled a great deal, and met many notable public figures in Germany and France.

That he read widely, and was influenced by what he read, cannot be doubted. It is a commonplace that he owed a great deal to Rousseau, and probably derived from him, as much as from Diderot and the French Enlightenment, his analytic, anti-historical ways of approaching social problems, in particular the tendency to treat them in terms of timeless logical, moral and metaphysical categories, and not look for their essence, as the German historical school advocated, in terms of growth, and of response to a changing historical environment. He remained an admirer of Rousseau, and late in life still recommended *Émile* as the best book ever written on education.[2] Rousseau must have strengthened, if he did not actually originate, his growing tendency to idealise the soil and its cultivators – the simple peasant, who for Tolstoy is a repository of almost as rich a stock of 'natural' virtues as Rousseau's noble savage. Rousseau, too, must have reinforced the

---

1   For example, both Shklovsky (*passim*) and Eikhenbaum (i 259–60) in the works cited above (29, note 1; 54, note 1).

2   'On n'a pas rendu justice à Rousseau [. . .] J'ai lu tout Rousseau, oui, tous les vingt volumes, y compris le *Dictionnaire de musique*. Je faisais mieux que l'admirer; je lui rendais une culte véritable'; 'Justice has not been done to Rousseau [. . .] I have read all of Rousseau, yes, all twenty volumes, including the *Dictionary of Music*. I did better than admire him, I truly worshipped him': loc. cit. (39 above, note 2).

coarse-grained, rough peasant in Tolstoy, with his strongly moralistic, puritanical strain, his suspicion of, and antipathy to, the rich,
the powerful, the happy as such, his streak of genuine vandalism,
and occasional bursts of blind, very Russian rage against Western
sophistication and refinement, and that adulation of 'virtue' and
simple tastes, of the 'healthy' moral life, the militant, anti-liberal
barbarism, which is one of Rousseau's specific contributions to
the stock of Jacobin ideas. Perhaps Rousseau influenced him also
in setting so high a value upon family life, and in his doctrine of
the superiority of the heart over the head, of moral over intellectual
or aesthetic virtues. This has been noted before, and it is true
and illuminating, but it does not account for Tolstoy's theory
of history, of which little trace can be found in the profoundly
unhistorical Rousseau. Indeed, in so far as Rousseau seeks to
derive the right of some men to authority over others from a
theory of the transference of power in accordance with the Social
Contract, Tolstoy contemptuously refutes him.

We get somewhat nearer to the truth if we consider the influence
upon Tolstoy of his romantic and conservative Slavophil contemporaries. He was close to some among them, particularly to
Pogodin and Samarin, in the mid-1860s when he was writing *War
and Peace*, and certainly shared their antagonism to the scientific
theories of history then fashionable, whether the metaphysical
positivism of Comte and his followers, or the more materialistic
views of Chernyshevsky and Pisarev, as well as those of Buckle
and Mill and Herbert Spencer, and the general British empiricist
tradition, tinged by French and German scientific materialism, to
which these very different figures all, in their various fashions,
belonged. The Slavophils (and perhaps especially Tyutchev, whose
poetry Tolstoy admired so deeply) may have done something to
discredit for him historical theories modelled upon the natural
sciences, which, for Tolstoy no less than for Dostoevsky, failed to
give a true account of what men did and suffered. They were
inadequate if only because they ignored man's 'inner' experience,
treated him as a natural object played upon by the same forces
as all the other constituents of the material world, and, taking
the French Encyclopedists at their word, tried to study social
behaviour as one might study a beehive or an anthill, and then

complained because the laws which they formulated failed to explain the behaviour of living men and women. These romantic medievalists may moreover have strengthened Tolstoy's natural anti-intellectualism and anti-liberalism, and his deeply sceptical and pessimistic view of the strength of non-rational motives in human behaviour, which at once dominate human beings and deceive them about themselves – in short that innate conservatism of outlook which very early made Tolstoy deeply suspect to the radical Russian intelligentsia of the 1850s and 1860s, and led them to think of him uneasily as being after all a count, an officer and a reactionary, not one of themselves, not genuinely enlightened or *révolté* at all, despite his boldest protests against the political system, his heterodoxies, his destructive nihilism.

But although Tolstoy and the Slavophils may have fought a common enemy, their positive views diverged sharply. The Slavophil doctrine derived principally from German Idealism, in particular from Schelling's view (despite much lip-service to Hegel and his interpreters) that true knowledge could not be obtained by the use of reason, but only by a kind of imaginative self-identification with the central principle of the universe – the soul of the world – such as artists and thinkers have in moments of divine inspiration. Some of the Slavophils identified this with the revealed truths of the Orthodox religion and the mystical tradition of the Russian Church, and bequeathed it to the Russian symbolist poets and philosophers of a later generation. Tolstoy stood at the opposite pole to all this. He believed that only by patient empirical observation could any knowledge be obtained; that this knowledge is always inadequate, that simple people often know the truth better than learned men, because their observation of men and nature is less clouded by empty theories, and not because they are inspired vehicles of the divine afflatus. There is a hard cutting edge of common sense about everything that Tolstoy wrote which automatically puts to flight metaphysical fantasies and undisciplined tendencies towards esoteric experience, or the poetical or theological interpretations of life which lay at the heart of the Slavophil outlook, and (as in the analogous case of the anti-industrial romanticism of the West) determined both its hatred of politics and economics in the ordinary sense, and its mystical

nationalism. Moreover, the Slavophils were worshippers of historical method as alone disclosing the true nature – revealed only
in its impalpable growth in time – of individual institutions and
abstract sciences alike.

None of this could possibly have found a sympathetic echo in
the very tough-minded, very matter-of-fact Tolstoy, especially the
realistic Tolstoy of the middle years; if the peasant Platon Karataev
has something in common with the agrarian ethos of the Slavophil
(and indeed pan-Slav) ideologists – simple rural wisdom as against
the absurdities of the overclever West – yet Pierre Bezukhov in
the early drafts of *War and Peace* ends his life as a Decembrist
and an exile in Siberia, and cannot be conceived in all his spiritual
wanderings as ultimately finding comfort in any metaphysical
system, still less in the bosom of the Orthodox or any other
established Church. The Slavophils saw through the pretensions
of Western social and psychological science, and that was sympathetic to Tolstoy; but their positive doctrines interested him
little. He was against unintelligible mysteries, against mists of
antiquity, against any kind of recourse to mumbo-jumbo: his
hostile picture of the Freemasons in *War and Peace* remained
symptomatic of his attitude until the end. This can only have been
reinforced by his interest in the writings of, and his visit in 1861 to,
the exiled Proudhon, whose confused irrationalism, puritanism,
hatred of authority and bourgeois intellectuals, and general
Rousseauism and violence of tone evidently pleased him. It is more
than possible that he took the title of his novel from Proudhon's
La Guerre et la paix, published in the same year.

If the classical German Idealists had had no direct effect upon
Tolstoy, there was at least one German philosopher for whom he
did express admiration. Indeed it is not difficult to see why he
found Schopenhauer attractive: that solitary thinker drew a
gloomy picture of the impotent human will beating desperately
against the rigidly determined laws of the universe; he spoke of
the vanity of all human passions, the absurdity of rational systems,
the universal failure to understand the non-rational springs of
action and feeling, the suffering to which all flesh is subject, and
the consequent desirability of reducing human vulnerability by
reducing man himself to the condition of the utmost quietism,

where, being passionless, he cannot be frustrated or humiliated or wounded. This celebrated doctrine reflected Tolstoy's later views – that man suffers much because he seeks too much, is foolishly ambitious and grotesquely overestimates his capacities. From Schopenhauer, too, may come the bitter emphasis laid on the familiar contrast of the illusion of free will with the reality of the iron laws which govern the world, in particular the account of the inevitable suffering which this illusion, since it cannot be made to vanish, must necessarily cause. This, for both Schopenhauer and Tolstoy, is the central tragedy of human life; if only men would learn how little the cleverest and most gifted among them can control, how little they can know of all the multitude of factors the orderly movement of which is the history of the world; above all, what presumptuous nonsense it is to claim to perceive an order merely on the strength of believing desperately that an order must exist, when all one actually perceives is meaningless chaos – a chaos of which the heightened form, the microcosm in which the disorder of human life is reflected in an intense degree, is war.

The best avowed of all Tolstoy's literary debts is, of course, that to Stendhal. In his celebrated interview in 1901 with Paul Boyer, Tolstoy coupled Stendhal and Rousseau as the two writers to whom he owed most, and added that all he had learnt about war he had learnt from Stendhal's description of the battle of Waterloo in *La Chartreuse de Parme*, where Fabrice wanders about the battlefield 'understanding "nothing"'. He added that this conception – war 'without panache' or 'embellishments' – of which his brother Nikolay had spoken to him, he later had verified for himself during his own service in the Crimean War.[1] Nothing ever won so much praise from active soldiers as Tolstoy's vignettes of episodes in the war, his descriptions of how battles appear to those who are actually engaged in them.

No doubt Tolstoy was right in declaring that he owed much of this dry light to Stendhal. But there is a figure behind Stendhal even drier, even more destructive, from whom Stendhal may well, at least in part, have derived his new method of interpreting social

1   ibid. ('il n'y a point de panache à la guerre').

life, a celebrated writer with whose works Tolstoy was certainly acquainted and to whom he owed a deeper debt than is commonly supposed; for the striking resemblance between their views can hardly be put down either to accident, or to the mysterious operations of the *Zeitgeist*. This figure was the famous Joseph de Maistre; and the full story of his influence on Tolstoy, although it has been noted by students of Tolstoy, and by at least one critic of Maistre,[1] still largely remains to be written.

                                        V

On 1 November 1865, in the middle of writing *War and Peace*, Tolstoy wrote down in his diary 'I am reading Maistre',[2] and on 7 September 1866 he wrote to the editor Bartenev, who acted as a kind of general assistant to him, asking him to send the 'Maistre archive', that is, his letters and notes. There is every reason why Tolstoy should have read this now relatively little-read author. Count Joseph de Maistre was a Savoyard royalist who had first made a name for himself by writing anti-revolutionary tracts during the last years of the eighteenth century. Although normally classified as an orthodox Catholic reactionary writer, a pillar of the Bourbon Restoration and a defender of the pre-Revolutionary status quo, in particular of papal authority, he was a great deal more than this. He held grimly unconventional and misanthropic views about the nature of individuals and societies, and wrote with a dry and ironical violence about the incurably savage and wicked nature of man, the inevitability of perpetual slaughter, the divinely instituted character of wars, and the overwhelming part played in human affairs by the passion for self-immolation, which, more than natural sociability or artificial agreements, creates armies and civil societies alike. He emphasised the need for absolute authority, punishment and continual repression if civilisation and order were to survive at all. Both the content and the tone of his writing are closer to Nietzsche, d'Annunzio and the heralds of

---

1   See Adolfo Omodeo, *Un reazionario: Il conte J. de Maistre* (Bari, 1939), 112,
     note 2.
2   'Chitayu Maistr'a', T xlviii 66.

modern fascism than to the respectable royalists of his own time, and caused a stir in their own day both among the legitimists and in Napoleonic France. In 1803 Maistre was sent by his master, the King of Piedmont–Sardinia, then living in exile in Rome as a victim of Napoleon and soon forced to move to Sardinia, as his semi-official representative to the Court of St Petersburg. Maistre, who possessed considerable social charm as well as an acute sense of his environment, made a great impression upon the society of the Russian capital as a polished courtier, a wit and a shrewd political observer. He remained in St Petersburg from 1803 to 1817, and his exquisitely written and often uncannily penetrating and prophetic diplomatic dispatches and letters, as well as his private correspondence and the various scattered notes on Russia and her inhabitants, sent to his government as well as to his friends and consultants among the Russian nobility, form a uniquely valuable source of information about the life and opinions of the ruling circles of the Russian Empire during and immediately after the Napoleonic period.

He died in 1821, the author of several theologico-political essays, but the definitive editions of his works, in particular of the celebrated *Les Soirées de Saint-Pétersbourg*, which in the form of Platonic dialogue dealt with the nature and sanctions of human government and other political and philosophical problems, as well as his *Correspondance diplomatique* and his letters, were published in full only in the 1850s and early 1860s by his son Rodolphe and by others. Maistre's open hatred of Austria, his anti-Bonapartism, as well as the rising importance of the Piedmontese kingdom before and after the Crimean War, naturally increased interest in his personality and his thought at this date. Books on him began to appear and excited a good deal of discussion in Russian literary and historical circles. Tolstoy possessed the *Soirées*, as well as Maistre's diplomatic correspondence and letters, and copies of them were to be found in the library at Yasnaya Polyana. It is in any case quite clear that Tolstoy used them extensively in *War and Peace*.[1] Thus the celebrated description of Paulucci's intervention in the debate of the Russian General

1   See Eikhenbaum, op. cit. (54 above, note 1), i 308–17.

Staff at Drissa is reproduced almost verbatim from a letter by Maistre. Similarly Prince Vasily's conversation at Mme Scherer's reception with the 'homme de beaucoup de mérite'[1] about Kutuzov is obviously based on a letter by Maistre, in which all the French phrases with which this conversation is sprinkled are to be found. There is, moreover, a marginal note in one of Tolstoy's early drafts, 'At Anna Pavlovna's J. Maistre', which refers to the raconteur who tells the beautiful Hélène and an admiring circle of listeners the idiotic anecdote about the meeting of Napoleon with the duc d'Enghien at supper with the celebrated actress Mlle Georges.[2] Again, old Prince Bolkonsky's habit of shifting his bed from one room to another is probably taken from a story which Maistre tells about the similar habit of Count Stroganov. Finally, the name of Maistre occurs in the novel itself,[3] as being among those who agree that it would be embarrassing and senseless to capture the more eminent princes and marshals of Napoleon's army, since this would merely create diplomatic difficulties. Zhikharev, whose memoirs Tolstoy is known to have used, met Maistre in 1807, and described him in glowing colours;[4] something of the atmosphere to be found in these memoirs enters into Tolstoy's description of the eminent émigrés in Anna Pavlovna Scherer's drawing-room, with which *War and Peace* opens, and his other references to fashionable Petersburg society at this date. These echoes and parallels have been collated carefully by Tolstoyan scholars, and leave no doubt about the extent of Tolstoy's borrowing.

Among these parallels there are similarities of a more important kind. Maistre explains that the victory of the legendary Horatius over the Curiatii – like all victories in general – was due to the intangible factor of morale, and Tolstoy similarly speaks of the supreme importance of this unknown quantity in determining the outcome of battles – the impalpable 'spirit' of troops and

1   *War and Peace*, vol. 3, part 2, chapter 6, T xi 127, 128; W 782, 783.
2   ibid. vol. 1, part 1, chapter 3, T ix 13–16; W 10–13. For the note see T xiii 687.
3   ibid. vol. 4, part 3, chapter 19, T xii 167; W 1182.
4   S. P. Zhikharev, *Zapiski sovremennika: dnevnik chinovnika* (Moscow, 1934), ii 112–13.

their commanders. This emphasis on the imponderable and the incalculable is part and parcel of Maistre's general irrationalism. More clearly and boldly than anyone before him, Maistre declared that the human intellect was but a feeble instrument when pitted against the power of natural forces; that rational explanations of human conduct seldom explained anything. He maintained that only the irrational, precisely because it defied explanation and could therefore not be undermined by the critical activities of reason, was able to persist and be strong. And he gave as examples such irrational institutions as hereditary monarchy and marriage, which survived from age to age, while such rational institutions as elective monarchy, or 'free' personal relationships, swiftly and for no obvious 'reason' collapsed wherever they were introduced. Maistre conceived of life as a savage battle at all levels, between plants and animals no less than individuals and nations, a battle from which no gain was expected, but which originated in some primal, mysterious, sanguinary, self-immolatory craving implanted by God. This instinct was far more powerful than the feeble efforts of rational men who tried to achieve peace and happiness (which was, in any case, not the deepest desire of the human heart – only of its caricature, the liberal intellect) by planning the life of society without reckoning with the violent forces which sooner or later would inevitably cause their puny structures to collapse like so many houses of cards.

Maistre regarded the battlefield as typical of life in all its aspects, and derided the generals who thought that they were in fact controlling the movements of their troops and directing the course of the battle. He declared that no one in the actual heat of battle can begin to tell what is going on:

On parle beaucoup de batailles dans le monde sans savoir ce que c'est; on est surtout assez sujet à les considérer comme des points, tandis qu'elles couvrent deux ou trois lieues de pays: on vous dit gravement: Comment ne savez-vous pas ce qui s'est passé dans ce combat puisque vous y étiez? tandis que c'est précisément le contraire qu'on pourrait dire assez souvent. Celui qui est à la droite sait-il ce qui se passe à la gauche? sait-il seulement ce qui se passe à deux pas de lui? Je me représente aisément une de ces scènes

épouvantables: sur un vaste terrain couvert de tous les apprêts du
carnage, et qui semble s'ébranler sous les pas des hommes et des
chevaux; au milieu du feu et des tourbillons de fumée; étourdi,
transporté par le retentissement des armes à feu et des instruments
militaires, par des voix qui commandent, qui hurlent ou qui s'éteign-
ent; environné de morts, de mourants, de cadavres mutilés; possédé
tour à tour par la crainte, par l'espérance, par la rage, par cinq ou
six ivresses différentes, que devient l'homme? que voit-il? que sait-il
au bout de quelques heures? que peut-il sur lui et sur les autres?
Parmi cette foule de guerriers qui ont combattu tout le jour, il n'y
en a souvent pas un seul, et pas même le général, qui sache où est le
vainqueur. Il ne tiendrait qu'à moi de vous citer des batailles
modernes, des batailles fameuses dont la mémoire ne périra jamais,
des batailles qui ont changé la face des affaires en Europe, et qui
n'ont été perdues que parce que tel ou tel homme a cru qu'elles
l'étaient; de manière qu'en supposant toutes les circonstances égales,
et pas une goutte de sang de plus versée de part et d'autre, un autre
général aurait fait chanter le *Te Deum* chez lui, et forcé l'histoire de
dire tout le contraire de ce qu'elle dira.[1]

And later: 'N'avons-nous pas fini même par voir perdre des
batailles gagnées? [. . .] Je crois en général que les batailles ne se

---

1   *Les Soirées de Saint-Pétersbourg* (1821), seventh conversation: OC v 33–4;
    SPD (from which the translations of this conversation in the notes are taken)
    222–3. 'People talk a lot about battles without knowing what they are really
    like. In particular, they tend to consider them as occurring at one place,
    whereas they cover two or three leagues of country. They ask you seriously:
    *How is it that you don't know what happened in this battle, since you were
    there?* Whereas it is precisely the opposite that would often have to be said.
    Does the one on the right know what is happening on the left? Does he even
    know what is happening two paces from him? I can easily imagine one of
    these frightful scenes. On a vast field covered with all the apparatus of carnage
    and seeming to shudder under the feet of men and horses, in the midst of fire
    and whirling smoke, dazed and carried away by the din of firearms and
    cannon, by voices that order, roar and die away, surrounded by the dead,
    the dying, the mutilated corpses, seized in turn by fear, hope and rage, by
    five or six different passions, what happens to a man? What does he see?
    What does he know after a few hours? What can he know about himself and
    others? Among this crowd of warriors who have fought the whole day, there
    is often not a single one, not even the general, who knows who the victor is.
    I will restrict myself to citing modern battles, famous battles whose memory

gagnent ni ne se perdent point physiquement.'[1] And again, in a similar strain: 'De même une armée de 40,000 hommes est inférieure physiquement à une autre armée de 60,000: mais si la première a plus de courage, d'expérience et de discipline, elle pourra battre la seconde; car elle a plus d'action avec moins de masse, et c'est ce que nous voyons à chaque page de l'histoire.'[2] And finally: 'C'est l'opinion qui perd les batailles, et c'est l'opinion qui les gagne.'[3] Victory is a moral or psychological, not a physical, issue:

> *qu'est ce qu'une bataille perdue?* [. . .] *C'est une bataille qu'on croit avoir perdue.* Rien n'est plus vrai. Un homme qui se bat avec un autre est vaincu lorsqu'il est tué ou terrassé, et que l'autre est debout; il n'en est pas ainsi de deux armées: l'une ne peut être tuée, tandis que l'autre reste en pied. Les forces se balancent ainsi que les morts, et depuis surtout que l'invention de la poudre a mis plus d'égalité dans les moyens de destruction, une bataille ne se perd plus matériellement; c'est-à-dire parce qu'il y a plus de morts d'un côté que de l'autre: aussi Frédéric II, qui s'y entendait un peu, disait: *Vaincre, c'est avancer.* Mais quel est celui qui avance? c'est celui dont la conscience et la contenance font reculer l'autre.[4]

---

will never perish, battles that have changed the face of Europe and that were lost only because such and such a man thought they were lost; they were battles where all circumstances being equal and without a drop of blood more being shed on either side, the other general could have had a *Te Deum* sung in his own country and forced history to record the opposite of what it will say.'

1 ibid. 35; SPD 223. 'Have we not even seen won battles lost? [. . .] In general, I believe that battles are not won or lost physically.'

2 ibid. 29; SPD 220. 'In the same way, an army of 40,000 men is physically inferior to another army of 60,000, but if the first has more courage, experience and discipline, it will be able to defeat the second, for it is more effective with less mass. This is what we can see on every page of history.'

3 ibid. 31 (omitted in SPD). 'It is opinion that loses battles, and it is opinion that wins them.'

4 ibid. 32; SPD 221. '*What is a lost battle?* [. . .] *It is a battle one believes one has lost.* Nothing is more true. One man fighting with another is defeated when he has been killed or brought to earth and the other remains standing. This is not the way it is with two armies; the one cannot be killed while the other remains on its feet. The forces are in equilibrium, as are the deaths, and especially since the invention of gunpowder has introduced more equality into the means of destruction, a battle is no longer lost materially, that is

There is and can be no military science, for 'C'est l'imagination qui perd les batailles',[1] and 'peu de batailles sont perdues physiquement – vous tirez, je tire [...] le véritable vainqueur, comme le véritable vaincu, c'est celui qui croit l'être'.[2]

This is the lesson which Tolstoy says he derives from Stendhal, but the words of Prince Andrey about Austerlitz – 'We lost because very early on we told ourselves we had lost'[3] – as well as the attribution of Russian victory over Napoleon to the strength of the Russian desire to survive, echo Maistre and not Stendhal.

This close parallelism between Maistre's and Tolstoy's views about the chaos and uncontrollability of battles and wars, with its larger implications for human life generally, together with the contempt of both for the naive explanations provided by academic historians to account for human violence and lust for war, was noted by the eminent French historian Albert Sorel, in a little-known lecture to the École des Sciences Politiques delivered on 7 April 1888.[4] He drew a parallel between Maistre and Tolstoy, and observed that although Maistre was a theocrat, while Tolstoy was a 'nihilist', yet both regarded the first causes of events as mysterious, involving the reduction of human wills to nullity. 'The

---

to say because there are more dead on one side than the other. It was Frederick II, who understood a little about these things, who said: *To win is to advance.* But who is the one who advances? It is the one whose conscience and countenance makes the other fall back.'

1   ibid. 33; SPD 222. 'It is imagination that loses battles.'

2   Letter of 14 September 1812 to Count de Front: OC xii 220–1. 'Few battles are lost physically – you fire, I fire [...] the real victor, like the real loser, is the one who believes himself to be so.'

3   [More literally: 'We told ourselves very early on that we had lost the battle, and we did lose it.'] *War and Peace*, vol. 3, part 2, chapter 25, T xi 206; W 855.

4   Albert Sorel, 'Tolstoï historien', *Revue bleue* 41 (January–June 1888), 460–9. This lecture, reprinted in revised form in Sorel's *Lectures historiques* (Paris, 1894), has been unjustly neglected by students of Tolstoy; it does much to correct the views of those – e.g. P. I. Biryukov, *L. N. Tolstoi: biografiya*, 3rd ed. (Berlin, 1921), and K. V. Pokrovsky, op. cit. (47 above, note 2), not to mention later critics and literary historians, who almost all rely upon their authority – who omit all reference to Maistre. Émile Haumant is almost unique among earlier scholars in ignoring secondary authorities and discovering the truth for himself: see his *La Culture française en Russie (1700–1900)* (Paris, 1910), 490–2.

distance', wrote Sorel, 'from the theocrat to the mystic, and from the mystic to the nihilist, is smaller than that from the butterfly to the larva, from the larva to the chrysalis, from the chrysalis to the butterfly.'[1] Tolstoy resembles Maistre in being, above all, curious about first causes, in asking such questions as Maistre's '*Expliquez pourquoi ce qu'il y a de plus honorable dans le monde, au jugement de tout le genre humain sans exception, est le droit de verser innocemment le sang innocent?*',[2] in rejecting all rationalist or naturalistic answers, in stressing impalpable psychological and 'spiritual' – and sometimes 'zoological' – factors as determining events, and in stressing these at the expense of statistical analyses of military strength, very much like Maistre in his dispatches to his government at Cagliari. Indeed, Tolstoy's accounts of mass movements – in battle, and in the flight of the Russians from Moscow or of the French from Russia – might almost be designed to give concrete illustrations of Maistre's theory of the unplanned and unplannable character of all great events. But the parallel runs deeper. The Savoyard Count and the Russian are both reacting, and reacting violently, against liberal optimism concerning human goodness, human reason, and the value or inevitability of material progress: both furiously denounce the notion that mankind can be made eternally happy and virtuous by rational and scientific means.

The first great wave of optimistic rationalism which followed the Wars of Religion broke against the violence of the great French Revolution and the political despotism and social and economic misery which ensued: in Russia a similar development was shattered by the long succession of repressive measures taken by Nicholas I to counteract firstly the effect of the Decembrist revolt, and, nearly a quarter of a century later, the influence of the European revolutions of 1848–9; and to this must be added the material and moral effect, a decade later, of the Crimean debacle. In both cases the emergence of naked force killed a great deal of tender-

---

1   op. cit. (previous note), 462. This passage is omitted from the 1894 reprint (270).

2   OC v 10; SPD 210. '*Explain why the most honourable thing in the world, according to the judgement of all of humanity, without exception, has always been the right to shed innocent blood innocently?*'

minded idealism, and resulted in various types of realism and toughness – among others, materialistic socialism, authoritarian neo-feudalism, blood-and-iron nationalism and other bitterly anti-liberal movements. In the case of both Maistre and Tolstoy, for all their unbridgeably deep psychological, social, cultural and religious differences, the disillusionment took the form of an acute scepticism about scientific method as such, distrust of all liberalism, positivism, rationalism, and of all the forms of high-minded secularism then influential in Western Europe; and led to a deliberate emphasis on the 'unpleasant' aspects of human history, from which sentimental romantics, humanist historians and optimistic social theorists seemed so resolutely to be averting their gaze.

Both Maistre and Tolstoy spoke of political reformers (in one interesting instance, of the same individual representative of them, the Russian statesman Speransky) in the same tone of bitterly contemptuous irony. Maistre was suspected of having had an actual hand in Speransky's fall and exile; Tolstoy, through the eyes of Prince Andrey, describes the pale face of Alexander's one-time favourite, his soft hands, his fussy and self-important manner, the artificiality and emptiness of his movements – as somehow indicative of the unreality of his person and of his liberal activities – in a manner which Maistre could only have applauded. Both speak of intellectuals with scorn and hostility. Maistre regards them not merely as grotesque casualties of the historical process – hideous cautions created by Providence to scare mankind into a return to the ancient Roman faith – but as beings dangerous to society, a pestilential sect of questioners and corrupters of youth against whose corrosive activity all prudent rulers must take measures. Tolstoy treats them with contempt rather than hatred, and represents them as poor, misguided, feeble-witted creatures with delusions of grandeur. Maistre sees them as a brood of social and political locusts, as a canker at the heart of Christian civilisation, which is of all things the most sacred and will be preserved only by the heroic efforts of the Pope and his Church. Tolstoy looks on them as clever fools, spinners of empty subtleties, blind and deaf to the realities which simpler hearts can grasp, and from time to time he lets fly at them with the brutal violence of a grim, anarchical old peasant, avenging himself, after years of silence, on the

Tolstoi + intellectuals

silly, chattering, town-bred monkeys, so knowing, and full of words to explain everything, and superior, and impotent and empty. Both dismiss any interpretation of history which does not place at the heart of it the problem of the nature of power, and both speak with disdain about rationalistic attempts to explain it. Maistre amuses himself at the expense of the Encyclopedists – their clever superficialities, their neat but empty categories – very much in the manner adopted by Tolstoy towards their descendants a century later, the scientific sociologists and historians. Both profess belief in the deep wisdom of the uncorrupted common people, although Maistre's mordant *obiter dicta* about the hopeless barbarism, venality and ignorance of the Russians cannot have been to Tolstoy's taste, if indeed he ever read them.

Both Maistre and Tolstoy regard the Western world as in some sense 'rotting', as being in rapid decay. This was the doctrine which the Roman Catholic counter-revolutionaries at the turn of the century virtually invented, and it formed part of their view of the French Revolution as a divine punishment visited upon those who strayed from the Christian faith, and in particular that of the Roman Church. From France this denunciation of secularism was carried by many devious routes, mainly by second-rate journalists and their academic readers, to Germany and to Russia (to Russia both directly and via German versions), where it found a ready soil among those who, having themselves avoided the revolutionary upheavals, found it flattering to their *amour propre* to believe that they, at any rate, might still be on the path to greater power and glory, while the West, destroyed by the failure of its ancient faith, was fast disintegrating morally and politically. No doubt Tolstoy derived this element in his outlook at least as much from Slavophils and other Russian chauvinists as directly from Maistre, but it is worth noting that this belief is exceptionally powerful in both these dry and aristocratic observers, and governs their oddly similar outlooks. Both were *au fond* unyieldingly pessimistic thinkers, whose ruthless destruction of current illusions frightened off their contemporaries even when they reluctantly conceded the truth of what was said. Despite the fact that Maistre was fanatically ultramontane and a supporter of established institutions, while Tolstoy, unpolitical in his earlier work, gave no evidence of radical

sentiment, both were obscurely felt to be nihilistic – the humane
values of the nineteenth century fell to pieces under their fingers.
Both sought for some escape from their own inescapable and
unanswerable scepticism in some vast, impregnable truth which
would protect them from the effects of their own natural inclinations and temperament: Maistre in the Church, Tolstoy in the
uncorrupted human heart and simple brotherly love – a state he
could have known but seldom, an ideal before the vision of
which all his descriptive skill deserts him, so that he usually writes
something inartistic, wooden and naive; painfully touching, painfully unconvincing, and conspicuously remote from his own
experience.

Yet the analogy must not be overstressed: it is true that both
Maistre and Tolstoy attach the greatest possible importance to
war and conflict, but Maistre, like Proudhon after him,[1] glorifies
war, and declares it to be mysterious and divine, while Tolstoy
detests it and regards it as in principle explicable if only we knew
enough of the many minute causes – the celebrated 'differential'
of history. Maistre believed in authority because it was an
irrational force, he believed in the need to submit, in the inevitability of crime and the supreme importance of inquisitions and
punishment. He regarded the executioner as the cornerstone of
society, and it was not for nothing that Stendhal called him *l'ami
du bourreau* and Lamennais said of him that there were only two
realities for him – crime and punishment – 'his works are all as

1   Tolstoy visited Proudhon in Brussels in 1861, the year in which the latter
     published a work which was called *La Guerre et la paix*, translated into
     Russian three years later. On the basis of this fact Eikhenbaum tries to deduce
     the influence of Proudhon upon Tolstoy's novel. Proudhon follows Maistre
     in regarding the origins of wars as a dark and sacred mystery; and there
     is much confused irrationalism, puritanism, love of paradox, and general
     Rousseauism in all his work. But these qualities are widespread in radical
     French thought, and it is difficult to find anything specifically Proudhonist in
     Tolstoy's *War and Peace*, besides the title. The extent of Proudhon's general
     influence on all kinds of Russian intellectuals during this period was, of
     course, very large; it would thus be just as easy, indeed easier, to construct a
     case for regarding Dostoevsky – or Maxim Gorky – as a *proudhonisant* as to
     look on Tolstoy as one; yet this would be no more than an idle exercise in
     critical ingenuity; for the resemblances are vague and general, while the
     differences are deeper, more numerous and more specific.

though written on the scaffold'.[1] Maistre's vision of the world is one of savage creatures tearing each other limb from limb, killing for the sake of killing, with violence and blood, which he sees as the normal condition of all animate life. Tolstoy is far from such horror, crime and sadism;[2] and he is not, *pace* Albert Sorel and Vogüé, in any sense a mystic: he has no fear of questioning anything, and believes that some simple answer must exist – if only we did not insist on tormenting ourselves with searching for it in strange and remote places, when it lies all the time at our feet.

Maistre supported the principle of hierarchy and believed in a self-sacrificing aristocracy, heroism, obedience, and the most rigid control of the masses by their social and theological superiors. Accordingly he advocated that education in Russia be placed in the hands of the Jesuits; they would at least inculcate into the barbarous Scythians the Latin language, which was the sacred tongue of humanity if only because it embodied the prejudices and superstitions of previous ages – beliefs which had stood the test of history and experience – alone able to form a wall strong enough to keep out the terrible acids of atheism, liberalism and freedom of thought. Above all he regarded natural science and secular literature as dangerous commodities in the hands of those not completely indoctrinated against them, a heady wine which would dangerously excite, and in the end destroy, any society not used to it.

Tolstoy all his life fought against open obscurantism and artificial repression of the desire for knowledge; his harshest words were directed against those Russian statesmen and publicists in the last quarter of the nineteenth century – Pobedonostsev and his friends and minions – who practised precisely these maxims of the great Catholic reactionary. The author of *War and Peace* plainly hated the Jesuits, and particularly detested their success in

---

1   Letter of 8 October 1834 to Gräfin Senfft von Pilsach: Félicité de Lamennais, *Correspondance générale*, ed. Louis le Guillou (Paris, 1971–81), letter 2338, vi 307.

2   Yet Tolstoy, too, says that millions of men kill each other, knowing that it is 'physically and morally evil', because it is 'necessary'; because 'in doing so men fulfilled [an] elemental, zoological law': op. cit. (49 above, note 2), 15. This is pure Maistre, and very remote from Stendhal or Rousseau.

converting Russian ladies of fashion during Alexander's reign –
the final events in the life of Pierre's worthless wife, Hélène, might
almost have been founded upon Maistre's activities as a missionary to the aristocracy of St Petersburg: indeed, there is every reason
to think that the Jesuits were expelled from Russia, and Maistre
himself was virtually recalled when his interference was deemed
too overt and too successful by the Emperor himself.

Nothing, therefore, would have shocked and irritated Tolstoy
so much as to be told that he had a great deal in common with
this apostle of darkness, this defender of ignorance and serfdom.
Nevertheless, of all writers on social questions, Maistre's tone
most nearly resembles that of Tolstoy. Both preserve the same
sardonic, almost cynical, disbelief in the improvement of society
by rational means, by the enactment of good laws or the propa-
gation of scientific knowledge. Both speak with the same angry
irony of every fashionable explanation, every social nostrum, particularly of the ordering and planning of society in accordance
with some man-made formula. In Maistre openly, and in Tolstoy
less obviously, there is a deeply sceptical attitude towards all
experts and all techniques, all high-minded professions of secular
faith and efforts at social improvement by well-meaning but, alas,
idealistic persons; there is the same distaste for anyone who deals
in ideas, who believes in abstract principles: and both are deeply
affected by Voltaire's temper, and bitterly reject his views. Both
ultimately appeal to some elemental source concealed in the souls
of men, Maistre even while denouncing Rousseau as a false
prophet, Tolstoy with his more ambiguous attitude towards him.
Both above all reject the concept of individual political liberty,
of civil rights guaranteed by some impersonal system of justice:
Maistre, because he regarded any desire for personal freedom –
whether political or economic or social or cultural or religious –
as wilful indiscipline and stupid insubordination, and supported
tradition in its most darkly irrational and repressive forms,
because it alone provided the energy which gave life, continuity
and safe anchorage to social institutions; Tolstoy rejected political
reform because he believed that ultimate regeneration could come
only from within, and that the inner life was lived truly only in
the untouched depths of the mass of the people.

VI

But there is a larger and more important parallel between Tolstoy's interpretation of history and Maistre's ideas, and it raises issues of fundamental principle concerning knowledge of the past. One of the most striking elements common to the thought of these dissimilar, and indeed antagonistic, *penseurs* is their preoccupation with the 'inexorable' character – the 'march' – of events. Both Tolstoy and Maistre think of what occurs as a thick, opaque, inextricably complex web of events, objects, characteristics, connected and divided by literally innumerable unidentifiable links – and gaps and sudden discontinuities too, visible and invisible. It is a view of reality which makes all clear, logical and scientific constructions – the well-defined, symmetrical patterns of human reason – seem smooth, thin, empty, 'abstract' and totally ineffective as means either of description or of analysis of anything that lives, or has ever lived. Maistre attributes this to the incurable impotence of human powers of observation and of reasoning, at least when they function without the aid of the superhuman sources of knowledge – faith, revelation, tradition, above all the mystical vision of the great saints and doctors of the Church, their unanalysable, special sense of reality to which natural science, free criticism and the secular spirit are fatal. The wisest of the Greeks, many among the great Romans, and after them the dominant ecclesiastics and statesmen of the Middle Ages, Maistre tells us, possessed this insight; from it flowed their power, their dignity and their success. The natural enemies of this spirit are cleverness and specialisation: hence the contempt so rightly shown for, in the Roman world, experts and technicians – the *Graeculus esuriens* – the remote but unmistakable ancestors of the sharp, wizened figures of the modern Alexandrian Age – the terrible Eighteenth Century – all the *écrivasserie et avocasserie*, the miserable crew of scribblers and attorneys, with the predatory, sordid, grinning figure of Voltaire at their head, destructive and self-destructive, because blind and deaf to the true word of God. Only the Church understands the 'inner' rhythms, the 'deeper' currents of the world, the silent march of things; *non in commotione Dominus*; not in noisy democratic manifestos nor in the rattle of constitutional formulae, nor in revolutionary violence, but in the eternal natural order, governed by 'natural' law. Only those who understand it know what can and what cannot be achieved, what should and what should not be attempted. They and they alone hold the key to secular success as well as to spiritual salvation. Omniscience belongs only to God. But only by immersing ourselves in his word, his theological or metaphysical principles, embodied at their lowest in instincts and ancient superstitions which are but primitive ways, tested by time, of divining and obeying his laws – whereas reasoning is an effort to substitute one's own arbitrary rules – dare we hope for wisdom. Practical wisdom is to a large degree knowledge of the inevitable: of what, given our world order, could not but happen; and, conversely, of how things cannot be, or could not have been, done; of why some schemes must, cannot help but, end in failure, although for this no demonstrative or scientific reason can be given. The rare capacity for seeing this we rightly call a 'sense of reality' – it is a sense of what fits with what, of what cannot exist with what; and it goes by many names: insight, wisdom, practical genius, a sense of the past, an understanding of life and of human character.

Tolstoy's view is not very different; save that he gives as the reason for the folly of our exaggerated claims to understand or determine events, not foolish or blasphemous efforts to do without special, that is, supernatural, knowledge, but our ignorance of too many among the vast number of interrelations – the minute determining causes of events. If we began to know the causal network in its infinite variety, we should cease to praise and blame, boast and regret, or look on human beings as heroes or villains, but should submit with due humility to unavoidable necessity. Yet to say no more than this is to give a travesty of his beliefs. It is indeed Tolstoy's explicit doctrine in *War and Peace* that all truth is in science – in the knowledge of material causes – and that we consequently render ourselves ridiculous by arriving at conclusions on too little evidence, comparing in this regard unfavourably with peasants or savages, who, being not so very much more ignorant, at least make more modest claims; but this is not the view of the world that, in fact, underlies either *War and Peace* or

Anna Karenina or any other work which belongs to this period of Tolstoy's life. Kutuzov is wise and not merely clever as, for example, the time-serving Drubetskoy or Bilibin are clever, and he is not a victim to abstract heroes or dogma as the German military experts are; he is unlike them, and is wiser than they – but this is so not because he knows more facts than they and has at his fingertips a greater number of the 'minute causes' of events than his advisers or his adversaries – than Pfuel or Paulucci or Berthier or the King of Naples. Karataev brings light to Pierre, whereas the Freemasons did not, but this is so not because he happens to have scientific information superior to that possessed by the Moscow lodges; Levin goes through an experience during his work in the fields, and Prince Andrey while lying wounded on the battlefield of Austerlitz, but in neither case has there been a discovery of fresh facts or of new laws in any ordinary sense. On the contrary, the greater one's accumulation of facts, the more futile one's activity, the more hopeless one's failure – as shown by the group of reformers who surround Alexander. They and men like them are saved from Faustian despair only by stupidity (like the Germans and the military experts and experts generally) or by vanity (like Napoleon) or by frivolity (like Oblonsky) or by heartlessness (like Karenin).

What is it that Pierre, Prince Andrey, Levin discover? And what are they searching for, and what is the centre and climax of the spiritual crisis resolved by the experience that transforms their lives? Not the chastening realisation of how little of the totality of facts and laws known to Laplace's omniscient observer they – Pierre, Levin and the rest – can claim to have discovered; not a simple admission of Socratic ignorance. Still less does it consist in what is almost at the opposite pole – in a new, a more precise awareness of the 'iron laws' that govern our lives, in a vision of nature as a machine or a factory, in the cosmology of the great materialists, Diderot or La Mettrie or Cabanis, or of the mid-nineteenth-century scientific writers idolised by the 'nihilist' Bazarov in Turgenev's *Fathers and Children*; nor yet in some transcendent sense of the inexpressible oneness of life to which poets, mystics and metaphysicians have in all ages testified. Nevertheless, something *is* perceived; there is a vision, or at least a glimpse, a moment of revelation which in some sense explains and reconciles, a theodicy, a justification of what exists and happens, as well as its elucidation. What does it consist in? Tolstoy does not tell us in so many words: for when (in his later, explicitly didactic works) he sets out to do so, his doctrine is no longer the same. Yet no reader of *War and Peace* can be wholly unaware of what he is being told. And that not only in the Kutuzov or Karataev scenes, or other quasi-theological or quasi-metaphysical passages – but even more, for example, in the narrative, non-philosophical section of the epilogue, in which Pierre, Natasha, Nikolay Rostov, Princess Marie are shown anchored in their new solid, sober lives with their established day-to-day routine. We are here plainly intended to see that these 'heroes' of the novel – the 'good' people – have now, after the storms and agonies of ten years and more, achieved a kind of peace, based on some degree of understanding: understanding of what? Of the need to submit: to what? Not simply to the will of God (not at any rate during the writing of the great novels, in the 1860s or 1870s), nor to the 'iron laws' of the sciences; but to the permanent relationships of things,[1] and the universal texture of human life, wherein alone truth and justice are to be found by a kind of 'natural' – somewhat Aristotelian – knowledge.

To do this is, above all, to grasp what human will and human reason can do, and what they cannot. How can this be known? Not by a specific enquiry and discovery, but by an awareness, not necessarily explicit or conscious, of certain general characteristics of human life and experience. And the most important and most pervasive of these is the crucial line that divides the 'surface' from the 'depths' – on the one hand the world of perceptible, describable, analysable data, both physical and psychological, both 'external' and 'inner', both public and private, with which the sciences can deal, although they have in some regions – those outside physics – made so little progress; and, on the other hand, the order which, as it were, 'contains' and determines the structure

---

1   Almost in the sense in which the phrase 'les rapports nécessaires qui dérivent de la nature des choses' ('necessary relationships which derive from the nature of things') is used by Montesquieu in the opening sentence of *De l'esprit des lois* (1748).

of experience, the framework in which it – that is, we and all that we experience – must be conceived as being set, that which enters into our habits of thought, action, feeling, our emotions, hopes, wishes, our ways of talking, believing, reacting, being. We – sentient creatures – are in part living in a world the constituents of which we can discover, classify and act upon by rational, scientific, deliberately planned methods; but in part (Tolstoy and Maistre, and many thinkers with them, say much the larger part) we are immersed and submerged in a medium that, precisely to the degree to which we inevitably take it for granted as part of ourselves, we do not and cannot observe as if from the outside; cannot identify, measure and seek to manipulate; cannot even be wholly aware of, inasmuch as it enters too intimately into all our experience, is itself too closely interwoven with all that we are and do to be lifted out of the flow (it *is* the flow) and observed with scientific detachment, as an object. It – the medium in which we are – determines our most permanent categories, our standards of truth and falsehood, of reality and appearance, of the good and the bad, of the central and the peripheral, of the subjective and the objective, of the beautiful and the ugly, of movement and rest, of past, present and future, of one and many; hence neither these, nor any other explicitly conceived categories or concepts, can be applied to it – for it is itself but a vague name for the totality that includes these categories, these concepts, the ultimate framework, the basic presuppositions wherewith we function.

Nevertheless, though we cannot analyse the medium without some (impossible) vantage point outside it (for there is no 'outside'), yet some human beings are better aware – although they cannot describe it – of the texture and direction of these 'submerged' portions of their own and everyone else's lives; better aware of this than others, who either ignore the existence of the all-pervasive medium (the 'flow of life'), and are rightly called superficial; or else try to apply to it instruments – scientific, metaphysical – adapted solely to objects above the surface, the relatively conscious, manipulable portion of our experience, and so achieve absurdities in their theories and humiliating failures in practice. Wisdom is ability to allow for the (at least by us) unalterable medium in which we act – as we allow for the pervasiveness, say, of time or space, which characterises all our experience; and to discount, less or more consciously, the 'inevitable trends', the 'imponderables', the 'way things are going'. It is not scientific knowledge, but a special sensitiveness to the contours of the circumstances in which we happen to be placed; it is a capacity for living without falling foul of some permanent condition or factor which cannot be either altered, or even fully described or calculated; an ability to be guided by rules of thumb – the 'immemorial wisdom' said to reside in peasants and other 'simple folk' – where rules of science do not, in principle, apply. This inexpressible sense of cosmic orientation is the 'sense of reality', the 'knowledge' of how to live.

Sometimes Tolstoy does speak as if science could in principle, if not in practice, penetrate and conquer everything; and if it did, then we should know the causes of all there is, and know we were not free, but wholly determined – which is all that the wisest can ever know. So, too, Maistre talks as if the schoolmen knew more than we, through their superior techniques: but what they knew was still, in some sense, 'the facts' – the subject-matter of the sciences. St Thomas knew incomparably more than Newton, and with more precision and more certainty, but what he knew was of the same kind. But despite this lip-service to the truth-finding capacities of natural science or theology, these avowals remain purely formal: and a very different belief finds expression in the positive doctrines of both Maistre and Tolstoy. Aquinas is praised by Maistre not for being a better mathematician than d'Alembert or Monge; Kutuzov's virtue does not, according to Tolstoy, consist in his being a better, more scientific theorist of war than Pfuel or Paulucci. These great men are wiser, not more knowledgeable; it is not their deductive or inductive reasoning that makes them masters; their vision is more 'profound', they see something the others fail to see; they see the way the world goes, what goes with what, and what never will be brought together; they see what can be and what cannot; how men live and to what ends, what they do and suffer, and how and why they act, and should act, thus and not otherwise.

This 'seeing' purveys, in a sense, no fresh information about the universe; it is an awareness of the interplay of the imponderable and the ponderable, of the 'shape' of things in general or of a specific situation, or of a particular character, which is precisely what cannot be deduced from, or even formulated in terms of, the laws of nature demanded by scientific determinism. Whatever can be subsumed under such laws scientists can and do deal with; that needs no 'wisdom'; and to deny science its rights because of the existence of this superior 'wisdom' is a wanton invasion of scientific territory, and a confusion of categories. Tolstoy, at least, does not go to the length of denying the efficacy of physics in its own sphere; but he thinks this sphere trivial in comparison with what is permanently out of the reach of science – the social, moral, political, spiritual worlds, which cannot be sorted out and described and predicted by any science, because the proportion in them of 'submerged', uninspectable life is too high. The insight that reveals the nature and structure of these worlds is not a mere makeshift substitute, an empirical *pis aller* to which recourse is had only so long as the relevant scientific techniques are insufficiently refined; its business is altogether different: it does what no science can claim to do; it distinguishes the real from the sham, the worthwhile from the worthless, that which can be done or borne from what cannot be; and does so without giving rational grounds for its pronouncements, if only because 'rational' and 'irrational' are terms that themselves acquire their meanings and uses in relation to – by 'growing out of' – it, and not vice versa. For what are the data of such understanding if not the ultimate soil, the framework, the atmosphere, the context, the medium (to use whatever metaphor is most expressive) in which all our thoughts and acts are felt, valued, judged, in the inevitable ways that they are?

It is the ever-present sense of this framework – of this movement of events, or changing pattern of characteristics – as something 'inexorable', universal, pervasive, not alterable by us, not in our power (in the sense of 'power' in which the progress of scientific knowledge has given us power over nature), that is at the root of Tolstoy's determinism, and of his realism, his pessimism, and his (and Maistre's) contempt for the faith placed in reason alike by science and by worldly common sense. It is 'there' – the framework, the foundation of everything – and the wise man alone has a sense of it; Pierre gropes for it; Kutuzov feels it in his bones;

Karataev is at one with it. All Tolstoy's heroes attain to at least intermittent glimpses of it — and this it is that makes all the conventional explanations, the scientific, the historical, those of unreflective 'good sense', seem so hollow and, at their most pretentious, so shamefully false. Tolstoy himself, too, knows that the truth is there, and not 'here' – not in the regions susceptible to observation, discrimination, constructive imagination, not in the power of microscopic perception and analysis of which he is so much the greatest master of our time; but he has not, himself, seen it face to face; for he has not, do what he might, a vision of the whole; he is not, he is remote from being, a hedgehog; and what he sees is not the one, but always, with an ever-growing minuteness, in all its teeming individuality, with an obsessive, inescapable, incorruptible, all-penetrating lucidity which maddens him, the many.

VII

We are part of a larger scheme of things than we can understand. We cannot describe it in the way in which external objects or the characters of other people can be described, by isolating them somewhat from the historical 'flow' in which they have their being, and from the 'submerged', unfathomed portions of themselves to which professional historians have, according to Tolstoy, paid so little heed; for we ourselves live in this whole and by it, and are wise only in the measure to which we make our peace with it. For until and unless we do so (only after much bitter suffering, if we are to trust Aeschylus and the Book of Job), we shall protest and suffer in vain, and make sorry fools of ourselves (as Napoleon did) into the bargain. This sense of the circumambient stream, defiance of whose nature through stupidity or overweening egotism will make our acts and thoughts self-defeating, is the vision of the unity of experience, the sense of history, the true knowledge of reality, the belief in the incommunicable wisdom of the sage (or the saint) which, *mutatis mutandis*, is common to Tolstoy and Maistre. Their realism is of a similar sort: the natural enemy of romanticism, sentimentalism and 'historicism' as much as of aggressive 'scientism'. Their purpose is not to distinguish the little that is known or done from the limitless ocean of what, in principle, could or one day will be known or done, whether by advance in the knowledge of the natural sciences or of metaphysics or of the historical sciences, or by a return to the past, or by some other method; what they seek to establish are the eternal frontiers of our knowledge and power, to demarcate them from what cannot in principle ever be known or altered by men. According to Maistre our destiny lies in original sin, in the fact that we are human – finite, fallible, vicious, vain – and that all our empirical knowledge (as opposed to the teachings of the Church) is infected by error and monomania. According to Tolstoy all our knowledge is necessarily empirical – there is no other – but it will never conduct us to true understanding, only to an accumulation of arbitrarily abstracted bits and pieces of information; yet that seems to him (as much as to any metaphysician of the Idealist school which he despised) worthless beside, and unintelligible save in so far as it derives from and points to, this inexpressible but very palpable kind of superior understanding which alone is worth pursuing.

Sometimes Tolstoy comes near to saying what it is: the more we know, he tells us, about a given human action, the more inevitable, determined it seems to us to be. Why? Because the more we know about all the relevant conditions and antecedents, the more difficult we find it to think away various circumstances, and conjecture what might have occurred without them; and as we go on removing in our imagination what we know to be true, fact by fact, this becomes not merely difficult but impossible. Tolstoy's meaning is not obscure. We are what we are, and live in a given situation which has the characteristics – physical, psychological, social – that it has; what we think, feel, do is conditioned by it, including our capacity for conceiving possible alternatives, whether in the present or future or past. Our imagination and ability to calculate, our power of conceiving, let us say, what might have been, if the past had, in this or that particular, been otherwise, soon reaches its natural limits, limits created both by the weakness of our capacity for calculating alternatives – 'might have beens' – and (we may add by a logical extension of Tolstoy's argument) even more by the fact that our thoughts, the terms in which they occur, the symbols themselves, are what they are, are themselves determined by the actual structure of our world. Our images and powers of conception are limited by the fact that our world possesses certain characteristics and not others: a world too different is (empirically) not conceivable at all; some minds are more imaginative than others, but all stop somewhere.

The world is a system and a network: to conceive of men as 'free' is to think of them as capable of having, at some past juncture, acted in some fashion other than that in which they did act; it is to think of what consequences would have come of such unfulfilled possibilities and in what respects the world would have been different, as a result, from the world as it now is. It is difficult enough to do this in the case of artificial, purely deductive systems, as for example in chess, where the permutations are finite in number, and clear in type – having been arranged so by us, artificially – so that the combinations are calculable. But if you apply this method to the vague, rich texture of the real world, and try to work out the implications of this or that unrealised plan or unperformed action – the effect of it on the totality of later events – basing yourself on such knowledge of causal laws and probabilities as you have, you will find that the greater the number of 'minute' causes you discriminate, the more appalling becomes the task of 'deducing' any consequence of the 'unhinging' of each of these, one by one; for each of the consequences affects the whole of the rest of the uncountable totality of events and things, which unlike chess is not defined in terms of a finite, arbitrarily chosen set of concepts and rules. And if, whether in real life or even in chess, you begin to tamper with basic notions – continuity of space, divisibility of time and the like – you will soon reach a stage in which the symbols fail to function, your thoughts become confused and paralysed. Consequently the fuller our knowledge of facts and of their connections the more difficult to conceive alternatives; the clearer and more exact the terms – or categories – in which we conceive and describe the world, the more fixed our world structure, the less 'free' acts seem. To know these limits, both of imagination and, ultimately, of thought itself, is to come face to face with the 'inexorable' unifying pattern of the world; to realise our identity with it, to submit to it, is to find truth and peace. This is not mere oriental fatalism, nor the mechanistic determinism of the celebrated German materialists of the day, Büchner and Vogt, or Moleschott, admired so deeply by the revolutionary 'nihilists' of Tolstoy's generation in Russia; nor is it a yearning for mystical illumination or integration. It is scrupulously empirical, rational, tough-minded and realistic. But its emotional cause is a passionate desire for a monistic vision of life on the part of a fox bitterly intent upon seeing in the manner of a hedgehog.

This is remarkably close to Maistre's dogmatic affirmations: we must achieve an attitude of assent to the demands of history which are the voice of God speaking through his servants and his divine institutions, not made by human hands and not destructible by them. We must attune ourselves to the true word of God, the inner 'go' of things; but what it is in concrete cases, how we are to conduct our private lives or public policies – of that we are told little by either critic of optimistic liberalism. Nor can we expect to be told. For the positive vision escapes them. Tolstoy's language – and Maistre's no less – is adapted to the opposite activity. It is in analysing, identifying sharply, marking differences, isolating concrete examples, piercing to the heart of each individual entity *per se* that Tolstoy rises to the full height of his genius; and similarly Maistre achieves his brilliant effects by pinning down and offering for public pillory – by a *montage sur l'épingle* – the absurdities committed by his opponents. They are acute observers of the varieties of experience: every attempt to represent these falsely, or to offer delusive explanations of them, they detect immediately and deride savagely. Yet they both know that the full truth, the ultimate basis of the correlation of all the ingredients of the universe with one another, the context in which alone anything that they, or anyone else, can say can ever be true or false, trivial or important – that resides in a synoptic vision which, because they do not possess it, they cannot express.

What is it that Pierre has learnt, of which Princess Marie's marriage is an acceptance, that Prince Andrey all his life pursued with such agony? Like Augustine, Tolstoy can say only what it is not. His genius is devastatingly destructive. He can only attempt to point towards his goal by exposing the false signposts to it; to isolate the truth by annihilating that which it is not – namely all that can be said in the clear, analytical language that corresponds to the all too clear, but necessarily limited, vision of the foxes. Like Moses, he must halt at the borders of the Promised Land; without it his journey is meaningless; but he cannot enter it; yet he knows that it exists, and can tell us, as no one else has ever told us, all that it is not – above all, not anything that art, or science or civilisation or rational criticism, can achieve.

So too Joseph de Maistre. He is the Voltaire of reaction. Every new doctrine since the ages of faith is torn to shreds with ferocious skill and malice. The pretenders are exposed and struck down one by one; the armoury of weapons against liberal and humanitarian doctrines is the most effective ever assembled. But the throne remains vacant, the positive doctrine is too unconvincing. Maistre sighs for the Dark Ages, but no sooner are plans for the undoing of the French Revolution – a return to the *status quo ante* – suggested by his fellow émigrés than he denounces them as childish nonsense – an attempt to behave as if what has occurred and changed us all irretrievably had never been. To try to reverse the Revolution, he wrote, was as if one had been invited to drain the Lake of Geneva by bottling its waters in a wine-cellar.

There is no kinship between him and those who really did believe in the possibility of some kind of return – neo-medievalists from Wackenroder and Görres and Cobbett to G. K. Chesterton, and Slavophils and Distributists and Pre-Raphaelites and other nostalgic romantics; for he believed, as Tolstoy also did, in the exact opposite: in the 'inexorable' power of the present moment; in our inability to do away with the sum of conditions which cumulatively determine our basic categories, an order which we can never fully describe or, otherwise than by some immediate awareness of it, come to know.

The quarrel between these rival types of knowledge – that which results from methodical enquiry, and the more impalpable kind that consists in the 'sense of reality', in 'wisdom' – is very old. And the claims of both have generally been recognised to have some validity: the bitterest clashes have been concerned with the precise line which marks the frontier between their territories. Those who made large claims for non-scientific knowledge have been accused by their adversaries of irrationalism and obscurantism, of the deliberate rejection, in favour of the emotions or blind prejudice, of reliable public standards of ascertainable truth; and have, in their turn, charged their opponents, the ambitious champions of science, with making absurd claims, promising the impossible, issuing false prospectuses, undertaking to explain history or the arts or the states of the individual soul (and to change them too) when quite plainly they do not begin to understand what they are; when the results of their labours, even when they are not nugatory, tend to take unpredicted, often catastrophic, directions – and all this because they will not, being vain and headstrong, admit that too many factors in too many situations are always unknown, and not discoverable by the methods of natural science. Better, surely, not to pretend to calculate the incalculable, not to pretend that there is an Archimedean point outside the world whence everything is measurable and alterable; better to use in each context the methods that seem to fit it best, that give the (pragmatically) best results; to resist the temptations of Procrustes; above all to distinguish what is isolable, classifiable and capable of objective study and sometimes of precise measurement and manipulation, from the most permanent, ubiquitous, inescapable, intimately present features of our world, which, if anything, are overfamiliar, so that their 'inexorable' pressure, being too much with us, is scarcely felt, hardly noticed, and cannot conceivably be observed in perspective, be an object of study.

This is the distinction that permeates the thought of Pascal and Blake, Rousseau and Schelling, Goethe and Coleridge, Chateaubriand and Carlyle; of all those who speak of the reasons of the heart, or of men's moral or spiritual nature, of sublimity and depth, of the 'profounder' insight of poets and prophets, of special kinds of understanding, of inwardly comprehending, or being at one with, the world. To these latter thinkers both Tolstoy and Maistre belong. Tolstoy blames everything on our ignorance of empirical causes, and Maistre on the abandonment of Thomist logic or the theology of the Catholic Church. But these avowed professions are belied by the tone and content of what in fact the two great critics say. Both stress, over and over again, the contrast between the 'inner' and the 'outer', the 'surface' which alone is lighted by the rays of science and of reason, and the 'depths' –

'the real life lived by men'. For Maistre, as later for Barrès, true knowledge – wisdom – lies in an understanding of, and communion with, *la terre et les morts* (what has this to do with Thomist logic?) – the great unalterable movement created by the links between the dead and the living and the yet unborn and the land on which they live; and it is this, perhaps, or something akin to it, that, in their respective fashions, Burke and Taine, and their many imitators, have attempted to convey.

As for Tolstoy, to him such mystical conservatism was peculiarly detestable, since it seemed to him to evade the central question by merely restating it, concealed in a cloud of pompous rhetoric, as the answer. Yet he, too, in the end, presents us with the vision, dimly discerned by Kutuzov and by Pierre, of Russia in her vastness, and what she could and what she could not do or suffer, and how and when – all of which Napoleon and his advisers (who knew a great deal but not of what was relevant to the issue) did not perceive; and so (although their knowledge of history and science and minute causes was perhaps greater than Kutuzov's or Pierre's) were led duly to their doom. Maistre's paeans to the superior science of the great Christian soldiers of the past and Tolstoy's lamentations about our scientific ignorance should not mislead anyone as to the nature of what they are in fact defending: awareness of the 'deep currents', the *raisons de cœur,* which they did not indeed themselves know by direct experience; but beside which, they were convinced, the devices of science were but a snare and a delusion.

Despite their deep dissimilarity and indeed violent opposition to one another, Tolstoy's sceptical realism and Maistre's dogmatic authoritarianism are blood brothers. For both spring from an agonised belief in a single, serene vision, in which all problems are resolved, all doubts stilled, peace and understanding finally achieved. Deprived of this vision, they devoted all their formidable resources, from their very different, and indeed often incompatible, positions, to the elimination of all possible adversaries and critics of it. The faiths for whose mere abstract possibility they fought were not, indeed, identical. It is the predicament in which they found themselves and that caused them to dedicate their strength to the lifelong task of destruction, it is their common enemies and the strong likeness between their temperaments that made them odd but unmistakable allies in a war which they were both conscious of fighting until their dying day.

VIII

Opposed as Tolstoy and Maistre were – one the apostle of the gospel that all men are brothers, the other the cold defender of the claims of violence, blind sacrifice, and eternal suffering – they were united by inability to escape from the same tragic paradox: they were both by nature sharp-eyed foxes, inescapably aware of sheer, *de facto* differences which divide and forces which disrupt the human world, observers utterly incapable of being deceived by the many subtle devices, the unifying systems and faiths and sciences, by which the superficial or the desperate sought to conceal the chaos from themselves and from one another. Both looked for a harmonious universe, but everywhere found war and disorder, which no attempt to cheat, however heavily disguised, could even begin to hide; and so, in a condition of final despair, offered to throw away the terrible weapons of criticism with which both, but particularly Tolstoy, were overgenerously endowed, in favour of the single great vision, something too indivisibly simple and remote from normal intellectual processes to be assailable by the instruments of reason, and therefore, perhaps, offering a path to peace and salvation.

Maistre began as a moderate liberal and ended by pulverising the new nineteenth-century world from the solitary citadel of his own variety of ultramontane Catholicism. Tolstoy began with a view of human life and history which contradicted all his knowledge, all his gifts, all his inclinations, and which, in consequence, he could scarcely be said to have embraced in the sense of practising it, either as a writer or as a man. From this, in his old age, he passed into a form of life in which he tried to resolve the glaring contradiction between what he believed about men and events, and what he thought he believed, or ought to believe, by behaving, in the end, as if factual questions of this kind were not the fundamental issues at all, only the trivial preoccupations of an idle, ill-conducted life, while the real questions were quite different. But it was of no use: the Muse cannot be cheated. Tolstoy was the least superficial of men: he could not swim with the tide without being drawn irresistibly beneath the surface to investigate the darker depths below; and he could not avoid seeing what he saw and doubting even that; he could close his eyes but not forget that he was doing so; his appalling, destructive sense of what was false frustrated this final effort at self-deception as it did all the earlier ones; and he died in agony, oppressed by the burden of his intellectual infallibility and his sense of perpetual moral error, the greatest of those who can neither reconcile, nor leave unreconciled, the conflict of what there is with what there ought to be.

Tolstoy's sense of reality was until the end too devastating to be compatible with any moral ideal which he was able to construct out of the fragments into which his intellect shivered the world, and he dedicated all of his vast strength of mind and will to the lifelong denial of this fact. At once insanely proud and filled with self-hatred, omniscient and doubting everything, cold and violently passionate, contemptuous and self-abasing, tormented and detached, surrounded by an adoring family, by devoted followers, by the admiration of the entire civilised world, and yet almost wholly isolated, he is the most tragic of the great writers, a desperate old man, beyond human aid, wandering self-blinded at Colonus.

HERZEN AND BAKUNIN ON
INDIVIDUAL LIBERTY

(1955) HERZEN 1812-70
BAKUNIN 1814-76

'Human life is a great social duty [said Louis Blanc]: man *must* constantly sacrifice himself for society.'

'Why?' I asked suddenly.

'How do you mean "Why?" – but surely the whole purpose and mission of man is the well-being of society?'

'But it will never be attained if everyone makes sacrifices and nobody enjoys himself.'

'You are playing with words.'

'The muddle-headedness of a barbarian,' I replied, laughing.
Alexander Herzen, *My Past and Thoughts*[1]

Since the age of thirteen [. . .] I have served one idea, marched under one banner – war against all imposed authority – against every kind of deprivation of freedom, in the name of the absolute independence of the individual. I should like to go on with my little guerrilla war – like a real Cossack – *auf eigene Faust*[2] – as the Germans say.   Alexander Herzen, letter to Mazzini[3]

I

Of all the Russian revolutionary writers of the nineteenth century, Herzen and Bakunin remain the most arresting. They were divided

---

1 'Byloe i dumy', part 6 ('Angliya (1852–1864)'), chapter 3 ('Emigratsii v Londone', 1870), H xi 48; 'England 1852–1855', 'The Emigrants in London', M iii 1060.
2 'On my own initiative'.
3 To G. Mazzini, 13 September 1850, H xxiv 140.

INDIVIDUAL LIBERTY - central to the thought of Herzen + Bakunin

by many differences both of doctrine and of temperament, but they were at one in placing the ideal of individual liberty at the centre of their thought and action. Both dedicated their lives to rebellion against every form of oppression, social and political, public and private, open and concealed; but the very multiplicity of their gifts has tended to obscure the relative value of their ideas on this crucial topic.

Bakunin was a gifted journalist, whereas Herzen was a writer of genius, whose autobiography remains one of the great masterpieces of Russian prose. As a publicist he had no equal in his century. He possessed a singular combination of fiery imagination, capacity for meticulous observation, moral passion, and intellectual gaiety, with a talent for writing in a manner at once pungent and distinguished, ironical and incandescent, brilliantly entertaining and at times rising to great nobility of feeling and expression. What Mazzini did for the Italians, Herzen did for his countrymen: he created, almost single-handed, the tradition and the 'ideology' of systematic revolutionary agitation, and thereby founded the revolutionary movement in Russia. Bakunin's literary endowment was more limited, but he exercised a personal fascination unequalled even in that heroic age of popular tribunes, and left behind him a tradition of political conspiracy which has played a major part in the great upheavals of our own century. Yet these very achievements, which have earned the two friends and companions-in-arms their claim to immortality, serve to conceal their respective importance as political and social thinkers. For whereas Bakunin, for all his marvellous eloquence, his lucid, clever, vigorous, at times devastating, critical power, seldom says anything which is precise, or profound, or authentic – in any sense personally 'lived through' – Herzen, despite his brilliance, his careless spontaneity, his notorious 'pyrotechnics', expresses bold and original ideas, and is a political (and consequently a moral) thinker of the first importance. To classify his views with those of Bakunin as forms of semi-anarchistic 'populism', or with those of Proudhon or Rodbertus or Chernyshevsky as yet another variant of early socialism with an agrarian bias, is to leave out his most arresting contribution to political theory. This injustice deserves to be remedied. Herzen's basic political ideas are unique not merely by Russian, but by European standards. Russia is not so rich in first-rate thinkers that she can afford to ignore one of the three moral preachers of genius born upon her soil.

11

Alexander Herzen grew up in a world dominated by French and German historical romanticism. The failure of the great French Revolution had discredited the optimistic naturalism of the eighteenth century as deeply as the Russian Revolution of our own day weakened the prestige of Victorian liberalism. The central notion of eighteenth-century enlightenment was the belief that the principal causes of human misery, injustice and oppression lay in men's ignorance and folly. Accurate knowledge of the laws governing the physical world, once and for all discovered and formulated by the divine Newton, would enable men in due course to dominate nature; by understanding and adjusting themselves to the unalterable causal laws of nature they would live as well and as happily as it is possible to live in the world as it is; at any rate, they would avoid the pains and disharmonies due to vain and ignorant efforts to oppose or circumvent such laws. Some thought that the world as explained by Newton was what it was *de facto*, for no discoverable reason – an ultimate, unexplained reality. Others believed they could discover a rational plan – a 'natural' or divine Providence, governed by an ultimate purpose for which all creation strove; so that man, by submitting to it, was not bowing to blind necessity, but consciously recognising the part which he played in a coherent, intelligible, and thereby justified process. But whether the Newtonian scheme was taken as a mere description or as a theodicy, it was the ideal paradigm of all explanation; it remained for the genius of Locke to point a way whereby the moral and spiritual worlds could at last also be set in order and explained by the application of the selfsame principles. If the natural sciences enabled men to shape the material world to their desire, the moral sciences would enable them so to regulate their conduct as to avoid for ever discord between beliefs and facts, and so end all evil, stupidity and frustration. If philosophers

Fall of the Enlightenment = French Rev.

(that is, scientists), both natural and moral, were put in charge of the world, instead of kings, noblemen, priests, and their dupes and factotums, universal happiness could in principle be achieved.

The consequences of the French Revolution broke the spell of these ideas. Among the doctrines which sought to explain what it was that must have gone wrong, German romanticism, both in its subjective-mystical and its nationalist forms, and in particular the Hegelian movement, acquired a dominant position. This is not the place to examine it in detail; suffice it to say that it retained the dogma that the world obeyed intelligible laws; that progress was possible, according to some inevitable plan, and identical with the development of 'spiritual' forces; that experts could discover these laws and teach understanding of them to others. For the followers of Hegel the gravest blunder that had been made by the French materialists lay in supposing that these laws were mechanical, that the universe was composed of isolable bits and pieces, of molecules, or atoms, or cells, and that everything could be explained and predicted in terms of the movement of bodies in space. Men were not mere collocations of bits of matter; they were souls or spirits obeying unique and intricate laws of their own. Nor were human societies mere collocations of individuals: they too possessed inner structures analogous to the psychical organisation of individual souls, and pursued goals of which the individuals who composed them might, in varying degrees, be unconscious. Knowledge was, indeed, liberating. Only people who knew why everything was as it was, and acted as it did, and why it was irrational for it to be or do anything else, could themselves be wholly rational: that is, would cooperate with the universe willingly, and not try to beat their heads in vain against the unyielding 'logic of the facts'. The only goals which were attainable were those embedded in the pattern of historical development; these alone were rational because the pattern was rational; human failure was a symptom of irrationality, of misunderstanding of what the times demanded, of what the next stage of the progress of reason must be; and values – the good and the bad, the just and the unjust, the beautiful and the ugly – were what a rational being would strive for at a specific stage of its growth as part of the rational pattern. To deplore the inevitable because it was cruel or unjust, to complain of what must be, was to reject rational answers to the problems of what to do, how to live. To oppose the stream was to commit suicide, which was mere madness. According to this view, the good, the noble, the just, the strong, the inevitable, the rational, were 'ultimately' one; conflict between them was ruled out, logically, a priori. Concerning the nature of the pattern there might be differences; Herder saw it in the development of the cultures of different tribes and races; Hegel in the development of the national State. Saint-Simon saw a broader pattern of a single Western civilisation, and distinguished in it the dominant role of technological evolution and the conflicts of economically conditioned classes, and within these the crucial influence of exceptional individuals – of men of moral, intellectual or artistic genius. Mazzini and Michelet saw it in terms of the inner spirit of each people seeking to assert the principles of their common humanity, each in its own fashion, against individual oppression or blind nature. Marx conceived it in terms of the history of the struggle of classes created and determined by growth of the forces of material production. Politico-religious thinkers in Germany and France saw it as *historia sacra*, the progress of fallen man struggling toward union with God – the final theocracy – the submission of secular forces to the reign of God on earth.

There were many variants of these central doctrines, some Hegelian, some mystical, some going back to eighteenth-century naturalism; furious battles were fought, heresies attacked, recalcitrants crushed. What they all had in common was the belief, firstly, that the universe obeys laws and displays a pattern, whether intelligible to reason, or empirically discoverable, or mystically revealed; secondly, that men are elements in wholes larger and stronger than themselves, so that the behaviour of individuals can be explained in terms of such wholes, and not vice versa; thirdly, that answers to the questions of what should be done are deducible from knowledge of the goals of the objective process of history in which men are willy-nilly involved, and must be identical for all those who truly know – for all rational beings; fourthly, that nothing can be vicious or cruel or stupid or ugly that is a means to the fulfilment of the objectively given cosmic purpose – it cannot, at least, be so 'ultimately', or 'in the last analysis' (however it might look on the face of it) – and conversely, that everything that opposes the great purpose is so. Opinions might vary as to whether such goals were inevitable – and progress therefore automatic; or whether, on the contrary, men were free to choose to realise them or to abandon them (to their own inevitable doom). But all were agreed that objective ends of universal validity could be found, and that they were the sole proper ends of all social, political and personal activity; for otherwise the world could not be regarded as a 'cosmos' with real laws and 'objective' demands; all beliefs, all values, might turn out merely relative, merely subjective, the plaything of whims and accidents, unjustified and unjustifiable, which was unthinkable.

Against this great despotic vision, the intellectual glory of the age, revealed, worshipped, and embellished with countless images and flowers by the metaphysical genius of Germany, and acclaimed by the profoundest and most admired thinkers of France, Italy and Russia, Herzen rebelled violently. He rejected its foundations and denounced its conclusions, not merely because it seemed to him (as it had to his friend Belinsky) morally revolting; but also because he thought it intellectually specious and aesthetically tawdry, and an attempt to force nature into a straitjacket of the poverty-stricken imagination of German philistines and pedants. In *Letters from France and Italy*, *From the Other Shore*, *Letters to an Old Comrade*, in *Open Letters* to Michelet, W. Linton, Mazzini, and, of course, throughout *My Past and Thoughts*, he enunciated his own ethical and philosophical beliefs. Of these, the most important were: that nature obeys no plan, that history follows no libretto; that no single key, no formula, can, in principle, solve the problems of individuals or societies; that general solutions are not solutions, universal ends are never real ends, that every age has its own texture and its own questions, that short cuts and generalisations are no substitute for experience; that liberty – of actual individuals, in specific times and places – is an absolute value; that a minimum area of free action is a moral necessity for all men, not to be suppressed in the name of abstractions or general principles so freely bandied by the great thinkers of this or any age, such as eternal salvation, or history, or humanity, or progress, still less the State or the Church or the proletariat – great names invoked to justify acts of detestable cruelty and despotism, magic formulae designed to stifle the voices of human feeling and conscience. This liberal attitude had an affinity with the thin but not yet dead tradition of Western libertarianism, of which elements persisted even in Germany – in Kant, in Wilhelm von Humboldt, in the early works of Schiller and of Fichte – surviving in France and French Switzerland among the Idéologues and in the views of Benjamin Constant, Tocqueville and Sismondi; and remained a hardy growth in England among the utilitarian radicals.

Like the early liberals of Western Europe, Herzen delighted in independence, variety, the free play of individual temperament. He desired the richest possible development of personal characteristics, valued spontaneity, directness, distinction, pride, passion, sincerity, the style and colour of free individuals; he detested conformism, cowardice, submission to the tyranny of brute force or pressure of opinion, arbitrary violence, and anxious submissiveness; he hated the worship of power, blind reverence for the past, for institutions, for mysteries or myths; the humiliation of the weak by the strong, sectarianism, philistinism, the resentment and envy of majorities, the brutal arrogance of minorities. He desired social justice, economic efficiency, political stability, but these must always remain secondary to the need for protecting human dignity, the upholding of civilised values, the protection of individuals from aggression, the preservation of sensibility and genius from individual or institutional bullying. Any society which, for whatever reason, failed to prevent such invasions of liberty, and opened the door to the possibility of insult by one side, and grovelling by the other, he condemned outright and rejected with all its works – all the social or economic advantages which it might, quite genuinely, offer. He rejected it with the same moral fury as that with which Ivan Karamazov spurned the promise of eternal happiness bought at the cost of the torture of one innocent child; but the arguments which Herzen employed in defence of his position, and the description of the enemy whom he picked out for pillory and destruction, were set forth in language which both in tone and substance had little in common with either the theological or the liberal eloquence of his age.

As an acute and prophetic observer of his times he is comparable, perhaps, to Marx and Tocqueville; as a moralist he is more interesting and original than either.

III

Man, it is commonly asserted, desires liberty. Moreover, human beings are said to have rights, in virtue of which they claim a certain degree of freedom of action. These formulae taken by themselves strike Herzen as hollow. They must be given some concrete meaning, but even then – if they are taken as hypotheses about what people actually believe – they are untrue; not borne out by history; for the masses have seldom desired freedom:

> The masses want to stay the hand which impudently snatches from them the bread which they have earned [. . .] They are indifferent to individual freedom, liberty of speech; the masses love authority. They are still blinded by the arrogant glitter of power, they are offended by those who stand alone. By equality they understand equality of oppression [. . .] they want a social government to rule for their benefit, and not, like the present one, against it. But to govern themselves doesn't enter their heads.[1]

On this topic there has been altogether too much 'romanticism for the heart' and 'idealism for the mind'[2] – too much craving for verbal magic, too much desire to substitute words for things. With the result that bloody struggles have been fought and many innocent human beings slaughtered and the most horrible crimes condoned in the name of empty abstractions:

> There is no nation in the world [. . .] which has shed so much blood for freedom as the French, and there is no people which understands it less, seeks to realise it less [. . .] on the streets, in the courts, in their homes [. . .] The French are the most abstract and religious

1   'S togo berega' (1850, 2nd. ed. 1855), H vi 124; F 133–4.
2   ibid. 23; F 24.

people in the world; the fanaticism of ideas with them goes hand in hand with lack of respect for persons, with contempt for their neighbours – the French turn everything into an idol, and then woe to him who does not bow the knee to the idol of the day. Frenchmen fight like heroes for freedom and without a thought drag you to jail if you don't agree with their opinions [. . .] The despotic *salus populi* and the bloody and inquisitorial *pereat mundus et fiat justitia* are engraved equally in the consciousness of royalists and democrats [. . .] Read George Sand, Pierre Leroux, Louis Blanc, Michelet – you will meet everywhere Christianity and romanticism adapted to our own morality; everywhere dualism, abstraction, abstract duty, enforced virtues and official and rhetorical morality without any relation to real life.[1]

Ultimately, Herzen goes on to say, this is heartless frivolity, the sacrifice of human beings to mere words which inflame the passions, and which, upon being pressed for their meaning, turn out to refer to nothing, a kind of 'political *gaminerie*' which 'excited and fascinated Europe',[2] but also plunged it into inhuman and unnecessary slaughter. 'Dualism' is for Herzen a confusion of words with facts, the construction of theories employing abstract terms which are not founded in discovered real needs, of political programmes deduced from abstract principles unrelated to real situations. These formulae grow into terrible weapons in the hands of fanatical doctrinaires who seek to bind them upon human beings, if need be, by violent vivisection, for the sake of some absolute ideal, for which the sanction lies in some uncriticised and uncriticisable vision – metaphysical, religious, aesthetic; at any rate, unconcerned with the actual needs of actual persons – in the name of which the revolutionary leaders kill and torture with a quiet conscience, because they know that this and this alone is – must be – the solution to all social and political and personal ills. And he develops this thesis along lines made familiar to us by Tocqueville and other critics of democracy, by pointing out that the masses detest talent, wish everyone to think

1   'Pis'ma iz Frantsii i Italii', tenth letter (1848), H v 175–6; L 160–1.
2   ibid., H v 176; L 161.

as they do, and are bitterly suspicious of independence of thought
and conduct:

> The submission of the individual to society – to the people – to
> humanity – to the idea – is a continuation of human sacrifice [. . .]
> the crucifixion of the innocent for the guilty [. . .] The individual,
> who is the true, real monad of society, has always been sacrificed to
> some general concept, some collective noun, some banner or other.
> What the purpose of [. . .] the sacrifice was [. . .] was never so much
> as asked.[1]

Since these abstractions – history, progress, the safety of the
people, social equality – have all been cruel altars upon which
innocents have been offered up without a qualm, they are deser-
ving of notice. Herzen examines them in turn.

If history has an inexorable direction, a rational structure, and
a purpose (perhaps a beneficial one), we must adjust ourselves to
it or perish. But what is this rational purpose? Herzen cannot
discern it; he sees no sense in history, only the story of 'hereditary,
chronic madness':[2]

> It seems unnecessary to cite examples, there are millions of them.
> Open any history you like and what is striking is that instead of real
> interests everything is governed by imaginary interests, fantasies.
> Look at the kind of causes in which blood is shed, in which people
> bear extreme sufferings; look at what is praised and what is blamed,
> and you will be convinced of a truth which at first seems sad – of a
> truth which on second thoughts is full of comfort, that all this is the
> result of a deranged intellect. Wherever you look in the ancient
> world, you will find madness almost as widespread as it is in our
> own. Here is Curtius throwing himself into a pit to save the city.
> There a father is sacrificing his daughter to obtain a fair wind, and
> he has found an old idiot to slaughter the poor girl for him, and this
> lunatic has not been locked up, has not been taken to a madhouse,
> but has been recognised as the high priest. Here the King of Persia

1   'S togo berega', H vi 125–6; F 135.
2   'Doktor Krupov' (1847), H iv 263.

orders the sea to be flogged, and understands the absurdity of his act as little as his enemies the Athenians, who wanted to cure the intellect and the understanding of human beings with hemlock. What frightful fever was it that made the emperors persecute Christianity? [. . .]

And after the Christians were torn and tortured by wild beasts, they themselves, in their turn, began to persecute and torture one another more furiously than they themselves had been persecuted. How many innocent Germans and Frenchmen perished just so, for no reason at all, while their demented judges thought they were merely doing their duty, and slept peacefully not many steps from the place where the heretics were being roasted to death.[1]

'History is the autobiography of a madman.'[2] This might have been written with equal bitterness by Voltaire and by Tolstoy. The purpose of history? We do not make history and are not responsible for it. If history is a tale told by an idiot, it is certainly criminal to justify the oppression and cruelty, the imposition of one's arbitrary will upon many thousands of human beings, in the name of hollow abstractions – the 'demands' of 'history' or of 'historical destiny', of 'national security', of 'the logic of the facts'. '*Salus populi suprema lex*, *pereat mundus et fiat justitia* have about them a strong smell of burnt bodies, blood, inquisition, torture, and generally of "*the triumph of order*".'[3] Abstractions, apart from their evil consequences, are a mere attempt to evade facts which do not fit into our preconceived schema.

A man looks at something freely only when he does not bend it to his theory, and does not himself bend before it; reverence before it, not free but enforced, limits a man, narrows his freedom; something in talking of which one is not allowed to smile without blasphemy [. . .] is a fetish, a man is crushed by it, he is frightened of confounding it with *ordinary* life.[4]

1   ibid. 263–4.   2   ibid. 264.
3   'S togo berega', H vi 140; F 159.
4   'Pis'ma iz Frantsii i Italii', fifth letter (1847), H v 89; L 80. See also the remarkable analysis of the universal desire to evade intellectual responsibility by the creation of idols and the transgression of the Second Commandment

It becomes an icon, an object of blind, uncomprehending worship, and so a mystery justifying excessive crimes. And in the same vein:

> The world will not know liberty until all that is religious, political, is transformed into something simple and human, is made susceptible to criticism and denial. Logic when it comes of age detests canonised truths [. . .] it thinks nothing sacrosanct, and if the republic arrogates to itself the same rights as the monarchy, it will despise it as much, nay, more [. . .] It is not enough to despise the crown – one must not be filled with awe before the Phrygian Cap; it is not enough not to consider *lèse-majesté* a crime: one must look on *salus populi* as being one.[1]

And he adds that patriotism – to sacrifice oneself for one's country – is doubtless noble; but it is better still if one survives together with one's country. So much for 'history'. Human beings 'will be cured of [such] idealism as they have been of other historical diseases – chivalry, Catholicism, Protestantism'.[2]

2. Then there are those who speak of 'progress', and are prepared to sacrifice the present to the future, to make men suffer today in order that their remote descendants might be happy; and condone brutal crimes and the degradation of human beings, because these are the indispensable means toward some guaranteed future felicity. For this attitude – shared equally by reactionary Hegelians and revolutionary communists, speculative utilitarians and ultramontane zealots, and indeed all who justify repellent means in the name of noble, but distant, ends – Herzen reserves his most violent contempt and ridicule. To it he devotes the best pages of *From the Other Shore* – his political *profession de foi*, written as a lament for the broken illusions of 1848.

> If progress is the goal, for whom are we working? Who is this Moloch who, as the toilers approach him, instead of rewarding them, draws back; and as a consolation to the exhausted and

---

in 'Novye variatsii na starye temy' (H ii 86–102), which originally appeared in *Sovremennik* in 1847.

1   'S togo berega', H vi 46; F 51.   2   ibid. 35; F 38.

doomed multitudes, shouting '*morituri te salutant*', can only give the [. . .] mocking answer that after their death all will be beautiful on earth. Do you truly wish to condemn the human beings alive today to the sad role of caryatids supporting a floor for others some day to dance on . . . or of wretched galley slaves who, up to their knees in mud, drag a barge [. . .] with the humble words 'progress in the future' upon its flag? [. . .] a goal which is infinitely remote is no goal, only [. . .] a deception; a goal must be closer – at the very least the labourer's wage, or pleasure in work performed. Each epoch, each generation, each life has had, has, its own fullness; and *en route* new demands grow, new experiences, new methods [. . .] The end of each generation is itself. Not only does Nature never make one generation the means for the attainment of some future goal, but she doesn't concern herself with the future at all; like Cleopatra, she is ready to dissolve the pearl in wine for a moment's pleasure [. . .]

[. . .] If humanity marched straight towards some result, there would be no history, only logic [. . .] Reason develops slowly, painfully, *it does not exist* in nature, nor outside nature [. . .] One has to arrange life with it as best one can, because there is no libretto. If history followed a set libretto it would lose all interest, become unnecessary, boring, ludicrous [. . .] Great men would be so many heroes strutting on a stage [. . .] History is all improvisation, all will, all extempore – there are no frontiers, no itineraries. Predicaments occur; sacred discontent; the fire of life; and the endless challenge to the fighters to try their strength, to go where they will, where there is a road; and where there is none, genius will blast a path.[1]

Herzen goes on to say that processes in history or nature may repeat themselves for millions of years; or stop suddenly; the tail of a comet may touch our planet and extinguish all life upon it; and this would be the finale of history. But nothing follows from this, it carries no moral with it. There is no guarantee that things will happen in one way rather than another. The death of a single human being is no less absurd and unintelligible than the death of the entire human race; it is a mystery that we accept, and with which there is no need to frighten children.

1   ibid. 34–5, 36; F 36–7, 38–9.

Nature is not a smooth, teleological development, certainly not a development designed for human happiness or the fulfilment of social justice. Nature is for Herzen a mass of potentialities which develop in accordance with no intelligible plan. Some develop, some perish; in favourable conditions they may be realised, but they may deviate, collapse, die. This leads some men to cynicism and despair. Is human life an endless cycle of growth and recession, achievement and collapse? Is there no purpose in it all? Is human effort bound to end in ruin, to be followed by a new beginning as foredoomed to failure as its predecessors? This is a misunderstanding of reality. Why should nature be conceived as a utilitarian instrument designed for man's progress or happiness? Why should utility – the fulfilment of purposes – be demanded of the infinitely rich, infinitely generous cosmic process? Is there not a profound vulgarity in asking of what use its marvellous colour, its exquisite scent is to the plant, or what its purpose can be when it is doomed to perish so soon? Nature is infinitely and recklessly fertile – 'she goes to extreme limits [. . .] until she reaches the outer frontier of all possible development – death – which cools her ardour and checks the excess of her poetic fancy, her unbridled creative passion.'[1] Why should nature be expected to follow our dreary categories? What right have we to insist that history is meaningless unless it obeys the patterns we impose upon it, pursues our goals, our transient, pedestrian ideals? History is an improvisation, it '"simultaneously knocks at a thousand doors . . . doors which may open . . . who knows?" "Baltic ones, perhaps – and then Russia will pour over Europe?" "Possibly."'[2] Everything in nature, in history, is what it is, and its own end. The present is its own fulfilment, it does not exist for the sake of some unknown future. If everything existed for the sake of something else, every fact, event, creature would be a means to something beyond itself in some cosmic plan. Or are we only puppets, pulled by invisible strings, victims of mysterious forces in a cosmic libretto? Is this what we mean by moral freedom? Is the culmination of a process *eo ipso* its purpose? Is old age the purpose of youth, merely because this is the order of human growth? Is the purpose of life death?

1   ibid. 31; F 33.   2   ibid. 32; F 34.

Why does a singer sing? Merely in order that, when he has stopped singing, his song might be remembered, so that the pleasure that his song has given may awaken a longing for that which cannot be recovered? No. This is a false and purblind and shallow view of life. The purpose of the singer is the song. And the purpose of life is to live it.

Everything passes, but what passes may reward the pilgrim for his sufferings. Goethe has told us that there is no insurance, no security, man must be content with the present; but he is not; he rejects beauty and fulfilment because he must own the future too. This is Herzen's answer to all those who, like Mazzini or Kossuth, or the socialists or the communists, called for supreme sacrifices and sufferings for the sake of civilisation, or equality, or justice, or humanity, if not in the present, then in the future. But this is 'idealism', metaphysical 'dualism', secular eschatology. The purpose of life is itself, the purpose of the struggle for liberty is the liberty here, today, of living individuals, each with his own individual ends, for the sake of which they move and fight and suffer, ends which are sacred to them; to crush their freedom, stop their pursuits, to ruin their ends for the sake of some ineffable felicity of the future, is blind, because that future is always too uncertain, and vicious, because it outrages the only moral values we know, tramples on real human lives and needs, and in the name of what? Of freedom, happiness, justice – fanatical generalisations, mystical sounds, abstractions. Why is personal liberty worth pursuing? Only for what it is in itself, because it is what it is, not because the majority desires freedom. Men in general do not seek freedom, despite Rousseau's celebrated exclamation that they are born free; that, remarks Herzen (echoing Joseph de Maistre), is as if you were to say 'Fish were born to fly, yet everywhere they swim.'[1] Ichthyophils may seek to prove that fish are 'by nature' made to fly; but they are not. And most people do not like liberators; they would rather continue in the ancient ruts, and bear the ancient yokes, than take the immense risks of building a new life. They prefer (Herzen repeats again and again) even the hideous cost of the present, muttering that modern life is at any rate better

[1]   ibid. 94; F 108.

than feudalism and barbarism. 'The people' do not desire liberty, only civilised individuals do; for the desire for freedom is bound up with civilisation. The value of freedom, like that of civilisation or education – none of which is 'natural' or obtainable without great effort – consists in the fact that without it the individual personality cannot realise all its potentialities – cannot live, act, enjoy, create in the illimitable fashions which every moment of history affords, and which differ in unfathomable ways from every other moment of history, and are wholly incommensurable with them. Man 'wants to be neither a passive grave-digger of the past, nor the unconscious midwife of the future'.[1] He wants to live in his own day. His morality cannot be derived from the laws of history (which do not exist), nor from the objective goals of human progress (there are none such – they change with changing circumstances and persons). Moral ends are what people want for their own sake. 'The truly free man *creates* his own morality.'[2]

This denunciation of general moral rules – without a trace of Byronic or Nietzschean hyperbole – is a doctrine not heard often in the nineteenth century; indeed, in its full extent, not until well into our own. It hits both right and left: against the romantic historians, against Hegel, and to some degree against Kant; against utilitarians and against supermen; against Tolstoy, and against the religion of art, against 'scientific' ethics, and all the Churches; it is empirical and naturalistic, recognises absolute values as well as change, and is overawed neither by evolution nor socialism. And it is original to an arresting degree.

If existing political parties are to be condemned, it is not, Herzen declares, because they do not satisfy the wishes of the majority, for the majority, in any case, prefer slavery to freedom, and the liberation of those who inwardly still remain slaves always leads to barbarism and anarchy: 'to dismantle the Bastille stone by stone will not of itself make free men out of the prisoners'.[3] 'The fatal error [of the French radicals in 1848] is [. . .] to have tried to free others before they were themselves liberated [. . .] They want, without altering the walls [of the prison], to give them

1   'Lettre sur le libre arbitre' (to his son Alexander, 1868), H xx/1 437–8.
2   'S togo berega', H vi 131; F 141.   3   ibid. 29; F 31.

a new function, as if a plan for a jail could be used for a free existence.'[1] Economic justice is certainly not enough: and this is ignored, to their own doom, by the socialist 'sects'. As for democracy, it can well be a 'razor' with which an immature people – like France with its universal suffrage in 1848 – nearly cut its own throat;[2] to try to remedy this by a dictatorship ('Petrograndism') leads to even more violent suppression. Gracchus Babeuf, who was disappointed by the results of the French Revolution, proclaimed the religion of equality – 'the equality of penal servitude'.[3] As for the communists of our own day, what is it they offer us? The 'forced labour of communism' of Cabet?[4] The 'organisation of labour in ancient Egypt à la Louis Blanc'?[5] The neatly laid-out little phalansteries of Fourier, in which a free man cannot breathe – in which one side of life is permanently repressed for the benefit of others?[6] Communism is merely a levelling movement, the despotism of frenzied mobs, of Committees of Public Safety invoking the security of the people – always a monstrous slogan, as vile as the enemy they seek to overthrow. Barbarism is abominable whichever side it comes from: 'Who will finish us off, put an end to it all? The senile barbarism of the sceptre or the wild barbarism of communism? A blood-stained sabre or the red flag?'[7] It is true that liberals are feeble, unrealistic and cowardly, and have no understanding of the needs of the poor and the weak, of the new proletarian class which is rising; it is true that the conservatives have shown themselves brutal, stupid, mean and despotic – although let it be remembered that priests and landowners are usually closer to the masses and understand their needs better than liberal intellectuals, even if their own intentions are less benevolent or honest. It is true that Slavophils are mere escapists, defenders of an empty throne, condoning a bad present in the name of an imaginary past. These men follow brutal and selfish instincts, or

1 ibid. 51; F 57.
2 'K staromu tovarishchu' (1869), H xx/2 584.
3 ibid. 578.   4 ibid.
5 'S togo berega', H vi 472 (variant of 'the slave labours of Egypt offered by the Communists', F 132).
6 'K staromu tovarishchu', H xx/2 578.
7 'Pis'ma iz Frantsii i Italii', fourteenth letter (1851), H v 211; L 194.

empty formulae. But the unbridled democracy of the present is no better, and can suppress men and their liberties even more brutally than the odious and sordid government of Napoleon III.

What do the masses care for 'us'? The masses can hurl in the teeth of the European ruling class, 'We were hungry and you gave us parliamentary chatter, we were naked and you sent us to our frontier to kill other hungry and naked men.'[1] Parliamentary government in England is certainly no answer, for it, in common with other so-called democratic institutions ('traps called oases of liberty'),[2] merely defends the rights of property, exiles men in the interests of public safety, and keeps under arms men who are ready, without asking why, to fire instantly as soon as ordered. Little do naive democrats know what it is that they believe in, and what the consequences will be. 'Why is belief in God [and] the Kingdom of Heaven silly, whereas belief in earthly Utopias is not silly?'[3] As for the consequences, one day there really will be democracy on earth, the rule of the masses. Then indeed something will occur.

> The whole of Europe will leave its normal courses and will be drowned in a general cataclysm [...] Cities taken by storm and looted will fall into poverty, education will decline, factories will come to a stop, villages will be emptied, the countryside will remain without hands to work it, as after the Thirty Years War. Exhausted and starving peoples will submit to everything, and military discipline will take the place of law and of every kind of orderly administration. Then the victors will begin to fight for their loot. Civilisation, industry, terrified, will flee to England and America, taking with them from the general ruin, some their money, others their scientific knowledge or their unfinished work. Europe will become a Bohemia after the Hussites.
>
> And then, on the brink of suffering and disaster, a new war will break out, home-grown, internal, the revenge of the *have-nots against the haves!*

1   'Myaso osvobozhdeniya' (1862), H xvi 29.
2   [Untraced, but cf. 'Du développement des idées révolutionnaires en Russie', H vii 185.]
3   'S togo berega', H vi 104; F 120.

[. . .] Communism will sweep across the world in a violent tempest – dreadful, bloody, unjust, swift; in thunder and lightning, amid the fire of the burning palaces, upon the ruin of factories and public buildings the New Commandments will be enunciated, [. . .] the New Symbols of the Faith.

They will be connected in a thousand fashions with the historic ways of life [. . .] but the basic tone will be set by socialism. The institutions and structure of our own time and *civilisation* will perish – will, as Proudhon politely puts it, be *liquidated*.

You regret the death of civilisation?

I, too, I am sorry.

But the masses will not regret it; the masses to whom it gave nothing but tears, want, ignorance and humiliation.[1]

It is prophecies of this type by the founding fathers of the New Order that cause embarrassment to contemporary Soviet critics and hagiographers. They are usually dealt with by omission.

Heine and Burckhardt too had seen nightmarish visions, and spoke of the demons called into being by the injustices and the 'contradictions' of the new world, which promised not Utopia but ruin. Like them, Herzen harbours no illusions:

Do you not perceive these [. . .] new barbarians, marching to destroy? [. . .] Like lava they are stirring heavily beneath the surface of the earth [. . .] When the hour strikes, Herculaneum and Pompeii will be wiped out, the good and the bad, the just and the unjust will perish equally. This will be not a judgement, not a vengeance, but a cataclysm, a total revolution . . . This lava, these barbarians, this new world, these Nazarenes who are coming to put an end to the impotent and decrepit [. . .], they are closer than you think. For it is they, none other, who are dying of cold and of hunger, it is they whose muttering you hear [. . .] from the garrets and the cellars, while you and I in our rooms on the first floor are chatting about socialism 'over pastry and champagne'.[2]

1   'Pis'ma iz Frantsii i Italii', fourteenth letter, H v 215–17; L 198–9.
2   'S togo berega', H vi 58–9; F 66–7.

Herzen is more consistently 'dialectical' than the 'scientific' social-ists who swept away the 'Utopias' of their rivals, only to succumb to millennial fantasies of their own. To set by the side of the classless idyll of Engels in the Communist Manifesto let us choose these lines by Herzen:

> Socialism will develop in all its phases until it reaches its own extremes and absurdities. Then there will again burst forth from the titanic breast of the revolting minority a cry of denial. Once more a mortal battle will be joined in which socialism will occupy the place of today's conservatism, and will be defeated by the coming revolution as yet invisible to us . . .[1]

The historical process has no 'culmination'. Human beings have invented this notion only because they cannot face the possibility of an endless conflict.

Such passages as these have their analogues in savage prophecies by Hegel and by Marx, who also predicted the doom of the bourgeoisie, and death and lava and a new civilisation. But, whereas there is in both Hegel and Marx an unmistakable note of sardonic, gloating joy in the very thought of vast, destructive powers unchained, and the coming holocaust of all the innocents and the fools and the contemptible philistines, so little aware of their terrible fate, Herzen is free from this prostration before the mere spectacle of triumphant power and violence, from contempt for weakness as such, and from the romantic pessimism which is at the heart of the nihilism and fascism that were to come; for he thinks the cataclysm neither inevitable nor glorious. He despises those liberals who begin revolutions and then try to extinguish their consequences, who at the same time undermine the old order and cling to it, light the fuse and try to stop the explosion, who are frightened by the emergence of that mythical creature, their 'unfortunate brother, cheated of his inheritance',[2] the worker, the proletarian who demands his rights, who does not realise that while he has nothing to lose, the intellectual may lose everything. It is the liberals who betrayed the revolution in 1848 in Paris, in

1   ibid. 110; F 147.   2   ibid. 53; F 60.

Rome, in Vienna, not only by taking flight and helping the defeated reactionaries to regain power and stamp out liberty, but by first running away, then pleading that the 'historical forces' were too strong to resist. If one has no answer to a problem, it is more honest to admit this, and to formulate the problem clearly, than first to obscure it, commit acts of weakness and betrayal, and then plead as an excuse that history was too much for one. True, the ideals of 1848 were themselves empty enough; at least they looked so to Herzen in 1869: 'not one constructive, organic idea [. . .], and economic blunders [which] lead not indirectly, like political ones, but directly and deeply, to ruin, stagnation, a hungry death'.[1] Economic blunders plus 'the arithmetical pantheism of universal suffrage', 'superstitious faith in republics'[2] or in parliamentary reform, is in effect his summary of some of the ideals of 1848. Nevertheless, the liberals did not fight even for their own foolish programme. And in any case liberty was not to be gained by such means. The claims of our time are clear enough, they are social more than economic; for mere economic change, as advocated by socialists, unaccompanied by a deeper transformation, will not suffice to abolish civilised cannibalism, monarchy and religion, courts and governments, moral beliefs and habits. The institutions of private life must be changed too.

> Is it not odd that man, liberated by modern science from penury and lawless rapacity, has nevertheless not been made free, but has somehow been swallowed up by society? To understand the entire breadth and reality, all the sanctity of the rights of man, and not to destroy society, not to reduce it to atoms, is the hardest of social problems; it will probably one day be resolved by history itself; in the past it has never been resolved.[3]

Science will not solve it, *pace* Saint-Simon, nor will preaching against the horrors of unbridled competition, nor advocacy of the abolition of poverty, if all they do is to dissolve individuals into a

---

1   'K staromu tovarishchu', H xx/2 576.
2   'Byloe i dumy', part 6, 'Dzhon-Styuart Mill' i ego kniga "On Liberty"' (1859), H xi 70; 'John Stuart Mill and his Book on Liberty', M iii 1079.
3   'Pis'ma iz Frantsii i Italii', fourth letter (1847), H v 62; L 56.

single, monolithic, oppressive community – Gracchus Babeuf's 'equality of penal servitude'.[1]

History is not determined. Life, fortunately, has no libretto, improvisation is always possible, nothing makes it necessary for the future to fulfil the programme prepared by the metaphysicians.[2] Socialism is neither impossible nor inevitable, and it is the business of the believers in liberty to prevent it from degenerating into either bourgeois philistinism or communist slavery. Life is neither good nor bad, men are what they make themselves. Without social sense they become orang-utans, without egoism, tame monkeys.[3] But there are not inexorable forces to compel them to be either. Our ends are not made for us, but by us; hence to justify trampling on liberty today by the promise of freedom tomorrow, because it is 'objectively' guaranteed, is to make use of a cruel and wicked delusion as a pretext for iniquitous action. 'If only people wanted, instead of saving the world, to save themselves – instead of liberating humanity, to liberate themselves, they would do much for the salvation of the world and the liberation of man.'[4]

Herzen goes on to say that man is of course dependent on his environment and his time – physiologically, educationally, biologically, as well as at more conscious levels; and he concedes that men reflect their own time and are affected by the circumstances of their lives.[5] But the possibility of opposition to the social medium, and protest against it, is nevertheless just as real; whether it is effective or not; whether it takes a social or an individual form. Belief in determinism is merely an alibi for weakness. There will always be those fatalists who will say 'the choice of the paths of history is not in the individual's power. Events do not depend on persons, but persons on events: we only seem to control our direction, but actually sail wherever the wave takes us.'[6] But this is not true.

1   loc. cit. (109 above, note 3).
2   'S togo berega', H vi 36, 93; F 39, 107.
3   ibid. 130; F 139–40.   4   ibid. 119; F 128.
5   ibid. 120; F 128–9.
6   'K staromu tovarishchu', H xx/2 588.

Our paths are not unalterable at all. On the contrary, they change with circumstances, with understanding, with personal energy. The individual is made by [...] events, but events are also made by individuals and bear their stamp upon them – there is perpetual interaction [...] To be passive tools of forces independent of us – [...] this is not for us; to be the blind instrument of fate – the scourge, the executioner of God, one needs naive faith, the simplicity of ignorance, wild fanaticism, a pure, uncontaminated, child-like quality of thought.[1]

To pretend that we are like this today would be a lie. Leaders arise, like Bismarck (or Marx), who claim to guide their nation or their class to the inevitable triumph reserved for them by destiny, whose chosen instruments they feel themselves to be; in the name of their sacred historic mission they ruin, torture, enslave. But they remain brutal impostors.

What thinking persons have forgiven Attila, the Committee of Public Safety, even Peter the First, they will not forgive us; we have heard no voice calling to us from on high to fulfil a destiny; no voice from the nether regions to point a path to us. For us, there is only one voice, one power, *the power of reason and understanding*. In rejecting them we become the unfrocked priests of science, renegades from civilisation.[2]

IV

If this is a condemnation of Bismarck or Marx, it is directed more obviously and expressly at Bakunin and the Russian Jacobins, at Karakozov's pistol and Chernyshevsky's axe, sanctified by the new young revolutionaries; at the terrorist propaganda of Zaichnevsky or of Serno-Solov'evich, and the culminating horror of Nechaev's activity and the final perversions of revolutionary doctrine, which went far beyond its Western origins, and treated honour, compassion and the scruples of civilisation as so many

1 ibid.   2 ibid. 588–9.

personal affronts. From this it is not far to Plekhanov's celebrated
formula of 1903, 'The safety of the revolution is the supreme
law',[1] which sanctioned the suspension of civil liberties; and so to
the April Theses, and the treatment of 'inviolability of the person'
as a luxury to be dispensed with in difficult moments.

The chasm between Herzen and Bakunin is not bridgeable.
And the half-hearted attempts by Soviet historians, if not to slur
over the differences, at any rate to represent them as necessary
and successive stages in the evolution of a single process – necessary both logically and historically (because history and the development of ideas obey 'logical' laws) – are melancholy failures.
The views of those who, like Herzen (or Mill), place personal
liberty in the centre of their social and political doctrine, to whom
it is the holy of holies the surrender of which makes all other
activities, whether of defence or attack, valueless;[2] and, as opposed
to them, of those for whom such liberty is only a desirable by-
product of the social transformation which is the sole end of their
activity, or else a transient stage of development made inevitable
by history – these two attitudes are opposed, and no reconciliation
or compromise between them is conceivable; for the Phrygian Cap
comes between them. For Herzen the issue of personal liberty
overshadows even such crucial questions as centralism against free
federation; revolution from above versus revolution from below;
political versus economic activity; peasants versus city workers;
collaboration with other parties versus refusal to transact and
the cry for 'political purity' and independence; belief in the
unavoidability of capitalist development versus the possibility of
circumnavigating it; and all the other great issues which divided
the liberal and revolutionary parties in Russia until the Revolution.
For those who stand 'in awe of the Phrygian Cap', *salus populi* is
a final criterion before which all other considerations must yield.
For Herzen it remains a 'criminal' principle, the greatest tyranny

1   *Vtoroi s"ezd RSDRP, iyul'–avgust 1903 goda: protokoly* (Moscow, 1959),
     182.
2   'However low [. . .] governments sank,' Herzen once remarked about the
     West in contrast to Russia, 'Spinoza was not sentenced to transportation, nor
     Lessing to be flogged or conscripted': 'S togo berega', H vi 15; F 12. The
     twentieth century has destroyed the force of this comparison.

of all; to accept it is to sacrifice the freedom of individuals to some huge abstraction – some monstrosity invented by metaphysics or religion, to escape from the real, earthly issues, to be guilty of 'dualism', that is, to divorce the principles of action from empirical facts, and deduce them from some other set of 'facts' provided by some special mode of vision; to take a path which in the end always leads to cannibalism – the slaughter of men and women today for the sake of 'future happiness'.[1] The *Letters to an Old Comrade* are aimed, above all, at this fatal fallacy. Herzen rightly held Bakunin guilty of it, and behind the ardent phrases, the lion-hearted courage, the broad Russian nature, the gaiety, the charm and the imagination of his friend – to whom he remained personally devoted to the end – he discerned a cynical indifference to the fate of individual human beings, a childish enthusiasm for playing with human lives for the sake of social experiment, a lust for revolution for revolution's sake, which went ill with his professed horror before the spectacle of arbitrary violence or the humiliation of innocent persons. He detected a certain genuine inhumanity in Bakunin (of which Belinsky and Turgenev were not unaware), a hatred of slavery, oppression, hypocrisy, poverty, in the abstract, without actual revulsion against their manifestations in concrete instances – a genuine Hegelianism of outlook – the feeling that it is useless to blame the instruments of history, when one can rise to a loftier height and survey the structure of history itself. Bakunin hated tsardom, but displayed too little specific loathing of Nicholas; he would never have given sixpences to little boys in Twickenham to cry, on the day of the Emperor's death, 'Zarnicoll is dead!' or felt the emancipation of the peasants as a personal happiness. The fate of individuals did not greatly concern him; his units were too vague and too large; 'First destroy, and then we shall see.' Temperament, vision, generosity, courage, revolutionary fire, elemental force of nature, these Bakunin had to overflowing. The rights and liberties of individuals play no great part in his apocalyptic vision.

Herzen's position on this issue is clear, and did not alter throughout his life. No distant ends, no appeals to overriding

1   ibid. 34; F 37.

principles or abstract nouns can justify the suppression of liberty, or fraud, violence and tyranny. Once the conduct of life in accordance with the moral principles that we actually live by, in the situation as we know it to be, and not as it might, or could, or should be, is abandoned, the path is open to the abolition of individual freedom and of all the values of humane culture. With genuine horror and disgust Herzen saw and denounced the militant, boorish anti-humanism of the younger generation of Russian revolutionaries – fearless but brutal, full of savage indignation, but hostile to civilisation and liberty, a generation of Calibans – 'the syphilis of [the] revolutionary passions'[1] of Herzen's own generation. They paid him back by a campaign of systematic denigration as a 'soft' aristocratic dilettante, a feeble liberal trimmer, a traitor to the revolution, a superfluous survival of an obsolete past. He responded with a bitter and accurate vignette of the 'new men': the new generation will say to the old: '"You are hypocrites, we will be cynics; you spoke like moralists, we shall speak like scoundrels; you were civil to your superiors, rude to your inferiors; we shall be rude to all; you bow without feeling respect, we shall push and jostle and make no apologies [. . .]".'[2]

It is a singular irony of history that Herzen, who wanted individual liberty more than happiness, or efficiency, or justice, who denounced organised planning, economic centralisation, governmental authority, because it might curtail the individual's capacity for the free play of fantasy, for unlimited depth and variety of personal life within a wide, rich, 'open' social milieu, who hated the Germans (and in particular the 'Russian Germans and German Russians')[3] of St Petersburg because their slavery was not (as in Russia or Italy) 'arithmetical', that is, reluctant submission to the numerically superior forces of reaction, but 'algebraical', that is, part of their 'inner formula' – the essence of their very being[4] – that Herzen, in

1   Letter to N. P. Ogarev, 1–2 May 1868, H xxix/1 330.
2   'Byloe i dumy', part 7, chapter 3 (1870), H xi 351; 'The Younger Emigrants: The Common Fund', M iii 1349.
3   The title of an article of 1859, 'Russkie nemtsy i nemetskie russkie', H xiv 148–89.
4   'Du développement des idées révolutionnaires en Russie', H vii 15. Arnold Ruge was outraged by this and protested vehemently in a letter to Herzen in

virtue of a casual phrase patronisingly dropped by Lenin, should today find himself in the holy of holies of the Soviet pantheon, placed there by a government the genesis of which he understood better and feared more deeply than Dostoevsky, and whose words and acts are a continuous insult to all that he believed and was.

Doubtless, despite all his appeals to concreteness, and his denunciation of abstract principles, Herzen was himself, at times, Utopian enough. He feared mobs, he disliked bureaucracy and organisation, and yet he believed in the possibility of establishing the rule of justice and happiness, not merely for the few, but for the many, if not in the Western world, at any rate in Russia; and that largely out of patriotism: in virtue of the Russian national character which had proved itself so gloriously by surviving Byzantine stagnation, and the Tatar yoke and the German truncheon, its own officials, and through it all preserving the inner soul of the people intact. He idealised Russian peasants, the village communes, free *artels*; similarly he believed in the natural goodness and moral nobility of the workers of Paris, in the Roman populace, and despite the increasingly frequent notes of 'sorrow, scepticism, irony [. . .] the three strings of the Russian lyre',[1] he grew neither cynical nor sceptical. Russian populism owes more to his ungrounded optimism than to any other single source of its inspiration.

Yet compared to Bakunin's doctrines, Herzen's views are a model of dry realism. Bakunin and Herzen had much in common: they shared an acute antipathy to Marxism and its founders, they saw no gain in the replacement of one class of despotism by another, they did not believe in the virtues of proletarians as such. But Herzen does at least face genuine political problems, such as the incompatibility of unlimited personal liberty with either social equality, or the minimum of social organisation and authority; the need to sail precariously between the Scylla of individualist 'atomisation' and the Charybdis of collectivist oppression; the sad disparity and conflict between many, equally noble, human ideals;

1854 when he received the German edition from him. See *Arnold Ruges Briefwechsel und Tagebuchblätter aus den Jahren 1825–1880*, ed. Paul Nerrlich (Berlin, 1886), ii (1848–1880) 147–9.

1   'Le Peuple russe et le socialisme: Lettre à Monsieur J. Michelet' (1851), H vii 295/330; F 194.

the non-existence of 'objective', eternal, universal moral and political standards, to justify either coercion or resistance to it; the mirage
of distant ends, and the impossibility of doing wholly without them.
In contrast to this, Bakunin, whether in his various Hegelian phases,
or his anarchist period, gaily dismisses such problems, and sails off
into the happy realm of revolutionary phraseology with the gusto
and the irresponsible delight in words which characterised his
adolescent and essentially frivolous outlook.

V

Bakunin, as his enemies and followers will equally testify, dedicated his entire life to the struggle for liberty. He fought for it in
action and in words. More than any other individual in Europe he
stood for ceaseless rebellion against every form of constituted authority, for ceaseless protest in the name of the insulted and oppressed
of every nation and class. His power of cogent and lucid destructive
argument is extraordinary, and has not, even today, obtained
proper recognition. His arguments against theological and metaphysical notions, his attacks upon the whole of the Western
Christian tradition – social, political and moral – his onslaughts
upon tyranny, whether of States or classes, or of special groups in
authority – priests, soldiers, bureaucrats, democratic representatives, scientists, bankers, revolutionary élites – are set forth in language which is still a model of eloquent polemical prose. With much
talent and wonderful high spirits he carried on the militant tradition
of the violent radicals among the eighteenth-century *philosophes*.
He shared their buoyancy but also their weaknesses, and his positive
doctrines, as so often theirs, turn out to be mere strings of ringing
commonplaces, linked together by vague emotional relevance or
rhetorical afflatus rather than a coherent structure of genuine ideas.
His affirmative doctrines are even thinner than theirs. Thus, as his
positive contribution to the problem of defining freedom, he offers:
'*Tous pour chacun et chacun pour tous.*'[1] This schoolboy jingle,

1   'Lettre à la Commission du journal l'*Égalité* à Genève', 19 December 1868,
     O v 15.

with its echo of *The Three Musketeers*, and the bright colours of historical romance, is more characteristic of Bakunin, with his irrepressible frivolity, his love of fantasy, and his lack of scruple in action and in the use of words, than the picture of the dedicated liberator painted by his followers and worshipped from afar by many a young revolutionary sent to Siberia or to death by the power of his unbridled eloquence. In the finest and most uncritical manner of the eighteenth century, without examining (despite his Hegelian upbringing and his notorious dialectical skill) whether they are compatible (or what they signify), Bakunin lumps all the virtues together into one vast undifferentiated amalgam: justice, humanity, goodness, freedom, equality ('the liberty of each through the equality of all'[1] is another of his empty incantations), science, reason, good sense, hatred of privilege and of monopoly, of oppression and exploitation, of stupidity and poverty, of weakness, inequality, injustice, snobbery – all these are represented as somehow forming one single, lucid, concrete ideal, for which the means would be only too ready to hand if only men were not too blind or too wicked to make use of them. Liberty will reign in 'a new heaven and a new earth, a new enchanting world in which all the dissonances will flow into one harmonious whole'[2] – the democratic and universal Church of human freedom.

1   See, e.g., (*a*) 'L'Instruction intégrale' (July–August 1869), O v 140 ('la liberté de chacun dans l'égalité et par l'égalité de tous'); Mikhail Bakunin, 'All-Round Education', in *From out of the Dustbin: Bakunin's Basic Writings 1869–1871*, trans. and ed. Robert M. Cutler (Ann Arbor, 1985), 113 ('the freedom of each individual through the equality of every individual and in that context'); (*b*) 'Organisation de la Fraternité Internationale révolutionnaire' (1865), in Daniel Guérin (ed.), *Ni Dieu ni maître* (Lausanne, [1969]), 197 ('il n'est point de liberté sans égalité'); 'The International Revolutionary Society or Brotherhood' (1865), 'The Program of the Brotherhood', in Daniel Guérin (ed.), *No Gods No Masters*, trans. Paul Sharkey (Edinburgh etc., 1998), 134 ('there is no liberty in the absence of equality').

2   From Bakunin's 'Die Reaction in Deutschland: Ein Fragment von einem Franzosen', *Deutsche Jahrbücher für Wissenschaft und Kunst*, Nos 247–51 (17–21 October 1842), 985–1002 (published under the pseudonym 'Jules Elysard'), at 986; Michael Bakunin, 'The Reaction in Germany: A Fragment from a Frenchman', in *Russian Philosophy*, ed. James M. Edie and others (Chicago, 1965), i 385–406, at 388; quoted by Arnold Ruge in his memoirs of Bakunin: 'Erinnerungen an Michael Bakunin', *Neue Freie Presse* (Vienna), 28 September 1876, 1–3, 29 September 1876, 1–3 (see the first part, 1).

Once launched upon the waves of this type of mid-nineteenth-century radical patter, one knows only too well what to expect. To paraphrase another passage, I am not free if you, too, are not free; my liberty must be 'reflected' in the freedom of others – the individualist is wrong who thinks that the frontier of my liberty is your liberty – liberties are complementary – are indispensable to each other – not competitive.[1] The 'juridical and political'[2] concept of liberty is part and parcel of that criminal use of words which equates society and the detested State. It deprives men of liberty for it sets the individual against society; upon this the thoroughly vicious theory of the social contract – by which men have to give up some portion of their original, 'natural' liberty in order to associate in harmony – is founded. But this is a fallacy, for it is only in society that men become both human and free – 'only collective and social labour liberates [man] from the yoke of [. . .] nature', and without such liberation 'no moral or intellectual liberty' is possible.[3] Liberty cannot occur in solitude, but is a form of reciprocity. I am free and human only so far as others are such. My freedom is limitless because that of others is also such; our liberties mirror one another – so long as there is one slave, I am not free, not human, have no dignity and no rights. Liberty is not a physical or a social condition but a mental one: it consists of universal reciprocal recognition of the individual's liberties; slavery is a state of mind and the slave-owner is as much a slave as his chattels.[4] The glib Hegelian claptrap of this kind with which the works of Bakunin abound has not even the alleged merits of Hegelianism, for it contrives to reproduce many of the worst confusions of eighteenth-century thought, including that whereby the comparatively clear, if negative, concept of personal liberty as a condition in which a man is not coerced by others into doing what he does not wish to do, is confounded with the Utopian and

1   'Trois conférences faites aux ouvriers du Val de Saint-Imier' (May 1871), in *Archives Bakounine*, ed. Arthur Lehning (Leiden, 1961–81), vi 228; 'Three Lectures to Swiss Members of the International', in Cutler, op. cit. (121 above, note 1), 48.
2   'L'Empire knouto-germanique et la Révolution sociale' (1870–1), in *Archives Bakounine* (see previous note), vii 171.
3   ibid.   4   ibid. 172.

perhaps unintelligible notion of being free from laws in a different sense of 'law' – from the necessities of nature or even of social coexistence. And from this it is inferred that since to ask for freedom from Nature is absurd, since I am what I am as part of her, therefore, because my relationships with other human beings are part of 'Nature', it is equally senseless to ask for freedom from them – what one should seek is a 'freedom' which consists in a 'harmonious solidarity' with them.

Bakunin rebelled against Hegel and professed to hate Christianity; but his language is a conventional amalgam of both. The assumption that all virtues are compatible, nay, mutually entailed by one another, that the liberty of one man can never clash with that of another if both are rational (for then they cannot desire conflicting ends), that unlimited liberty is not only compatible with unlimited equality but inconceivable without it; reluctance to attempt a serious analysis of the notion either of liberty or of equality; the belief that it is only avoidable human folly and wickedness which are responsible for preventing the natural goodness and wisdom of man from making a paradise upon earth almost instantaneously, or at least as soon as the tyrannical State, with its vicious and idiotic legal system, is destroyed root and branch – all these naive fallacies, intelligible enough in the eighteenth century, but endlessly criticised in Bakunin's own sophisticated century, form the substance of his sermons *urbi et orbi*; and in particular of his fiery allocutions to the fascinated watchmakers of La Chaux-de-Fonds and the Valley of Saint-Imier.

Bakunin's thought is almost always simple, shallow and clear; the language is passionate, direct and imprecise, riding from climax to climax of rhetorical evidence, sometimes expository, more often hortatory or polemical, usually ironical, sometimes sparkling, always gay, always entertaining, always readable, seldom related to facts of experience, never original or serious or specific. 'Liberty' – the word – occurs ceaselessly. Sometimes Bakunin speaks of it in exalted semi-religious terms, and declares that the instinct to mutiny – defiance – is one of the three basic 'moments' in the development of humanity, denounces God and pays homage to Satan, the first rebel, the true friend of freedom. In such 'Acherontic' moods, in words which resemble the opening

of a revolutionary marching song, he declares that the only true
revolutionary element in Russia (or anywhere else) is the doughty
(*likhoi*) world of brigands and desperadoes, who, having nothing
to lose, will destroy the old world – after which the new will arise
spontaneously like the phoenix from the ashes.[1] He puts his hopes
in the sons of the ruined gentry, in all those who drown their
sorrows and indignation in violent outbreaks against their cramping milieu. Like Weitling, he calls upon the dregs of the under-
world, and, in particular, the disgruntled peasants, the Pugachevs
and Razins, to rise like modern Samsons and bring down the
temple of iniquity. At other times, more innocently, he calls merely
for a revolt against all fathers and all schoolmasters: children must
be free to choose their own careers; we want 'neither demigods
nor slaves',[2] but an equal society, above all not differentiated by
university education, which creates intellectual superiority and
leads to more painful inequalities than even aristocracy or pluto-
cracy. Sometimes he speaks of the necessity for an 'iron dictatorship'[3] during the transitional period between the vicious society
of today with its 'knouto-German'[4] army and police, and the
stateless society of tomorrow confined by no restraints. Other
times he says that all dictatorships tend inevitably to perpetuate
themselves, and that the dictatorship of the proletariat is yet one
more detestable despotism of one class over another. He cries that
all 'imposed' laws, being man-made, must be thrown off at once;
but allows that 'social' laws which are 'natural' and not 'arbitrary'
will have to be obeyed[5] – as if these latter are fixed and immutable
and beyond human control. Few of the optimistic confusions of
the eighteenth-century rationalists fail to make an appearance
somewhere in his works. After proclaiming the right – the duty –

1 See his pamphlet of 1869, 'Postanovka revolyutsionnogo voprosa', in M. P.
   Dragomanov (ed.), *Pis'ma M. A. Bakunina k A. I. Gertsenu i N. P. Ogarevu*
   (Geneva, 1896), 469–77, at 472–4.
2 op. cit. (121 above, note 1, (*a*)), O v 147; Cutler 116.
3 Letters to Herzen of 7 November and 8 December 1860, M. A. Bakunin,
   Sobranie sochinenii i pisem, ed. Yu. M. Steklov (Moscow, 1934–5), vol. 4,
   V tyur'makh i ssylke 1849–1861, 305, 360.
4 op. cit. (122 above, note 1), 221; Cutler 41. See also the work cited at 122
   above, note 2.
5 op. cit. (121 above, note 1, (*a*)), 158–9; Cutler 121.

to mutiny, and the urgent necessity for the violent overthrow of
the State, he happily proclaims his belief in absolute historical and
sociological determinism, and approvingly quotes the words of
the Belgian statistician Quételet: 'Society prepares crimes, criminals are only the instruments necessary for executing them.'[1]
Belief in free will is irrational, for like Engels he believes that
'freedom is [. . .] the inescapable end result of natural and social
necessity'.[2] Our human, as well as natural, environment shapes us
entirely: yet we must fight for man's independence not of 'the laws
of nature and society' but of all the laws, 'political, criminal
and civil', imposed on him by other men 'against his personal
convictions'.[3] That is Bakunin's final, most sophisticated definition
of liberty, and the meaning of this phrase is for anybody to seek.
All that clearly emerges is that Bakunin is opposed to the imposition of any restraints upon anyone at any time under any conditions. Moreover he believes, like Holbach or Godwin, that once
the artificial restraints imposed upon mankind by blind tradition,
or folly, or 'interested vice',[4] are lifted, all will automatically be
set right, and justice, virtue, happiness, pleasure and freedom will
immediately commence their united sway on earth. The search for
something more solid in Bakunin's utterances is unrewarding.[5] He
used words principally not for descriptive but for inflammatory
purposes, and was a great master of his medium; even today his
words have not lost their power to stir.

Like Herzen he disliked the new ruling class, the Figaros in
power, Figaro-bankers and Figaro-ministers whose livery could

1   op. cit. (121 above, note 1, (a)), O v 161; Cutler 122.
2   'Programma obshchestva mezhdunarodnoi revolyutsii' (c.1865), in V. A.
     Polonsky (ed.), Materialy dlya biografii M. Bakunina (Moscow, 1923–8), iii
     121.
3   ibid. 122–3; cf. 124 above, note 5.
4   [Normally referred to by IB as 'interested error', a phrase from Samuel
     Wilkinson's translation (London, 1820–1) of Holbach's 'recourons à nos
     sens, que l'on nous a faussement fait regarder comme suspects', Système de
     la nature (1770), part 1, chapter 1, as 'let us recover our senses, which
     interested error has taught us to suspect'); cf. 'erreurs utiles' ('useful errors'),
     ibid., part 2, chapter 12, and 'hommes fortement intéressés à l'erreur' ('people
     with a strong interest in error'), Le Bon Sens, § 82.]
5   Herzen, in a letter to Turgenev of 22 November 1862, justly called it 'fatras
     bakuninskoi demagogii' ('Bakunin's demagogic hotchpotch'), H xxvii/1 264.

not be shed because it had become part of their skins.[1] He liked free men and unbroken personalities. He detested spiritual slavery more than any other quality. And like Herzen he looked on the Germans as irredeemably servile, and said so with insulting repetitiveness:

When an Englishman or an American says 'I am an Englishman', 'I am an American', they are saying 'I am a free man'; when a German says 'I am a German' he is saying 'I am a slave, but my Emperor is stronger than all the other Emperors, and the German soldier who is strangling me will strangle you all' [. . .] Every people has tastes of its own – the Germans are obsessed by the big stick of the State.[2]

Bakunin recognised oppression when he saw it; he genuinely rebelled against every form of established authority and order, and he knew an authoritarian when he met one, whether he was Tsar Nicholas and Bismarck, or Lassalle and Marx (the latter triply authoritarian, in his view, as a German, a Hegelian and a Jew).[3] But he is not a serious thinker; he is neither a moralist nor a psychologist; what is to be looked for in him is not social theory or political doctrine, but an outlook and a temperament. There are no coherent ideas to be extracted from his writings of any period, only fire and imagination, violence and poetry, and an ungovernable desire for strong sensations, for life at a high tension, for the disintegration of all that is peaceful, secluded, tidy, orderly, small-scale, philistine, established, moderate, part of the monotonous prose of daily life. His attitude and his teaching were profoundly frivolous, and, on the whole, he knew this well, and laughed good-naturedly whenever he was exposed.[4] He wanted to

1   'Pis'ma iz Frantsii i Italii', second letter (1847), H v 35, 33; L 30, 28.
2   'Gosudarstvennost' i anarkhiya' (1873), Archives Bakounine (122 above, note 1), iii 159/358; Michael Bakunin, Statism and Anarchy, trans. and ed. Marshall S. Shatz (Cambridge, 1990), 192.
3   ibid. 119/317; Shatz 142.
4   'By nature I am not a charlatan,' he said in his letter to the Tsar of July–August 1851, '[. . .] but the unnatural and unhappy predicament for which, in point of fact, I was myself responsible sometimes made me a charlatan against my will.' 'Ispoved'', in Steklov, op. cit. (124 above, note 3), iv 143; The

set on fire as much as possible as swiftly as possible; the thought of any kind of chaos, violence, upheaval he found boundlessly exhilarating. When in his famous *Confession* (written in prison to the Tsar) he said that what he hated most was a quiet life, that what he longed for most ardently was always something – anything – fantastic, unheard-of adventures, perpetual movement, action, battle, that he suffocated in peaceful conditions, he summed up the content as well as the quality of his writings.

VI

Despite their prima facie similarities – their common hatred of the Russian regime, their belief in the Russian peasant, their theoretical federalism and Proudhonian socialism, their hatred of bourgeois society and contempt for middle-class virtues, their anti-liberalism and their militant atheism, their personal devotion, and the similarity of their social origin, tastes and education – the differences of the two friends are deep and wide. Herzen (although this has been seldom recognised even by his greatest admirers) is an original thinker, independent, honest and unexpectedly profound. At a time when general nostrums, vast systems and simple solutions were in the air, preached by the disciples of Hegel, of Feuerbach, of Fourier, of Christian and neo-Christian social mystics, when utilitarians and neo-medievalists, romantic pessimists and nihilists, peddlers of 'scientific' ethics and 'evolutionary' politics, and every brand of communist and anarchist, offered short-term remedies and long-term Utopias – social, economic, theosophical, metaphysical – Herzen retained his incorruptible sense of reality. He realised that general and abstract terms like 'liberty' or 'equality', unless they were translated into specific terms applicable to actual situations, were likely, at best, merely to stir the poetical imagination and inspire men with generous sentiments, at worst to justify stupidities or crimes. He saw – and in his day it was a discovery of genius – that there was something

Confession of Mikhail Bakunin, trans. Robert C. Lowes, ed. Lawrence D. Orton (Ithaca, NY, 1977), 79.

absurd in the very asking of such general questions as 'What is the meaning of life?' or 'What accounts for the fact that things in general happen as they do?' or 'What is *the* goal or *the* pattern or *the* direction of history?' He realised that such questions made sense only if they were made specific, and that the answers depended on the specific ends of specific human beings in specific situations. To ask always for 'ultimate' purposes was not to know what a purpose is; to ask for the ultimate goal of the singer in singing was to be interested in something other than songs or music. For men acted as they did each for the sake of his own personal ends (however much, and however rightly, he might believe them to be connected or identical with those of others), which were sacred to him, ends for the sake of which he was prepared to live and to die. It is for this reason that Herzen so seriously and passionately believed in the independence and freedom of individuals; and understood what he believed in, and reacted so painfully against the adulteration or obfuscation of the issues by metaphysical or theological patter and democratic rhetoric. In his view all that is ultimately valuable are the particular purposes of particular persons; and to trample on these is always a crime because there is, and can be, no principle or value higher than the ends of the individual, and therefore no principle in the name of which one could be permitted to do violence to or degrade or destroy individuals – the sole authors of all principles and all values. Unless a minimum area is guaranteed to all men within which they can act as they wish, the only principles and values left will be those guaranteed by theological or metaphysical or scientific systems claiming to know the final truth about man's place in the universe, and his functions and goals therein. And these claims Herzen regarded as fraudulent, one and all. It is this particular species of non-metaphysical, empirical, 'eudaemonistic' individualism that makes Herzen the sworn enemy of all systems, and of all claims to suppress liberties in their name, whether in the name of utilitarian considerations or authoritarian principles, of mystically revealed ends, or of reverence before irresistible power, or 'the logic of the facts', or any other similar reason.

What can Bakunin offer that is remotely comparable? Bakunin, with his gusto and his logic and his eloquence, his desire and

capacity to undermine and burn and shiver to pieces, now dis-
armingly childlike, at other times pathological and inhuman; with
his odd combination of analytical acuteness and unbridled ex-
hibitionism; carrying with him, with superb unconcern, the multi-
coloured heritage of the eighteenth century, without troubling to
consider whether some among his ideas contradicted others – the
'dialectic' would look after that – or how many of them had
become obsolete, discredited, or had been absurd from the beginning – Bakunin, the official friend of absolute liberty, has not
bequeathed a single idea worth considering for its own sake;
there is not a fresh thought, not even an authentic emotion, only
amusing diatribes, high spirits, malicious vignettes, and a memorable epigram or two. A historical figure remains – the 'Russian
Bear', as he liked to describe himself – morally careless, intellectually irresponsible, a man who, in his love for humanity in the
abstract, was prepared, like Robespierre, to wade through seas of
blood; and thereby constitutes a link in the tradition of cynical
terrorism and unconcern for individual human beings, the practice
of which is the main contribution of our own century, thus far,
to political thought. And this aspect of Bakunin, the Stavrogin
concealed inside Rudin, the fascist streak, the methods of Attila,
'Petrograndism', sinister qualities so remote from the lovable
'Russian Bear' – *die grosse Lise*[1] – was detected not merely by
Dostoevsky, who exaggerated and caricatured it, but by Herzen
himself, who drew up a formidable indictment against it in the
Letters to an Old Comrade, perhaps the most instructive, prophetic, sober and moving essays on the prospects of human
freedom written in the nineteenth century.

---

[1]   'The big Lise', as Herzen used to call him after his three-year-old daughter,
Bakunin's friend.

A REMARKABLE DECADE

(1955 -56)

I

The Birth of the Russian Intelligentsia

I

My title – 'A Remarkable Decade' – and my subject are both taken from a long essay in which the nineteenth-century Russian critic and literary historian Pavel Annenkov described his friends more than thirty years after the period with which he deals. Annenkov was an agreeable, intelligent and exceedingly civilised man, and a most understanding and dependable friend. He was not, perhaps, a very profound critic, nor was the range of his learning wide – he was a scholarly dilettante, a traveller about Europe who liked to meet eminent men, an eager and observant intellectual tourist.

It is clear that in addition to his other qualities he possessed considerable personal charm, so much, indeed, that he even succeeded in captivating Karl Marx, who wrote him at least one letter considered important by Marxists, on the subject of Proudhon. Indeed, Annenkov has left us an exceedingly vivid description of the physical appearance and ferocious intellectual manner of the young Marx – an admirably detached and ironical vignette, perhaps the best portrait of him that has survived.

It is true that, after he went back to Russia, Annenkov lost interest in Marx, who was so deeply snubbed and hurt by this desertion by a man on whom he thought he had made an indelible impression that in after years he expressed himself with extreme bitterness about the Russian intellectual *flâneurs* who fluttered around him in Paris in the 1840s, but turned out not to have any serious intentions after all. But although not very loyal to the figure of Marx, Annenkov did retain the friendship of his compatriots

Belinsky, Turgenev and Herzen to the end of his days. And it is about them that he is most interesting.

'A Remarkable Decade' is a description by him of the life of some among the early members – the original founders – of the Russian intelligentsia, between 1838 and 1848, when they were all young men, some still at the university, some just emerged from it. The subject is of more than literary or psychological interest because these early Russian intellectuals created something which was destined ultimately to have worldwide social and political consequences. The largest single effect of the movement, I think it would be fair to say, was the Russian Revolution itself. These *révoltés* early Russian intellectuals set the moral tone for the kind of talk and action which continued throughout the nineteenth and early twentieth centuries, until the final climax in 1917.

It is true that the Russian Revolution (and no event had been more discussed and speculated about during the century which preceded it – not even the great French Revolution) did not follow the lines that most of these writers and talkers had anticipated. Yet despite the tendency to minimise the importance of such activity by such thinkers as, for example, Tolstoy or Karl Marx, general ideas do have great influence. The Nazis seemed to grasp this fact when they took care at once to eliminate intellectual leaders in conquered countries, as likely to be among the most dangerous figures in their path; to this degree they had analysed history correctly. But whatever may be thought about the part played by thought in affecting human lives, it would be idle to deny that the influence of ideas – and in particular of philosophical ideas – at the beginning of the nineteenth century did make a considerable difference to what happened later. Without the kind of outlook of which, for example, the Hegelian philosophy, then so prevalent, was both the cause and the symptom, a great deal of what happened might, perhaps, either not have happened, or else have happened differently. Consequently the chief importance of these writers and thinkers, historically speaking, lies in the fact that they set in train ideas destined to have cataclysmic effects not merely in Russia itself, but far beyond her borders.

And these men have more specific claims to fame. It is difficult to imagine that the Russian literature of the mid-century, and, in

particular, the great Russian novels, could have come into being
save for the specific atmosphere which these men created and
promoted. The works of Turgenev, Tolstoy, Goncharov, Dostoevsky, and of minor novelists too, are penetrated with a sense
of their own time, of this or that particular social and historical
milieu and its ideological content, to an even higher degree than
the 'social' novels of the West. To this topic I propose to revert
later.

Lastly, they invented social criticism. This may seem a very bold
and even absurd claim to make; but by social criticism I do not
mean the appeal to standards of judgement which involve a view
of literature and art as having, or as obliged to have, a primarily
didactic purpose; nor yet the kind of criticism developed by romantic essayists, especially in Germany, in which heroes or villains are
regarded as quintessential types of humanity and examined as
such; nor yet the critical process (in which the French in particular
showed superlative skill) which attempts to reconstruct the process
of artistic creation mainly by analysing the social, spiritual and
psychological environment and the origins and economic position
of the artist, rather than his purely artistic methods or character
or specific quality; although, to some degree, the Russian intellectuals did all this too.

Social criticism in this sense had, of course, been practised
before them, and far more professionally, scrupulously and profoundly, by critics in the West. The kind of social criticism that I
mean is the method virtually invented by the great Russian essayist
Belinsky – the kind of criticism in which the line between life and
art is of set purpose not too clearly drawn; in which praise and
blame, love and hatred, admiration and contempt are freely
expressed both for artistic forms and for the human characters
drawn, both for the personal qualities of authors and for the
content of their novels, and the criteria involved in such attitudes,
whether consciously or implicitly, are identical with those in terms
of which living human beings are in everyday life judged or
described.

This is, of course, a type of criticism which has itself been much
criticised. It is accused of confusing art with life, and thereby
derogating from the purity of art. Whether these Russian critics did

perpetrate this confusion or not, they introduced a new attitude towards the novel, derived from their particular outlook on life. This outlook later came to be defined as that peculiar to members of the intelligentsia – and the young radicals of 1838–48, Belinsky, Turgenev, Bakunin, Herzen, whom Annenkov so devotedly describes in his book, are its true original founders. 'Intelligentsia' is a Russian word invented in the nineteenth century that has since acquired worldwide significance. The phenomenon itself, with its historical and literally revolutionary consequences, is, I suppose, the largest single Russian contribution to social change in the world.

The concept of intelligentsia must not be confused with the notion of intellectuals. Its members thought of themselves as united by something more than mere interest in ideas; they conceived themselves as being a dedicated order, almost a secular priesthood, devoted to the spreading of a specific attitude to life, something like a gospel. Historically their emergence requires some explanation.

II

Most Russian historians are agreed that the great social schism between the educated and the 'dark folk' in Russian history sprang from the wound inflicted on Russian society by Peter the Great. In his reforming zeal Peter sent selected young men into the Western world, and when they had acquired the languages of the West and the various new arts and skills which sprang from the scientific revolution of the seventeenth century, brought them back to become the leaders of that new social order which, with ruthless and violent haste, he imposed upon his feudal land. In this way he created a small class of new men, half Russian, half foreign – educated abroad, even if they were Russian by birth; these, in due course, became a small managerial and bureaucratic oligarchy, set above the people, no longer sharing in their still-medieval culture; cut off from them irrevocably. The government of this large and unruly nation became constantly more difficult, as social and economic conditions in Russia increasingly diverged from the progressing West. With the widening of the gulf, greater and greater repression had to be exercised by the ruling élite. The small group of governors thus grew more and more estranged from the people they were set to govern.

The rhythm of government in Russia in the eighteenth and early nineteenth centuries is one of alternate repression and liberalisation. Thus, when Catherine the Great felt that the yoke was growing too heavy, or the appearance of things became too barbarous, she relaxed the brutal rigidity of the despotism and was duly acclaimed by Voltaire and Grimm. When this seemed to lead to too much sudden stirring from within, too much protest, and too many educated persons began to compare conditions in Russia unfavourably with conditions in the West, she scented the beginnings of something subversive; the French Revolution finally terrified her; she clamped down again. Once more the regime grew stern and repressive.

The situation scarcely altered in the reign of Alexander I. The vast majority of the inhabitants of Russia still lived in a feudal darkness, with a weak and, on the whole, ignorant priesthood exercising relatively little moral authority, while a large army of fairly faithful and at times not inefficient bureaucrats pressed down on the more and more recalcitrant peasantry. Between the oppressors and the oppressed there existed a small cultivated class, largely French-speaking, aware of the enormous gap between the way in which life could be lived – or was lived – in the West and the way in which it was lived by the Russian masses. They were, for the most part, men acutely conscious of the difference between justice and injustice, civilisation and barbarism, but aware also that conditions were too difficult to alter, that they had too great a stake in the regime themselves, and that reform might bring the whole structure toppling down. Many among them were reduced either to an easy-going quasi-Voltairean cynicism, at once subscribing to liberal principles and whipping their serfs; or to noble, eloquent and futile despair.

This situation altered with the invasion of Napoleon, which brought Russia into the middle of Europe. Almost overnight, Russia found herself a great power in the heart of Europe, conscious of her crushing strength, dominating the entire scene, and accepted by Europeans, with some terror and great reluctance, as not merely equal but superior to them in sheer brute force.

The triumph over Napoleon and the march to Paris were events in the history of Russian ideas as vitally important as the reforms of Peter. They made Russia aware of her national unity, and generated in her a sense of herself as a great European nation, recognised as such; as being no longer a despised collection of barbarians teeming behind a Chinese wall, sunk in medieval darkness, half-heartedly and clumsily imitating foreign models. Moreover, since the long Napoleonic war had brought about great and lasting patriotic fervour, and, as a result of a general participation in a common ideal, an increase in the feeling of equality between the orders, a number of relatively idealistic young men began to feel new bonds between themselves and their nation which their education could not by itself have inspired. The growth of patriotic nationalism brought with it, as its inevitable concomitant, a growth of the feeling of responsibility for the chaos, the squalor, the poverty, the inefficiency, the brutality, the appalling disorder in Russia. This general moral uneasiness affected the least sentimental and perceptive, the hardest-hearted of the semi-civilised members of the ruling class.

III

There were other factors which contributed to this collective sense of guilt. One, certainly, was the coincidence (for coincidence it was) of the rise of the romantic movement with the entrance of Russia into Europe. One of the cardinal romantic doctrines (connected with the cognate doctrines that history proceeds according to discoverable laws or patterns, and that nations are unitary 'organisms', not mere collections, and 'evolve' in an 'organic', not a mechanical or haphazard fashion) is that everything in the world is as and where and when it is because it participates in a single universal purpose. Romanticism encourages the idea that not only individuals but groups, and not only groups but institutions – States, Churches, professional bodies, associations that have ostensibly been created for definite, often purely utilitarian purposes – come to be possessed by a 'spirit' of which they themselves might well be unaware – awareness of which is, indeed, the very process of enlightenment.

The doctrine that every human being, country, race, institution has its own unique, individual, inner purpose which is itself an 'organic' element in the wider purpose of all that exists, and that in becoming conscious of that purpose it is, by this very fact, participating in the march towards light and freedom – this secular version of an ancient religious belief powerfully impressed the minds of the young Russians. They imbibed it all the more readily as a result of two causes, one material, one spiritual.

The material cause was the unwillingness of the government to let its subjects travel to France, which was thought of, particularly after 1830, as a chronically revolutionary country, liable to perpetual upheavals, blood-letting, violence and chaos. By contrast, Germany lay peaceful under the heel of a very respectable despotism. Consequently, young Russians were encouraged to go to German universities, where they would obtain a sound training in civic principles that would, so it was supposed, make them still more faithful servants of the Russian autocracy.

The result was the exact opposite. Crypto-Francophile sentiment in Germany itself was at this time so violent, and enlightened Germans themselves believed in ideas – in this case those of the French Enlightenment – so much more intensely and fanatically than the French themselves, that the young Russian Anacharsises who dutifully went to Germany were infected by dangerous ideas far more violently there than they could ever have been had they gone to Paris in the easy-going early years of Louis-Philippe. The government of Nicholas I could hardly have foreseen the chasm into which it was destined to fall.

If this was the first cause of romantic ferment, the second was its direct consequence. The young Russians who had travelled to Germany, or read German books, became possessed with the simple idea that if, as ultramontane Catholics in France and nationalists in Germany were sedulously maintaining, the French Revolution and the decadence that followed were scourges sent upon the people for abandoning their ancient faith and ways, the Russians were surely free from these vices, since, whatever else might be true of them, no revolution had been visited upon them. The German romantic historians were particularly zealous in preaching the view that, if the West was declining because of its scepticism, its rationalism, its materialism, and its abandonment of its own spiritual tradition, then the Germans, who had not suffered this melancholy fate, should be viewed as a fresh and youthful nation, with habits uncontaminated by the corruption of a Rome in decay, barbarous indeed, but full of violent energy, about to come into the inheritance falling from the feeble hands of the French.

The Russians merely took this process of reasoning one step further. They rightly judged that if youth, barbarism and lack of education were criteria of a glorious future, they had an even more powerful hope of it than the Germans. Consequently the vast outpouring of German romantic rhetoric about the unexhausted forces of the Germans and the unexpended German language with its pristine purity and the young, unwearied German nation, directed as it was against the 'impure', Latinised, decadent Western nations, was received in Russia with understandable enthusiasm. Moreover, it stimulated a wave of social idealism which began to possess all classes, from the early 1820s until well into the early 1840s. The proper task of a man was to dedicate himself to the ideal for which his 'essence' was intended. This could not consist in scientific rationalism (as the French eighteenth-century materialists had taught), for it was a delusion to think that life was governed by mechanical laws. It was an even worse delusion to suppose that it was possible to apply a scientific discipline, derived from the study of inanimate matter, to the rational government of human beings and the organisation of their lives on a worldwide scale. The duty of man was something very different – to understand the texture, the 'go', the principle of life of all there is, to penetrate to the soul of the world (a theological and mystical notion wrapped by the followers of Schelling and Hegel in rationalist terminology), to grasp the hidden, 'inner' plan of the universe, to understand his own place in it, and to act accordingly.

The task of the philosopher was to discern the march of history, or of what was, somewhat mysteriously, called 'the Idea', and discover whither it was carrying mankind. History was an enormous river, the direction of which could, however, be observed only by people with a capacity for a special kind of deep, inner contemplation. No amount of observation of the outer world would ever teach you where this inward *Drang*, this subterranean current, led. To uncover it was to be at one with it; the development both of your individual self as a rational being, and of society, depended upon a correct assessment of the spiritual direction of the larger 'organism' to which you belonged. To the question of how this organism was to be identified – what it was – the various metaphysicians who founded the principal romantic schools of philosophy replied differently. Herder declared this unit to be a spiritual culture or way of life; the Roman Catholic *penseurs* identified it with the life of the Christian Church; Fichte somewhat obscurely, and after him Hegel unequivocally, declared it to be the national State.

The whole notion of organic method militated in favour of supposing that the favourite instrument of the eighteenth century – chemical analysis into constituent bits, into ultimate, irreducible atoms, whether of inanimate matter or of social institutions – was an inadequate way of apprehending anything. 'Growth' was the great new term – new, that is, in its application far beyond the bounds of scientific biology; and in order to apprehend what growth was, you had to have a special inner sense capable of apprehending the invisible kingdom, an intuitive grasp of the impalpable principle in virtue of which a thing grows as it does; grows not simply by successive increments of 'dead' parts, but by some kind of occult vital process that needs a quasi-mystical power of vision, a special sense of the flow of life, of the forces of history, of the principles at work in nature, in art, in personal relationships, of the creative spirit unknown to empirical science, to seize upon its essence.

IV

This is the heart of political romanticism, from Burke to our own day, and the source of many passionate arguments directed against liberal reform and every attempt to remedy social evils by rational means, on the grounds that these were based on a 'mechanical' outlook – a misunderstanding of what society was and of how it developed. The programmes of the French Encyclopedists or of the adherents of Lessing in Germany were condemned as so many ludicrous and Procrustean attempts to treat society as if it were an amalgam of bits of inanimate stuff, a mere machine, whereas it was a palpitating, living whole.

The Russians were highly susceptible to this propaganda, which drew them in both a reactionary and a progressive direction. You could believe that life or history was a river, which it was useless and perilous to resist or deflect, and with which you could only merge your identity – according to Hegel by discursive, logical, rational activity of the Spirit; according to Schelling intuitively and imaginatively, by a species of inspiration the depth of which is the measure of human genius, from which spring myths and religions, art and science. This led in the conservative direction of eschewing everything analytical, rational, empirical, everything founded upon experiment and natural science. On the other hand, you might declare that you felt within the earth the pangs of a new world struggling to be born. You felt – you knew – that the crust of the old institutions was about to crack under the violent inner heavings of the Spirit. If you genuinely believed this, then you would, if you were a reasonable being, be ready to risk identifying yourself with the revolutionary cause, for otherwise it would destroy you. Everything in the cosmos was progressive, everything moved. And if the future lay in the fragmentation and the explosion of your present universe into a new form of existence, it would be foolish not to collaborate with this violent and inevitable process.

German romanticism, in particular the Hegelian school, was divided on this issue; there were movements in both directions in Germany, and consequently also in Russia, which was virtually an intellectual dependency of German academic thought. But whereas in the West ideas of this kind had for many years been prevalent – theories and opinions, philosophical, social, theological, political, had, since the Renaissance at least, clashed and collided with each other in a vast variety of patterns, and formed a general process of rich intellectual activity in which no one idea or opinion could for long hold undisputed supremacy – in Russia this was not the case.

One of the great differences between the areas dominated by the Eastern and the Western Churches was that the former had had no Renaissance and no Reformation. The Balkan people could blame the Turkish conquest for their backwardness. But the case was little better in Russia, which did not have a gradually expanding, literate, educated class, connecting – by a series of social and intellectual steps – the most and the least enlightened. The gap between the illiterate peasants and those who could read and write was wider in Russia than in other European States, in so far as Russia could be called European at this time.

Thus the number and variety of social or political ideas to be heard if you moved in the salons of St Petersburg and Moscow were nothing like so great as you would find in the intellectual ferment of Paris or Berlin. Paris was, of course, the great cultural Mecca of the time. But even Berlin was scarcely less agitated with intellectual, theological, artistic controversies, despite the repressive Prussian censorship.

You must therefore imagine in Russia a situation dominated by three main factors: a dead, oppressive, unimaginative government chiefly engaged in holding its subjects down, preventing change largely because this might lead to yet further change, even though its more intelligent members obscurely realised that reform – and that of a very radical kind – for instance with regard to the serf system or the systems of justice and education – was both desirable and inevitable. The second factor was the condition of the vast mass of the Russian population – an ill-treated, economically wretched peasantry, sullen and inarticulately groaning, but plainly too weak and unorganised to act effectively in its own defence. Finally, between the two, a small, educated class, deeply and sometimes resentfully influenced by Western ideas, with minds tantalised by visits to Europe and by the great new social and intellectual movement at work in the centres of its culture.

May I remind you again that there was in the air, as much in Russia as in Germany, a romantic conviction that every man had a unique mission to fulfil if only he could know what it was; and that this created a general enthusiasm for social and metaphysical ideas, perhaps as a kind of ethical substitute for a dying religion, that was not dissimilar to the fervour with which philosophical systems and political Utopias had, for more than a century, been acclaimed in France and Germany, by men in search of a new theodicy uncompromised by association with some discredited political or religious Establishment. But in Russia there was, in addition, among the educated classes, a moral and intellectual vacuum due to the absence of a Renaissance tradition of secular education, and maintained by the rigid censorship exercised by the government, by widespread illiteracy, by the suspicion and disfavour with which all ideas as such were regarded, by the acts of a nervous and often massively stupid bureaucracy. In this situation, ideas which in the West competed with a large number of other doctrines and attitudes, so that to become dominant they had to emerge victorious from a fierce struggle for survival, in Russia came to lodge in the minds of gifted individuals and, indeed, obsess them, often enough simply for lack of other ideas to satisfy their intellectual needs. Moreover, there existed in the capital cities of the Russian Empire a violent thirst for knowledge, indeed for mental nourishment of any kind, together with an unparalleled sincerity (and sometimes a disarming naivety) of feeling, intellectual freshness, passionate resolve to participate in world affairs, a troubled consciousness of the social and political problems of a vast country, and very little to respond to this new state of mind. What there was, was mostly imported from abroad – scarcely one single political and social idea to be found in Russia in the nineteenth century was born on native soil. Perhaps Tolstoy's idea of non-resistance was something genuinely Russian – a restatement of a Christian position so original that it had the force of a new idea when he preached it. But, in general, I do not think that Russia has contributed a single new social or political idea: nothing that was not traceable, not merely to some ultimate Western root, but to some doctrine discoverable in the West eight or ten or twelve years earlier than its first appearance in Russia.

V

You must conceive, therefore, of an astonishingly impressionable society with an unheard-of capacity for absorbing ideas – ideas which might waft across, in the most casual fashion, because someone brought back a book or collection of pamphlets from Paris (or because some audacious bookseller had smuggled them in); because someone attended the lectures of a neo-Hegelian in Berlin, or had made friends with Schelling, or had met an English missionary with strange ideas. Genuine excitement was generated by the arrival of a new 'message' emanating from some disciple of Saint-Simon or Fourier, of a book by Proudhon, by Cabet, by Leroux, the latest social Messiahs in France; or again, by an idea attributed to David Strauss or Ludwig Feuerbach or Lamennais or some other forbidden author. Because of their relative scarcity in Russia, these ideas and fragments of ideas would be seized upon with the utmost avidity. The social and economic prophets in Europe seemed full of confidence in the new revolutionary future, and their ideas had an intoxicating effect upon the young Russians.

When such doctrines were promulgated in the West, they sometimes excited their audience, and occasionally led to the formation of parties or sects, but they were not regarded by the majority of those whom they reached as the final truth; and even those who thought them crucially important did not immediately begin to put them into practice with every means at their disposal. The Russians were liable to do just this; to argue to themselves that if the premises were true and the reasoning correct, true conclusions followed: and further, that if these conclusions dictated certain actions as being necessary and beneficial, then if one was honest and serious one had a plain duty to try to realise them as swiftly and as fully as possible. Instead of the generally held view of the Russians as a gloomy, mystical, self-lacerating, somewhat religious nation, I should like to suggest, at least as far as the articulate intelligentsia are concerned, that they were somewhat exaggerated Westerners of the nineteenth century; and that so far from being liable to irrationalism or neurotic self-absorption, what they possessed in a high, perhaps excessive, degree was extremely developed powers of reasoning, extreme logic and lucidity.

It is true that when people tried to put these Utopian schemes into operation and were almost immediately frustrated by the police, disillusionment followed, and with it a liability to fall into a state of apathetic melancholy or violent exasperation. But this came later. The original phase was neither mystical nor introspective, but on the contrary rationalist, bold, extroverted and optimistic. I think it was the celebrated terrorist Kravchinsky who once said about the Russians that, whatever other qualities they might have, they never recoiled from the consequences of their own reasoning. If you study the Russian 'ideologies' of the nineteenth and indeed the twentieth century, I think you will find, on the whole, that the more difficult, the more paradoxical, the more unpalatable a conclusion is, the greater is the degree of passion and enthusiasm with which some Russians, at any rate, tend to embrace it; for to do so seems to them no more than a proof of a man's moral sincerity, of the genuineness of his devotion to the truth and of his seriousness as a human being; and although the consequences of one's reasoning may appear prima facie unplausible or even downright absurd, one must not for that reason recoil from them, for what would that be but cowardice, weakness or – worst of all – the setting up of comfort before the truth? Herzen once said: 'We are great doctrinaires and *raisonneurs*. To this German capacity we add our own national [. . .] element, ruthless, fanatically dry: we are only too willing to cut off heads [. . .] With fearless step we march *to the very limit*, and go beyond it; never out of step with the dialectic, only with the *truth* [. . .]'.[1] And this characteristically acid comment is, as a verdict on some of his contemporaries, not altogether unjust.

---

1   'Byloe i dumy', part 5, 'Russkie teni', 'I: N. I. Sazonov' (1863), H x 320; 'C. Russian Shadows', '1. N. I. Sazonov', M ii 956.

VI

Imagine, then, a group of young men, living under the petrified regime of Nicholas I – men with a degree of passion for ideas perhaps never equalled in a European society, seizing upon ideas as they come from the West with unconscionable enthusiasm, and making plans to translate them swiftly into practice – and you will have some notion of what the early members of the intelligentsia were like. They were a small group of *littérateurs*, both professional and amateur, conscious of being alone in a bleak world, with a hostile and arbitrary government on the one hand, and a completely uncomprehending mass of oppressed and inarticulate peasants on the other, conceiving of themselves as a kind of self-conscious army, carrying a banner for all to see – of reason and science, of liberty, of a better life.

Like persons in a dark wood, they tended to feel a certain solidarity simply because they were so few and far between; because they were weak, because they were truthful, because they were sincere, because they were unlike the others. Moreover, they had accepted the romantic doctrine that every man is called upon to perform a mission beyond mere selfish purposes of material existence; that because they had had an education superior to that of their oppressed brothers they had a direct duty to help them toward the light; that this duty was uniquely binding upon them, and that, if they fulfilled it, as history surely intended them to do, the future of Russia might yet be as glorious as her past had been empty and dark; and that for this they must preserve their inner solidarity as a dedicated group. They were a persecuted minority who drew strength from their very persecution; they were the self-conscious bearers of a Western message, freed from the chains of ignorance and prejudice, stupidity or cowardice, by some great Western liberator – a German romantic, a French socialist – who had transformed their vision.

The act of liberation is something not uncommon in the intellectual history of Europe. A liberator is one who does not so much answer your problems, whether of theory or conduct, as transform them – he ends your anxieties and frustrations by placing you within a new framework where old problems cease to have meaning, and new ones appear which have their solutions, as it were, already to some degree prefigured in the new universe in which you find yourself. I mean that those who were liberated by the humanists of the Renaissance or the *philosophes* of the eighteenth century did not merely think their old questions answered more correctly by Plato or Newton than by Albertus Magnus or the Jesuits – rather they had a sense of a new universe. Questions which had troubled their predecessors suddenly appeared to them senseless and unnecessary. The moment at which ancient chains fall off, and you feel yourself recreated in a new image, can make a life. One cannot tell by whom a man might not, in this sense, be set free – Voltaire probably emancipated a greater number of human beings in his own lifetime than anyone before or after him; Schiller, Kant, Mill, Ibsen, Nietzsche, Samuel Butler, Freud have liberated human beings. For all I know Anatole France, or even Aldous Huxley, may have had this effect.

The Russians of whom I speak were 'liberated' by the great German metaphysical writers, who freed them on the one hand from the dogmas of the Orthodox Church, on the other from the dry formulae of the eighteenth-century rationalists, which had been not so much refuted as discredited by the failure of the French Revolution. What Fichte, Hegel, Schelling and their numerous expositors and interpreters provided was little short of a new religion. A corollary of this new frame of mind is the Russian attitude to literature.

VII

There may be said to exist at least two attitudes towards literature and the arts in general, and it may not be uninteresting to contrast them. For short, I propose to call one French, the other Russian. But these will be mere labels used for brevity and convenience. I hope I shall not be thought to maintain that every French writer held what I propose to call the 'French' attitude, or every Russian the 'Russian'. The distinction taken in any literal sense would, of course, be gravely misleading.

The French writers of the nineteenth century on the whole believed that they were purveyors. They thought that an intellectual or an artist had a duty to himself and to the public – to produce as good an object as possible. If you were a painter, you produced as beautiful a picture as you could. If you were a writer you produced the best piece of writing of which you were capable. That was your duty to yourself, and it was what the public rightly expected. If your works were good, they were recognised, and you were successful. If you possessed little taste, or skill, or luck, then you were unsuccessful; and that was that.

In this 'French' view, the artist's private life was of no more concern to the public than the private life of a carpenter. If you order a table, you are not interested in whether the carpenter has a good motive for making it or not; or whether he lives on good terms with his wife and children. And to say of the carpenter that his table must in some way be degraded or decadent, because his morality is degraded or decadent, would be regarded as bigoted, and indeed as silly: certainly as a grotesque criticism of his merit as a carpenter.

This attitude of mind (which I have deliberately exaggerated) was rejected with the utmost vehemence by almost every major Russian writer of the nineteenth century; and this was so whether they were writers with an explicit moral or social bias, or aesthetic writers believing in art for art's sake. The 'Russian' attitude (at least in the last century) is that man is one and cannot be divided; that it is not true that a man is a citizen on the one hand and, quite independently of this, a money-maker on the other, and that these functions can be kept in separate compartments; that a man is one kind of personality as a voter, another as a painter, and a third as a husband. Man is indivisible. To say 'Speaking as an artist, I feel this; and speaking as a voter, I feel that' is always false; and immoral and dishonest too. Man is one, and what he does, he does with his whole personality. It is the duty of men to do what is good, speak the truth, and produce beautiful objects. They must speak the truth in whatever media they happen to work. If they are novelists they must speak the truth as novelists. If they are ballet dancers they must express the truth in their dancing.

This idea of integrity, of total commitment, is the heart of the romantic attitude. Certainly Mozart and Haydn would have been exceedingly surprised if they were told that as artists they were peculiarly sacred, lifted far above other men, priests uniquely dedicated to the worship of some transcendent reality, to betray which is mortal sin. They conceived of themselves as true craftsmen, sometimes as inspired servants of God or of Nature, seeking to celebrate their divine Maker in whatever they did; but in the first place they were composers who wrote works to order and strove to make them as melodious as possible. By the nineteenth century, the notion of the artist as a sacred vessel, set apart, with a unique soul and unique status, was exceedingly widespread. It was born, I suppose, mainly among the Germans, and is connected with the belief that it is the duty of every man to give himself to a cause; that upon the artist and poet this duty is binding in a special degree, for he is a wholly dedicated being; and that his fate is peculiarly sublime and tragic, for his form of self-surrender is to sacrifice himself totally to his ideal. What this ideal is, is comparatively unimportant. The essential thing is to offer oneself without calculation, to give all one has for the sake of the light within (whatever it may illuminate) from pure motives. For only motives count.

Every Russian writer was made conscious that he was on a public stage, testifying; so that the smallest lapse on his part, a lie, a deception, an act of self-indulgence, lack of zeal for the truth, was a heinous crime. If you were principally engaged in making money, then, perhaps, you were not quite so strictly accountable to society. But if you spoke in public at all, be it as poet or novelist or historian or in whatever public capacity, then you accepted full responsibility for guiding and leading the people. If this was your calling then you were bound by a Hippocratic oath to tell the truth and never to betray it, and to dedicate yourself selflessly to your goal.

There are certain clear cases – Tolstoy is one of them – where this principle was accepted literally and followed to its extreme consequences. But this tendency in Russia was far wider than Tolstoy's peculiar case would indicate. Turgenev, for example, who is commonly thought of as the most Western among Russian writers, a man who believed in the pure and independent nature of art more than, say, Dostoevsky or Tolstoy, who consciously and deliberately avoided moralising in his novels, and was, indeed, sternly called to order by other Russian authors for an excessive – and, it was indicated, regrettably Western – preoccupation with aesthetic principles, for devoting too much time and attention to the mere form and style of his works, for insufficient probing into the deep moral and spiritual essence of his characters – even the 'aesthetic' Turgenev is wholly committed to the belief that social and moral problems are the central issues of life and of art, and that they are intelligible only in their own specific historical and ideological context.

I was once astonished to see it stated, in a review by an eminent literary critic in a Sunday newspaper, that, of all authors, Turgenev was not particularly conscious of the historical forces of his time. This is the very opposite of the truth. Every novel of Turgenev deals explicitly with social and moral problems within a specific historical setting; it describes human beings in particular social conditions at an identifiable date. The mere fact that Turgenev was an artist to his marrow-bones, and understood the universal aspects of human character or predicament, need not blind us to the fact that he fully accepted his duty as a writer to speak the objective truth – social no less than psychological – in public, and not to betray it.

If someone had proved that Balzac was a spy in the service of the French government, or that Stendhal conducted immoral operations on the Stock Exchange, it might have upset some of their friends, but it would not, on the whole, have been regarded as derogating from their status and genius as artists. But there is scarcely any Russian writer in the nineteenth century who, if something of the sort had been discovered about himself, would have doubted for an instant whether the charge was relevant to his activity as a writer. I can think of no Russian writer who would have tried to slip out with the alibi that he was one kind of person as a writer, to be judged, let us say, solely in terms of his novels, and quite another as a private individual. That is the gulf between the characteristically 'Russian' and 'French' conceptions of life and art, as I have christened them. I do not mean that every

Western writer would accept the ideal which I have attributed to the French, nor that every Russian would subscribe to what I have called the 'Russian' conception. But, broadly speaking, I think it is a correct division, and holds good even when you come to the aesthetic writers – for instance, the Russian symbolist poets at the turn of the nineteenth century, who despised every form of utilitarian or didactic or 'impure' art, took not the slightest interest in social analysis or psychological novels, and accepted and exaggerated the aestheticism of the West to an *outré* degree. Even these Russian symbolists did not think that they had no moral obligation. They saw themselves, indeed, as Pythian priestesses upon some mystical tripod, as seers of a reality of which this world was merely a dark symbol and occult expression, and, remote though they were from social idealism, believed with moral and spiritual fervour in their own sacred vows. They were witnesses to a mystery; that was the ideal which they were morally not permitted, by the rules of their art, to betray. This attitude is utterly different from anything that Flaubert laid down about the fidelity of the artist to his art, which to him is identical with the proper function of the artist, or the best method of becoming as good an artist as one could be. The attitude which I attribute to the Russians is a specifically moral attitude; their attitude to life and to art is identical, and it is ultimately a moral attitude. This is something not to be confused with the notion of art with a utilitarian purpose, in which, of course, some of them believed. Certainly, the men of whom I propose to speak – the men of the 1830s and early 1840s – did not believe that the business of novels and the business of poetry was to teach men to be better. The ascendancy of utilitarianism came much later, and it was propagated by men of far duller and cruder minds than those with whom I am here concerned.

The most characteristic Russian writers believed that writers are, in the first place, men; and that they are directly and continually responsible for all their utterances, whether made in novels or in private letters, in public speeches or in conversation. This view, in turn, affected Western conceptions of art and life to a marked degree, and is one of the arresting contributions to thought of the Russian intelligentsia. Whether for good or ill, it made a very violent impact upon the European conscience.

VIII

At the time of which I speak, Hegel and Hegelianism dominated the thought of young Russia. With all the moral ardour of which they were capable, the emancipated young men believed in the necessity of total immersion in his philosophy. Hegel was the great new liberator; therefore it was a duty – a categorical duty – to express in every act of your life, whether as a private individual or as a writer, truths which you had absorbed from him. This allegiance – later transferred to Darwin, to Spencer, to Marx – is difficult to understand for those who have not read the fervid literature, above all, the literary correspondence of the period. To illustrate it, let me quote some ironical passages from Herzen, the great Russian publicist, who lived the latter part of his life abroad, written when, looking back, he described the atmosphere of his youth. It is, as so often with this incomparable satirist, a somewhat exaggerated picture – in places a caricature – but nevertheless it successfully conveys the mood of the time.

After saying that an exclusively contemplative attitude is wholly opposed to the Russian character, he goes on to talk about the fate of the Hegelian philosophy when it was brought over to Russia:

There is no paragraph in all the three parts of the *Logic*, two parts of the *Aesthetic*, of the *Encyclopedia* [. . .] which was not captured after the most desperate debates lasting several nights. People who adored each other became estranged for entire weeks because they could not agree on a definition of 'transcendental spirit', were personally offended by opinions about 'absolute personality' and 'being in itself'. The most worthless tracts of German philosophy that came out of Berlin and other [German] provincial towns and villages, in which there was any mention of Hegel, were written for and read to shreds – till they came out in yellow stains, till pages dropped out after a few days. Thus, just as Professor Francoeur was moved to tears in Paris when he heard that he was regarded as a great mathematician in Russia, that his algebraical symbolism was used for differential equations by our younger generation, so might they all have wept for joy – all these forgotten Werders, Marheineckes, Michelets, Ottos, Vatkes, Schallers, Rosenkranzes, and Arnold Ruge himself [. . .] – if they had known what duels, what battles they had started in Moscow between the Maroseika and Mokhovaya [two Moscow streets], how they were read, how they were *bought* [. . .]

I have a right to say this because, carried away by the torrents of those days, I myself wrote just like this, and was, in fact, startled when our famous astronomer, Perevoshchikov, referred to it all as 'bird talk'. Nobody at this time would have disowned a sentence like this: 'The concrescence of abstract ideas in the sphere of the plastic represents that phase of the self-questing spirit in which it, defining itself for itself, is potentialised from natural immanence into the harmonious sphere of formal consciousness in beauty.'[1]

He continues:

A man who went for a walk in Sokolniki [a Moscow suburb], went there not just for a walk, but in order to surrender himself to the pantheistic feeling of his identification with the cosmos. If, on the way, he met a tipsy soldier or a peasant woman who said something to him, the philosopher did not simply talk with them, but determined the substantiality of the popular element, both in its immediate and its accidental presentation. The very tear which might rise to his eye was strictly classified and referred to its proper category – *Gemüt*, or 'the tragic element in the heart' . . .[2]

Herzen's ironical sentences need not be taken too literally. But they show vividly the kind of *exalté* intellectual mood in which his friends had lived.

Let me now offer you a passage from Annenkov – from the excellent essay called 'A Remarkable Decade' to which I referred at the outset. It gives a different picture of these same people at the same period, and it is worth quoting if only to correct Herzen's amusing sketch, which may, quite unjustly, suggest that all this

1   'Byloe i dumy', part 4 ('Moskva, Peterburg i Novgorod (1840–1847)'), chapter 25 (1855), H ix 18–19; 'Moscow, Petersburg and Novgorod 1840–1847', 'Return to Moscow and Intellectual Debate', M ii 398–9.
2   ibid. 20 (400).

intellectual activity was so much worthless gibberish on the part
of a ridiculous collection of overexcited young intellectuals.
Annenkov describes life in a country house, in the village of
Sokolovo in 1845, that had been taken for the summer by three
friends – Granovsky, who was a professor of history in the University of Moscow, Ketcher, who was an eminent translator, and
Herzen himself, who was a rich young man of no very fixed
profession, then still vaguely in government service. They took the
house for the purpose of entertaining their friends and enjoying
intellectual conversation in the evenings.

> Only one thing was not allowed, and that was to be a philistine.
> Not that what was expected were flights of eloquence or flashes of
> brilliant wit – on the contrary, students absorbed in their own special
> fields were respected deeply. But what was demanded was a certain
> intellectual level and certain qualities of character [. . .] They pro-
> tected themselves against contacts with anything that seemed cor-
> rupt [. . .] and were worried by its intrusion, however casual and
> unimportant. They did not cut themselves off from the world, but
> stood aloof from it, and attracted attention for that very reason; and
> because of this they developed a special sensitiveness to everything
> artificial and spurious. Any sign of a morally doubtful sentiment,
> evasive talk, dishonest ambiguity, empty rhetoric, insincerity, was
> detected at once, and [. . .] provoked immediate storms of ironical
> mockery and merciless attack [. . .] The circle [. . .] resembled an
> order of knighthood, a brotherhood of warriors; it had no written
> constitution. Yet it knew all its members scattered over our vast
> country; it was not organised, but a tacit understanding prevailed.
> It stretched, as it were, across the stream of the life of its time, and
> protected it from aimlessly flooding its banks. Some adored it; others
> detested it.[1]

---

1   P. V. Annenkov, 'Zamechatel'noe desyatiletie' (1880), *Literaturnye vospomi-*
    naniya (Moscow, 1960), chapter 26, 269–70; P. V. Annenkov, *The Extra-*
    ordinary Decade: Literary Memoirs, ed. Arthur P. Mendel, trans. Irwin R.
    Titunik (Ann Arbor, 1968), 137–8.

IX

The sort of society which Annenkov described, although it may have about it a slight suggestion of priggishness, is the sort of society which tends to crystallise whenever there is an intellectual minority (say in Bloomsbury or anywhere else) which sees itself as divided by its ideals from the world in which it lives, and tries to promote certain intellectual and moral standards, at any rate within itself. That is what these Russians from 1838 to 1848 tried to do. They were unique in Russia in that they did not automatically come from any one social class, even though few among them were of humble origin. They had to be moderately well-born, otherwise their chance of obtaining an adequate, that is to say Western, education was too small.

Their attitude to each other was genuinely free from bourgeois self-consciousness. They were not impressed by wealth, nor were they self-conscious about poverty. They did not admire success. Indeed they almost tried to avoid it. Few among them became successful persons in the worldly sense of that word. A number went into exile, others were professors perpetually under the eye of tsarist police; some were poorly paid hacks and translators; some simply disappeared. One or two of them left the movement and were regarded as renegades. There was Mikhail Katkov, for example, a gifted journalist and writer who had been an original member of the movement and had then crossed over to the tsarist government, and there was Vasily Botkin, the intimate friend of Belinsky and Turgenev, who started as a philosophical tea-merchant and became a confirmed reactionary in later years. But these were exceptional cases.

Turgenev was always regarded as a case somewhat betwixt and between: a man whose heart was in the right place, who was not devoid of ideals and knew well what enlightenment was, and yet not quite reliable. Certainly he was vehement against the serf system, and his book *A Sportsman's Sketches* had admittedly had a more powerful social effect upon the public than any other book hitherto published in Russia – something like *Uncle Tom's Cabin* in the United States at a later date, from which it differed

principally in being a work of art, indeed of genius. Turgenev was
regarded by the young radicals, on the whole, as a supporter
of the right principles, on the whole a friend and an ally, but
unfortunately weak, flighty, liable to indulge his love of pleasure
at the expense of his convictions; apt to vanish unaccountably –
and a little guiltily – and be lost to his political friends; yet still
'one of us'; still a member of the party; still with us rather than
against us, in spite of the fact that he often did things which had
to be severely criticised, and which seemed mainly due to his
unfortunate infatuation with the French *diva* Pauline Viardot,
which led him to sell his stories – surreptitiously – to reactionary
newspapers in order to obtain enough money to be able to buy a
box at the opera, since the virtuous left-wing periodicals could
not afford to pay as much. A vacillating and unreliable friend;
still, and despite everything, fundamentally on our side; a man
and a brother.

There was a very self-conscious sense of literary and moral
solidarity amongst these people, which created between them a
feeling of genuine fraternity and of purpose which certainly no
other society in Russia has ever had. Herzen, who later met a great
many celebrated people, and was a critical and intolerant, often
an exceedingly sardonic and at times cynical judge of men, and
Annenkov, who had travelled a good deal in Western Europe and
had a variegated acquaintance among the notables of his day –
both these connoisseurs of human beings, in later years, confessed
that never in their lives had they again found anywhere a society
so civilised and gay and free, so enlightened, spontaneous and
agreeable, so sincere, so intelligent, so gifted and attractive in
every way.

2

German Romanticism in Petersburg and Moscow

All – or nearly all – historians of Russian thought or literature, whatever their other differences, seem agreed upon one thing: that the dominant influence upon Russian writers in the second quarter of the nineteenth century is that of German romanticism. This judgement, like most such generalisations of its type, is not quite true. Even if Pushkin is held to belong to an earlier generation, neither Lermontov nor Gogol nor Nekrasov, to take only the most notable writers of this time, can be regarded as disciples of these thinkers. Nevertheless, it is true that German metaphysics did radically alter the direction of ideas in Russia, both on the right and on the left, among nationalists, Orthodox theologians, and political radicals equally, and profoundly affected the outlook of the more wide-awake students at the universities, and intellectually inclined young men generally. These philosophical schools, and in particular the doctrines of Hegel and Schelling, are still, in their modern transformations, not without influence today. Their principal legacy to the modern world is a notorious and powerful political mythology, which in both its right- and left-wing forms has been used to justify the most obscurantist and oppressive movements of our own times. At the same time the great historical achievements of the romantic school have become so deeply absorbed into the very texture of civilised thought in the West that it is not easy to convey how novel, and to some minds intoxicating, they once proved to be.

The works of the early German romantic thinkers – Herder, Fichte, Schelling, Friedrich Schlegel and their followers, are not easy to read. The treatises of Schelling, for instance – vastly admired in their day – are like a dark wood into which I do not, here at least, propose to venture – *vestigia terrent*, too many eager enquirers have entered it never to return. Yet the art and thought of this period, at any rate in Germany, and also in Eastern Europe and Russia, which were, in effect, intellectual dependencies of Germany, are not intelligible without some grasp of the fact that these metaphysicians – in particular Schelling – caused a major shift in human thought: from the mechanistic categories of the eighteenth century to explanation in terms of aesthetic or biological notions. The romantic thinkers and poets successfully undermined the central dogma of eighteenth-century enlightenment, that the only reliable method of discovery or interpretation was that of the triumphant mechanical sciences. The French *philosophes* may have exaggerated the virtue, and the German romantics the absurdity, of the application of the criteria of the natural sciences to human affairs. But, whatever else it may have done, the romantic reaction against the claims of scientific materialism did set up permanent doubts about the competence of the sciences of man – psychology, sociology, anthropology, physiology – to take over, and put an end to the scandalous chaos of, such human activities as history, or the arts, or religious, philosophical, social and political thought. As Bayle and Voltaire had mocked the theological reactionaries of their time, so the romantics derided the dogmatic materialists of the school of Condillac and Holbach; and their favourite field of battle was that of aesthetic experience.

If you wanted to know what it was that made a work of art; if you wanted to know, for example, why particular colours and forms produced a particular piece of painting or sculpture; why particular styles of writing or collocations of words produced particularly strong or memorable effects upon particular human beings in specific states of awareness; or why certain musical sounds, when they were juxtaposed, were sometimes called shallow and at other times profound, or lyrical, or vulgar, or morally noble or degraded or characteristic of this or that national or individual trait; then no general hypothesis of the kind adopted in physics, no general description or classification or subsumption under scientific laws of the behaviour of sound, or of patches of paint, or of black marks on paper, or the utterances of human beings, would begin to suffice to answer these questions.

What were the non-scientific modes of explanation which could explain life, thought, art, religion, as the sciences could not? The romantic metaphysicians returned to ways of knowing which they attributed to the Platonic tradition: spiritual insight, 'intuitive' knowledge of connections incapable of scientific analysis. Schelling (whose views on the working of the artistic imagination, and in particular about the nature of genius, are, for all their obscurity, arrestingly original and imaginative) spoke in terms of a universal mystical vision. He saw the universe as a single spirit, a great, animate organism, a soul or self, evolving from one spiritual stage into another. Individual human beings were, as it were, 'finite centres', 'aspects', 'moments' of this enormous cosmic entity – the 'living whole', the world soul, the transcendental Spirit or Idea, descriptions of which almost recall the fantasies of early gnosticism. Indeed the sceptical Swiss historian Jakob Burckhardt said that when he listened to Schelling he began to see creatures with many arms and feet advancing upon him. The conclusions drawn from this apocalyptic vision are less eccentric. The finite centres – the individual human beings – understand each other, their surroundings and themselves, the past and to some degree the present and the future too, but not in the same sort of way in which they communicate with one another. When, for example, I maintain that I understand another human being – that I am sympathetic to him, follow, 'enter into' the workings of his mind, and that I am for this reason particularly well qualified to form a judgement of his character – of his 'inner' self – I am claiming to be doing something which cannot be reduced to, on the one hand, a set of systematically classified operations and, on the other, a method of deriving further information from them which, once discovered, could be reduced to a technique, and taught to, and applied more or less mechanically by, a receptive pupil. Understanding men or ideas or movements, or the outlooks of individuals or groups, is not reducible to a sociological classification into types of behaviour with predictions based on scientific experiment and carefully tabulated statistics of observations.

There is no substitute for sympathy, understanding, insight, 'wisdom'.

Similarly, Schelling taught that if you wanted to know what it was, for example, that made a work of art beautiful, or what it was that gave its own unique character to a historical period, it was necessary to employ methods different from those of experiment, classification, induction, deduction or the other techniques of the natural sciences. According to this doctrine, if you wished to understand what, for example, had brought about the vast spiritual upheaval of the French Revolution, or why Goethe's *Faust* was a profounder work than the tragedies of Voltaire, then to apply the methods of the kind of psychology and sociology adumbrated by, say, Condillac or Condorcet would not prove rewarding. Unless you had a capacity for imaginative insight – for understanding the 'inner', the mental and emotional – the 'spiritual' – life of individuals, societies, historical periods, the 'inner purposes' or 'essences' of institutions, nations, Churches, you would for ever remain unable to explain why certain combinations form 'unities', whereas others do not: why particular sounds or words or acts are relevant to, fit with, certain other elements in the 'whole', while others fail to do so. And this no matter whether you are 'explaining' the character of a man, the rise of a movement or a party, the process of artistic creation, the characteristics of an age, or of a school of thought, or of a mystical view of reality. Nor is this, according to the view I am discussing, an accident. For reality is not merely organic but unitary: which is a way of saying that its ingredients are not merely connected by causal relationships – they do not merely form a pattern or harmony so that each element is seen to be 'necessitated' by the disposition of all the other elements – but each 'reflects' or 'expresses' the others; for there is a single 'Spirit' or 'Idea' or 'Absolute' of which all that exists is a unique aspect, or an articulation – and the more of an aspect, the more vividly articulated, the 'deeper', the 'more real' it is. A philosophy is 'true' in the proportion in which it expresses the phase which the Absolute or the Idea has reached at each stage of development. A poet possesses genius, a statesman greatness, to the degree to which they are inspired by, and express, the 'spirit' of their milieu – State, culture, nation – which is itself an 'incarnation' of the self-realisation of the spirit of the universe conceived pantheistically as a kind of ubiquitous divinity. And a work of art is dead or artificial or trivial if it is a mere accident in this development. Art, philosophy, religion are so many efforts on the part of finite creatures to catch and articulate an 'echo' of the cosmic harmony. Man is finite, and his vision will always be fragmentary; the 'deeper' the individual, the larger and richer the fragment. Hence the lofty contempt which such thinkers express for the 'merely' empirical or 'mechanical', for the world of every-day experience whose denizens remain deaf to the inner harmony in terms of which alone anything – and everything – is 'truly' to be understood.

The romantic critics in some cases supposed themselves not merely to be revealing the nature of types of knowledge or thought or feeling hitherto unrecognised or inadequately analysed, but to be building new cosmological systems, new faiths, new forms of life, and indeed to be direct instruments of the process of the spiritual redemption, or 'self-realisation', of the universe. Their metaphysical fantasies are – fortunately, I may add – all but dead today; but the incidental light which they shed on art, history and religion transformed the outlook of the West. By paying a great deal of attention to the unconscious activity of the imagination, to the role of irrational factors, to the part played in the mind by symbols and myths, to awareness of unanalysable affinities and contrasts, to fundamental but impalpable connections and differences which cut across the conventional lines of rational classification, they often succeeded in giving an altogether novel account of such phenomena as poetical inspiration, religious experience, political genius, of the relationship of art to social development, or of the individual to the masses, or of moral ideals to aesthetic or biological facts. This account was more convincing than any that had been given before; at any rate than the doctrines of the eighteenth century, which had not treated such topics systematic-ally, and largely left them to the isolated utterances of mystically inclined poets and essayists.

So too Hegel, despite all the philosophical obfuscation for which *Hegel* he was responsible, set in motion ideas which have become so universal and familiar that we think in terms of them without being aware of their relative novelty. This is true, for example, of the idea of the history of thought as a continuous process, capable of independent study. There existed, of course, accounts – usually mere *catalogues raisonnés* – of particular philosophical systems in the ancient world or in the Middle Ages, or monographs devoted to particular thinkers. But it was Hegel who developed the notion of a specific cluster of ideas as permeating an age or a society, of the effect of those ideas upon other ideas, of the many invisible links whereby the feelings, the sentiments, the thoughts, the religions, the laws and the general outlook – what is nowadays called ideology – of one generation are connected with the ideology of other times or places. Unlike his predecessors Vico and Herder, Hegel tried to present this as a coherent, continuous, rationally analysable development – the first in the fatal line of cosmic historians which stretches through Comte and Marx to Spengler and Toynbee and all those who find spiritual comfort in the discovery of vast imaginary symmetries in the irregular stream of human history.

Although much of this programme is a fantasy, or at any rate a form of highly subjective poetry in prose, yet the notion that the many activities of the human spirit are interrelated, that the artistic or scientific thought of an age is best understood in its interplay with the social, economic, theological, legal activities pursued in the society in which artists and scientists live and work – the very notion of cultural history as a source of light – is itself a cardinal step in the history of thought. And again Schelling (following Herder) is largely responsible for the characteristically romantic notion that poets or painters may understand the spirit of their age more profoundly and express it in a more vivid and lasting manner than academic historians; this is so because artists tend to have a greater degree of sensibility to the contours of their own age (or of other ages and cultures) than either trained antiquaries or professional journalists, inasmuch as they are irritable organisms; more responsive to, and conscious of, inchoate, half-understood factors which operate beneath the surface in a given milieu, factors which may come to full maturity only at a later period. This was the sense in which, for example, Karl Marx used to maintain that Balzac in his novels had depicted the life and character not so much of his own time, as of the men of the 1860s and 1870s, whose lineaments, while they were still in embryo, impinged upon the sensibilities of artists long before they emerged into the full light of day. The romantic philosophers vastly exaggerated the power and reliability of this kind of intuitive or poetical insight; but their fervid vision, which remained mystical and irrationalist no matter how heavily disguised in quasi-scientific or quasi-lyrical terminology, captivated the imagination of the young Russian intellectuals of the 1830s and 1840s, and seemed to open a door to a nobler and calmer world from the sordid reality of the Empire ruled by Tsar Nicholas I.

The man who, more persuasively than anyone else in Russia, taught the educated young men of the 1830s to soar above empirical facts into a realm of pure light where all was harmonious and eternally true, was a student of Moscow University called Nicholas Stankevich, who, while still in his early twenties, gathered round him a circle of devoted admirers. Stankevich was an aristocratic young man of great distinction of mind and appearance, a gentle and idealistic personality, and exceptional sweetness of character, with a passion for metaphysics and a gift for lucid exposition. He was born in 1813, and in the course of his short life (he died at twenty-seven) exercised a remarkable moral and intellectual ascendancy over his friends. They idolised him in his lifetime, and after his death worshipped his memory. Even Turgenev, who was not addicted to uncritical admiration, painted a portrait of him in his novel *Rudin* under the name of Pokorsky in which there is not a trace of irony. Stankevich had read widely in German romantic literature, and preached a secular, metaphysical religion which for him had taken the place of the doctrines of the Orthodox Church, in which neither he nor his friends any longer believed.

He taught that a proper understanding of Kant and Schelling (and later Hegel) led one to realise that beneath the apparent disorder and the cruelty, the injustice and the ugliness of daily life, it was possible to discern eternal beauty, peace and harmony. Artists and scientists were travelling their different roads to the selfsame goal (a very Schellingian idea) of communion with this inner harmony. Art (and this included philosophical and scientific truth) alone was immortal, stood up unscathed against the chaos of the empirical world, against the unintelligible and shapeless flow of political, social, economic events which would soon vanish and be forgotten. The masterpieces of art and thought were permanent memorials to the creative power of men, because they alone embodied moments of insight into some portion of the everlasting pattern which lies beyond the flux of appearances. Stankevich believed (as many have believed, particularly after some great fiasco in the life of their society, in this case perhaps the failure of the Decembrist revolution of 1825) that in the place of social reforms, which merely affected the outer texture of life, men should seek rather to reform themselves within, and everything else would be added unto them: the kingdom of heaven – the Hegelian self-transcending Spirit – lies within. Salvation comes from individual self-regeneration, and to achieve truth, reality, happiness, men must learn from those who truly know: the philosophers, the poets, the sages. Kant, Hegel, Homer, Shakespeare, Goethe were harmonious spirits, saints and sages who saw what the multitude would never see. Study, endless study alone could afford a glimpse into their Elysian world, the sole reality in which the broken fragments came together again into their original unity. Only those who could attain to this beatific vision were wise and good and free. To pursue material values – social reforms or political goals of any kind – was to pursue phantoms, to court broken hopes, frustration and misery.

For anyone who was young and idealistic in Russia between 1830 and 1848, or simply human enough to be depressed by the social conditions of the country, it was comforting to be told that the appalling evils of Russian life – the ignorance and poverty of the serfs, the illiteracy and hypocrisy of the clergy, the corruption, inefficiency, brutality, arbitrariness of the governing class, the pettiness, sycophancy and inhumanity of the merchants – that the entire barbarous system, according to the sages of the West, was a mere bubble upon the surface of life. It was all ultimately unimportant, the inevitable attribute of the world of appearances which, seen from a superior vantage point, did not disturb the deeper harmony. Musical images are frequent in the metaphysics of this time. You were told that if you simply listened to the isolated notes of a given musical instrument you might find them ugly and meaningless and without purpose; but if you understood the entire work, if you listened to the orchestra as a whole, you would see that these apparently arbitrary sounds conspired with other sounds to form a harmonious whole which satisfied your craving for truth and beauty. This is a kind of translation into aesthetic terms of the scientific method of explanation of an earlier time. Spinoza – and some among the rationalists of the eighteenth century – had taught that if you could understand the pattern of the universe (some said by metaphysical intuition, others by perceiving a mathematical or mechanical order) then you would cease to kick against the pricks, for you would realise that whatever was real was necessarily what and when and where it was, part of the rational order of the harmony of the cosmos. And if you saw this you became reconciled and achieved inner peace: for you could no longer, as a rational human being, rebel in an arbitrary and capricious fashion against a logically necessary order.

The transposition of this into aesthetic terms is the dominant factor of the German romantic movement. Instead of talking about necessary connections of a scientific kind, or of logical or mathematical reasoning to be employed in the unravelling of these mysteries, you are invited to use a new kind of logic which unfolds to you the beauty of a picture, the depth of a piece of music, the truth of a literary masterpiece. If you conceive of life as the artistic creation of some cosmic divinity, and of the world as the progressive revelation of a work of art – if, in short, you are converted from a scientific to a mystical or 'transcendental' view of life and history, you may well experience a sense of liberation. Previously you were the victim of unexplained chaos, which rendered you indignant and unhappy, a prisoner in a system which you vainly tried to reform and correct, with the result that you only suffered failure and defeat. But now you acquired a sense of yourself willingly and eagerly participating in the cosmic enterprise: whatever befell necessarily fulfilled the universal, and thereby your own personal, design. You were wise, happy and free: for you were at one with the purposes of the universe.

Under the conditions of literary censorship then prevalent in Russia, where it was difficult to give open expression to political and social ideas, where literature was the only vehicle in which such ideas could, however cryptically, be conveyed, a programme which invited you to ignore the repulsive (and, after the fate of the Decembrists, perilous) political scene, and concentrate upon personal – moral, literary, artistic – self-improvement, offered great comfort to people who did not wish to suffer too much. Stankevich believed in Hegel deeply and sincerely, and preached his quietist sermons with an eloquence which sprang from a pure and sensitive heart and an unswerving faith which never left him. Such doubts as he had, he stilled within himself; and remained until his early end an unworldly saint in whose presence his friends felt a sense of spiritual peace which flowed from the beauty of his singularly unbroken personality, and the feminine delicacy and charm with which he used to bind his gentle spell upon them. This influence ceased with his death: he left a few graceful, faded poems, a handful of fragmentary essays, and a bundle of letters to his friends and to various German philosophers; among them moving avowals to the most admired of his friends, a young playwright and professor in Berlin in whom he discerned something akin to genius, a disciple of Hegel whose very name is now justly forgotten. From this scanty material it is scarcely possible to reconstruct the personality of this leader of Russian Idealism.

His most gifted and impressionable disciple was a man of very different cast, Mikhail Bakunin, at this time an amateur philosopher, and already notorious for his turbulent and despotic character. Bakunin had, by the late 1830s, resigned his commission in the army and was living in Moscow largely by his wits. Endowed with an exceptional capacity for absorbing other people's doctrines, he expounded them with fervour and enthusiasm as though they were his own, and in the course of this changed them somewhat, making them, as a rule, simpler, clearer, cruder, and at times more convincing. Bakunin had a considerable element of cynicism in his character, and cared little what the exact effect of his sermons might be on his friends – provided only that it was powerful enough; he did not ask whether they excited or demoralised them, or ruined their lives, or bored them, or turned them into fanatical zealots for some wildly Utopian scheme. Bakunin was a born agitator with sufficient scepticism in his system not to be taken in himself by his own torrential eloquence. To dominate individuals and sway assemblies was his *métier*: he belonged to that odd, fortunately not very numerous, class of persons who contrive to hypnotise others into throwing themselves into causes – if need be killing and dying for them – while themselves remaining coldly, clearly and ironically aware of the effect of the spells which they cast. When his bluff was called, as occasionally it was, for example, by Herzen, Bakunin would laugh with the greatest good nature, admit everything freely, and continue to cause havoc, if anything with greater unconcern than before. His path was strewn with victims, casualties, and faithful, idealistic converts; he himself remained a gay, easy-going, mendacious, irresistibly agreeable, calmly and coldly destructive, fascinating, generous, undisciplined, eccentric Russian landowner to the end.

He played with ideas with adroitness and boyish delight. They came from many sources: from Saint-Simon, from Holbach, from Hegel, from Proudhon, from Feuerbach, from the Young Hegelians, from Weitling. He would imbibe these doctrines during periods of short but intensive application, and then he would expound them with a degree of fervour and personal magnetism which was, perhaps, unique even in that century of great popular tribunes. During the decade which Annenkov describes, he was a fanatically orthodox Hegelian, and preached the paradoxical principles of the new metaphysics to his friends night after night with lucidity and stubborn passion. He proclaimed the existence of iron and inexorable laws of history, and indeed of everything else. Hegel – and Stankevich – were right. It was idle to rebel against them, or to protest against the cruelties and injustices which they seemed to entail; to do so was simply a sign of immaturity, of not understanding the necessity and beauty of the rationally organised cosmos – to fail to grasp the divine goal in which the sufferings and disharmonies of individual lives must, if you understood them properly, inevitably culminate and be resolved.

Hegel taught that the spirit evolved not continuously, but by a 'dialectical' struggle of 'opposites' which (somewhat, it seems, like a diesel engine) moved by a series of sharp explosions. This notion suited Bakunin's temperament well, since, as he himself was fond of saying, he detested nothing more than peace, order, bourgeois contentment. Mere bohemianism, disorganised rebellion have been discredited too often. Hegelianism presented its tragic and violent view of life beneath the guise of an eternal rational system, an objective 'science', with all the logical paraphernalia of reasoned judgement. First to justify the need to submit to a brutal government and a stupid bureaucracy in the name of eternal Reason, then to justify rebellion with the selfsame arguments, was a paradoxical task that delighted Bakunin. In Moscow he enjoyed his power of turning peaceful students into dervishes, ecstatic seekers after some aesthetic or metaphysical goal. In later life he applied these talents on a wider scale, and stirred some exceedingly unpromising human material – Swiss watchmakers and German peasants – into unbelievable frenzies of enthusiasm, which no one ever induced in them before or after.

During the period of which I am speaking, he concentrated these sinister talents upon the relatively humble task of expounding Hegel's *Encyclopedia*, paragraph by paragraph, to his admiring friends. Among these friends was another intimate of Stankevich, Nikolay Granovsky, a gentle and high-minded historian who had studied in Germany and there became a moderate Hegelian, and came back to lecture on Western medieval history in Moscow. Granovsky succeeded in making his apparently remote subject into a means of inducing in his audiences respect for the Western tradition. He dwelt in particular on the civilising effect of the Roman Church, of Roman law, and of the institutions of feudalism, developing his theses in the face of the growing chauvinism – with its emphasis on the Byzantine roots of Russian culture – which was at this time encouraged by the Russian government as an antidote to the dangerous ideas of the West. Granovsky combined erudition with a very balanced intellect, and was not carried away by extravagant theories. Nevertheless he was Hegelian enough to believe that the universe must have a pattern and a goal; that this goal was slowly being approached, that humanity was marching towards freedom, although the path was by no means smooth or straight: obstacles occurred – relapses were frequent and difficult to avert. Unless a sufficient number of human beings with personal courage, strength and a sense of dedication emerged, humanity tended to subside into long nights of reaction, swamps from which it extricated itself at terrible cost. Nevertheless, slowly and painfully, but inexorably, humanity was moving towards an ideal state of happiness, justice, truth and beauty. Granovsky's lectures in Moscow University in the early 1840s on the apparently recondite subject of the late Merovingian and early Carolingian kings attracted a very large and distinguished audience. These lectures were treated both by the 'Westerners' and their nationalist Slavophil opponents as a quasi-political demonstration of pro-Western, liberal and rationalist sentiment: above all of faith in the transforming power of enlightened ideas, against mystical nationalism and ecclesiasticism.

I quote the example of Granovsky's famous lectures – passionately acclaimed by his friends, and attacked by the conservatives – as an illustration of the peculiar disguises which in Russia (as to a lesser extent in Germany) social and political liberalism had to adopt if it was to find voice at all. The censorship was at once a heavy fetter and a goad – it brought into being a peculiar brand of crypto-revolutionary writing, made more tortuous and more intense by repression, which in the end turned the whole of Russian literature into what Herzen described as 'one vast bill of indictment' against Russian life.[1]

The censor was the official enemy, but unlike his modern successor, he was almost wholly negative. The tsarist censorship imposed silence but it did not directly tell professors what to teach; it did not dictate to authors what to say and how to say it; and it did not command composers to induce this or that mood in their audiences. It was merely designed to prevent the expression of a certain number of selected 'dangerous ideas'. It was an obstacle, at times a maddening one. But because it was, like so much in old Russia, inefficient, corrupt, indolent, often stupid, or deliberately lenient – and because so many loopholes could always be found by the ingenious and the desperate, not much that was subversive was stopped effectively. The Russian writers who belonged to the radical intelligentsia did, after all, publish their works, and published them, by and large, in an almost undistorted form. The main effect of repression was to drive social and political ideas into

---

1   'Du développement des idées révolutionnaires en Russie', H vii 247.

the relatively safe realm of literature. This had already occurred in
Germany, and it did so on a much larger scale in Russia.

Yet it would be a mistake to exaggerate the role of government repression in compelling literature to become political in
character. The romantic movement was itself an equally potent
factor in creating 'impure' literature, in filling it with ideological
content. Turgenev himself, the 'purest' of all the men of letters of
his time, and often taken to task for this sin by censorious
preachers like Dostoevsky or the 'materialist' critics of the 1860s,
did, after all, at one time, contemplate an academic career – as
a professor of philosophy. He was dissuaded from this; but his
early Hegelian infatuation proved a lasting influence on his whole
view of life. Hegel's teaching drove some to revolution, others to
reaction; in either case it emancipated its adherents from the
oversimplified classifications of men by the eighteenth-century
pamphleteers into the virtuous and the vicious, the benighted or
the enlightened, of events into good and bad, and from the view
of both men and things as intelligible and predictable in terms of
clear, mechanically conceived, causal chains. For Turgenev, on
the contrary, everything is compounded of characteristics in a
perpetual process of transformation, infinitely complex, morally
and politically ambivalent, blending into constantly changing
combinations, explicable only in terms of flexible and often
impressionistic psychological and historical concepts, which allow
for the elaborate interplay of factors that are too many and too
fleeting to be reduced to scientific schemata or laws. Turgenev's
liberalism and moderation, for which he was so much criticised,
took the form of holding everything in solution – of remaining
outside the situation in a state of watchful and ironical detachment, uncommitted, evenly balanced – an agnostic oscillating
contentedly between atheism and faith, belief in progress and
scepticism, an observer in a state of cool, emotionally controlled
doubt before a spectacle of life where nothing is quite what it
seems, where every quality is infected by its opposite, where paths
are never straight, never cross in geometrically regular patterns.
For him (this is his version of the Hegelian dialectic) reality for
ever escapes all artificial ideological nets, all rigid, dogmatic
assumptions, defies all attempts at codification, upsets all sym-

metrical moral or sociological systems, and yields itself only to cautious, emotionally neutral, scrupulously empirical attempts to describe it bit by bit, as it presents itself to the curious eye of the morally disinterested observer. Herzen, too, rejects cut and dried systems and programmes: neither he nor Turgenev accepted the positive Hegelian doctrines, the vast cosmological fantasy – the historical theodicy which unhinged so many of their contemporaries. Both were profoundly affected by its negative aspect – the undermining of the uncritical faith in the new social sciences which animated the optimistic thinkers of the previous century.

These were some of the more prominent and celebrated among the avant-garde young Russians of the late 1830s and 1840s – and there were many members of this group whom there is not room to mention – Katkov, who began as a philosopher and a radical and later became a famous and influential reactionary journalist; the philosopher Redkin, the essayist Korsh, and the translator Ketcher; the actor Shchepkin; wealthy young dilettanti like Botkin, Panaev, Sazonov, Ogarev, Galakhov, the great poet Nekrasov, and many lesser figures whose lives are of interest only to literary or social historians. But over all these towers the figure of the critic Vissarion Belinsky. His defects both of education and taste were notorious; his appearance was unimpressive, his prose style left much to be desired. But he became the moral and literary dictator of his generation. Those who came under his influence remained affected by it long after his death; and whether for good or ill it transformed Russian writing – in particular criticism – radically, and, it would seem, for ever.

3

Vissarion Belinsky *(1811-1848)*

[1960]

In 1856 Ivan Aksakov, one of two famous Slavophil brothers, who had no sympathy for political radicalism, wrote an account of one of his tours of the provincial centres of European Russia. The tour was conceived by him as a kind of nationalist pilgrimage, intended at once to draw comfort and inspiration from direct contact with the untouched mass of the Russian people, and to warn those who needed warning against the horrors of the West and the snares of Western liberalism. Aksakov was bitterly disappointed.

> The name of Belinsky is known to every thinking young man [he wrote], to everyone who is hungry for a breath of fresh air in the reeking bog of provincial life. There is not a country schoolmaster who does not know – and know by heart – Belinsky's letter to Gogol [. . .] If you want to find honest people, people who care about the poor and the oppressed, an honest doctor, an honest lawyer not afraid of a fight, you will find them among Belinsky's followers [. . .][1]

Slavophil influence was negligible. Belinsky's proselytes were increasing.

Plainly we are dealing with a major phenomenon of some kind – someone to whom, eight years after his death, idealistic young men, during one of the worst moments of repression in the nineteenth century, looked as their leader. The literary reminiscences of the young radicals of the 1830s and 1840s – Panaev and his

1   *Ivan Sergeevich Aksakov v ego pis'makh* (Moscow, 1888–96), iii 290–1.

wife, Turgenev, Herzen, Annenkov, Ogareva, Dostoevsky – agree in stressing this aspect of Belinsky as the 'conscience' of the Russian intelligentsia, the inspired and fearless publicist, the ideal of the young *révoltés*, the writer who almost alone in Russia had the character and the eloquence to proclaim clearly and harshly what many felt, but either could not or would not openly declare.

We can easily imagine the kind of young man Aksakov was speaking of. In Turgenev's novel *Rudin* there is a mildly ironical, but sympathetic and touching, portrait of a typical radical of that time, employed as tutor in a country house. He is a plain-looking, awkward, clumsy university student, neither intelligent nor interesting; indeed he is dim, provincial, rather a fool, but pure-hearted, embarrassingly sincere and self-revealing, and comically naive. The student is a radical not in the sense that he holds clear intellectual or moral-political views, but because he is filled with a vague but bitter hostility towards the government of his country, the grey, brutish soldiers, the dull, dishonest, and frightened officials, the illiterate, superstitious, and sycophantic priests; with a deep distaste for the peculiar mixture, compounded of fear, greed and a dislike of everything new or connected with the forces of life, which formed the prevailing Russian atmosphere. He is in full reaction against the queer variety of cynical resignation which accepted the starved and semi-barbarous condition of the serfs and the deathly stagnation of provincial Russian society as something not merely natural, but possessing a deep, traditional value, almost a kind of spiritual beauty, the object of a peculiar, nationalist, quasi-religious mystique of its own. Rudin is the life and soul of the house-party, and the young tutor is completely taken in by his specious liberal rhetoric, worships the ground Rudin treads on, and fills his easy generalisations with all his own moral enthusiasm and faith in truth and material progress. When Rudin, still gay and charming and irresistible, still overflowing with empty liberal platitudes, refuses to face a moral crisis, makes feeble excuses, behaves like a craven and a fool, and gets himself out of an awkward predicament by a squalid piece of minor treachery, his follower, the simple seeker after truth, is left dazed, helpless and outraged, not knowing what to believe or which way to turn, in a typical Turgenev situation in which everyone ends by behaving with weakness and irresponsibility that is human, disarming and disastrous. The tutor Basistov is a very minor figure, but he is a direct if humble descendant of the foil – and sometimes the dupe – of the original 'superfluous man'[1] of Russian society, of Pushkin's Lensky (as opposed to Onegin); he is of the same stock as Pierre Bezukhov (as against Prince Andrey) in *War and Peace*, as Levin in *Anna Karenina* and all the Karamazovs, as Krutsifersky in Herzen's novel *Who Is To Blame?*, as the student in *The Cherry Orchard*, as Colonel Vershinin and the Baron in *The Three Sisters*. He is, in the context of the 1840s, the figure that came to be thought of as one of the characteristic figures in the Russian social novel, the perplexed idealist, the touchingly naive, over-enthusiastic, pure-hearted man, the victim of misfortunes which could be averted but in fact never are. Sometimes comical, some-times tragical, often confused, blundering and inefficient, he is incapable of any falseness, or, at least, of irremediable falseness, of anything in any degree sordid or treacherous; sometimes weak and self-pitying, like Chekhov's heroes – sometimes strong and furious like Bazarov in *Fathers and Children* – he never loses an inner dignity and an indestructible moral personality in contrast with which the ordinary philistines who form the vast majority of normal society appear at once pathetic and repulsive.

The original prototype of these sincere, sometimes childish, at other times angry, champions of persecuted humanity, the saints and martyrs in the cause of the humiliated and the defeated – the actual, historical embodiment of this most Russian type of moral and intellectual heroism – is Vissarion Grigor'evich Belinsky. His name became the greatest Russian myth in the nineteenth century, detestable to the supporters of autocracy, the Orthodox Church, and fervid nationalism, disturbing to elegant and fastidious lovers of Western classicism, and for the same reasons the idealised ances-tor of both the reformers and the revolutionaries of the second half of the century. In a very real sense he was one of the founders of the movement which culminated in 1917 in the overthrow of

1   [The concept of the 'superfluous man' was given its familiar name by Tur-genev in *Dnevnik lishnego cheloveka* ('Diary of a superfluous man', 1850): see entry for 23 March 1850, S v 185–9. The term was also used as a catchphrase by Dostoevsky in *Zapiski iz podpol'ya* (1864), D vi 7–80.]

the social order which towards the end of his life he increasingly denounced. There is scarcely a radical Russian writer – and few liberals – who did not at some stage claim to be descended from him. Even such timid and half-hearted members of the opposition as Annenkov and Turgenev worshipped his memory, even the conservative government censor Goncharov spoke of him as the best man he had ever known. As for the true left-wing authors of the 1860s – the revolutionary propagandists Dobrolyubov and Chernyshevsky, Nekrasov, Lavrov and Mikhailovsky, and the socialists who followed them, Plekhanov, Martov, Lenin and his followers – they formally recognised him as one of the earliest and, with Herzen, the greatest of the heroes of the heroic 1840s, when the organised struggle for full social as well as political freedom, economic as well as civil equality, was held to have begun in the Russian Empire.

Clearly, then, he was, to say the least, an arresting figure in the history of Russian social thought. Those who have read the memoirs of his friends, Herzen, Turgenev, and of course Annenkov, will discover for themselves the reason for this. But in the West Belinsky is even now relatively unknown. Yet, as anyone knows who has read at all widely in his works, he is the father of the social criticism of literature, not only in Russia but perhaps even in Europe, the most gifted and formidable enemy of the aesthetic and religious and mystical attitudes to life. Throughout the nineteenth century his views were the great battlefield between Russian critics, that is, between two incompatible views of art and indeed of life. He was always very poor, and he wrote to keep alive, and, therefore, too much. Much of his writing was composed in fearful haste, and a great deal is uninspired hackwork. But in spite of all the hostile criticism to which he has been exposed from his earliest beginnings as a critic (and let me add that Belinsky is to this day the subject of heated controversy – no other figure dead for over a century has excited so much devotion and so much odium among Russians), his best work is in Russia regarded as classical and immortal. In the Soviet Union his place is all too secure, for (despite his lifelong war against dogma and conformism) he has there long been canonised as a founding father of the new form of life. But the moral and political issue with which he was concerned is, in the West, open still. This alone makes him a figure of interest at the present time.

His life was outwardly uneventful. He was born in poverty in 1810 or 1811, at Sveaborg in Finland, and brought up in the remote town of Chembar in the province of Penza. His father was a retired naval doctor who settled down to a small practice and to drink. He grew up a thin, consumptive, overserious, pinched little boy, prematurely old, unsmiling and always in deadly earnest, who soon attracted the attention of his schoolmasters by his single-minded devotion to literature, and his grim, unseasonable and apparently devouring passion for the truth. He went to Moscow as a poor scholar with a government stipend, and after the normal troubles and misfortunes of impoverished students of humble birth in what was still the home of the gentry and nobility – the University of Moscow – was expelled for reasons which are still obscure, but probably connected with lack of solid knowledge, and the writing of a play denouncing serfdom. The play, which survives, is very badly written, rhetorical, mildly subversive, and worthless as a work of literature, but the moral was plain enough for the intimidated University censors, and the author was poor and lacked protectors. Nadezhdin, then a liberal young professor of European literature at the University, who edited an avant-garde periodical, was impressed by Belinsky's obvious seriousness and passion for literature, thought that he detected a spark of inspiration, and engaged him to write reviews. From 1835 until his death thirteen years later, Belinsky poured out a steady stream of articles, critical notices and reviews in various journals. They split educated Russian opinion into rival camps, and became the gospel of the progressive young men in every corner of the Empire, particularly of the university students who became his most devoted and fanatical followers.

In appearance Belinsky was of middle height, thin, bony and slightly stooped; his face was pale, slightly mottled, and flushed easily when he was excited. He was asthmatic, tired easily, and usually looked worn out, haggard and rather grim. His movements were awkward, like a peasant's, nervous and abrupt, and before strangers he tended to be shy, brusque and sullen. With his intimates, the young radicals, Turgenev, Botkin, Bakunin,

Granovsky, he was full of life and irrepressible gusto. In the heat of a literary or philosophical discussion his eyes would shine, his pupils dilate, he would walk from corner to corner talking loudly, rapidly and with violent intensity, coughing and waving his arms. In society he was clumsy and uncomfortable and tended to be silent, but if he heard what he regarded as wicked or unctuous sentiments he intervened on principle, and Herzen testifies that on such occasions no opponent could stand before the force of his terrible moral fury. He was at his best when excited by argument. Let me quote Herzen's words:

> Without controversy, unless he was irritated, he did not talk well; but when he felt wounded, when his dearest convictions were touched, and the muscles of his cheeks began to quiver and his voice broke – one should have seen him then: he would fling himself at his victim like a leopard, he would tear him to pieces, make him ridiculous, make him pitiful, and in the course of it would develop his own thought with astonishing power and poetry. The argument would often end in blood which poured from the sick man's throat; pale, choking, with eyes fixed on whoever he was addressing, he would, with a trembling hand, lift the handkerchief to his mouth, and stop – terribly upset, undone by his lack of physical strength. How I loved and how I pitied him at those moments![1]

At dinner with some decayed and respectable official who had survived from the reign of the Empress Catherine, Belinsky went out of his way to praise the execution of Louis XVI. Someone ventured to say in front of him that Chaadaev (a Russian sympathiser with Roman Catholicism who had denounced the barbarism of his country) had, in a civilised country, been very properly declared insane by the Tsar for insulting the dearest convictions of his people. Belinsky, after vainly tugging at Herzen's sleeve and whispering to him to intervene, finally broke in himself, and said in a dead, dull voice that in still more civilised countries the guillotine was invented for people who advanced that kind of opinion. The victim was crushed, the host was alarmed, and the

1 'Byloe i dumy', part 4, chapter 25 (see 151 above, note 1), H ix 31; M ii 411.

party quickly broke up. Turgenev, who disliked extremes, and detested scenes, loved and respected Belinsky for precisely this social fearlessness that he himself conspicuously lacked.

With his friends Belinsky played cards, cracked commonplace jokes, talked through the night, and charmed and exhausted them all. He could not bear solitude. He was married unsuitably, from sheer misery and loneliness. He died of consumption in the early summer of 1848. The head of the gendarmerie later expressed fierce regret that Belinsky had died, adding: 'We would have rotted him in a fortress.'[1] He was thirty-seven or thirty-eight at the time of his death, and at the height of his powers.

For all the external monotony of his days, Belinsky lived a life of abnormal intensity, punctuated by acute crises, intellectual and moral, which helped to destroy him physically. The subject which he had chosen, the subject from which he cannot be separated even in thought, was literature, and although he was, despite his detractors' charges of lack of authentic capacity, acutely sensitive to pure literary quality, to the sounds and rhythms and nuances of words, to images and poetical symbolism and the purely sensuous emotions directed towards them, yet that was not the central factor of his life. This centre was the influence of ideas; not merely in the intellectual or rational sense in which ideas are judgements or theories, but in that sense which is perhaps even more familiar, but more difficult to express, in which ideas embody emotions as well as thoughts, inarticulate as well as explicit attitudes to the inner and to the outer worlds. This is the sense in which ideas are something wider and more intrinsic to the human beings who hold them than opinions or even principles, the sense in which ideas constitute, and indeed are, the central complex of relations of a man towards himself and to the external world, and may be shallow or deep, false or true, closed or open, blind or endowed with the power of insight. This is something which is discovered in behaviour, conscious and unconscious, in style, in gestures and actions and minute mannerisms at least as much as in any explicit doctrine or profession of faith. It is ideas and beliefs in this sense, as they are manifested in the lives and works of human beings –

1   loc. cit. (p. 14 above, note 1).

what is sometimes vaguely called ideology – that perpetually
excited Belinsky to enthusiasm or anxiety or loathing, and kept
him in a state sometimes amounting to a kind of moral frenzy. He
believed what he believed very passionately, and sacrificed his
entire nature to it. When he doubted he doubted no less passionately, and was prepared to pay any price for the answers to the
questions which tormented him. These questions were, as might
be supposed, about the proper relation of the individual to himself
and to other individuals, to society, about the springs of human
action and feeling, about the ends of life, but in particular about
the imaginative work of the artist, and his moral purpose.

All serious questions to Belinsky were always, in the end, moral
questions: about what it is that is wholly valuable and worth
pursuing for its own sake. To him this meant the question of what
is alone worth knowing, saying, doing and, of course, fighting for
– if need be, dying for. The ideas which he found in books or in
conversation were not for him, in the first place, intrinsically
interesting or delightful or even intellectually important, to be
examined, analysed, reflected about in some detached and impartial fashion. Ideas were, above all, true or false. If false, then like
evil spirits to be exorcised. All books embody ideas, even when
least appearing to do so; and it is for these that, before anything
else, the critic must probe. To illustrate this I shall give you a
curious, indeed a grotesque, but nevertheless, it seems to me, an
illuminating example of his method. His critics and biographers
do not mention it, since it is a trivial piece of writing. In the course
of his day-to-day journalism Belinsky published a short review of
a Russian version of some nineteenth-century French translation
of *The Vicar of Wakefield*.[1] The review starts conventionally
enough, but gradually assumes an irritated and hostile tone: Belinsky does not like Goldsmith's masterpiece, because he thinks it

1   [At the time this essay was written it was generally assumed by Belinsky
    scholars that this (unsigned) review, published in *Sovremennik* in November
    1847 (1847 vol. 6 No 1, part 3 ['Russkaya literatura'], 77–86), was by
    Belinsky. It has since emerged, however, that it was in fact written by A. D.
    Galakhov, who mentions it in 'Moe sotrudnichestvo v zhurnalakh', *Istori-
    cheskii vestnik* 26 (1886), 312–35, at 323. But Galakhov's attitude echoes
    Belinsky's closely, and may indeed have been influenced by it.]

falsifies the moral facts. He complains that in the character of the
Vicar, Goldsmith represents apathy, placid stupidity and incompetence as being ultimately superior to the qualities of the fighter,
the reformer, the aggressive champion of ideas. The Vicar is represented as a simple soul, full of Christian resignation, unpractical,
and constantly deceived; and this natural goodness and innocence,
it is implied, is somehow both incompatible with, and superior to,
cleverness, intellect, action. This to Belinsky is a deep and dam-
nable heresy. All books embody points of view, rest on underlying
assumptions, social, psychological and aesthetic, and the basis on
which the *Vicar* rests is, according to Belinsky, philistine and false.
It is a glorification of persons who are not engaged in the struggle
of life, who stand on the edge, uncommitted, *dégagés*, and enter
only to be bamboozled and compromised by the active and the
crooked; which leads them to material defeat but moral victory.
But this, he exclaims, is to pander to irrationalism – to the faith
in 'muddling through' clung to by the average bourgeois everywhere – and to that extent it is a dishonest representation of
cowardice as a deeper wisdom, of failure, temporising, appease-
ment as a profound understanding of life. One may reply that this
is an absurd exaggeration; and places a ludicrously heavy burden
on the shoulders of the poor Vicar. But it illustrates the beginning
of a new kind of social criticism, which searches in literature
neither for ideal 'types' of men or situations (as the earlier German
romantics had taught), nor for an ethical instrument for the direct
improvement of life; but for the attitude to life of an individual
author, of his milieu, or age or class. This attitude then requires
to be judged as it would be in life in the first place for its degree
of genuineness, its adequacy to its subject-matter, its depth, its
truthfulness, its ultimate motives.

'I am a *littérateur*,' he wrote. 'I say this with a painful and yet
proud and happy feeling. Russian literature is my life and my
blood.'[1] And this is intended as a declaration of moral status.
When the radical writer Vladimir Korolenko at the beginning of

---

1   Letter to V. P. Botkin, [14–]15 March 1840, B xi 494. [Belinsky also says
    'I am a *littérateur*' in a letter to Bakunin of 10 September 1838, B xi 293.]

this century said, 'Russian literature became my homeland',[1] it is this position that was being so demonstratively defended. Korolenko was speaking in the name of a movement which, quite correctly, claimed Belinsky as its founder, of a creed for which literature alone was free from the betrayals of everyday Russian life, and alone offered a hope of justice, freedom, truth.

Books and ideas to Belinsky were crucial events, matters of life and death, salvation and damnation, and he therefore reacted to them with the most devastating violence. He was by temperament not religious, nor a naturalist, nor an aesthete, nor a scholar. He was a moralist, secular and anti-clerical through and through. Religion was to him a detestable insult to reason, theologians were charlatans, the Church a conspiracy. He believed that objective truth was discoverable in nature, in society, and in the hearts of men. He was not an impressionist, he was not prepared to confine himself to ethically neutral analysis, or meticulous description without bias or comment, of the texture of life or of art. This he would have thought, like Tolstoy, or Herzen, shallow, self-indulgent or frivolous, or else (if you knew the moral truth but preferred the outer texture) deliberate and odious cynicism. The texture was an outer integument, and if you wanted to understand what life was really like (and therefore what it could become), you had to distinguish what is eternal and desperately important from the ephemeral, however attractive. It was not enough to look at or even recreate what Virginia Woolf called the 'semi-transparent envelope'[2] which encloses our existence from life to death; you had to sink beneath the mere flow of life, and examine the structure of the ocean bed, and how the winds blow and how the tides flow, not as an end in itself (for no man may be indifferent to his own fate), but in order to master the elements and to steer your craft, it may be with unending suffering and heroism, it may be against infinitely great odds, towards the goal of truth and social justice

1   [More literally: 'I discovered my country, and Russian literature became my country first and foremost.'] *Istoriya moego sovremennika*, chapter 27: V. G. Korolenko, *Sobranie sochinenii v pyati tomakh* (Leningrad, 1989–91), iv 270.

2   Virginia Woolf, 'Modern Fiction' (1918), in her *The Common Reader* (London, 1925), 189.

which you in fact know to be (because this cannot be doubted) the only goal worth seeking for its own sake. To linger on the surface, to spend yourself in increasingly elaborate descriptions of its properties and of your own sensations, was either moral idiocy or calculated immoralism, either blindness or a craven lie which would in the end destroy the man who told it. The truth alone was beautiful and it was always beautiful, it could never be hideous or destructive or bleak or trivial, and it did not live in the outer appearance. It lay 'beneath' (as Schelling, Plato, Hegel taught) and was revealed only to those who cared for the truth alone, and was therefore not for the neutral, the detached, the cautious, but for the morally committed, for those who were prepared to sacrifice all they had in order to discover and vindicate the truth, and liberate themselves and others from the illusions, conventions and self-deceptions which blinded men about the world and their duty in it. This creed was the creed, then enunciated for the first time, of the Russian intelligentsia, of the moral and political opposition to autocracy, to the Orthodox Church, and to the national way of life, the triple slogan of the supporters of the regime.

Naturally, with the temperament of a Lucretius or a Beethoven, Belinsky as a critic was, unlike his Western contemporaries, neither a classically pure connoisseur of Platonic forms like Landor, nor a sharp, pessimistic, disillusioned observer of genius like Sainte-Beuve; he was a moralist, painfully and hopefully sifting the chaff from the grain. If anything seemed to him new or valuable or important or even true, he would fly into ecstasies of enthusiasm and proclaim his discovery to the world in hurrying, ill-written, impassioned sentences, as if to wait might be fatal because the attention of the vacillating public might be distracted. Moreover one must herald the truth tumultuously, for to speak in an even voice would perhaps not indicate its crucial importance. And in this way Belinsky, in his exuberance, did discover and overpraise a handful of comparatively unknown and worthless writers and critics whose names are today justly forgotten. But he also revealed, and for the first time, the full glory of the great sun of Russian literature, Alexander Pushkin, and he discovered and assessed at their true worth Lermontov, Gogol, Turgenev and Dostoevsky, not to mention such writers of the second rank as

Goncharov, or Grigorovich, or Kol'tsov. Of course Pushkin had been recognised as a writer of genius before Belinsky had begun writing, but it was Belinsky's eleven famous essays that established his importance, not merely as a poet of magnificent genius, but as being, in the literal sense, the creator of Russian literature, of its language, its direction, and its place in the national life. Belinsky created the image of Pushkin, which henceforth dominated Russian writing, as a man who stood to literature as Peter the Great to the Russian State, the radical reformer, the breaker of the old, the creator of the new; the implacable enemy and the faithful child of the national tradition, as at once the invader of hitherto remote foreign territory and the integrator of the deepest and most national elements of the Russian past. With consistency and passionate conviction, Belinsky paints the portrait of a poet who justly saw himself as a herald and a prophet, because by his art he had made Russian society aware of itself as a spiritual and political entity, with its appalling inner conflicts, its anachronisms, its anomalous position among other nations, its huge untried strength and dark and tantalising future. With a multitude of examples he demonstrates that this was Pushkin's achievement, and not that of his predecessors – the official trumpeters of Russia's spirit and Russia's might – even of the most civilised and talented, such as the epic poet Derzhavin, the admired historian Karamzin, or his own mentor, the generous, romantic, mellifluous, always delightful Zhukovsky.

This unique domination of literature over life, and of one man over the entire consciousness and imagination of a vast nation, is a fact to which there is no precise parallel, not even in the place occupied in the consciousness of their nations by Dante or Shakespeare, Homer or Vergil or Goethe. And this extraordinary phenomenon, whatever may be thought of it, is, to a degree still unrecognised, the work of Belinsky and his disciples, who first saw in Pushkin the central planet, the source of light in whose radiance Russian thought and feeling grew so wonderfully. Pushkin himself, who was a gay, elegant, and, in his social life, an arrogant, disdainful and whimsical man, thought this embarrassing and spoke of the angular and unfashionable Belinsky as 'a queer character who for some extraordinary reason seems to adore me'.[1] He was a little frightened of him, half suspected that he had something to say, thought of asking him to contribute to the journal which he edited, recollected that his friends thought him unpresentable, and successfully avoided a personal meeting.

Pushkin's snobbery, his intermittent attempts to pretend that he was an aristocratic dilettante and not a professional man of letters at all, touched the socially sensitive Belinsky on the raw, just as the mask of worldly cynicism which Lermontov adopted had offended him at their first meeting. Nevertheless, in the presence of genius Belinsky forgot everything. He forgot Pushkin's coldness, he realised that behind Lermontov's Byronic mask, his insulting cynicism and desire to wound and be wounded, there was a great lyrical poet, a serious and penetrating critic, and a tormented human being of great tenderness and depth. The genius of these men had bound its spell upon him, and it is really in terms of their, and in particular Pushkin's, art and personality that Belinsky, whether he was aware of it or not, tried to define his own ideas of what a creative artist is and should be.

As a critic he remained, all his life, a disciple of the great German romantics. He sharply rejected the didactic and utilitarian doctrines of the function of art, then enjoying a vogue among the French socialists: 'Poetry has no purpose beyond itself. It is its own end, as truth is of knowledge, and the good of action.'[2] Earlier in the same article he says:

> The whole world, [its ...] colours and sounds, all the forms of nature and of life, can be poetical phenomena; but its essence is that which is concealed in these phenomena [. . .] that in them which enchants by the play of life [... The poet] is an impressionable, irritable organism, always active, which at the lightest touch gives off electric sparks, suffers more painfully than others, savours

---

1   [Untraced. Other sources for Pushkin's view of Belinsky include Pushkin, 'Pis'mo k izdatelyu' (23 April 1836), *Polnoe sobranie sochinenii* (Leningrad, 1937–59), xii 97; reply to Pushkin (October/November 1836) by P. V. Nashchokin, ibid. xvi 181 (Pushkin's letter does not survive); Belinsky to Gogol (1843), B xii 109.]

2   'Stikhotvoreniya M. Lermontova' (1841), B iv 496.

pleasures more fiercely, loves more violently, hates with more passion [. . .][1]

And again, literature is 'the fruit of free inspiration, of the united though not the premeditated efforts of men [. . .] who fully express [. . .] the spirit of the people [. . .] whose inward life they manifest [. . .] in its most hidden depths and pulsations.'[2] He rejected with passion the notion of art as a social weapon then preached by George Sand and Pierre Leroux: 'Do not worry about the incarnation of ideas. If you are a poet, your works will contain them without your knowledge – they will be both moral and national if you follow your inspiration freely.'[3]

This is an echo of August Wilhelm Schlegel and his allies. And from this early view Belinsky never retreated. Annenkov says that he looked in art for an 'integral'[4] answer to all human needs – to repair the gaps left by other, less adequate forms of experience; that he felt that perpetual return to the great classical works would regenerate and ennoble the reader, that they alone would resolve – by transforming his vision until the true relations of things were revealed – all moral and political problems; provided always that they remained spontaneous and self-subsistent works of art: worlds in themselves, and not the sham structures of moral or social propaganda. Belinsky altered his opinions often and painfully; but to the end of his days he believed that art – and in particular literature – gave the truth to those who sought it; that the purer the artistic impulse – the more purely artistic the work – the clearer and profounder the truth revealed; and he remained faithful to the romantic doctrine that the best and least alloyed art was necessarily the expression not merely of the individual artist but always of a milieu, a culture, a nation, whose voice, conscious

1   ibid. 494–5.
2   'Literaturnye mechtaniya' (1834), B i 24.
3   'O kritike i literaturnykh mneniyakh "Moskovskogo nablyudatelya"' (1836), B ii 154. [More literally, the second sentence runs 'If you are a poet – your works will contain an idea without your knowledge; do not try to be national: follow your inspiration freely – and you'll be national without knowing how; do not worry about morality, just create, don't make – and you'll be moral, even in spite of yourself, even if you try to be immoral! . . .']
4   op. cit. (152 above, note 1), chapter 35, 359; Titunik 221.

and unconscious, the artist was, a function without which he became trivial and worthless, and in the context of which alone his own personality possessed any significance. None of this would have been denied by his Slavophil opponents: their disagreements lay elsewhere.

And yet, despite his historicism – common to all romantics – Belinsky does not belong to those whose main purpose and skill consist in a careful critical or historical analysis of artistic phenomena, in relating a work of art or an artist to a precise social background, analysing specific influences upon his work, examining and describing the methods which he uses, providing psychological or historical explanations of the success or failure of the particular effects which he achieves. Belinsky did indeed now and then perform such tasks; and was, in effect, the first and greatest of Russian literary historians. But he detested detail and had no bent for scrupulous scholarship; he read unsystematically and widely; he read and read in a feverish, frantic way until he could bear it no longer, and then he wrote. This gives his writing an unceasing vitality, but it is scarcely the stuff of which balanced scholarship is made. Yet his criticism of the eighteenth century is not as blind and sweeping as his detractors have maintained. His work in assigning their due place to earlier Russian writers (for example, Tredyakovsky, Khemnitser, Lomonosov, Fonvizin and Dmitriev), and in particular his pages on the poet Derzhavin and the fabulist Krylov, are a model of insight and lucid judgement. And he did kill the reputations of a number of eighteenth-century mediocrities and imitators once and for all.

But a capacity for lasting literary verdicts is not where his genius lay. His unique quality as a literary critic, the quality which he possessed to a degree scarcely equalled by anyone in the West, is the astonishing freshness and fullness with which he reacts to any and every literary impression, whether of style or of content, and the passionate devotion and scruple with which he reproduces and paints in words the vivid original character, the colour and shape, above all the moral quality of his direct impressions. His life, his whole being, went into the attempt to seize the essence of the literary experience which he was at any given moment trying to convey. He had an exceptional capacity both for understanding and for articulating, but what distinguished him from other, at least in this respect equally gifted, critics, Sainte-Beuve for example, or Matthew Arnold, was that his vision was wholly direct – there is, as it were, nothing between him and the object. Several of his contemporaries, among them Turgenev, noted an almost physical likeness to a hawk or a falcon: and indeed he used to pounce upon a writer like a bird of prey, and tear him limb from limb until he had said all he had to say. His expositions were often too prolix, the style is uneven and sometimes tedious and involved; his education was haphazard, and his words have little elegance and little intrinsic magic. But when he has found himself, when he is dealing with an author worthy of him, whether he is praising or denouncing, speaking of ideas and attitudes to life, or of prosody and idiom, the vision is so intense, he has so much to say, and says it in so first-hand a fashion, the experience is so vivid and conveyed with such uncompromising and uninterrupted force, that the effect of his words is almost as powerful and unsettling today as it was upon his own contemporaries. He himself said that no one could understand a poet or a thinker who did not for a time become wholly immersed in his world, letting himself be dominated by his outlook, identified with his emotions; who did not, in short, try to live through the writer's experiences, beliefs and convictions. In this way he did in fact 'live through' the influence of Shakespeare and Pushkin, Gogol and George Sand, Schiller and Hegel, and as he changed his spiritual domicile he altered his attitude and denounced what he had previously praised, and praised what he had previously denounced. Later critics have accused him of being a chameleon, a sensitive surface which re-flected too much and altered too quickly, an unreliable guide, without a permanent core of inner principle, too impressionable, too undisciplined, vivid and eloquent, but without a specific, firm, critical personality, without a definite approach or an identifiable point of view. But this is unjust, and none of his contemporaries who knew him best would have begun to understand such a judgement. If ever there lived a man of rigorous, indeed over-rigorous, and narrow principle, dominated all his life by a remorseless, never-ceasing, fanatical passion for the truth, unable to compromise or adapt himself, even for a short time and superficially, to anything

which he did not wholly and utterly believe, it was Belinsky. If a
man does not alter his views about life and art, it is because he is
devoted to his own vanity rather than to the truth, he said.[1]
Belinsky radically altered his opinions twice, each time after a
painful crisis. On each occasion he suffered with an intensity
which Russians seem particularly capable of conveying by the use
of words, and he gave a full account of it, principally in his letters,
the most moving in the Russian language. Those who have read
them will know what I mean by the heroic quality of his grimly
undeviating, perpetually self-scrutinising honesty of mind and
feeling.

   Belinsky held several intellectual positions in his life, and turned
from one to another and exhausted each to the uttermost until,
with great tormenting effort, he would liberate himself from it, to
begin the struggle over again. He arrived at no final or consistent
outlook, and the efforts by tidy-minded biographers to divide his
thought into three or more distinct 'periods', each neatly self-
contained and coherent, ignore too many facts: Belinsky is always
'relapsing' towards earlier, 'abandoned', positions; his consistency
was moral, not intellectual. He began to philosophise in the mid-
1830s, as a young man of twenty-three, with that disgust and
sense of being asphyxiated by the police State of Nicholas I which
all young intellectuals with hearts and consciences felt, and he
adopted the philosophy then preached by the young Moscow
philosophers, Stankevich and Bakunin, to whose circle he
belonged. Idealism was a reaction to the grim suppression which
followed the abortive Decembrist revolt in 1825. The young Russian intellectuals, encouraged as they were to go to Germany
rather than to Louis-Philippe's dangerously fermenting France,
returned full of German metaphysics. Life on earth, material existence, above all politics, was repulsive but fortunately unimportant.
The only thing that mattered was the ideal life created by the
spirit, the great imaginative constructions by means of which man
transcended the frustrating material environment, freed himself
from its squalor, and identified himself with nature and with
God. The history of Western Europe revealed many such sublime

1   'Rech' o kritike' (1842), B vi 276.

achievements, and it was idle nationalistic cant to pretend that
Russia had anything to put beside this. Russian culture (so Belinsky in the 1830s was telling his readers) was an artificial, imported
growth, and till Pushkin arose could not be spoken of in the same
breath as Shakespeare, Dante, Goethe and Schiller, or even such
great realistic writers as Walter Scott and (of all writers) Fenimore
Cooper. Russian folk-song and *byliny* and popular epics were
more contemptible than even the second- and third-rate imitations
of French models which formed the miserable collection of repro-
ductions dignified under the name of national Russian literature.
As for the Slavophils, their passion for old Russian ways and
manners, for traditional Slav dress and Russian song and dances,
for archaic musical instruments, for the rigidities of Byzantine
Orthodoxy, their contrast of the spiritual depth and wealth of the
Slavs with the decadent and 'rotting' West, corrupted by superstition and sordid materialism – this was childish vanity and
delusion. What had Byzantium given? Its direct descendants, the
southern Slavs, were among the deadest and dullest of all European nations. If all the Montenegrins died tomorrow, Belinsky
cried in one of his reviews, the world would be none the poorer.
Compared to one noble voice from the eighteenth century, one
Voltaire, one Robespierre, what had Byzantium and Russia to
offer? Only the great Peter, and he belonged to the West. As for
the glorification of the meek and pious peasant – the holy fool
touched with grace – Belinsky, who, unlike the Slavophils, was by
birth not a nobleman or a gentleman, but the son of a sodden
small-town doctor, looked on agriculture not as romantic and
ennobling, but merely as degrading and stupefying. The Slavophils
infuriated him by talking romantic and reactionary nonsense in
their attempt to arrest scientific progress by appeals to ancient
and, as often as not, non-existent traditions. Nothing was more
contemptible than false, twopence-coloured nationalism, archaic
clothes, a hatred of foreigners, and a desire to undo the great
heroic work which Peter the Great had so boldly and magnificently
begun. Like the Encyclopedists of the eighteenth century in France,
whose temper his much resembled, Belinsky at the beginning of his
career (and again towards the end of his life) believed that only an
enlightened despot – by enforcing education, technical progress,

material civilisation – could rescue the benighted, barbarous
Russian nation. In a letter to a friend written in 1837 he writes:

> Above all you should abandon politics and guard yourself against
> the influence of politics on your ways of thought. Here in Russia,
> politics has no meaning, and only empty heads can have anything
> to do with it [. . .] If each of the individuals who compose Russia
> could reach perfection by means of love, Russia would be the
> happiest country in the world without any politics – education, that
> is the road to happiness.[1]

and again (in the same letter):

> Peter is clear evidence that Russia will not develop her liberty and
> her civil structure out of her own resources, but will obtain it at the
> hands of her tsars, as so much else. True, we do not as yet possess
> rights – we are, if you like, slaves; but that is because we still need
> to be slaves. Russia is an infant and needs a nurse in whose breast
> there beats a heart full of love for her fledgling, and in whose hand
> there is a rod ready to punish it if it is naughty. To give the child
> complete liberty is to ruin it. To give Russia in her present state a
> constitution is to ruin her. To our people liberty simply means
> *licence*. The liberated Russian nation would not go to a parliament,
> but run to the taverns to drink wine, break glass, and hang the
> gentry because they shave their beards and wear European clothes
> [. . .] The hope of Russia is education, not [. . .] revolutions and
> constitutions. France has had two revolutions, and as a result of
> them a constitution [. . .] And in this constitutional France there is
> far less liberty of thought than in autocratic Prussia.[2]

and again:

> Our autocracy gives us complete freedom of thought and reflection,
> but limits our freedom to raise our voices and interfere in her affairs.
> It allows us to import books from abroad which it forbids us to trans-

1   Letter to D. P. Ivanov, 7 August 1837, B xi 148.
2   ibid. 148–9.

late or publish. And this is right and just, because what you may know the *muzhik* may not; an idea which might be good for you, might be fatal to the *muzhik*, who would naturally misunderstand it [. . .] Wine is good for adults who know what to do with it, but fatal to children, and politics is wine which in Russia may even turn into opium [. . .] And so to the devil with the French. Their influence has brought us nothing but harm. We imitated their literature, and killed our own [. . .] Germany – that is the Jerusalem of modern humanity [. . .][1]

Even the Russian nationalist school did not go so far. At a time when even so Western a thinker as Herzen, not to speak of mild liberals such as Granovsky and Kavelin, was prepared to temporise, and indeed to some degree shared the Slavophils' deep and sincere feeling for the Russian tradition and older forms of life, Belinsky would not bend. Western Europe, more particularly enlightened despotism, was responsible for the major achievements of mankind. There and only there were the forces of life and the critical canons of scientific and philosophical truth, which alone made progress possible. The Slavophils had turned their backs on this, and however worthy their motives, they were blind and leaders of the blind, returning to the ancient slough of ignorant barbarism and weakness from which it had taken the great Peter such efforts to lift, or half-lift, his primitive people; salvation lay in this alone. This doctrine is radical, individualist, enlightened, and anti-democratic. Soviet authors in search of texts to justify the progressive role of ruthless governing élites find much to quote from Belinsky's early writings.

Meanwhile Bakunin had begun to preach Hegel to Belinsky, who knew no German. Night after night he preached the new objectivism to him, as he did later in Paris to Proudhon. Finally, after a fearful inner struggle, Belinsky was converted to the new anti-individualist faith. He had earlier toyed with the idealism of Fichte and Schelling, as expounded by Stankevich, the effect of which had been to turn him away from political issues altogether, as a sordid chaos of the trivial, empirical world, a delusive curtain concealing the harmonious reality beyond. This was now finished and done with. He moved to St Petersburg, and under the influence

1   ibid. 150, 152.

of his new religion wrote two celebrated articles in 1839–40, one reviewing a poem and a work of prose on an anniversary of the Battle of Borodino, the other a criticism of an attack by a German Hegelian on Goethe. 'The real is the rational', the new doctrine had said. It was childish and shallow and short-sighted to attack or seek to alter reality. What is, is, because it must be. To understand it is to understand the beauty and the harmony of everything as it falls into its own appointed time and place in accordance with intelligible and necessary laws. Everything has its place in the vast scheme of nature unrolling its pattern like a great carpet of history. To criticise is only to show that you are not adjusted to reality and that you do not sufficiently understand it. There were no half-measures for Belinsky. Herzen tells us that once Belinsky finally adopted a view, 'he [. . .] did not quail before any [. . .] consequences. He would not stop at considerations of moral propriety, or the opinion of others, which tends to frighten weaker and less independent natures. He knew no fear, because he was strong and sincere; his conscience was clear.'[1] His (or Bakunin's) interpretation of Hegel's doctrine had convinced him that contemplation and understanding was an attitude spiritually superior to that of active fighting: consequently he threw himself into 'acceptance of reality' with the same frenzy of passion as that with which only two years later he was to attack the quietists and demand active resistance to Nicholas I's abominations.

In 1838–40 Belinsky proclaimed that might was right; that history itself – the march of the inevitable forces – sanctified the actual; that autocracy was, coming when it did, sacred; that Russia was as it was as part of a divine scheme marching towards an ideal goal; that the government – the representative of power and coercion – was wiser than its citizens; that protests against it were frivolous, wicked and vain. Resistance to cosmic forces is always suicidal. 'Reality is a monster,' he wrote to Bakunin, 'armed with iron talons, a huge mouth and huge jaws. Sooner or later she will devour everyone who resists her, who cannot live at peace with her. To be free – and instead of a terrible monster to see in her the source of happiness – there is only one means – *to know*

1   'Byloe i dumy', part 4, chapter 25 (see 151 above, note 1), H ix 22; M ii 402.

her.'[1] And again: 'I look upon reality, which I used to hold in such contempt, and tremble with mystic joy, recognising its rationality, realising that nothing of it may be rejected, nothing in it may be condemned or spurned.'[2] And in the same vein: 'Schiller was [. . .] my personal enemy, and it was only with great effort that I was able to prevent my hatred of him from going beyond the bounds of such decency as I was capable of. Why this hatred?'[3] Because, he goes on to say, Schiller's works *Die Räuber, Kabale und Liebe* and *Fiesco* 'induced in me a wild hatred of the social order, in the name of an abstract ideal of society, cut off from the geographical and historical conditions of development, built in mid-air.'[4]

This echoes, but in a politically far more sinister form, the relatively harmless maxims of earlier, Fichtean Idealism, when he would declare that society is always more right than the individual, or 'The individual is real and not a phantom only to the degree to which he is an individual expression of the universal.'[5]

His friends were stupefied into silence. This was nothing less than a major betrayal by the most single-minded and most fearless of all the radical leaders. The shock was so painful that in Moscow it could scarcely be discussed at all. Belinsky knew precisely what effect his secession would cause, and said so in his letters; nevertheless he saw no way out. He had reached his conclusion by a rational process, and if the choice was between betraying the truth and betraying his friends, he must be man enough to betray his friends. Indeed the thought of the appalling pain that this would cause him somehow merely underlined the inescapable necessity of this great sacrifice to principle. This acceptance of the 'iron laws' of social development and the march of history as being not merely inevitable but just, rational, morally liberating, was nevertheless marked, both then and later, by a profound disgust with the conditions of Russian society in general and of his own society in particular.

Our life [he wrote to Konstantin Aksakov in 1840], what sort of life is it to be? Where is it and what is it about? We are so many

---

1   Letter to M. A. Bakunin, 10 September 1838, B xi 288.
2   ibid. 282.
3   Letter to N. V. Stankevich, 2 October 1839, B xi 385.
4   ibid.   5   'Gore ot uma' (1840), B iii 480.

individuals outside a society, because Russia is not a society. We possess neither a political nor a religious nor a scientific nor a literary life. Boredom, apathy, frustration, fruitless efforts – that is our life [. . .] China is a disgusting State, but more disgusting is a State which possesses rich materials for life but which is held in an iron frame like a rickety child.[1]

And the remedy? Conformity to the powers that be: adjustment to 'reality'. Like many a Communist of a later date Belinsky gloried in the very weight of the chains with which he had chosen to bind his limbs, in the very narrowness and darkness which he had willed to suffer; the shock and disgust of his friends was itself evidence of the vastness, and therefore of the grandeur and the moral necessity, of the sacrifice. There is no ecstasy to compare to that of self-immolation.

This condition lasted for a year, and then he could bear it no longer. Herzen paid a visit to him in St Petersburg; it had begun in a frigid and awkward manner, and then in a great burst of emotion Belinsky broke down, and admitted that the Hegelian year, with its wilful 'acceptance' and glorification of the black reaction of the regime, was a heavy nightmare, an offering upon the altar not of truth but of an insane logical consistency. What he cared about, what he had never ceased to care about, was not the historical process or the condition of the universe or the solemn march of the Hegelian God through the world, but the lives and liberties and aspirations of individual men and women whose sufferings no sublime universal harmony could explain away or redeem. From that moment he never looked back. The relief was immense:

I abominate [he wrote to Botkin] my contemptible desire to reconcile myself with a contemptible reality! Long live the great Schiller, noble advocate of humanity, bright star of salvation, the emancipator of society from the blood-stained prejudices of tradition! 'Long live reason, and may the darkness perish' as great Pushkin used to exclaim! *The human personality* is now above history, above society, above humanity for me [. . .] Good Lord, it frightens me to think of

1   Letter to K. S. Aksakov, 23 August 1840, B xi 546.

what must have been happening to me – fever, madness – I feel like a convalescent now [. . .] I will not make my peace or adjust myself to vile realities. I look for happiness only in the world of fancy, only fantasies make me happy. As for reality–reality is an executioner.[1]

And in the same year:

I am tormented by the thought of the pleasures I have let go because of the contemptible idealism and feebleness of my character [. . .] God knows what vile, revolting nonsense I have talked in print, with all the sincerity and fanaticism of deep, wild conviction! [. . .] And oh the mad nonsense which I have poured out [. . .] against the French, that energetic and noble nation, shedding its blood for the most sacred rights of mankind [. . .] I have awoken and recollect my dreams with horror [. . .] What horrible zigzags my path towards truth seems to involve, what a terrible price I have had to pay, what fearful blunders I have had to commit for the sake of truth, and what a bitter truth it is – how vile the world is, especially in our neighbourhood.[2]

And apropos the inexorable march of the Spirit (Herzen records): 'So it is not for myself that I create, but for the Spirit [. . .] Really what kind of an idiot does it take me for? I'd rather not think at all – what do I care about *Its* consciousness?'[3] And in his letters there are passages in which such sacred metaphysical entities as Universality – Cosmic Consciousness – the Spirit – the rational State and so forth are denounced as a Moloch of abstraction devouring living human beings.

A year later he finally settled accounts with the master himself:

1   Letter to V. P. Botkin, 4 October 1840, B xi 556, 559.
2   Letter to V. P. Botkin, 11 December 1840, B xi 576–7.
3   [Probably a paraphrase of Herzen's report of Belinsky's views in 'Du développement des idées révolutionnaires en Russie', H vii 107: ' "You want to make me believe that the aim of man is to bring the absolute spirit to self-consciousness, and you are satisfied with that role; as for me, I'm not stupid enough to serve as anybody's unwitting mouthpiece. If I think, if I suffer, it is for myself. Your absolute spirit, if it exists, is alien to me. I have no need to know it, since I have nothing in common with it." ']

All Hegel's talk about morality is utter nonsense, since in the objective realm of thought there is no morality [. . .] Even if I attained to
the actual top of the ladder of human development, I should at that
point still have to ask [Hegel] to account for all the victims of life
and of history, all the victims of accident and superstition, of the
Inquisition and Philip II, and so on and so forth; otherwise I will
throw myself off head-downwards. I am told that disharmony is a
condition of harmony. This may be found agreeable [. . .] by musical
persons, but is not quite so satisfactory from the point of view
of those whose fate it is to express in their lives the element of
disharmony.[1]

And in the same year he tries to explain the aberration:

[. . .] because [. . .] we understood that for us there is no life in real
life, and because our nature was such that without life we could not
live, we ran away into the world of books, and began to live and to
love according to books, and made life and love a kind of occupa-
tion, a kind of work, an anxious labour [. . . In the end] we bored
and irritated and maddened each other [. . .]

   Be social or die! That is my slogan. What is it to me that something
universal lives, so long as the individual suffers, that genius on earth
should live in heaven, while the common herd rolls in the mud?
What is it to me if *I* apprehend [. . .] the essence of art or religion
or history, if I cannot share this with all those who should be my
human brothers, my brethren in Christ, but are in fact strangers and
enemies because of their ignorance? [. . .] I cannot bear the sight of
barefoot boys playing [. . .] in the gutter, poor men in tatters, the
drunken cab-driver, the soldier coming off duty, the official padding
along with a portfolio under his arm, the self-satisfied army officer,
the haughty grandee. When I give a penny to a soldier I almost cry,
when I give a penny to a beggar I run from him as if I had done
something terrible, as if I did not wish to hear the sound of my own
steps [. . .] Has a *human being* the right to forget himself in art or
science, while this goes on?[2]

1   Letter to V. P. Botkin, 1 March 1841, B xii 22–3.
2   Letter to V. P. Botkin, 8 September 1841, B xii 67, 69–70.

He read the materialist Feuerbach and became a revolutionary democrat, denouncing tyranny, ignorance, and the bestial lives of his fellow countrymen with ever-increasing ferocity. After his escape from the spell of a half-understood German metaphysics he felt a sense of extreme liberation. As always the reaction took an external form and poured itself out in passionate paeans to individualism. In a letter to his friend Botkin he denounced his intellectual milieu for its lack of seriousness and personal dignity:

[. . .] we are the unhappy Anacharsises of the new Scythia. Why do we all gape, yawn, bustle and hurry and take an interest in everything and stick to nothing, and consume everything and remain hungry? [. . .] We love one another, we love warmly and deeply [. . .] and how have we shown our friendship? We used to be tremendously excited about one another, enthusiastic, ecstatic, we hated one another, we wondered about each other, we despised one another [. . .] When separated from each other for long we pined and wept salt tears at the mere thought of meeting, we were sick with love and affection: when we met, our meetings were cold and oppressive, and we would separate without regret. That is how it was, and it is time that we stopped deceiving ourselves [. . .] Our learned professors are pedants, a mass of social corruption [. . .] We are orphans [. . .] men without a country [. . .] The ancient world is enchanting: its life contains the seed of everything that is great, noble, valiant, because the foundation of its life is personal pride; the dignity and sanctity of the individual.[1]

There follows an ecstatic comparison of Schiller to Tiberius Gracchus and of himself to Marat. 'The human personality has become the point on which I fear I will go off my head. I am beginning to love mankind *à la* Marat: to make the smallest portion of it happy I am ready, I do believe, to destroy the rest by fire and sword.'[2] He loves only the Jacobins – only they are effective: 'the two-edged sword of word and deed – the Robespierres and the St Justs'; not 'the sugary and ecstatic turns of phrase, the pretty

---

1   Letter to V. P. Botkin, 27/28 June 1841, B xii 49, 50, 52.
2   ibid. 52.

idealism of the Gironde',[1] and this leads to socialism – of that pre-
Marxist, 'Utopian' kind, which Belinsky embraced before he understood it, because of its promise of equality: '[. . .] *socialism* [. . .] idea
of ideas, essence of essences [. . .] the alpha and omega of faith and
science [. . .] The day will come when nobody will be burnt alive,
nobody will have his head chopped off . . . There will be no rich,
no poor, no kings and subjects, but [men] will be brothers [. . .]'.[2]

It is this mystical vision that Dostoevsky had in mind when a good
many years after Belinsky's death he said: 'he believed [. . .] that
socialism not only does not destroy the freedom of the individual
personality but, on the contrary, restores it to unheard-of splendour, on new and this time adamantine foundations'.[3] Belinsky was
the first man to tell Dostoevsky, then still young and obscure, that
in his *Poor Folk* he had done in one stroke what the critics vainly
tried to do in lengthy essays – he had revealed the life of the grey,
humiliated, Russian minor official as nobody had ever done before;
but he disliked Dostoevsky personally and detested his Christian
convictions, and deliberately scandalised him by violent atheistic
and blasphemous tirades. His attitude to religion was that of Holbach or Diderot, and for the same reasons: 'in the words *God* and
religion I see only black darkness, chains and the knout'.[4]

In 1847 Gogol, whose genius Belinsky had acclaimed, published
a violently anti-liberal and anti-Western tract, calling for a return
to ancient patriarchal ways, a spiritually regenerated land of serfs,
landlords, the tsar. The cup brimmed over. In a letter written from
abroad Belinsky, in the last stages of his wasting disease, accused
Gogol of betraying the light:

> [. . .] one cannot be silent when, under cover of religion, backed by
> the whip, falsehood and immorality are preached as truth and virtue.
>
>   Yes, I loved you, with all the passion with which a man tied by
> ties of blood to his country loves its hope, its honour, its glory, one
> of its great leaders along the path of consciousness, development
> and progress [. . .] Russia sees her salvation not in mysticism or

1   Letter to V. P. Botkin, 15 April 1842, B xii 105.
2   Letter to V. P. Botkin, 8 September 1841, B xii 66, 70–1.
3   Dostoevsky, *Dnevnik pisatelya* (1873), D xi 12.
4   Letter to Herzen, 26 January 1845, B xii 250.

aestheticism, or piety, but in the achievements of education, civilisation and humane culture. She has no need of sermons (she has heard too many), nor of prayers (she has mumbled them too often), but of the awakening in the people of a feeling of human dignity, lost for so many ages in mud and filth. It needs laws and rights in accordance not with the teachings of the Church, but with those of common sense and justice [. . .] Instead of which she offers the terrible spectacle of a land where men buy and sell other men without even the cant of the American planters, who say that Negroes are not human beings, a country [. . .] where there are no guarantees of personal security or honour or property; not even a police State, only huge corporations of official thieves and robbers [. . .] The government [. . .] knows well what the landlords do to their peasants, and how many landlords are massacred by their serfs every year [. . .]

Preacher of the whip, apostle of ignorance, champion of obscurantism and black reaction, defender of a Tatar way of life – what are you doing? . . . Look at the ground beneath your feet. You are standing on the edge of an abyss . . . You found your teachings upon the Orthodox Church, and that I understand, for the Church has always favoured whips, it has always grovelled to despotism. But what has this to do with Christ? [. . .] Of course a Voltaire whose ridicule put out the flames of fanaticism and ignorance in Europe is far more a son of Christ, flesh of His flesh, and bone of His bone, than all your priests, bishops, metropolitans, patriarchs [. . .]

About whom do the Russian people tell obscene tales? [. . .] Is not the Russian priest in the eyes of all Russians a symbol of gluttony, miserliness, sycophancy and shamelessness? [. . .] Most of our clergy have always been distinguished by their fat bellies, theological pedantry and utter ignorance [. . .]

Only in literature, in spite of our Tatar censorship, there is still some life and forward movement. This is why the writer's calling enjoys such respect among us, why literary success is so easy here even when there is little talent. The title of poet, the profession of letters has thrown into the shade the glitter of epaulettes and gaudy uniforms. This is why, especially amongst us, universal attention is paid to every manifestation of any so-called liberal trend, no matter how poor the writer's gifts, while great poets who sincerely or insincerely sell their gifts to serve Orthodoxy, autocracy and the national

way of life quickly lose their popularity [. . .] And in this the public
is right. It sees in Russian writers its only leaders, defenders, and
saviours from the darkness of autocracy, Orthodoxy and the national
way of life. It can forgive a bad book but not a harmful one.[1]

He read this letter to his friends in Paris. 'This is a work of genius,'
Herzen said in a low voice to Annenkov, who records the scene,
'and I think his last will and testament.'[2] This celebrated document
became the bible of Russian revolutionaries. Indeed it is for reading it to an illicit discussion circle that Dostoevsky was condemned
to death, then sent to Siberia.

   Belinsky in his final phase was a humanist, an enemy of theology
and metaphysics, and a radical democrat, and by the extreme
force and vehemence of his convictions turned purely literary
disputes into the beginnings of social and political movements.
Turgenev said of him that there are two types of writer: a writer
may be brilliantly imaginative and creative, but remain on the
periphery of the collective experience of the society to which he
belongs. Or he may live at the centre of his society, being connected
'organically' with the emotions and state of mind of his community. Belinsky knew, as only true social critics do, where the
centre of moral gravity of a book, an opinion, an author, a movement, an entire society could be found. The central issue of Russian
society was not political but social and moral. The intelligent and
awakened Russian wanted above all to be told what to do, how
to live as an individual, as a private person. Turgenev testifies that
never were people more interested in the problems of life, and
never less in those of pure aesthetic theory, than in the 1840s and
1850s. The mounting repression made literature the only medium
within which any degree of free discussion of social questions
could take place. Indeed the great controversy between Slavophils
and 'Westerners', between the view of Russia as a still uncorrupted
spiritual and social organism, bound by impalpable links of
common love, natural piety and reverence for authority, to which

1   Letter to Gogol, 15 July 1847, B x 212–15, 217–18; *Belinsky, Chernyshev-
    sky, and Dobrolyubov: Selected Criticism*, ed. Ralph E. Matlaw (Bloom-
    ington and London, 1962), 83–7, 89.
2   op. cit. (152 above, note 1), chapter 35, 363; Titunik 224.

the application of artificial, 'soulless' Western forms and institutions had done, and would do, fearful damage; and, on the
other hand, the view of it held by the 'Westerners' as a retarded
semi-Asiatic despotism lacking even the rudiments of social justice
and individual liberty – this crucial debate, which split educated
Russians in the nineteenth century, was carried on principally
in the semi-disguise of literary and philosophical argument. The
authorities viewed neither side with favour, and, with some justice,
regarded public discussion of any serious issue as in itself a menace
to the regime. Nevertheless the effective techniques of suppression,
as we know them now, had not as yet been invented; and the
half-clandestine controversy continued, sharpened and rendered
more personal by the acute consciousness of their own social
origins which infected the opinions and quality of feeling of the
principal adversaries themselves.

Russia in Belinsky's day, in the 1830s and the 1840s, was still,
in the main, a feudal society. It was pre-industrial and, in certain
parts of it, semi-colonial. The State was based on sharply drawn
divisions which separated the peasantry from the merchants and
from the lower clergy, and there was a still wider gap which
divided the gentry from the nobility. It was not altogether impossible, although it was very difficult and very uncommon, to rise
from a lower to a higher stratum. But in order to do this a man
had to have not merely exceptional energy, exceptional ambition
and talent, but also a certain willingness and capacity to jettison
his past and to identify himself morally, socially and mentally
with the higher milieu, which on certain terms, if he tried hard
enough, might be prepared to receive and assimilate him. The
most remarkable Russian in the eighteenth century, the father of
polite letters and of the natural sciences in his country, Mikhail
Lomonosov – 'the Russian Leonardo' – was a man of obscure and
humble origin, but he rose and was transformed. There is a good
deal that is robust and vigorous, but nothing primitive, no trace of
a rustic accent, in his writing. He had all the zeal of a convert and
a self-taught one at that, and did more than anyone to establish the
formal conventions of Russian literary prose and verse in the later
eighteenth century, rigorously modelled on the most elaborate
European – that is to say French – practice of the time. Until the

second quarter of the nineteenth century the social élite alone possessed enough education, leisure and trained taste to pursue the fine arts, and in particular literature: they looked to the mandarins of the West, and borrowed little – at most here and there a touch of local colour – from the traditional arts and crafts still practised with skill and imagination by peasants and artisans in forgotten corners of the great Empire. Literature was an elegant accomplishment and was practised largely by aristocratic dilettanti and their protégés in St Petersburg, and to a lesser extent in Moscow – the first the seat of the government, the second the home of wealthy merchants and of the more solid and old-fashioned nobility, who looked with distaste on the chilly and sophisticated atmosphere of the Europeanised capital. The most characteristic names in the first generation of the great literary renaissance – Karamzin and Zhukovsky, Pushkin and Griboedov, Baratynsky and Venevitinov, Vyazemsky and Shakhovskoy, Ryleev and both Odoevskys – belong to this social stratum. A few individuals from outside were, indeed, permitted to enter: the critic and journalist Polevoy, the pioneer of literary naturalism in Russia, was the son of a merchant in Siberia; the lyrical poet Kol'tsov was a peasant to the end of his days. But such exceptions did not greatly affect the established literary hierarchy. The socially humble Polevoy, after beginning bravely enough as a *frondeur* against the élite, gradually assimilated himself completely to the style and methods of the dominant group, and ended his life (it is true, after persecution by the authorities) as a tame and frightened supporter of the Orthodox Church and the autocratic government. Kol'tsov, who retained his country idiom to the end, achieved fame precisely as such – as a primitive of genius, the simple peasant unspoilt by fame who charmed the sophisticated salons by the freshness and spontaneity of his gifts, and touched his well-born admirers by the almost exaggerated humility of his manner, and by his unhappy and self-effacing life.

Belinsky broke this tradition and broke it for ever. This he did because he entered the company of his social superiors on his own terms – without surrendering anything. He was an uncouth provincial when he arrived in Moscow, and he retained many of the tastes, prejudices and habits of his class to the end of his life.

He was born in poverty and bred in the atmosphere, at once bleak and coarse, of an obscure country town in a backward province. Moscow did, to some degree, soften and civilise him, but there remained to the end a core of crudeness, and a self-conscious, rough, sometimes aggressive tone in his writing. This tone enters Russian literature, never to leave it. Throughout the nineteenth century it is the distinguishing characteristic of the political radicals impatient of the urbanity of the non-political or conservative intelligentsia. As the revolutionary movement grew in intensity, this note becomes by turns strident and violent, or muted and ominous. Its use gradually became a matter of principle: a weapon deliberately employed by the intellectual *sans-culottes* against the supporters of the established order, the rude and defiant tone of the leaders of the underprivileged and oppressed, determined to do away once and for all with the polite fictions which merely conceal the deadness, futility, and above all the heartless wickedness of the prevailing system. Belinsky spoke with this accent because this kind of harshness was natural to him, because he was widely-read but half-educated, violently emotional, and unrestrained by conventional breeding or a naturally moderate temper, liable to storms of moral indignation, constantly boiling and protesting and crying out against iniquity or falsehood without regard to time or place or company. His followers adopted his manner because they were the party of the *enragés*, and this became the traditional accent of the new truth which had to be spoken with anger, with a sense of freshly suffered insult.

In this sense the real heir of Belinsky is the 'nihilist' Bazarov in Turgenev's *Fathers and Children*. When the cultivated but insufferable uncle in that novel, who stands for elegant manners and Pushkin and an aesthetic view of life (with which Turgenev himself feels to some degree identified, although not without a sense of guilt), enquires why the dissection of frogs and the other sordid paraphernalia of modern anatomy should be regarded as so supremely interesting or important, Bazarov replies with deliberate harshness and arrogance that this is so because they are 'true'. This kind of violent *boutade*, asserting the primacy of the material facts of life and nature, became the official battle-cry of the rebellious section of the intelligentsia, and it became a duty not merely to tell the unpalatable truth but to say it as loudly, as harshly, as disagreeably as possible, to trample with excessive brutality upon the delicate aesthetic values of the older generation, to employ shock tactics. The enemy was numerous, powerful and well-entrenched, and therefore the cause of truth could not triumph without wholesale destruction of his defence works, however valuable or attractive they might be in themselves. Belinsky did not himself develop this attitude to its fullest and most destructive extent, although Bakunin had begun to do so in his lifetime; he was too sensitive to artistic experience as such, too deeply under the spell of literary genius, whether it came from a radical or a reactionary source, and too honest to practise ruthlessness for its own sake. But the unbending, puritanical attitude to the truth, and particularly the passion for the seamy, the unmentionable side of everything, the insistence on asserting it at whatever cost, at whatever sacrifice of literary or social amenities, and consequently a certain exaggerated emphasis on angular, blunt, unambiguous terms calculated to provoke some kind of sharp reaction – that came from him and him alone, and it altered the style and content of the great political and artistic controversies of the hundred years and more since his death.

In the polite, elegant, spirited, gay, socially accomplished society of the intellectuals of Moscow and Petersburg he continued to speak, indeed at times to shout, in his own dissonant idiom, and remained independent, violent, maladjusted, and, indeed, what later came to be called 'class-conscious', to the end of his days; and he was felt to be a profoundly disturbing figure for precisely this reason, an unassimilable outsider, a dervish, a moral fanatic, a man whose unbridled behaviour threatened the accepted conventions upon which a civilised literary and artistic world rested. He secured this independence at a cost; he overdeveloped the harsher side of his nature, and sometimes flung off needlessly crude judgements, he was too intolerant of refinement and fastidiousness as such, too suspicious of the merely beautiful, and was sometimes artistically and morally blinded by the violence of his own moral dogmatism. But his individuality was so strong, the power of his words so great, his motives so pure and so intense, that (as I said before) the very roughness and clumsiness of his style created its

own tradition of literary sincerity. This tradition of protest and
revolt is of a quality wholly different from that of the well-born
and well-bred radicals of the 1840s who shook and in the end
destroyed the classical aristocratic façade of the 'Augustan age' of
Russian literature. The circle – or the two overlapping circles – in
which he moved, in his day still consisted principally of the sons of
land-owning squires. But in due course this aristocratic opposition
gave way to more violent figures drawn from the middle class and
the proletariat. Of these latter Belinsky is the greatest and most
direct ancestor.

Those left-wing writers of a later day inevitably tended to
imitate the defects of his qualities, and in particular the brutal
directness and carelessness of his diction as a measure of their
own contempt for the careful and often exquisite taste of the
polite *belles lettres* against which they were in such hot rebellion.
But whereas the literary crudities of such radical critics of the
1860s as Chernyshevsky or Pisarev were deliberate – a conscious
weapon in the war for materialism and the natural sciences, and
against the ideals of pure art, refinement, and the cultivation of
aesthetic, non-utilitarian attitudes to personal and social questions – Belinsky's case is more painful and more interesting. He
was not a crude materialist, and certainly not a utilitarian. He
believed in his critical calling as an end valuable in itself. He wrote
as he spoke – in shapeless, overlong, awkward, hurrying, tangled
sentences – only because he possessed no better means of
expression; because that was the natural medium in which he felt
and thought.

Let me remind you once again that Russian writing for several
decades, before and after Pushkin, practised, as it was, almost
exclusively by the 'awakened' members of the upper and upper-
middle class, drew on foreign, principally French and later German, sources, and was marked with an altogether exceptional
sensibility to style and subtlety of feeling. Belinsky's preoccupations, for all his insight into the process of artistic creation,
were predominantly social and moral. He was a preacher, he
preached with fervour, and could not always control the tone and
accent of his utterance. He wrote, as he spoke, with a grating,
occasionally shrill intonation, and Pushkin's friends – aesthetes

and mandarins – instinctively recoiled from this noisy, frantically
excited, half-educated vulgarian. Belinsky, whose admiration of
their magnificent achievement was wholehearted and boundless,
felt (as so often) wounded and socially humiliated. But he could
not alter his nature, nor could he alter or modify or pass over
the truth as he saw it, painfully but, from time to time, with
overwhelming clearness. His pride was great, and he was dedicated
to a cause; the cause was that of the unadorned truth, and in her
service he would live and die.

The literary élite, the friends of Pushkin, the Arzamas group as
they were called, despite radical ideas acquired abroad in the
victorious war against Napoleon, despite the Decembrist inter-
lude, was on the whole conservative, if not always politically, yet
in social habits and temper; it was connected with the Court and
the army and deeply patriotic. Belinsky, to whom this seemed a
retrograde outlook, a sin against the light of science and education,
was convinced that Russia had more to learn from the technologic-
ally progressive West than to teach it, that the Slavophil movement
was a romantic illusion, and, in its extreme form, blind nationalistic megalomania, that Western arts and sciences and forms of
civilised life offered the first and only hope of lifting Russia from
her backward state. Herzen, Bakunin, Granovsky believed this
too, of course. But then they had had a semi-Western education,
and found it both easy and agreeable to travel and live abroad
and to enter into social and personal relations with civilised
Frenchmen or Germans. Even the Slavophils who spoke of the
West as worthless and decadent were delighted by their visits to
Berlin or Baden-Baden or Oxford or even Paris itself.

Belinsky, who intellectually was so ardent a Westerner, was
emotionally more deeply and unhappily Russian than any of his
contemporaries, spoke no foreign languages, could not breathe
freely in any environment save that of Russia, and felt miserable
and persecution-ridden abroad. He found Western culture worthy
of respect and emulation, but Western habits of life were to him
personally quite insufferable. He began to sigh bitterly for home
as soon as he had left his native shore on a sea voyage to Germany;
the Sistine Madonna and the wonders of Paris did not comfort
him; after a month abroad he was almost insane with nostalgia.

In a very real sense he embodied the uncompromising elements of a Slav temperament and way of life to a sharper degree than his friends and contemporaries – whether like Turgenev they felt contented in Germany and Paris and unhappy in Russia, or, like the Slavophils, wore traditional Russian dress and secretly preferred a poem by Goethe or a tragedy by Schiller to any number of ancient Russian ballads or Slav chronicles. This deep inner conflict between intellectual beliefs and emotional, sometimes almost physical, needs is a characteristically Russian disease. As the nineteenth century developed, and as the struggle between social classes became sharper and more articulate, the contradiction, which tormented Belinsky, emerged more clearly. The Marxists or agrarian socialists or anarchists, when they are not noblemen or university professors, that is to say, to some degree professionally members of an international society, make their bow with great conviction and sincerity to the West in the sense that they believe in its civilisation, above all its sciences, its techniques, its political thought and practice, but when they are forced to emigrate, find life abroad more agonising than other exiles. Herzen, Bakunin, Turgenev, Lavrov were by birth gentlemen, and lived abroad, if not happily, at any rate without becoming embittered specifically by contact with it. Herzen did not greatly love Switzerland and he disliked Twickenham and London a great deal, but he preferred either to St Petersburg under Nicholas I, and he was happy in the society of his French and Italian friends. Turgenev seemed more than contented on Madame Viardot's estate at Bougival. But Belinsky can no more be thought of as a voluntary émigré than Dr Johnson or Cobbett. He stormed and ranted and denounced the most sacrosanct Russian institutions, but he did not leave his country. And although he must have known that imprisonment and slow and painful death were inevitable if he persisted, he did not, and obviously could not for a moment, contemplate emigrating beyond the frontiers of the Russian Empire: the Slavophils and the reactionaries were the enemy, but the battle could be fought only on native soil. He could not be silent and he would not go abroad. His head was with the West, but his heart and his ill-kept body were with the mass of inarticulate peasants and small traders – the 'poor folk' of

Dostoevsky, the inhabitants of the teeming world of Gogol's terrible comic imagination. Speaking of the Westerners' attitude to
the Slavophils, Herzen said:

> Yes, we were their opponents, but very peculiar ones. We had only
> *one* love, but *it did not take the same form.*
>
> From our earliest years, we were possessed by one powerful,
> unaccountable, physiological, passionate feeling, which they took
> for memory of the past, we for a vision of the future – a feeling of
> love, limitless, embracing all our being, love for the Russian people,
> the Russian way of life, the Russian type of mind. We, like Janus or
> the double-headed eagle, looked in opposite directions, while *one
> heart beat in us all.*[1]

Belinsky was not torn between incompatible ideals. He was an
integrated personality in the sense that he believed in his own
feelings, and was therefore free from the self-pity and the sentimentality which spring from indulgence in feelings which one does
not respect in oneself. But there was a division within him which
arose from a simultaneous admiration for Western values and
ideals, and a profound lack of sympathy with, indeed dislike and
lack of respect for, the characters and form of life of the Western
bourgeoisie and typical Western intellectuals. This ambivalence
of feeling, created by history – by the social and psychological
conditions which formed the Russian intellectuals in the nineteenth century – was inherited by and became prominent in the
next generation of radical intellectuals – in Chernyshevsky and
Nekrasov, in the populist movement, in the assassins of Alexander
II, and indeed in Lenin too, Lenin who could not be accused of
ignoring or despising the contributions of Western culture, but
felt far more alien in London or Paris than the more 'normal' type
of international exile. To some degree this peculiar amalgam of
love and hate is still intrinsic to Russian feelings about Europe: on
the one hand, intellectual respect, envy, admiration, desire to
emulate and excel; on the other, emotional hostility, suspicion and
contempt, a sense of being clumsy, *de trop*, of being outsiders;

1   loc. cit. (7 above, note 1).

leading, as a result, to an alternation between excessive self-prostration before, and aggressive flouting of, Western values. No visitor to the Soviet Union can have failed to remark something of this phenomenon: a combination of intellectual inadequacy and emotional superiority, a sense of the West as enviably self-restrained, clever, efficient and successful: but also as being cramped, cold, mean, calculating and fenced in, without capacity for large views or generous emotion, for feeling which must, at times, rise too high and overflow its banks, for heedless self-abandonment in response to some unique historical challenge, and consequently condemned never to know a rich flowering of life.

This spontaneity of feeling and passionate idealism are in themselves sufficient to distinguish Belinsky from his more methodical disciples. Unlike later radicals, he was not himself a utilitarian, least of all where art was concerned. Towards the end of his life he pleaded for a wider application of science, and more direct expression in art. But he never believed that it was the duty of the artist to prophesy or to preach – to serve society directly by telling it what to do, by providing slogans, by putting its art in the service of a specific programme. This was the view of Chernyshevsky and Nekrasov in the 1860s; of Lunacharsky and Mayakovsky and Soviet critics today. Belinsky, like Gorky, believed in the duty of the artist to tell the truth as he alone, being uniquely qualified to see and to utter, sees it and can say it; that this is the whole duty of a writer, whether he be a thinker or an artist. Moreover he believed that since man lives in society, and is largely made by society, this truth must necessarily be largely social, and that, for this reason, all forms of insulation and escape from environment must, to that degree, be falsifications of the truth, and treason to it. For him the man and the artist and the citizen are one; and whether you write a novel, or a poem, or a work of history or philosophy, or an article in a newspaper, or compose a symphony or a picture, you are, or should be, expressing the whole of your nature, not merely a professionally trained part of it, and you are morally responsible as a man for what you do as an artist. You must always bear witness to the truth, which is one and indivisible, in every act and in every word. There are no purely aesthetic truths or aesthetic canons. Truth, beauty, morality are attributes of life and cannot be abstracted from it, and what is intellectually false or morally ugly cannot be artistically beautiful, or vice versa. He believed that human existence was – or should be – a perpetual and desperate war between truth and falsehood, justice and injustice, in which no man had the right to be neutral or have relations with the enemy, least of all the artist. He declared war on the official nationalists because they suppressed and distorted or coloured the facts: and this was thought unpatriotic. He denounced copybook sentiments, and with a certain brutality of expression tried to formulate the crude truth behind them, and that was thought cynical. He admired first the German romantics, then only their radical wing, and then the French socialists, and was thought subversive. He told the Slavophils that inner self-improvement and spiritual regeneration cannot occur on an empty stomach, nor in a society which lacks social justice and suppresses elementary rights, and this was thought materialistic.

His life and personality became a myth. He lived as an idealised, severe and morally immaculate figure in the hearts of so many of his contemporaries that, after mention of his name was once again tolerated by the authorities, they vied with each other in composing glowing epitaphs to his memory. He established the relation of literature to life in a manner which even writers not at all sympathetic to his point of view, such as Leskov and Goncharov and Turgenev, all of whom in some sense pursued the ideal of pure art, were forced to recognise; they might reject his doctrine, but they were forced by the power of his invisible presence into having to settle accounts with him – if they did not, like Dostoevsky or Gogol, follow him, they at least felt it necessary to explain themselves on this matter. No one felt this need more acutely than Turgenev. Pulled one way by Flaubert, another by the awful apparition of his dead friend which perpetually arose before him, Turgenev vainly tried to placate both, and so spent much of his life in persuading himself and his Russian public that his position was not morally indefensible, and involved no betrayals or evasions. This search for one's proper place in the moral and the social universe continued as a central tradition in Russian literature virtually until the revolt in the 1890s of the neoclassicist aesthetes and the symbolists under Ivanov and

Bal'mont, Annensky and Blok. But these movements, splendid as their fruit was, did not last long as an effective force. And the Soviet revolution returned, albeit in a crude and distorted utilitarian form, to the canons of Belinsky and the social criteria of art.

Many things have been said against Belinsky, particularly by the opponents of naturalism, and some of them it is difficult to deny. He was wildly erratic, and all his enthusiasm and seriousness and integrity do not make up for lapses of insight or intellectual power. He declared that Dante was not a poet; that Fenimore Cooper was the equal of Shakespeare; that *Othello* was the product of a barbarous age; that Pushkin's poem *Ruslan and Lyudmila* was 'infantile',[1] that his *Tales of Belkin* and *Fairy Tales* were worthless, and Tatyana in *Evgeny Onegin* 'a moral embryo'.[2] There are equally wild remarks about Racine and Corneille and Balzac and Hugo. Some of these are due to irritation caused by the pseudo-medievalism of the Slavophils, some to an oversharp reaction against his old master Nadezhdin and his school, which laid down that it was inartistic to deal with what is dark or ugly or monstrous, when life and nature contain so much that is beautiful and harmonious; but it is mostly due to sheer critical blindness. He did damn the magnificent poet Baratynsky out of hand, and erased a gifted minor contemporary of Pushkin – the lyrical poet Benediktov – out of men's minds for half a century, for no better reason than that he disliked mere delicacy without moral fervour. And he began to think that he was mistaken in proclaiming the genius of Dostoevsky, who was perhaps no more than an exasperating religious neurotic with persecution mania. His criticism is very uneven. His essays in artistic theory, despite good pages, seem arid and artificial and conceived under the influence of Procrustean German systems, alien to his concrete, impulsive and direct sense of life and art. He wrote and talked a very great deal, and said far too much about too many unrelated things, and too often spoke incoherently and naively, with the uncritical exaggeration and half-baked dogmatism of an auto-didact – always in a dither of excitement, always frantic, always

1   'Sochineniya Aleksandra Pushkina', No 6 (1844), B vii 358.
2   ibid. No 9 (1845), B vii 499.

hurrying, falling and rising and stumbling on, sometimes pathetically ill-equipped, hurrying desperately wherever the battle
between truth and falsehood, life and death, seemed most critical.
He was the more erratic because he took pride in what seemed to
him freedom from petty qualities, from neatness and tidiness and
scholarly accuracy, from careful judgement and knowing how far
to go. He could not bear the cautious, the morally timid, the
intellectually genteel, the avoiders of crises, the *bien pensant* seekers of compromise, and attacked them in long and clumsy periods
full of fury and contempt. Perhaps he was too intolerant, and
morally lop-sided, and overplayed his own feelings. He need not,
perhaps, have hated Goethe quite so much for his, to him, maddening serenity, or the whole of Polish literature for being Polish and
in love with itself. And these are not accidental blemishes, they
are the defects inherent in everything that he is and stands for.
To dislike them overmuch is ultimately to condemn his positive
attitude too. The value and influence of his position reside precisely
in his lack of, and conscious opposition to, artistic detachment:
for he saw in literature the expression of everything that men have
felt and thought and have had to say about life and society,
their central attitude to man's situation and to the world, the
justification of their whole life and activity, and consequently
looked on it with the deepest possible concern. He abandoned no
view, however eccentric, until he had tried it out on himself as it
were, until he had 'lived himself' through it, and paid the price in
nervous waste and a sense of inadequacy, and sometimes total
failure. He put truth, however fitfully glimpsed, however dull or
bleak it might turn out to be, so far above other aims that he
communicated a sense of its sanctity to others and thereby transformed the standards of criticism in Russia.

Because his consuming passion was confined to literature and
books, he attached immense importance to the appearance of new
ideas, new literary methods, above all new concepts of the relation
of literature and life. Because he was naturally responsive to everything that was living and genuine, he transformed the concept of
the critic's calling in his native country. The lasting effect of his
work was in altering, and altering crucially and irretrievably,
the moral and social outlook of the leading younger writers and

thinkers of his time. He altered the quality and the tone both of
the experience and of the expression of so much Russian thought
and feeling that his role as a dominant social influence overshadows his attainments as a literary critic. Every age has its official
preachers and prophets who castigate its vices and call men to a
better life. Yet it is not by them that its deepest *malaise* is revealed,
but in the artists and thinkers dedicated to the more painful and
difficult task of creation, description and analysis – it is they, the
poets, the novelists, the critics, who live through the moral agony
of their society in their own personal experience; and it is they,
their victories and their defeats, that affect the fate of their generation and leave the most authentic testimony of the battle itself for
the benefit of interested posterity. Nekrasov was a very gifted poet,
but before everything he was a preacher and a propagandist of
genius; consequently it was not he but Belinsky who first saw the
central issue and saw it more clearly and directly and simply than
anyone would ever see it again. Nor did the thought ever seem to
arise in his mind that it might be possible not to face it with all its
implications, to practise caution, to be more circumspect in one's
choice of a moral and political position, or perhaps even to retire
to a neutral and disinterested attitude above the din of the battle.
'He knew no fear, because he was strong and sincere; his conscience was clear.'[1] It is because he committed himself so violently
and irrevocably to a very specific vision of the truth, and to a very
specific set of moral principles to govern both thought and action,
at a price which grew greater continually to himself and those
who chose to follow him, that his life and his outlook alternately
appalled and inspired the generation which came after him. No
final verdict had been declared upon him in his own lifetime. Not
even official canonisation in his native country has finally laid the
ghost of his doubts and torments or stilled his indignant voice.
The issues on which he spent his life are today more alive – and,
in consequence of revolutionary forces which he himself did so
much to set in motion, more pressing and more threatening – than
ever before.

1   loc. cit. (190 above, note 1).

4
Alexander Herzen (1812~ 1870)

Alexander Herzen is the most arresting Russian political writer in the nineteenth century. No good biographies of him exist, perhaps because his own autobiography is a great literary masterpiece. It is not widely known in English-speaking countries, and that for no good reason, for it has been translated into English, the first part magnificently by J. D. Duff, and the whole adequately by Constance Garnett; unlike some works of political and literary genius, it is, even in translation, marvellously readable.

In some respects, it resembles Goethe's *Dichtung und Wahrheit* more than any other book. For it is not a collection of wholly personal memoirs and political reflections. It is an amalgam of personal detail, descriptions of political and social life in various countries, of opinions, personalities, outlooks, accounts of the author's youth and early manhood in Russia, historical essays, notes of journeys in Europe, France, Switzerland, Italy, of Paris and Rome during the revolutions of 1848 and 1849 (these last are incomparable, and the best personal documents about these events that we possess), discussions of political leaders, and of the aims and purposes of various parties. All this is interspersed with a variety of comment, pungent observation, sharp and spontaneous, occasionally malicious, vignettes of individuals, of the character of peoples, analyses of economic and social facts, discussions and epigrams about the future and past of Europe and about the author's own hopes and fears for Russia; and interwoven with this is a detailed and poignant account of Herzen's personal tragedy, perhaps the most extraordinary self-revelation on the part of a sensitive and fastidious man ever written down for the benefit of the general public.

Alexander Ivanovich Herzen was born in Moscow in 1812, not long before the capture of the city by Napoleon, the illegitimate son of Ivan Yakovlev, a rich and well-born Russian gentleman, descended from a cadet branch of the Romanovs, a morose, difficult, possessive, distinguished and civilised man, who bullied his son, loved him deeply, embittered his life, and had an enormous influence upon him both by attraction and repulsion. His mother, Luise Haag, was a mild German lady from Stuttgart in Württemberg, the daughter of a minor official. Ivan Yakovlev had met her while travelling abroad, but never married her. He took her to Moscow, established her as mistress of his household, and called his son Herzen in token, as it were, of the fact that he was the child of his heart, but not legitimately born and therefore not entitled to bear his name.

The fact that Herzen was not born in wedlock probably had a considerable effect on his character, and may have made him more rebellious than he might otherwise have been. He received the regular education of a rich young nobleman, went to the University of Moscow, and there early asserted his vivid, original, impulsive character. He was born (in later years he constantly came back to this) into the generation of what in Russia came to be called *lishnie lyudi*, 'superfluous men',[1] with whom Turgenev's early novels are so largely concerned.

These young men have a place of their own in the history of European culture in the nineteenth century. They belonged to the class of those who are by birth aristocratic, but who themselves go over to some freer and more radical mode of thought and of action. There is something singularly attractive about men who retain, throughout life, the manners, the texture of being, the habits and style of a civilised and refined milieu. Such men exercise a peculiar kind of personal freedom which combines spontaneity with distinction. Their minds see large and generous horizons, and, above all, reveal a unique intellectual gaiety of a kind that aristocratic education tends to produce. At the same time, they are intellectually on the side of everything that is new, progressive, rebellious, young, untried, of that which is about to come into

1   [See 172 above, note 1.]

being, of the open sea, whether or not there is land that lies beyond. To this type belong those intermediate figures, like Mirabeau, Charles James Fox, Franklin Roosevelt, who live near the frontier that divides old from new, between the *douceur de la vie* which is about to pass and the tantalising future, the dangerous new age that they themselves do much to bring into being.

Herzen belonged to this milieu. In his autobiography he has described what it was like to be this kind of man in a suffocating society, where there was no opportunity of putting to use one's natural gifts, what it meant to be excited by novel ideas which came drifting in from all kinds of sources, from classical texts and the old Utopias of the West, from French social preachers and German philosophers, from books, journals, casual conversations, only to remember that the milieu in which one lived made it absurd even to begin to dream of creating in one's own country those harmless and moderate institutions which had long become forms of life in the civilised West.

This normally led to one of two results: either the young enthusiast simply subsided, and came to terms with reality, and became a wistful, gently frustrated landowner, who lived on his estate, turned the pages of serious periodicals imported from Petersburg or abroad, and occasionally introduced new pieces of agricultural machinery or some other ingenious device which had caught his fancy in England or in France. Such enthusiasts would endlessly discuss the need for this or that change, but always with the melancholy implication that little or nothing could or would be done; or, alternatively, they would give in entirely and fall into a species of gloom or stupor or violent despair, becoming self-devouring neurotics, destructive personalities slowly poisoning both themselves and the life round them.

Herzen was resolved to escape from both these familiar predicaments. He was determined that of him, at any rate, nobody would say that he had done nothing in the world, that he had offered no resistance and collapsed. When he finally emigrated from Russia in 1847 it was to devote himself to a life of activity. His education was that of a dilettante. Like most young men brought up in an aristocratic milieu, he had been taught to be too many things to too many men, to reflect too many aspects of life, and situations, to be able to concentrate sufficiently upon any one particular activity, any one fixed design.

Herzen was well aware of this. He talks wistfully about the good fortune of those who enter peacefully upon some steady, fixed profession, untroubled by the many countless alternatives open to gifted and often idealistic young men who have been taught too much, are too rich, and are offered altogether too wide an opportunity of doing too many things, and who, consequently, begin, and are bored, and go back and start down a new path, and in the end lose their way and drift aimlessly and achieve nothing. This was a very characteristic piece of self-analysis: filled with the idealism of his generation in Russia that both sprang from and fed the growing sense of guilt towards 'the people', Herzen was passionately anxious to do something memorable for himself and his country. This anxiety remained with him all his life. Driven by it he became, as everyone knows who has any acquaintance with the modern history of Russia, perhaps the greatest of European publicists of his day, and founded the first free – that is to say, anti-tsarist – Russian press in Europe, thereby laying the foundation of revolutionary agitation in his country.

In his most celebrated periodical, which he called the *Bell* (*Kolokol*), he dealt with anything that seemed to be of topical interest. He exposed, he denounced, he derided, he preached, he became a kind of Russian Voltaire of the mid-nineteenth century. He was a journalist of genius, and his articles, written with brilliance, gaiety and passion, although, of course, officially forbidden, circulated in Russia and were read by radicals and conservatives alike. Indeed it was said that the Emperor himself read them; certainly some among his officials did so; during the heyday of his fame Herzen exercised a genuine influence within Russia itself – an unheard-of phenomenon for an émigré – by exposing abuses, naming names, but, above all, by appealing to liberal sentiment, which had not completely died, even at the very heart of the tsarist bureaucracy, at any rate during the 1850s and 1860s.

Unlike many who find themselves only on paper, or on a public platform, Herzen was an entrancing talker. Probably the best description of him is to be found in the essay from which I have taken my title – 'A Remarkable Decade', by his friend Annenkov. It was written some twenty years after the events that it records.

I must own [Annenkov wrote] that I was puzzled and overwhelmed, when I first came to know Herzen – by this extraordinary mind which darted from one topic to another with unbelievable swiftness, with inexhaustible wit and brilliance; which could see in the turn of somebody's talk, in some simple incident, in some abstract idea, that vivid feature which gives expression and life. He had a most astonishing capacity for instantaneous, unexpected juxtaposition of quite dissimilar things, and this gift he had in a very high degree, fed as it was by the powers of the most subtle observation and a very solid fund of encyclopedic knowledge. He had it to such a degree that, in the end, his listeners were sometimes exhausted by the inextinguishable fireworks of his speech, the inexhaustible fantasy and invention, a kind of prodigal opulence of intellect which astonished his audience. After the always ardent but remorselessly severe Belinsky, the glancing, gleaming, perpetually changing and often paradoxical and irritating, always wonderfully clever, talk of Herzen demanded of those who were with him not only intense concentration, but also perpetual alertness, because you had always to be prepared to respond instantly. On the other hand, nothing cheap or tawdry could stand even half an hour of contact with him. All pretentiousness, all pompousness, all pedantic self-importance, simply fled from him or melted like wax before a fire. I knew people, many of them what are called serious and practical men, who could not bear Herzen's presence. On the other hand, there were others [. . .] who gave him the most blind and passionate adoration [. . .]

He had a natural gift for criticism – a capacity for exposing and denouncing the dark sides of life. And he showed this trait very early, during the Moscow period of his life of which I am speaking. Even then Herzen's mind was in the highest degree rebellious and unmanageable, with a kind of innate, organic detestation of anything which seemed to him to be an accepted opinion sanctified by general silence about some unverified fact. In such cases the predatory powers of his intellect would rise up in force and come into the open, sharp, cunning, resourceful. He lived in Moscow [. . .] still unknown to the public, but in his own familiar circle he was already known as a witty and a dangerous observer of his friends. Of course, he could not altogether conceal the fact that he kept secret dossiers, secret protocols of his own, about his dearest friends and distant acquaintances, within the privacy of his own thoughts. People who stood by his side, all innocence and trustfulness, were invariably amazed, and sometimes extremely annoyed, when they suddenly came on one or other side of this involuntary activity of his mind. Strangely enough, Herzen combined with this the tenderest, most loving relations with his chosen intimates, although even they could never escape his pungent analyses. This is explained by another side of his character.

As if to restore the equilibrium of his moral organism, nature took care to place in his soul one unshakeable belief, one unconquerable inclination. Herzen believed in the noble *instincts* of the human heart. His analysis grew silent and reverent before the instinctive impulses of the moral organism as the sole, indubitable truth of existence. He admired anything which he thought to be a noble or passionate impulse, however mistaken; and he never amused himself at its expense. This ambivalent, contradictory play of his nature – suspicion and denial on the one hand and blind faith on the other – often led to perplexity and misunderstandings between him and his friends, and sometimes to quarrels and scenes. But it is precisely in this crucible of argument, in its flames, that up to the very day of his departure for Europe, people's devotion to him used to be tested and strengthened instead of disintegrating. And this is perfectly intelligible. In all that Herzen did and all that Herzen thought at this time there never was the slightest trace of anything false, no malignant feeling nourished in darkness, no calculation, no treachery. On the contrary, the whole of him was always there, in every one of his words and deeds. And there was another reason which made one sometimes forgive him even insults, a reason which may seem unplausible to people who did not know him.

With all this proud, strong, energetic intellect, Herzen had a wholly gentle, amiable, almost feminine character. Beneath the stern outward aspect of the sceptic, the satirist, under the cover of a most unceremonious, and exceedingly unreticent humour, there dwelt the heart of a child. He had a curious, angular kind of charm, an angular kind of delicacy, [. . . but it was given] particularly to those who were beginning, who were seeking after something, people who were trying out their powers. They found a source of strength and confidence in his advice. He took them into the most intimate communion with himself and with his ideas – which, nevertheless, did not stop him, at times, from using his full destructive, analytic powers, from performing exceedingly painful, psychological experiments on these very same people at the very same time.[1]

This vivid and sympathetic vignette tallies with the descriptions left to us by Turgenev, Belinsky and others of Herzen's friends. It is borne out, above all, by the impression which the reader gains if he reads his own prose, his essays or the autobiographical memoirs collected under the title *My Past and Thoughts.* The impression that it leaves is not conveyed even by Annenkov's devoted words.

The chief influence on Herzen as a young man in Moscow University, as upon all the young Russian intellectuals of his time, was of course that of Hegel. But although he was a fairly orthodox Hegelian in his early years, he turned his Hegelianism into something peculiar, personal to himself, very dissimilar from the theoretical conclusions which the more serious-minded and pedantic of his contemporaries deduced from that celebrated doctrine.

The chief effect upon him of Hegelianism seems to have been the belief that no specific theory or single doctrine, no one interpretation of life, above all, no simple, coherent, well-constructed schema – neither the great French mechanistic models of the eighteenth century, nor the romantic German edifices of the nineteenth, nor the visions of the great Utopians Saint-Simon, Fourier, Owen, nor the socialist programmes of Cabet or Leroux or Louis Blanc – could conceivably be true solutions to real problems, at least not in the form in which they were preached.

He was sceptical if only because he believed (whether or not he derived this view from Hegel) that there could not in principle be any simple or final answer to any genuine human problem; that if a question was serious and indeed agonising, the answer could

1   op. cit. (152 above, note 1), chapter 17, 218–20; Titunik 86–8.

never be clear-cut and neat. Above all, it could never consist in some symmetrical set of conclusions, drawn by deductive means from a collection of self-evident axioms.

This disbelief begins in Herzen's early, forgotten essays which he wrote at the beginning of the 1840s, on what he called dilettantism and Buddhism in science; where he distinguishes two kinds of intellectual personality, against both of which he inveighs. One is that of the casual amateur who never sees the trees for the wood; who is terrified, Herzen tells us, of losing his own precious individuality in too much pedantic preoccupation with actual, detailed facts, and therefore always skims over the surface without developing a capacity for real knowledge; who looks at the facts, as it were, through a kind of telescope, with the result that nothing ever gets articulated save enormous, sonorous generalisations floating at random like so many balloons.

The other kind of student – the Buddhist – is the person who escapes from the wood by frantic absorption in the trees; who becomes an intense student of some tiny set of isolated facts, which he views through more and more powerful microscopes. Although such a man might be deeply learned in some particular branch of knowledge, almost invariably – and particularly if he is a German (and almost all Herzen's gibes and insults are directed against the hated Germans, and that despite the fact that he was half German himself) – he becomes intolerably tedious, pompous and blindly philistine; above all, always repellent as a human being.

Between these poles it is necessary to find some compromise, and Herzen believed that if one studied life in a sober, detached and objective manner, one might perhaps be able to create some kind of tension, a sort of dialectical compromise, between these opposite ideals; for if neither of them can be realised fully and equally, neither of them should be altogether deserted; only thus could human beings be made capable of understanding life in some profounder fashion than if they committed themselves recklessly to one or the other of the two extremes.

This ideal of detachment, moderation, compromise, dispassionate objectivity which Herzen at this early period of his life was preaching was something deeply incompatible with his temperament. And indeed, not long after, he bursts forth with a great

paean to partiality. He declares that he knows that this will not
be well received. There are certain concepts which simply are not
received in good society – rather like people who have disgraced
themselves in some appalling way. Partiality is not something
which is well thought of in comparison, for example, with abstract
justice. Nevertheless, nobody has ever said anything worth saying
unless he was deeply and passionately partial.

There follows a long and typically Russian diatribe against the
chilliness, meanness, impossibility and undesirability of remaining
objective, of being detached, of not committing oneself, of not
plunging into the stream of life. The passionate voice of his friend
Belinsky is suddenly audible in Herzen's writings in this phase of
his development.

The fundamental thesis which emerges at this time, and is then
developed throughout his later life with marvellous poetry and
imagination, is the terrible power over human lives of ideological
abstractions (I say poetry advisedly; for as Dostoevsky in later
years very truly said, whatever else might be said about Herzen,
he was certainly a Russian poet; which saved him in the eyes of
this jaundiced but, at times, uncannily penetrating critic: Herzen's
views or mode of life naturally found little favour in his eyes).

Herzen declares that any attempt to explain human conduct in
terms of, or to dedicate human beings to the service of, any
abstraction, be it never so noble – justice, progress, nationality –
even if preached by impeccable altruists like Mazzini or Louis
Blanc or Mill, always leads in the end to victimisation and human
sacrifice. Men are not simple enough, human lives and relationships are too complex for standard formulae and neat solutions,
and attempts to adapt individuals and fit them into a rational
schema, conceived in terms of a theoretical ideal, be the motives
for doing it never so lofty, always lead in the end to a terrible
maiming of human beings, to political vivisection on an ever-
increasing scale. The process culminates in the liberation of some
only at the price of enslavement of others, and the replacing of an
old tyranny with a new and sometimes far more hideous one – by
the imposition of the slavery of universal socialism, for example,
as a remedy for the slavery of the universal Roman Church.

There is a typical piece of dialogue between Herzen and Louis

Blanc, the French socialist (whom he respected greatly), which Herzen quotes, and which shows the kind of levity with which Herzen sometimes expressed his deepest convictions. The conversation is described as having taken place in London somewhere in the early 1850s. One day Louis Blanc observed to Herzen that human life was a great social duty, that man must always sacrifice himself to society.

> 'Why?' I asked suddenly.
>
> 'How do you mean "Why?" [said Louis Blanc] – but surely the whole purpose and mission of man is the well-being of society?'
>
> 'But it will never be attained if everyone makes sacrifices and nobody enjoys himself.'
>
> 'You are playing with words.'
>
> 'The muddle-headedness of a barbarian,' I replied, laughing.[1]

In this gay and apparently casual passage, Herzen embodies his central principle – that the goal of life is life itself, that to sacrifice the present to some vague and unpredictable future is a form of delusion which leads to the destruction of all that alone is valuable in men and societies – to the gratuitous sacrifice of the flesh and blood of live human beings upon the altar of idealised abstractions.

Herzen is revolted by the central substance of what was being preached by some of the best and purest-hearted men of his time, particularly by socialists and utilitarians, namely that vast suffering in the present must be undergone for the sake of an ineffable felicity in the future, that thousands of innocent men may be forced to die that millions might be happy – battle cries that were common even in those days, and of which a great deal more has been heard since. The notion that there is a splendid future in store for humanity, that it is guaranteed by history, and that it justifies the most appalling cruelties in the present – this familiar piece of political eschatology, based on belief in inevitable progress, seemed to him a fatal doctrine directed against human life.

The profoundest and most sustained – and the most brilliantly

1   loc. cit. (93 above, note 1).

written – of all Herzen's statements on this topic is to be found in
the volume of essays which he called *From the Other Shore*, and
wrote as a memorial to his disillusionment with the European
revolutions of 1848 and 1849. This great polemical masterpiece
is Herzen's profession of faith and his political testament. Its
tone and content are well conveyed in the characteristic (and
celebrated) passage in which he declares that one generation must
not be condemned to the role of being a mere means to the welfare
of its remote descendants, which is in any case none too certain.
A distant goal is a cheat and a deception. Real goals must be closer
than that – 'at the very least the labourer's wage or pleasure in
work performed'.[1] The end of each generation is itself – each life
has its own unique experience; the fulfilment of its wants creates
new needs, claims, new forms of life. Nature, he declares (perhaps
under the influence of Schiller), is careless of human beings and
their needs, and crushes them heedlessly. Has history a plan, a
libretto? If it did 'it would lose all interest, become unnecessary,
boring, ludicrous'. There are no timetables, no cosmic patterns;
there is only the 'fire of life', passion, will, improvisation; sometimes roads exist, sometimes not; where there is no road 'genius
will blast a path'.[2]

But what if someone were to ask, 'Supposing all this is suddenly
brought to an end? Supposing a comet strikes us and brings to an
end life on earth? Will history not be meaningless? Will all this
talk suddenly end in nothing? Will it not be a cruel mockery of all
our efforts, all our blood and sweat and tears, if it all ends in some
sudden, unexplained brute fashion with some mysterious, totally
unexplained event?' Herzen replies that to think in these terms is
a great vulgarity, the vulgarity of mere numbers. The death of
a single human being is no less absurd and unintelligible than
the death of the entire human race; it is a mystery we accept;
merely to multiply it enormously and ask 'Supposing millions of
human beings die?' does not make it more mysterious or more
frightening. 'In nature, as in the souls of men, there slumber
endless possibilities and forces, and in suitable conditions – they

1   'S togo berega', H vi 34; F 37. [See also 105 above.]
2   ibid. 36; F 39.

develop, and will develop furiously. They may fill a world, or they may fall by the roadside. They may take a new direction. They may stop. They may collapse [. . .] Nature is perfectly indifferent to what happens . . .'[1]

What is all this for? The life of people becomes a pointless game. Men build something with pebbles and sand only to see it all collapse again; and human creatures crawl out from underneath the ruins and again start clearing spaces and build huts of moss and planks and broken capitals and, after centuries of endless labour, it all collapses again. Not in vain did Shakespeare say that history was a tedious tale told by an idiot [. . .]

[To this I reply that . . .] you are like [. . .] those very sensitive people who shed a tear whenever they recollect that 'man is born but to die'. To look at the end and not at the action itself is a cardinal error. Of what use to the flower is its bright magnificent bloom? Or this intoxicating scent, since it will only pass away? None at all. But nature is not so miserly. She does not disdain what is transient, what is only in the present. At every point she achieves all she can achieve [. . .] Who will find fault with nature because flowers bloom in the morning and die at night, because she has not given the rose or the lily the hardness of flint? And this miserable pedestrian principle *we* wish to transfer to the world of history! [. . .] Life has no obligation to realise the fantasies and ideas [of civilisation . . .] Life loves novelty [. . .]

[. . .] History seldom repeats itself, it uses every accident, simultaneously knocks at a thousand doors . . . doors which may open . . . who knows?[2]

And again:

Human beings have an instinctive passion to preserve anything they like. Man is born and therefore wishes to live for ever. Man falls in love and wishes to be loved, and loved for ever as in the very first moment of his avowal [. . . But life gives no guarantees.] Life does not ensure existence, nor pleasure; she does not answer for their

1   ibid. 37; F 40.   2   ibid. 30–2; F 32–4.

continuance [. . .] Every historical moment is full and is beautiful, is self-contained in its own fashion. Every year has its own spring and its own summer, its own winter and autumn, its own storms and fair weather. Every period is new, fresh, filled with its own hopes and carries within itself its own joys and sorrows. The present belongs to it. But human beings are not content with this, they must needs own the future too [. . .]

What is the purpose of the song the singer sings? [. . .] If you look beyond your pleasure in it for something else, for some other goal, the moment will come when the singer stops and then you will only have memories and vain regrets because, instead of listening, you were waiting for something else . . . You are confused by categories that are not fitted to catch the flow of life. What is this goal for which you [Mazzini and the liberals and the socialists] are seeking – is it a programme? An order? Who conceived it? To whom was the order given? Is it something inevitable? Or not? If it is, are we simply puppets? Are we morally free or are we wheels within a machine? I would rather think of life, and therefore of history, as a goal attained, not as a means to something else.[1]

And 'We think that the purpose of the child is to grow up because it does grow up. But its purpose is to play, to enjoy itself, to be a child. If we merely look to the end of the process, the purpose of all life is death.'[2]

This is Herzen's central political and social thesis, and it enters henceforth into the stream of Russian radical thought as an antidote to the exaggerated utilitarianism of which its adversaries have so often accused it. The purpose of the singer is the song, and the purpose of life is to be lived. Everything passes, but what passes may sometimes reward the pilgrim for all his sufferings. Goethe has told us that there can be no guarantee, no security. Man could be content with the present. But he is not. He rejects beauty, he rejects fulfilment today, because he must own the future also. That is Herzen's answer to all those who, like Mazzini, or the socialists of his time, called for supreme sacrifices and sufferings for the sake of nationality, or human civilisation, or socialism,

1   ibid. 32–3; F 34–6.   2   ibid. 93; F 107.

or justice, or humanity – if not in the present, then in the future.
Herzen rejects this violently. The purpose of the struggle for
liberty is not liberty tomorrow, it is liberty today, the liberty of
living individuals with their own individual ends, the ends for
which they move and fight and perhaps die, ends which are sacred
to them. To crush their freedom, their pursuits, to ruin their ends
for the sake of some vague felicity in the future which cannot be
guaranteed, about which we know nothing, which is simply the
product of some enormous metaphysical construction that itself
rests upon sand, for which there is no logical, or empirical, or any
other rational guarantee – to do that is in the first place blind,
because the future is uncertain; and in the second place vicious,
because it offends against the only moral values we know; because
it tramples on human demands in the name of abstractions –
freedom, happiness, justice – fanatical generalisations, mystical
sounds, idolised sets of words. Why is liberty valuable? Because it
is an end in itself, because it is what it is. To bring it as a sacrifice
to something else is simply to perform an act of human sacrifice.

This is Herzen's ultimate sermon, and from this he develops the
corollary that one of the deepest of modern disasters is to be
caught up in abstractions instead of realities. And this he maintains
not merely against the Western socialists and liberals among whom
he lived (let alone the enemy – priests or conservatives) but even
more against his own close friend Bakunin, who persisted in trying
to stir up violent rebellion, involving torture and martyrdom, for
the sake of dim, confused and distant goals. For Herzen, one of
the greatest of sins that any human being can perpetrate is to
seek to transfer moral responsibility from his own shoulders to
those of an unpredictable future order, and, in the name of something which may never happen, perpetrate crimes today which no
one would deny to be monstrous if they were performed for
some egoistic purpose, and do not seem so only because they are
sanctified by faith in some remote and intangible Utopia.

For all his hatred of despotism, and in particular of the Russian
regime, Herzen was all his life convinced that equally fatal dangers
threatened from his own socialist and revolutionary allies. He
believed this because there was a time when, with his friend the
critic Belinsky, he too had believed that a simple solution was

feasible; that some great system – a world adumbrated by Saint-Simon or by Proudhon – did provide it: that if one regulated social life rationally and put it in order, and created a clear and tidy organisation, human problems could be finally resolved. Dostoevsky once said of Belinsky that his socialism was nothing but a simple belief in a marvellous life of 'unheard-of splendour, on new and [. . .] adamantine foundations'.[1] Because Herzen had himself once believed in these foundations (although never with simple and absolute faith) and because this belief came toppling down and was utterly destroyed in the fearful cataclysms of 1848 and 1849 in which almost every one of his idols proved to have feet of clay, he denounces his own past with peculiarly intense indignation: we call upon the masses, he writes, to rise and crush the tyrants. But the masses are indifferent to individual freedom and independence, and suspicious of talent: 'they want a [. . .] government to rule for their benefit, and not [. . .] against it. But to govern themselves doesn't enter their heads.'[2] 'It is not enough to despise the Crown; one must not be filled with awe before the Phrygian Cap [. . .]'.[3] He speaks with bitter scorn about monolithic, oppressive communist idylls, about the barbarous 'equality of penal servitude', about the 'forced labour' of socialists like Cabet, about barbarians marching to destroy.[4]

Who will finish us off? The senile barbarism of the sceptre or the wild barbarism of communism; the bloody sabre, or the red flag? . . .

[. . .] Communism will sweep across the world in a violent tempest – dreadful, bloody, unjust, swift [. . .]

[Our] institutions [. . .] will, as Proudhon politely puts it, be *liquidated*. [. . .]

I am sorry [for the death of civilisation].

But the masses will not regret it; the masses to whom it gave nothing but tears, want, ignorance and humiliation.[5]

1   loc. cit. (196 above, note 3).
2   'S togo berega', H vi 124; F 133–4.
3   ibid. 46; F 51.
4   loc. cit. (109 above, note 3).
5   'Pis'ma iz Frantsii i Italii', fourteenth letter, H v 211, 216–17; L 194, 199.
     [See also 110–11 above.]

He is terrified of the oppressors, but he is terrified of the liberators
too. He is terrified of them because for him they are the secular
heirs of the religious bigots of the ages of faith; because anybody
who has a cut and dried scheme, a straitjacket which he wishes to
impose on humanity as the sole possible remedy for all human
ills, is ultimately bound to create a situation intolerable for free
human beings, for men like himself who want to express themselves, who want to have some area in which to develop their
own resources, and are prepared to respect the originality, the
spontaneity, the natural impulse towards self-expression on the
part of other human beings too. He calls this Petrograndism –
the methods of Peter the Great. He admires Peter the Great. He
admires him because he did at least overthrow the feudal rigidity,
the dark night, as he thinks of it, of medieval Russia. He admires
the Jacobins because the Jacobins dared to do something instead
of nothing. Yet he is clearly aware, and became more and more
so the longer he lived (he says all this with arresting clarity in his
open letters *To an Old Comrade* – Bakunin – written in the late
1860s), that Petrograndism, the behaviour of Attila, the behaviour
of the Committee of Public Safety in 1792 – the use of methods
which presuppose the possibility of simple and radical solutions –
always in the end lead to oppression, bloodshed and collapse. He
declares that whatever the justification in earlier and more innocent ages of acts inspired by fanatical faith, nobody has any right
to act in this fashion who has lived through the nineteenth century
and has seen what human beings are really made of – the complex,
crooked texture of men and institutions. Progress must adjust
itself to the actual pace of historical change, to the actual economic
and social needs of society, because to suppress the bourgeoisie by
violent revolution – and there was nothing he despised more than
the bourgeoisie, and the mean, grasping, philistine financial bourgeoisie of Paris most of all – before its historical role has been played
out, would merely mean that the bourgeois spirit and bourgeois
forms would persist into the new social order. They want, without
altering the walls [of the prison], to give them a new function, as if
a plan for a jail could be used for a free existence.'[1] Houses for

---

1   loc. cit. (109 above, note 1).

free men cannot be built by specialists in prison architecture. And who shall say that history has proved that Herzen was mistaken?

His loathing of the bourgeoisie is frantic, yet he does not want a violent cataclysm. He thinks that it may be inevitable, that it may come, but he is frightened of it. The bourgeoisie seems to him like a collection of Figaros, but of Figaros grown fat and prosperous. He declares that, in the eighteenth century, Figaro wore a livery, a mark of servitude to be sure, but still something different from, detachable from, his skin; the skin, at least, was that of a palpitating, rebellious human being. But today Figaro has won. Figaro has become a millionaire. He is judge, commander-in-chief, president of the republic. Figaro now dominates the world, and, alas, the livery is no longer a mere livery. It has become part of his skin. It cannot be taken off; it has become part of his living flesh.

Everything that was repellent and degrading in the eighteenth century, against which the noble revolutionaries had protested, has grown into the intrinsic texture of the mean middle-class beings who now dominate us. And yet we must wait. Simply to cut off their heads, as Bakunin wanted, can only lead to a new tyranny and a new slavery, to the rule of the revolted minorities over majorities, or, worse still, the rule of majorities – monolithic majorities – over minorities, the rule of what John Stuart Mill, in Herzen's view with justice, called 'collective mediocrity'.[1]

Herzen's values are undisguised: he likes only the style of free beings, only what is large, generous, uncalculating. He admires pride, independence, resistance to tyrants; he admires Pushkin because he was defiant; he admires Lermontov because he dared to suffer and to hate; he even approves of the Slavophils, his reactionary opponents, because at least they detested authority, at least they would not let the Germans in. He admires Belinsky because he was incorruptible, and told the truth in the face of the arrayed battalions of German academic or political authority. The dogmas of socialism seem to him no less stifling than those of capitalism or of the Middle Ages or of the early Christians. What he hated most of all was the despotism of formulae – ∫

1   loc. cit. (xxx above, note 2).

the submission of human beings to arrangements arrived at by deduction from some kind of a priori principles which had no foundation in actual experience. That is why he feared the new liberators so deeply. 'If only people wanted,' he says, '[. . .] instead of liberating humanity, to liberate themselves, they would do much for [. . .] the liberation of man.'[1] He knew that his own perpetual plea for more individual freedom contained the seeds of social atomisation, that a compromise had to be found between the two great social needs – for organisation and for individual freedom – some unstable equilibrium that would preserve a minimal area within which the individual could express himself and not be utterly pulverised, and he utters a great appeal for what he calls the value of egoism. He declares that one of the great dangers to our society is that individuals will be tamed and suppressed disinterestedly by idealists in the name of altruism, in the name of measures designed to make the majority happy. The new liberators may well resemble the inquisitors of the past, who drove herds of innocent Spaniards, Dutchmen, Belgians, Frenchmen, Italians to the autos-da-fé, and then went home peacefully with a quiet conscience, with the feeling that they had done their duty, with the smell of roasting human flesh still in their nostrils, and slept – the sleep of the innocent after a day's work well done.[2] Egoism is not to be condemned without qualification. Egoism is not a vice. Egoism gleams in the eye of an animal. Moralists bravely thunder against it, instead of building on it. What moralists try to deny is the great, inner citadel of human dignity. They want to make men tearful, sentimental, insipid, kindly creatures, asking to be made slaves. But to tear egoism from a man's heart is to rob him of his living principles, of the yeast and salt of his personality. Fortunately this is impossible. Of course it is sometimes suicidal to try to assert oneself. One cannot try and go up a staircase down which an army is trying to march. That is done by tyrants, conservatives, fools and criminals. 'Destroy a man's altruism, and you get a savage orang-utan, but if you destroy his egoism you generate a tame monkey.'[3]

1   ibid. 119; F 128.
2   loc. cit. (103 above, note 1), 264.
3   'S togo berega', H vi 129–30 (quotation at 130); F 138–40 (139–40).

Human problems are too complex to demand simple solutions. Even the peasant commune in Russia, in which Herzen believed so deeply as a 'lightning conductor', because he believed that peasants in Russia at least had not been infected by the distorting, urban vices of the European proletariat and the European bourgeoisie – even the peasant commune did not, after all, as he points out, preserve Russia from slavery. Liberty is not to the taste of the majority – only of the educated. There are no guaranteed methods, no sure paths to social welfare. We must try to do our best; and it is always possible that we shall fail.

The heart of his thought is the notion that the basic problems are perhaps not soluble at all, that all one can do is to try to solve them, but that there is no guarantee, either in socialist nostrums or in any other human construction, no guarantee that happiness or a rational life can be attained, in private or in public life. This curious combination of idealism and scepticism – not unlike, for all his vehemence, the outlook of Erasmus, Montaigne, Montesquieu – runs through all his writings.

Herzen wrote novels, but they are largely forgotten, because he was not a born novelist. His stories are greatly inferior to those of his friend Turgenev, but they have something in common with them. For in Turgenev's novels, too, you will find that human problems are not treated as if they were soluble. Bazarov in *Fathers and Children* suffers and dies; Lavretsky in *A Nest of Gentlefolk* is left in melancholy uncertainty at the end of the novel, not because something had not been done which could have been done, not because there is a solution round the corner which someone simply had not thought of, or had refused to apply, but because, as Kant once said, 'From the crooked timber of humanity no straight thing was ever made.'[1] Everything is partly the fault of circumstance, partly the fault of the individual character, partly of the nature of life itself. This must be faced, it must be stated, and it is a vulgarity and, at times, a crime to believe that permanent solutions are always possible.

Herzen wrote a novel called *Who Is To Blame?* about a typical

---

1   Immanuel Kant, 'Idee zu einer allgemeinen Geschichte in weltbürgerlicher Absicht' ('Idea for a Universal History with a Cosmopolitan Purpose', 1784), *Kant's gesammelte Schriften* (Berlin, 1900–), viii 23, line 22.

tragic triangle in which one of the 'superfluous men' of whom I spoke earlier falls in love with a lady in a provincial town who is married to a virtuous, idealistic, but dull and naive husband. It is not a good novel, and its plot is not worth recounting, but the main point, and what is most characteristic of Herzen, is that the situation possesses, in principle, no solution. The lover is left broken-hearted, the wife falls ill and probably dies, the husband contemplates suicide. It sounds like a typically gloomy, morbidly self-centred caricature of the Russian novel. But it is not. It rests on an exceedingly delicate, precise and at times profound description of an emotional and psychological situation to which the theories of a Stendhal, the method of a Flaubert, the depth and moral insight of a George Eliot are inapplicable because they are seen to be too literary, derived from obsessive ideas, ethical doctrines not fitted to the chaos of life.

At the heart of Herzen's outlook (and of Turgenev's too) is the notion of the complexity and insolubility of the central problems, and, therefore, of the absurdity of trying to solve them by means of political or sociological instruments. But the difference between Herzen and Turgenev is this. Turgenev is, in his innermost being, not indeed heartless but a cool, detached, at times slightly mocking observer who looks upon the tragedies of life from a comparatively remote point of view; oscillating between one vantage point and another, between the claims of society and of the individual, the claims of love and of daily life; between heroic virtue and realistic scepticism, the morality of Hamlet and the morality of Don Quixote, the necessity for efficient political organisation and the necessity for individual self-expression; remaining suspended in a state of agreeable indecision, sympathetic melancholy, ironical, free from cynicism and sentimentality, perceptive, scrupulously truthful and uncommitted. Turgenev neither quite believed nor quite disbelieved in a deity, personal or impersonal; religion is for him a normal ingredient of life, like love, or egoism, or the sense of pleasure. He enjoyed remaining in an intermediate position, he enjoyed almost too much his lack of will to believe, and because he stood aside, because he contemplated in tranquillity, he was able to produce great literary masterpieces of a finished kind, rounded stories told in peaceful retrospect, with well-constructed beginnings, middles and ends. He detached his art from himself; he did not, as a human being, deeply care about solutions; he saw life with a peculiar chilliness, which infuriated both Tolstoy and Dostoevsky, and he achieved the exquisite perspective of an artist who treats his material from a certain distance. There is a chasm between him and his material, within which alone his particular kind of poetical creation is possible.

Herzen, on the contrary, cared far too violently. He was looking for solutions for himself, for his own personal life. His novels were certainly failures. He obtrudes himself too vehemently into them, himself and his agonised point of view. On the other hand, his autobiographical sketches, when he writes openly about himself and about his friends, when he speaks about his own life in Italy, in France, in Switzerland, in England, have a kind of palpitating directness, a sense of first-handness and reality, which no other writer in the nineteenth century begins to convey. His reminiscences are a work of critical and descriptive genius with the power of absolute self-revelation that only an astonishingly imaginative, impressionable, perpetually reacting personality, with an exceptional sense both of the noble and the ludicrous, and a rare freedom from vanity and doctrine, could have attained. As a writer of memoirs he is unequalled. His sketches of England, or rather of himself in England, are better than Heine's or Taine's. To demonstrate this, one need only read his wonderful account of English political trials, of how judges, for example, looked to him when they sat in court trying foreign conspirators for having fought a fatal duel in Windsor Great Park. He gives a vivid and entertaining description of bombastic French demagogues and gloomy French fanatics, and of the impassable gulf which divides this agitated and slightly grotesque émigré society from the dull, frigid and dignified institutions of mid-Victorian England, typified by the figure of the presiding judge at the Old Bailey, who looks like the wolf in *Red Riding Hood*, in his white wig, his long skirts, with his sharp little wolf-like face, thin lips, sharp teeth, and harsh little words that come with an air of specious benevolence from the face encased in disarming feminine curls – giving the impression of a sweet, grandmotherly old lady, belied by the small gleaming eyes and the dry, acrid, malicious judicial humour.

He paints classical portraits of German exiles, whom he detested, of Italian and Polish revolutionaries, whom he admired, and gives little sketches of the differences between the nations, such as the English and the French, each of which regards itself as the greatest nation on earth, and will not yield an inch, and does not begin to understand the other's ideals – the French with their gregariousness, their lucidity, their didacticism, their neat formal gardens, as against the English with their solitudes and dark suppressed romanticism, and the tangled undergrowth of their ancient, illogical, but profoundly civilised and humane institutions. And there are the Germans, who regard themselves, he declares, as an inferior fruit of the tree of which the English are the superior products, and come to England, and after three days 'say "yes" instead of "ja", and "well" where it is not required'.[1] It is invariably for the Germans that both he and Bakunin reserved their sharpest taunts, not so much from personal dislike as because the Germans to them seemed to stand for all that was middle-class, cramping, philistine and boorish, the sordid despotism of grey and small-minded drill sergeants, aesthetically more disgusting than the generous, magnificent tyrannies of great conquerors of history. 'Where they are stopped by their conscience, we are stopped by a policeman. Our weakness is arithmetical, and so we yield; their weakness is an algebraic weakness, it is part of the formula itself.'[2] This was echoed by Bakunin a decade later: 'When an Englishman or an American says "I am an Englishman", "I am an American", they are saying "I am a free man"; when a German says "I am a German" he is saying "[. . .] my Emperor is stronger than all the other Emperors, and the German soldier who is strangling me will strangle you all".'[3]

This kind of sweeping prejudice, these diatribes against entire nations and classes, are characteristic of a good many Russian writers of this period. They are often ill-founded, unjust and violently exaggerated, but they are the authentic expression of an indignant reaction against an oppressive milieu, and of a genuine

1   'Byloe i dumy', part 6, chapter 3 (see 93 above, note 1), H xi 34; M iii 1047.
2   'Du développement des idées révolutionnaires en Russie', H vii 15/143.
3   loc. cit. (p. 126 above, note 2).

and highly personal moral vision which makes them lively reading even now.

His irreverence and the irony, the disbelief in final solutions, the conviction that human beings are complex and fragile, and that there is value in the very irregularity of their structure, which is violated by attempts to force it into patterns or straitjackets – this and the irrepressible pleasure in exploding all cut and dried social and political schemata which serious-minded and pedantic saviours of mankind, both radical and conservative, were perpetually manufacturing, inevitably made Herzen unpopular among the earnest and the devout of all camps. In this respect he resembled his sceptical friend Turgenev, who could not, and had no wish to, resist the desire to tell the truth, however 'unscientific' – to say something psychologically telling, even though it might not fit in with some generally accepted, enlightened system of ideas. Neither accepted the view that because he was on the side of progress or revolution he was under a sacred obligation to suppress the truth, or to pretend to think that it was simpler than it was, or that certain solutions would work although it seemed patently improbable that they could, simply because to speak otherwise might give aid and comfort to the enemy.

This detachment from party and doctrine, and the tendency to utter independent and sometimes disconcerting judgements, brought violent criticism on both Herzen and Turgenev, and made their position difficult. When Turgenev wrote *Fathers and Children*, he was duly attacked both from the right and from the left, because neither was clear which side he was supporting. This indeterminate quality particularly irritated the 'new' young men in Russia, who assailed him bitterly for being too liberal, too civilised, too ironical, too sceptical, for undermining noble idealism by the perpetual oscillation of political feelings, by excessive self-examination, by not engaging himself and declaring war upon the enemy, and perpetrating instead what amounted to a succession of evasions and minor treacheries. Their hostility was directed at all the 'men of the '40s', and in particular at Herzen, who was rightly looked on as their most brilliant and most formidable representative. His answer to the stern, brutal young revolutionaries of the 1860s is exceedingly characteristic. The new revolutionaries had attacked him for nostalgic love of an older style of life, for being a gentleman, for being rich, for living in comfort, for sitting in London and observing the Russian revolutionary struggle from afar, for being a member of a generation which had merely talked in the salons, and speculated and philosophised, when all round them were squalor and misery, bitterness and injustice; for not seeking salvation in some serious, manual labour – in cutting down a tree, or making a pair of boots, or doing something 'concrete' and real in order to identify himself with the suffering masses, instead of endless brave talk in the drawing-rooms of wealthy ladies with other well-educated, noblyborn, equally feckless young men – self-indulgence and escapism, deliberate blindness to the horrors and agonies of their world.

Herzen understood his opponents, and declined to compromise. He admits that he cannot help preferring cleanliness to dirt; decency, elegance, beauty, comfort to violence and austerity, good literature to bad, poetry to prose. Despite his alleged cynicism and 'aestheticism', he declines to admit that only scoundrels can achieve things, that in order to achieve a revolution that will liberate mankind and create a new and nobler form of life on earth one must be unkempt, dirty, brutal and violent, and trample with hob-nailed boots on civilisation and the rights of men. He does not believe this, and sees no reason why he should believe it.

As for the new generation of revolutionaries, they are not sprung from nothing: they are the fault of his generation, which begat them by its idle talk in the 1840s. These are men who come to avenge the world against the men of the '40s – 'the syphilis of our revolutionary passions'.[1] The new generation will say to the old: '"You are hypocrites, we will be cynics; you spoke like moralists, we shall speak like scoundrels; you were civil to your superiors, rude to your inferiors; we shall be rude to all; you bow without feeling respect, we shall push and jostle and make no apologies [. . .]".'[2] He says in effect: Organised hooliganism can solve nothing. Unless civilisation – the recognition of the difference of good and bad, noble and ignoble, worthy and unworthy – is preserved,

---

1   Letter to N. P. Ogarev, 1–2 May 1868, H xxix/1 330.
2   loc. cit. (118 above, note 2).

unless there are some people who are both fastidious and fearless, and are free to say what they want to say, and do not sacrifice their lives upon some large, nameless altar, and sink themselves into a vast, impersonal, grey mass of barbarians marching to destroy, what is the point of the revolution? It may come whether we like it or not. But why should we welcome, still less work for, the victory of the barbarians who will sweep away the wicked old world only to leave ruins and misery, on which nothing but a new despotism can be built? The 'vast bill of indictment which Russian literature has been drafting against Russian life'[1] does not demand a new philistinism in place of the old: 'sorrow, scepticism, irony [. . .] the three strings of the Russian lyre'[2] are closer to reality than the crude and vulgar optimism of the new materialists.

Herzen's most constant goal is the preservation of individual liberty. That is the purpose of the guerrilla war which, as he once wrote to Mazzini, he had fought from his earliest youth. What made him unique in the nineteenth century is the complexity of his vision, the degree to which he understood the causes and nature of conflicting ideals simpler and more fundamental than his own. He understood what made – and what in a measure justified – radicals and revolutionaries: and at the same time he grasped the frightening consequences of their doctrines. He was in full sympathy with, and had a profound psychological understanding of, what it was that gave the Jacobins their severe and noble grandeur, and endowed them with a moral magnificence which raised them above the horizon of that older world which he found so attractive and which they had ruthlessly crushed. He understood only too well the misery, the oppression, the suffocation, the appalling inhumanity, the bitter cries for justice on the part of the crushed elements of the population under the *ancien régime*, and at the same time he knew that the new world which had risen to avenge these wrongs must, if it was given its head, create its own excesses and drive millions of human beings to useless mutual extermination. Herzen's sense of reality, in particular of the need for, and the price of, revolution, is unique in his own, and perhaps in any, age. His sense of the critical moral and

1   loc. cit. (167 above, note 1).   2   loc. cit. (119 above, note 1).

political issues of his time is a good deal more specific and concrete than that of the majority of the professional philosophers of the nineteenth century, who tended to try to derive general principles from observation of their society, and to recommend solutions which are deduced by rational methods from premises formulated in terms of the tidy categories in which they sought to arrange opinions, principles and forms of conduct. Herzen was a publicist and an essayist whom his early Hegelian training had not ruined: he had acquired no taste for academic classifications; he had a unique insight into the 'inner feel' of social and political predicaments, and with it a remarkable power of analysis and exposition. Consequently he understood and stated the case, both emotional and intellectual, for violent revolution, for saying that a pair of boots was of more value than all the plays of Shakespeare (as the 'nihilistic' critic Pisarev once said in a rhetorical moment),[1] for denouncing liberalism and parliamentarism, which offered the masses votes and slogans when what they needed was food, shelter, clothing; and understood no less vividly and clearly the aesthetic and even moral value of civilisations which rest upon slavery, where a minority produces divine masterpieces, and only a small

1   [This remark, whose first use is often mistakenly attributed to Pisarev (even by Gorky), appears to have its true origins in a satirical 'extract' from a 'novel' ('Otryvok iz romana *Shchedrodarov*'), contributed by Dostoevsky in 1864 to his journal *Epokha*: see 'Gospodin Shchedrin ili raskol v nigilistakh', D v 266–81, at 267–78. This pastiche is aimed against the nihilists, who appear in it under thinly disguising pseudonyms. At 271 the eponymous character Shchedrodarov (Saltykov-Shchedrin), who has recently joined the editorial board of the journal *Svoevremennyi* – a board whose members include Pravdolyubov (Dobrolyubov) and Skribov (Pisarev) – encounters the board's editorial principle that 'a pair of boots are, in every sense, better than Pushkin, because [. . .] Pushkin is mere luxury and nonsense'; and, a little later, 'Shakespeare too is mere nonsense and luxury'. Perhaps Dostoevsky had in mind Pushkin's own remark in a letter to P. A. Vyazemsky of March 1823 that he looked on his poems 'as a cobbler looks on a pair of boots that he has made. I sell for profit [. . .]', even though this letter was not published until 1903: Pushkin, *Polnoe sobranie sochinenii* (Leningrad, 1937–59), xiii 59. Versions of this 'principle', mentioning Pushkin rather than Shakespeare, appear in Saltykov-Shchedrin's *Gentlemen of Tashkent* (1869–72), *Sobranie sochinenii* (9 above, note 1), x 102, and Dostoevsky's *The Possessed* (1871–2), part 1, chapter 1, section 6, D ix 21. In due course the Shakespearian version became current, and its coinage began to be credited to Pisarev.]

number of persons have the freedom and the self-confidence, the imagination and the gifts, to be able to produce forms of life that endure, works which can be shored up against the ruin of our time.

This curious ambivalence, the alternation of indignant championship of revolution and democracy against the smug denunciation of them by liberals and conservatives, with no less passionate attacks upon revolutionaries in the name of free individuals; the defence of the claims of life and art, human decency, equality and dignity, with the advocacy of a society in which human beings shall not exploit or trample on one another even in the name of justice or progress or civilisation or democracy or other abstractions – this war on two, and often more, fronts, wherever and whoever the enemies of freedom might turn out to be – makes Herzen the most realistic, sensitive, penetrating and convincing witness to the social life and the social issues of his own time. His greatest gift is that of untrammelled understanding: he understood the value of the so-called 'superfluous' Russian idealists of the 1840s because they were exceptionally free, and morally attractive, and formed the most imaginative, spontaneous, gifted, civilised and interesting society which he had ever known. At the same time he understood the protest against it of the exasperated, deeply earnest, *révoltés* young radicals, repelled by what seemed to them gay and irresponsible chatter among a group of aristocratic *flâneurs*, unaware of the mounting resentment of the sullen mass of the oppressed peasants and lower officials that would one day sweep them and their world away in a tidal wave of violent, blind, but justified hatred which it is the business of true revolutionaries to foment and direct. Herzen understood this conflict, and his autobiography conveys the tension between individuals and classes, personalities and opinions both in Russia and in the West, with marvellous vividness and precision.

My Past and Thoughts is dominated by no single clear purpose, it is not committed to a thesis; its author was not enslaved by any formula or any political doctrine, and for this reason it remains a profound and living masterpiece, and Herzen's greatest title to immortality. He possesses other claims: his political and social views were arrestingly original, if only because he was among the very few thinkers of his time who in principle rejected all general solutions, and grasped, as very few thinkers have ever done, the crucial distinction between words that are about words, and words that are about persons or things in the real world. Nevertheless it is as a writer that he survives. His autobiography is one of the great monuments to Russian literary and psychological genius, worthy to stand beside the great novels of Turgenev and Tolstoy. Like *War and Peace*, like *Fathers and Children*, it is wonderfully readable, and, save in inferior translation, not dated, not Victorian, still astonishingly contemporary in feeling.

One of the elements in political genius is a sensibility to characteristics and processes in society while they are still in embryo and invisible to the naked eye. Herzen possessed this capacity to a high degree, but he viewed the approaching cataclysm neither with the savage exultation of Marx or Bakunin nor with the pessimistic detachment of Burckhardt or Tocqueville. Like Proudhon he believed the destruction of individual freedom to be neither desirable nor inevitable, but, unlike him, as being highly probable, unless it was averted by deliberate human effort. The strong tradition of libertarian humanism in Russian socialism, defeated only in October 1917, derives from his writings. His analysis of the forces at work in his day, of the individuals in whom they were embodied, of the moral presuppositions of their creeds and words, and of his own principles, remains to this day one of the most penetrating, moving and morally formidable indictments of the great evils which have grown to maturity in our own time.

RUSSIAN POPULISM

(1960)

Russian populism is the name not of a single political party, nor of a coherent body of doctrine, but of a widespread radical movement in Russia in the middle of the nineteenth century. It was born during the great social and intellectual ferment which followed the death of Tsar Nicholas I and the defeat and humiliation of the Crimean War, grew to fame and influence during the 1860s and 1870s, and reached its culmination with the assassination of Tsar Alexander II, after which it swiftly declined. Its leaders were men of very dissimilar origins, outlooks and capacities; it was not at any stage more than loose congeries of small independent groups of conspirators or their sympathisers, who sometimes united for common action, and at other times operated in isolation. These groups tended to differ both about ends and about means. Nevertheless they held certain fundamental beliefs in common, and possessed sufficient moral and political solidarity to entitle them to be called a single movement. Like their predecessors, the Decembrist conspirators in the 1820s, and the circles that gathered round Alexander Herzen and Belinsky in the 1830s and 1840s, they looked on the government and the social structure of their country as a moral and political monstrosity – obsolete, barbarous, stupid and odious – and dedicated their lives to its total destruction. Their general ideas were not original. They shared the democratic ideals of the European radicals of their day, and in addition believed that the struggle between social and economic classes was the determining factor in politics; they held this theory not in its Marxist form (which did not effectively reach Russia until the 1870s) but in the form in which it was taught by Proudhon and Herzen, and before them by Saint-Simon, Fourier and other French socialists and radicals whose writings had entered Russia, legally and illegally, in a thin but steady stream for several decades.

The theory of social history as dominated by the class war – the heart of which is the notion of the coercion of the 'have-nots' by the 'haves' – was born in the course of the Industrial Revolution in the West; and its most characteristic concepts belong to the capitalist phase of economic development. Economic classes, capitalism, cut-throat competition, proletarians and their exploiters, the evil power of unproductive finance, the inevitability of increasing centralisation and standardisation of all human activities, the transformation of men into commodities and the consequent 'alienation' of individuals and groups and degradation of human lives – these notions are fully intelligible only in the context of expanding industrialism. Russia, even as late as the 1850s, was one of the least industrialised States in Europe. Nevertheless, exploitation and misery had long been amongst the most familiar and universally recognised characteristics of its social life, the principal victims of the system being the peasants, both serfs and free, who formed over nine-tenths of its population. An industrial proletariat had indeed come into being, but by mid-century did not exceed two or three per cent of the population of the Empire. Hence the cause of the oppressed was still at that date overwhelmingly that of the agricultural workers, who formed the lowest stratum of the population, the vast majority being serfs in State or private possession. The populists looked upon them as martyrs whose grievances they were determined to avenge and remedy, and as embodiments of simple uncorrupted virtue, whose social organisation (which they largely idealised) was the natural foundation on which the future of Russian society must be rebuilt.

The central populist goals were social justice and social equality. Most of them were convinced, following Herzen, whose revolutionary propaganda in the 1850s influenced them more than any other single set of ideas, that the essence of a just and equal society existed already in the Russian peasant commune – the *obshchina* organised in the form of a collective unit called the *mir*. The *mir* was a free association of peasants which periodically redistributed the agricultural land to be tilled; its decisions bound all its members, and constituted the cornerstone on which, so the populists maintained, a federation of socialised, self-governing units, conceived along lines popularised by the French socialist Proudhon, could be erected. The populist leaders believed that this form of cooperation offered the possibility of a free and democratic social system in Russia, originating as it did in the deepest moral instincts and traditional values of Russian, and indeed all human, society, and they believed that the workers (by which they meant all productive human beings), whether in town or country, could bring this system into being with a far smaller degree of violence or coercion than had occurred in the industrial West. This system, since it alone sprang naturally from fundamental human needs and a sense of the right and the good that existed in all men, would ensure justice, equality and the widest opportunity for the full development of human faculties. As a corollary of this, the populists believed that the development of large-scale centralised industry was not 'natural', and therefore led inexorably to the degradation and dehumanisation of all those who were caught in its tentacles: capitalism was an appalling evil, destructive of body and soul; but it was not inescapable. They denied that social or economic progress was necessarily bound up with the Industrial Revolution. They maintained that the application of scientific truths and methods to social and individual problems (in which they passionately believed), although it might, and often did, lead to the growth of capitalism, could be realised without this fatal sacrifice. They believed that it was possible to improve life by scientific techniques without necessarily destroying the 'natural' life of the peasant village, or creating a vast, pauperised, faceless city proletariat. Capitalism seemed irresistible only because it had not been sufficiently resisted. However it might be in the West, in Russia 'the curse of bigness'[1] could still be successfully fought, and federations of small self-governing units of producers, as Fourier and Proudhon had advocated, could be fostered, and

1   [From the title of a collection of essays by Justice Brandeis, *The Curse of Bigness: Miscellaneous Papers of Louis D. Brandeis*, ed. Osmond K. Fraenkel (New York, 1934). This title itself derives from 'A Curse of Bigness', chapter 8 of Louis D. Brandeis, *Other People's Money and How the Bankers Use It* (New York, 1914).]

indeed created, by deliberate action. Like their French masters, the Russian disciples held the institution of the State in particular hatred, since to them it was at once the symbol, the result and the main source of injustice and inequality – a weapon wielded by the governing class to defend its own privileges – and one that, in the face of increasing resistance from its victims, grew progressively more brutal and blindly destructive.

The defeat of liberal and radical movements in the West in 1848–9 confirmed them in their conviction that salvation did not lie in politics or political parties: it seemed clear to them that liberal parties and their leaders had neither understood nor made a serious effort to forward the fundamental interests of the oppressed populations of their countries. What the vast majority of peasants in Russia (or workers in Europe) needed was to be fed and clothed, to be given physical security, to be rescued from disease, ignorance, poverty and humiliating inequalities. As for political rights, votes, parliaments, republican forms, these were meaningless and useless to ignorant, barbarous, half-naked and starving men; such programmes merely mocked their misery. The populists shared with the nationalistic Russian Slavophils (with whose political ideas they had otherwise little in common) a loathing of the rigidly class-conscious social pyramid of the West that was complacently accepted, or fervently believed in, by the conformist bourgeoisie and the bureaucracy to whom this bourgeoisie looked up.

The satirist Saltykov, in his famous dialogue between a German and a Russian boy, immortalised this attitude when he declared his faith in the Russian boy, hungry and in rags, stumbling in the mud and squalor of the accursed, slave-owning tsarist regime, because he had not, like the neat, docile, smug, well-fed, well-dressed German boy, bartered away his soul for the few pence that the Prussian official had offered him, and was consequently capable, if only he was allowed to do so (as the German boy no longer was), of rising one day to his full human height. Russia was in darkness and in chains, but her spirit was not captive; her past was black, but her future promised more than the death in life of the civilised middle classes in Germany or France or England, who had long ago sold themselves for material security and had become so apathetic in their shameful, self-imposed servitude that they no longer knew how to want to be free.

The populists, unlike the Slavophils, did not believe in the unique character or destiny of the Russian people. They were not mystical nationalists. They believed only that Russia was a backward nation which had not reached the stage of social and economic development at which the Western nations (whether or not they could have avoided this) had entered upon the path of unrestrained industrialism. They were not, for the most part, historical determinists; consequently they believed that it was possible for a nation in such a predicament to avoid this fate by the exercise of intelligence and will. They saw no reason why Russia could not benefit by Western science and Western technology without paying the appalling price paid by the West. They argued that it was possible to avoid the despotism of a centralised economy or a centralised government by adopting a loose, federal structure composed of self-governing, socialised units both of producers and of consumers. They held that it was desirable to organise, but not to lose sight of other values in the pursuit of organisation as an end in itself; to be governed primarily by ethical and humanitarian and not solely by economic and technological – 'ant-hill' – considerations. They declared that to protect human individuals against exploitation by turning them into an industrial army of collectivised robots was self-stultifying and suicidal. The ideas of the populists were often unclear, and there were sharp differences among them, but there was an area of agreement wide enough to constitute a genuine movement. Thus they accepted, in broad outline, the educational and moral lessons, but not the State worship, of Rousseau. Some of them – indeed perhaps the majority – shared Rousseau's belief in the goodness of simple men, his conviction that the cause of corruption is the crippling effect of bad institutions, his acute distrust of all forms of cleverness, of intellectuals and specialists, of all self-isolating coteries and factions. They accepted the anti-political ideas, but not the technocratic centralism, of Saint-Simon. They shared the belief in conspiracy and violent action preached by Babeuf and his disciple Buonarroti, but not their Jacobin authoritarianism. They stood with Sismondi and Proudhon and Lamennais and the other originators of the notion of the Welfare State, against, on the one hand, laissez-faire, and, on the other, central authority, whether nationalist or socialist, whether temporary or permanent, whether preached by List, or Mazzini, or Lassalle, or Marx. They came close at times to the positions of Western Christian socialists, without, however, any religious faith, since, like the French Encyclopedists of the previous century, they believed in 'natural' morality and scientific truth. These were some of the beliefs that held them together. But they were divided by differences no less profound.

The first and greatest of their problems was their attitude towards the peasants in whose name all that they did was done. Who was to show the peasants the true path to justice and equality? Individual liberty is not, indeed, condemned by the populists, but it tends to be regarded as a liberal catchword, liable to distract attention from immediate social and economic tasks. Should one train experts to teach the ignorant younger brothers – the tillers of the soil – and, if need be, stimulate them to resist authority, to revolt and destroy the old order before the rebels had themselves fully grasped the need or meaning of such acts? That is the view of such dissimilar figures as Bakunin and Speshnev in the 1840s; it was preached by Chernyshevsky in the 1850s, and was passionately advocated by Zaichnevsky and the Jacobins of 'Young Russia' in the 1860s; it was preached by Lavrov in the 1870s and 1880s, and equally by his rivals and opponents – the believers in disciplined professional terrorism – Nechaev and Tkachev, and their followers who include – for this purpose alone – not only the Socialist Revolutionaries but also some of the most fanatical Russian Marxists, in particular Lenin and Trotsky.

Some among them asked whether this training of revolutionary groups might not create an arrogant élite of seekers of power and autocracy, men who would, at best, believe it their duty to give the peasants not what the peasants asked for but what they – their self-appointed mentors – thought good for them, namely, that which the masses ought to ask for, whether they in fact did so or not. They pushed the question farther, and asked whether this would not, in due course, breed fanatical men who would pay too little heed to the actual wants of the vast majority of the Russian population, intent on forcing upon them only what they – the dedicated order of professional revolutionaries, cut off from the life of the masses by their own special training and conspiratorial lives – had chosen for them, ignoring the hopes and protests of the people itself. Was there not a terrible danger here of the substitution of a new yoke for the old, of a despotic oligarchy of intellectuals in the place of the nobility and the bureaucracy and the tsar? What reason was there for thinking that the new masters would prove less oppressive than the old?

This was argued by some among the terrorists of the 1860s – Ishutin and Karakozov, for example – and even more forcibly by the majority of the idealistic young men, who 'went among the people' in the 1870s and later, with the aim not so much of teaching others as of themselves learning how to live, in a state of mind inspired by Rousseau (and perhaps by Nekrasov or Tolstoy) at least as much as by the more tough-minded social theorists. These young men, the so-called 'repentant gentry', believed themselves to have been corrupted not merely by an evil social system but by the very process of liberal education which makes for deep inequalities, and inevitably lifts scientists, writers, professors, experts, civilised men in general, too high above the heads of the masses, and so itself becomes the richest breeding-ground of injustice and class oppression; everything that obstructs understanding between individuals or groups or nations, that creates and keeps in being obstacles to human solidarity and fraternity, is *eo ipso* evil; specialisation and university education build walls between men, prevent individuals and groups from 'connecting', kill love and friendship, and are among the major causes responsible for what, after Hegel and his followers, came to be called the 'alienation' of entire orders or classes or cultures.

Some among the populists contrived to ignore or evade this problem. Bakunin, for example, who, if not a populist himself, influenced populism profoundly, denounced faith in intellectuals and experts as liable to lead to the most ignoble of tyrannies – the rule of scientists and pedants – but would not face the problem of whether the revolutionaries had come to teach or to learn. It was left unanswered by the terrorists of 'The People's Will' and their sympathisers. More sensitive and morally scrupulous thinkers – Chernyshevsky and Kropotkin, for example – felt the oppressive weight of the question, and did not attempt to conceal it from themselves; yet whenever they asked themselves by what right they proposed to impose this or that system of social organisation on the mass of peasants who had grown up in a wholly different way of life, and one that might embody far profounder values of its own, they gave no clear reply. The question became even more acute when it was asked (as it increasingly came to be in the 1860s) what was to be done if the peasants actually resisted the revolutionaries' plans for their liberation? Must the masses be deceived, or, worse still, coerced? No one denied that in the end it was the people and not the revolutionary élite that must govern, but in the meanwhile how far was one allowed to go in ignoring the majority's wishes, or in forcing them into courses which they plainly loathed?

This was by no means a merely academic problem. The first enthusiastic adherents of radical populism – the missionaries who went 'to the people' in the famous summer of 1874 – were met by mounting indifference, suspicion, resentment, and sometimes active hatred and resistance, on the part of their would-be beneficiaries, who, as often as not, handed them over to the police. The populists were thus forced to define their attitude explicitly, since they believed passionately in the need to justify their activities by rational argument. Their answers, when they came, were far from unanimous. The activists, men like Tkachev, Nechaev and, in a less political sense, Pisarev, whose admirers came to be known as 'nihilists', anticipated Lenin in their contempt for democratic methods. Since the days of Plato it has been argued that the spirit is superior to the flesh, and that those who know must govern those who do not. The educated cannot listen to the uneducated and ignorant masses. The masses must be rescued by whatever means were available, if necessary against their own foolish wishes, by guile or fraud, or violence if need be. But it was only a minority in the movement who accepted this division and the authoritarianism that it entailed. The majority were horrified by the open advocacy of such Machiavellian tactics, and thought that no end, however good, could fail to be destroyed by the adoption of monstrous means.

A similar conflict broke out over the attitude to the State. All

Russian populists were agreed that the State was the embodiment
of a system of coercion and inequality, and therefore intrinsically
evil; neither justice nor happiness was possible until it was eliminated. But in the meanwhile what was to be the immediate aim of
the revolution? Tkachev is quite clear that until the capitalist
enemy had been finally destroyed, the weapon of coercion – the
pistol torn from his hand by the revolutionaries – must on no
account be thrown away, but must itself be turned against him. In
other words the machinery of the State must not be destroyed, but
must be used against the inevitable counter-revolution; it cannot
be dispensed with until the last enemy has been – in Proudhon's
immortal phrase – successfully liquidated, and mankind consequently has no further need of any instrument of coercion. In this
doctrine he was followed by Lenin more faithfully than mere
adherence to the ambivalent Marxist formula about the dictatorship of the proletariat seemed to require. Lavrov, who represents
the central stream of populism, and reflects all its vacillations and
confusions, characteristically advocated not indeed the immediate
or total elimination of the State but its systematic reduction to
something vaguely described as the minimum. Chernyshevsky,
who is the least anarchistic of the populists, conceives of the State
as the organiser and protector of the free associations of peasants
or workers, and contrives to see it at once as centralised and
decentralised, a guarantee of order and efficiency, and of equality
and individual liberty too.

All these thinkers share one vast apocalyptic assumption: that
once the reign of evil – autocracy, exploitation, inequality – is
consumed in the fire of the revolution, there will arise naturally
and spontaneously out of its ashes a natural, harmonious, just
order, needing only the gentle guidance of the enlightened revolutionaries to attain its proper perfection. This great Utopian dream,
based on simple faith in regenerated human nature, was a vision
which the populists shared with Godwin and Bakunin, Marx and
Lenin. Its heart is the pattern of sin and death and resurrection –
of the road to the earthly paradise, the gates of which will open
only if men find the one true way and follow it. Its roots lie deep
in the religious imagination of mankind; and there is therefore
nothing surprising in the fact that this secular version of it had

strong affinities with the faith of the Russian Old Believers – the dissenting sects – for whom, since the great religious schism of the seventeenth century, the Russian State and its rulers, particularly Peter the Great, represented the rule of Satan upon earth; this persecuted religious underground provided a good many potential allies whom the populists made efforts to mobilise.

There were deep divisions among the populists; they differed about the future role of the intellectuals, as compared with that of the peasants; they differed about the historical importance of the rising class of capitalists, gradualism versus conspiracy, education and propaganda versus terrorism and preparation for immediate risings. All these questions were interrelated and they demanded immediate solutions. But the deepest rift among the populists arose over the urgent question of whether a truly democratic revolution could possibly occur before a sufficient number of the oppressed had become fully conscious – that is, capable of understanding and analysing the causes of their intolerable condition. The moderates argued that no revolution could justly be called democratic unless it sprang from the rule of the revolutionary majority. But in that event, there was perhaps no alternative to waiting until education and propaganda had created this majority – a course that was being advocated by almost all Western socialists – Marxist and non-Marxist alike – in the second half of the nineteenth century.

Against this the Russian Jacobins argued that to wait, and in the meanwhile to condemn all forms of revolt organised by resolute minorities as irresponsible terrorism, or, worse still, as the replacement of one despotism by another, would lead to catastrophic results: while the revolutionaries procrastinated, capitalism would develop rapidly; the breathing space would enable the ruling class to develop a social and economic base incomparably stronger than that which it possessed at present; the growth of a prosperous and energetic capitalism would create opportunities of employment for the radical intellectuals themselves: doctors, engineers, educators, economists, technicians and experts of all types would be assigned profitable tasks and positions; their new bourgeois masters (unlike the existing regime) would be intelligent enough not to force them into any kind of political conformity; the intelligentsia would obtain special privileges, status and wide opportunities for self-expression – harmless radicalism would be tolerated, a good deal of personal liberty permitted – and in this way the revolutionary cause would lose its more valuable recruits. Once those whom insecurity and discontent had driven into making common cause with the oppressed had been partially satisfied, the incentive to revolutionary activity would be weakened, and the prospects of a radical transformation of society would become exceedingly dim. The radical wing of the revolutionaries argued with great force that the advance of capitalism, whatever Marx might say, was not inevitable; it might be so in Western Europe, but in Russia it could still be arrested by a revolutionary coup, destroyed in the root before it had had time to grow too strong. If recognition of the need to awaken the 'political consciousness' of the majority of the workers and peasants (which by this time, and partly as a result of the failure of the intellectuals in 1848, had been pronounced absolutely indispensable to the revolution both by Marxists and by the majority of the populist leaders) was tantamount to the adoption of a gradualist programme, the moment for action would surely be missed; and in place of the populist or socialist revolution would there not arise a vigorous, imaginative, predatory, successful capitalist regime which would succeed Russian semi-feudalism as surely as it had replaced the feudal order in Western Europe? And then who could tell how many decades or centuries might elapse before the arrival, at long last, of the revolution? When it did arrive, who could tell what kind of order it would, by that time, install – resting upon what social basis?

All populists were agreed that the village commune was the ideal embryo of those socialist groups on which the future society was to be based. But would the development of capitalism not automatically destroy the commune? And if it was maintained (although perhaps this was not explicitly asserted before the 1880s) that capitalism was already destroying the *mir*, that the class struggle, as analysed by Marx, was dividing the villages as surely as the cities, then the plan of action was clear: rather than sit with folded hands and watch this disintegration fatalistically, resolute men could and must arrest this process, and save the village commune. Socialism, so the Jacobins argued, could be introduced by the capture of power to which all the energies of the revolutionaries must be bent, even at the price of postponing the task of educating the peasants in moral, social and political realities; indeed, such education could surely be promoted more rapidly and efficiently after the revolution had broken the resistance of the old regime.

This line of thought, which bears an extraordinary resemblance, if not to the actual words, then to the policies pursued by Lenin in 1917, was basically very different from the older Marxist determinism. Its perpetual refrain was that there was no time to lose. Kulaks were devouring the poorer peasants in the country, capitalists were breeding fast in the towns. If the government possessed even a spark of intelligence, it would make concessions and promote reforms, and by this means divert educated men whose will and brains were needed for the revolution into the peaceful paths of the service of the reactionary State; propped up by such liberal measures, the unjust order would continue and be strengthened. The activists argued that there was nothing inevitable about revolutions: they were the fruit of human will and human reason. If there were not enough of these, the revolution might never take place at all. It was only the insecure who craved social solidarity and communal life; individualism was always a luxury, the ideal of the socially established. The new class of technical specialists – the modern, enlightened, energetic men celebrated by liberals like Kavelin and Turgenev, and at times even by the radical individualist Pisarev – were for the Jacobin Tkachev worse than cholera or typhus,[1] for by applying scientific methods to social life they were playing into the hands of the new, rising capitalist oligarchs and thereby obstructing the path to freedom. Palliatives were fatal when only an operation could save the patient: they merely prolonged his disease and weakened him so much that in the end not even an operation could save him. One must strike before these new, potentially conformist, intellectuals had grown too numerous and too comfortable and had obtained too much power, for otherwise it would be too late: a Saint-Simonian élite

---

1   'Printsipy i zadachi sovremennoi kritiki' (1872), in P. N. Tkachev, *Izbrannye sochineniya na sotsial'no-politicheskie temy v semi tomakh*, ed. B. P. Koz'min (Moscow, 1932–7), vi 297.

of highly-paid managers would preside over a new feudal order –
an economically efficient but socially immoral society, inasmuch
as it was based on permanent inequality.

The greatest of all evils was inequality. Whenever any other
ideal came into conflict with equality, the Russian Jacobins always
called for its sacrifice or modification; the first principle upon
which all justice rested was that of equality; no society was equit-
able in which there was not a maximum degree of equality between
men. If the revolution was to succeed, three major fallacies had to
be fought and rooted out. The first was that men of culture alone
created progress. This was not true, and had the bad consequence
of inducing faith in élites. The second was the opposite illusion –
that everything must be learnt from the common people. This was
equally false. Rousseau's Arcadian peasants were so many idyllic
figments. The masses were ignorant, brutal, reactionary, and did
not understand their own needs or good. If the revolution depended upon their maturity, or capacity for political judgement
or organisation, it would certainly fail. The last fallacy was that
only a proletarian majority could successfully make a revolution.
No doubt a proletarian majority might do that, but if Russia was
to wait until it possessed one, the opportunity of destroying a
corrupt and detested government would pass, and capitalism
would be found to be too firmly in the saddle.

What, then, must be done? Men must be trained to make the
revolution and destroy the present system and all obstacles to
social equality and democratic self-government. When this was
achieved, a democratic assembly was to be convened, and if those
who made the revolution took care to explain the reasons for it,
and the social and economic situation that made it necessary,
then the masses, benighted though they might be today, would
assuredly, in the view of the Jacobins, grasp their condition sufficiently to allow themselves to be – indeed to welcome the opportunity of being – organised into the new free federation of
productive associations.

But supposing they were still, on the morrow of a successful
coup d'état, not mature enough to see this? Herzen did indeed ask
this awkward question again and again in his writings in the late
1860s. The majority of the populists were deeply troubled by it.

But the activist wing had no doubt of the answer: strike the chains from the captive hero, and he will stretch himself to his full height and live in freedom and happiness for ever after. The views of these men were astonishingly simple. They believed in terrorism and more terrorism to achieve complete, anarchist liberty. The purpose of the revolution, for them, was to establish absolute equality, not only economic and social, but physical and physiological: they saw no discrepancy between this bed of Procrustes and absolute freedom. This order would be imposed in the beginning by the power and authority of the State, after which the State, having fulfilled its purpose, would swiftly 'liquidate' itself.

Against this, the spokesmen of the main body of the populists argued that Jacobin means tended to bring about Jacobin consequences: if the purpose of the revolution was to liberate, it must not use the weapons of despotism that were bound to enslave those whom they were designed to liberate: the remedy must not prove more destructive than the disease. To use the State to break the power of the exploiters and to impose a specific form of life upon a people, the majority of whom had not been educated to understand the need for it, was to exchange the tsarist yoke for a new, not necessarily less crushing, one – that of the revolutionary minority. The majority of the populists were deeply democratic; they believed that all power tended to corrupt, that all concentration of authority tended to perpetuate itself, that all centralisation was coercive and evil, and, therefore, that the sole hope of a just and free society lay in the peaceful conversion of men by rational argument to the truths of social and economic justice and democratic freedom. In order to obtain the opportunity of converting men to this vision, it might indeed be necessary to break the existing obstacles to free and rational intercourse – the police State, the power of capitalists or of landowners – and to use force in the process, whether mass mutiny or individual terrorism. But this concept of temporary measures presented itself to them as something wholly different from leaving absolute power in the hands of any party or group, however virtuous, once the power of the enemy had been broken. Their case is the classical case, during the last two centuries, of every libertarian and federalist against Jacobins and centralisers; it is Voltaire's case against both

Helvétius and Rousseau; that of the left wing of the Gironde against the Mountain; Herzen used these arguments against doctrinaire communists of the immediately preceding period – Cabet and the disciples of Babeuf; Bakunin denounced the Marxist demand for the dictatorship of the proletariat as something that would merely transfer power from one set of oppressors to another; the populists of the 1880s and 1890s urged this against all those whom they suspected of conspiring (whether they realised it or not) to destroy individual spontaneity and freedom, whether they were laissez-faire liberals who allowed factory owners to enslave the masses, or radical collectivists who were ready to do so themselves; whether they were capitalist entrepreneurs (as Mikhailovsky wrote to Dostoevsky in his celebrated criticism of his novel *The Possessed*) or Marxist advocates of centralised authority; he looked upon both as far more dangerous than the pathological fanatics pilloried by Dostoevsky – as brutal, amoral social Darwinists, profoundly hostile to variety and individual freedom and character.

This, again, was the main political issue which, at the turn of the century, divided the Russian Socialist Revolutionaries from the Social Democrats; and over which, a few years later, both Plekhanov and Martov broke with Lenin: indeed the great quarrel between the Bolsheviks and the Mensheviks (whatever its ostensible cause) turned upon it. In due course Lenin himself, two or three years after the October Revolution, while he never abandoned the central Marxist doctrine, expressed his bitter disappointment with those very consequences of it which his opponents had predicted – bureaucracy and the arbitrary despotism of the party officials; and Trotsky accused Stalin of this same crime. The dilemma of means and ends is the deepest and most agonising problem that torments the revolutionary movements of our own day in all the continents of the world, not least in Asia and Africa. That this debate took so clear and articulate a form within the populist movement makes its development exceptionally relevant to our own predicament.

All these differences occurred within the framework of a common revolutionary outlook, for, whatever their disagreements, all populists were united by an unshakeable faith in the revolution. This faith derived from many sources. It sprang from the needs and outlook of a society still overwhelmingly pre-industrial, which gave the craving for simplicity and fraternity, and the agrarian idealism which derives ultimately from Rousseau, a reality which can still be seen in India and Africa today, and which necessarily looks Utopian to the eyes of social historians born in the industrialised West. It was a consequence of the dis-illusionment with parliamentary democracy, liberal convictions and the good faith of bourgeois intellectuals that resulted from the fiasco of the European revolutions of 1848–9, and from the particular conclusion drawn by Herzen that Russia, which had not suffered this revolution, might find her salvation in the un-destroyed natural socialism of the peasant *mir*. It was deeply influenced by Bakunin's violent diatribes against all forms of central authority, and in particular the State; and by his vision of men as being by nature peaceful and productive, and rendered violent only when they are perverted from their proper ends, and forced to be either jailers or convicts. But it was also fed by the streams that flowed in a contrary direction: by Tkachev's faith in a Jacobin élite of professional revolutionaries as the only force capable of destroying the advance of capitalism, helped on its fatal path by innocent reformists and humanitarians and careerist intellectuals, and concealed behind the repulsive sham of parlia-mentary democracy; even more by the passionate utilitarianism of Pisarev, and his brilliant polemics against all forms of idealism and amateurishness, and, in particular, the sentimental idealisation of the simplicity and beauty of peasants in general, and of Russian peasants in particular, as beings touched by grace, remote from the corrupting influences of the decaying West. It was supported by the appeal which these 'critical realists' made to their com-patriots to save themselves by self-help and hard-headed energy – a kind of neo-Encyclopedist campaign in favour of natural science, skill and professionalism, directed against the humanities, clas-sical learning, history and other forms of 'sybaritic' self-indulgence. Above all, it contrasted 'realism' with the literary culture which had lulled the best men in Russia into a condition where corrupt bureaucrats, stupid and brutal landowners and an obscurantist Church could exploit them or let them rot, while aesthetes and liberals looked the other way.

But the deepest strain of all, the very centre of the populist outlook, was the individualism and rationalism of Lavrov and Mikhailovsky. With Herzen they believed that history followed no predetermined pattern, that it possessed 'no libretto',[1] that neither the violent conflicts between cultures, nations, classes (which for Hegelians constituted the essence of human progress), nor the struggles for power by one class over another (represented by Marxists as being the motive force of history) were inevitable. Faith in human freedom was the cornerstone of populist humanism: the populists never tired of repeating that ends were chosen by men, not imposed upon them, and that men's wills alone could construct a happy and honourable life – a life in which the interests of intellectuals, peasants, manual workers and the liberal professions could be reconciled; not indeed made wholly to coincide, for that was an unattainable ideal; but adjusted in an unstable equilibrium, which human reason and constant human care could adjust to the largely unpredictable consequences of the interaction of men with each other and with nature. It may be that the tradition of the Orthodox Church with its conciliar and communal principles and deep antagonism both to the authoritarian hierarchy of the Roman Church, and to the individualism of the Protestants, also exercised its share of influence. These doctrines and these prophets and their Western masters – French radicals before and after the French Revolution, as well as Fichte and Buonarroti, Fourier and Hegel, Mill and Proudhon, Owen and Marx – played their part. But the largest figure in the populist movement, the man whose temperament, ideas and activities dominated it from beginning to end, is undoubtedly Nikolay Gavrilovich Chernyshevsky. The influence of his life and teachings, despite a multitude of monographs, still awaits its interpreter.

Nikolay Chernyshevsky was not a man of original ideas. He did not possess the depth, the imagination or the brilliant intellect and literary talent of Herzen; nor the eloquence, the boldness, the temperament or the reasoning power of Bakunin, nor the moral genius and unique social insight of Belinsky. But he was a man of unswerving integrity, immense industry, and a capacity rare

1   'S togo berega', H vi 36, 338 (variant); F 39. [See also 105 above.]

among Russians for concentration upon concrete detail. His deep, steady, lifelong hatred of slavery, injustice and irrationality did not express itself in large theoretical generalisations, or the creation of a sociological or metaphysical system, or violent action against authority. It took the form of slow, uninspired, patient accumulation of facts and ideas – a crude, dull, but powerful intellectual structure on which one might found a detailed policy of practical action appropriate to the specific Russian environment which he desired to alter. Chernyshevsky was in greater sympathy with the concrete, carefully elaborated socialist plans, however mistaken they might be, of the Petrashevsky group (to which Dostoevsky had belonged in his youth), crushed by the government in 1849, than with the great imaginative constructions of Herzen, Bakunin and their followers.

A new generation had grown up during the dead years after 1849. These young men had witnessed vacillation and outright betrayals on the part of liberals, which had led to the victories of the reactionary parties in 1849. Twelve years later they saw the same phenomenon in their own country when the manner in which the peasants had been emancipated in Russia seemed to them to be a cynical travesty of all their plans and hopes. Such men as these found the plodding genius of Chernyshevsky – his attempts to work out specific solutions to specific problems in terms of concrete statistical data; his constant appeals to facts; his patient efforts to indicate attainable, practical, immediate ends rather than desirable states of affairs to which there was no visible road; his flat, dry, pedestrian style, his very dullness and lack of inspiration – more serious and ultimately more inspiring than the noble flights of the romantic idealists of the 1840s. His relatively low social origin (he was the son of a parish priest) gave him a natural affinity with the humble folk whose condition he was seeking to analyse, and an abiding distrust, later to turn into fanatical hatred, of all liberal theorists, whether in Russia or the West. These qualities made Chernyshevsky a natural leader of a disenchanted generation of socially mingled origins, no longer dominated by good birth, embittered by the failure of their own early ideals, by government repression, by the humiliation of Russia in the Crimean War, by the weakness, heartlessness, hypocrisy and chaotic incompetence of the ruling class. To these tough-minded, socially insecure, angry, suspicious young radicals, contemptuous of the slightest trace of eloquence or 'literature', Chernyshevsky was a father and a confessor as neither the aristocratic and ironical Herzen nor the wayward and ultimately frivolous Bakunin could ever become.

Like all populists, Chernyshevsky believed in the need to preserve the peasant commune and to spread its principles to industrial production. He believed that Russia could profit directly by learning from the scientific advances of the West, without going through the agonies of an industrial revolution. Human development is a form of chronological unfairness, Herzen had once characteristically observed, since latecomers are able to profit by the labours of their predecessors without paying the same price.[1] 'History is fond of her grandchildren,' Chernyshevsky repeated after him, 'for it offers them the marrow of the bones, which the previous generation had hurt its hands in breaking.'[2] For Chernyshevsky history moved along a spiral, in Hegelian triads, since every generation tends to repeat the experience not of its parents, but of its grandparents, and repeats it at a 'higher level'.

But it is not this historicist element in his doctrine that bound its spell upon the populists. They were most of all influenced by his acute distrust of reforms from above, by his belief that the essence of history was a struggle between the classes, above all by his conviction (which derives nothing, so far as we know, from Marx, but draws upon socialist sources common to both) that the State is always the instrument of the dominant class, and cannot,

1   [Probably paraphrase rather than direct quotation. For passages in which Herzen makes similar remarks, see 'La Russie' (1849), H vi 167–8; 'La Russie et le vieux monde' (1854), H xii 152, where he says that Russia will pass through some of the phases through which Western nations have passed only 'in the same way that a foetus passes through the inferior stages of zoological existence'; and the article cited at 118 above, note 3, section 3, 'Si vieillesse pouvait, si jeunesse savait!', 170 ff.]

2   'Kritika filosofskikh predubezhdenii protiv obshchinnogo vladeniya' (1858), C v 387. [For a more literal translation see 'A Critique of Philosophical Prejudices against Communal Ownership', in Teodor Shanin (ed.), Late Marx and the Russian Road: Marx and 'the Peripheries of Capitalism' (London etc., 1984), 187.]

whether it consciously desires this or not, embark on those necessary reforms, the success of which would end its own domination.
No order can be persuaded to undertake its own dissolution.
Hence all attempts to convert the tsar, all attempts to evade the
horrors of revolution, must (he concluded in the early 1860s)
remain necessarily vain. There was a moment in the late 1850s
when, like Herzen, he had hoped for reforms from above. The final
form of the Emancipation, and the concessions which the government had made to the landowners, cured him of this illusion. He
pointed out with a good deal of historical justification that liberals,
who hoped to influence the government by Fabian tactics, had
thus far merely succeeded in betraying both the peasants and
themselves: first they compromised themselves with the peasants
by their relations with their masters; after that, the governing
class found little difficulty whenever this suited their convenience
in representing them as false friends to the peasants, and turning
the latter against them. This had occurred in both France and
Germany in 1849. Even if the moderates withdrew in time,
and advocated violent measures, their ignorance of conditions
and blindness to the peasants' and workers' actual needs usually
led them to advocate Utopian schemes which in the end cost their
followers a terrible price.

Chernyshevsky had evolved a simple form of historical materialism, according to which social factors determined political ones,
and not vice versa. Consequently, he held with Fourier and
Proudhon that liberal and parliamentary ideals merely evaded the
central issues: the peasants and the workers needed food, shelter,
boots; as for the right to vote, or to be governed by liberal consti-
tutions, or to obtain guarantees of personal liberty, these meant
little to hungry and half-naked men. The social revolution must
come first: appropriate political reforms would follow of themselves. For Chernyshevsky the principal lesson of 1848 was that
the Western liberals, the brave no less than the cowardly, had
demonstrated their political and moral bankruptcy, and with it
that of their Russian disciples – Herzen, Kavelin, Granovsky and
the rest. Russia must pursue her own path. Unlike the Slavophils,
and like the Russian Marxists of the next generation, he maintained with a wealth of economic evidence that the historical

development of Russia, and in particular the peasant *mir*, were in no sense unique, but followed the social and economic laws that governed all human societies. Like the Marxists (and the Comtian positivists), he believed that such laws could be discovered and stated; but unlike the Marxists, he was convinced that by adopting Western techniques, and educating a body of men of trained and resolute wills and rational outlook, Russia could 'leap over' the capitalist stage of social development, and transform her village communes and free cooperative groups of craftsmen into agricultural and industrial associations of producers who would constitute the embryo of the new socialist society. Technological progress did not, in his view, automatically break up the peasant commune: savages can be taught to use Latin script and safety-matches;[1] factories can be grafted on to workers' *artels* without destroying them; large-scale organisation could eliminate exploitation, and yet preserve the predominantly agricultural nature of the Russian economy.[2]

Chernyshevsky believed in the decisive historical role of the application of science to life, but, unlike Pisarev, did not regard individual enterprise, still less capitalism, as indispensable to this process. He retained enough of the Fourierism of his youth to look upon the free associations of peasant communes and craftsmen's *artels* as the basis of all freedom and progress. But at the same

1   See ibid. 380–4; 'A Critique of Philosophical Prejudices against Communal Landholding', in *A Documentary History of Russian Thought: From the Enlightenment to Marxism*, trans. and ed. W. J. Leatherbarrow and D. C. Offord (Ann Arbor, 1987), 210–12; cf. Shanin 187–90.

2   In chapter 15 of *Il Populismo russo* – translated into English as *Roots of Revolution* (London, 1960) – Franco Venturi very aptly quotes populist statistics (which seem plausible enough) according to which the proportion of peasants to that of landowners in the 1860s was of the order of 134:1, while the land owned by them stood to that of their masters in the ratio of 1:11.5, and their incomes were 2.5:97.5; as for industry, the proportion of city workers to peasants was 1:100 (403–4 in the English edition). Given these figures, it is perhaps not surprising that Marx should have declared that his prognosis applied to the Western economies, and not necessarily to that of the Russians, even though his Russian disciples ignored this concession, and insisted that capitalism was making enormous strides in Russia, and would soon obliterate the differences that divided it from the West. Plekhanov (who stoutly denied that Chernyshevsky had ever been a populist) elaborated this theory; Lenin acted upon it.

time, like the Saint-Simonians, he was convinced that little would be achieved without collective action – State socialism on a vast scale. These incompatible beliefs were never reconciled; Chernyshevsky's writings contain statements both in favour of and against the desirability of large-scale industry. He is similarly ambivalent about the part to be played (and the part to be avoided) by the State as the stimulator and controller of industry, about the function of managers of large collective industrial enterprises, about the relations of the public and private sectors of the economy, and about the political sovereignty of the democratically elected parliament and its relation to the State as the source of centralised economic planning and control.

The outlines of Chernyshevsky's social programme remained vague or inconsistent, and often both. It is the concrete detail which, founded as it was on real experience, spoke directly to the representatives of the great popular masses, who had at last found a spokesman and interpreter of their own needs and feelings. His deepest aspirations and emotions were poured into *What Is To Be Done?*, a social *Utopia* which, grotesque as a work of art, had a literally epoch-making effect on Russian opinion. This didactic novel described the 'new men' of the free, morally pure, co-operative socialist commonwealth of the future; its touching sincerity and moral passion bound their spell upon the imaginations of the idealistic and guilt-stricken sons of prosperous parents, and provided them with an ideal model in the light of which an entire generation of revolutionaries educated and hardened itself to the defiance of existing laws and conventions and to the acceptance of exile and death with sublime unconcern.

Chernyshevsky preached a naive utilitarianism. Like James Mill, and perhaps Bentham, he held that basic human nature was a fixed, physiologically analysable pattern of natural processes and faculties, and that the maximisation of human happiness could therefore be scientifically planned and realised. Having decided that imaginative writing and criticism were the only available media in Russia for propagating radical ideas, he filled the *Contemporary*, a review which he edited together with the poet Nekrasov, with as high a proportion of direct socialist doctrine as could be smuggled in under the guise of literature. In his work he was helped by the violent young critic Dobrolyubov, a genuinely gifted man of letters (which Chernyshevsky was not) who, at times, went even further in his passionate desire to preach and educate. The aesthetic views of the two zealots were severely practical. Chernyshevsky laid it down that the function of art was to help men to satisfy their wants more rationally, to disseminate knowledge, to combat ignorance, prejudice and the anti-social passions, to improve life in the most literal and narrow sense of these words. Driven to absurd consequences, he embraced them gladly. Thus he explained that the chief value of marine paintings was that they showed the sea to those who, like, for instance, the inhabitants of central Russia, lived too far away from it ever to see it for themselves; or that his friend and patron Nekrasov, because by his verse he moved men to greater sympathy with the oppressed than other poets had done, was for this reason the greatest Russian poet, living or dead. His earlier collaborators, civilised and fastidious men of letters like Turgenev and Botkin, found his grim fanaticism increasingly difficult to bear. Turgenev could not long live with this art-hating and dogmatic schoolmaster. Tolstoy despised his dreary provincialism, his total lack of aesthetic sense, his intolerance, his rationalism, his maddening self-assurance. But these very qualities, or, rather, the outlook of which they were characteristic, helped to make him the natural leader of the 'hard' young men who had succeeded the idealists of the 1840s. Chernyshevsky's harsh, flat, dull, humourless, grating sentences, his preoccupation with concrete detail, his self-discipline, his dedication to the material and moral good of his fellow men, the grey, self-effacing personality, the tireless, passionate, devoted, minute industry, the hatred of style or of any concessions to the graces, the unquestionable sincerity, utter self-forgetfulness, brutal directness, indifference to the claims of private life, innocence, personal kindness, pedantry, disarming moral charm, capacity for self-sacrifice, created the image that later became the prototype of the Russian revolutionary hero and martyr. More than any other publicist he was responsible for drawing the final line between 'us' and 'them'. All his life he preached that there must be no compromise with 'them', that the war must be fought to the death and on every front; that there were no neutrals; that, so long as this war was being fought, no work could be too trivial, too repulsive or too tedious for a revolutionary to perform. His personality and outlook set their seal upon two generations of Russian revolutionaries; not least upon Lenin, who admired him devotedly.

In spite of his emphasis on economic or sociological arguments, the basic approach, the tone and outlook of Chernyshevsky and of the populists generally is moral, and at times religious. These men believed in socialism not because it was inevitable, nor because it was effective, not even because it alone was rational, but because it was just. Concentrations of political power, capitalism, the centralised State, trampled on the rights of men and crippled them morally and spiritually. The populists were stern atheists, but socialism and orthodox Christian values coalesced in their minds. They shrank from the prospect of industrialism in Russia because of its brutal cost, and they disliked the West because it had paid this price too heartlessly. Their disciples, the populist economists of the 1880s and 1890s, Daniel'son and Vorontsov for example, for all their strictly economic arguments about the possibility of capitalism in Russia (some of which seem a good deal sounder than their Marxist opponents have represented them as being), were in the last analysis moved by moral revulsion from the sheer mass of suffering that capitalism was destined to bring, that is to say, by a refusal to pay so appalling a price, no matter how valuable the results. Their successors in the twentieth century, the Socialist Revolutionaries, sounded the note which runs through the whole of the populist tradition in Russia: that the purpose of social action is not the power of the State, but the welfare of the people; that to enrich the State and provide it with military and industrial power, while undermining the health, the education, the morality, the general cultural level of its citizens, was feasible but wicked. They compared the progress of the United States, where, they maintained, the welfare of the individual was paramount, with that of Prussia, where it was not. They committed themselves to the view (which goes back at least to Sismondi) that the spiritual and physical condition of the individual citizen matters more than the power of the State, so that if, as often happened, the two stood in inverse ratio to one another, the rights and welfare of the individual must come first. They rejected as historically false the proposition that only powerful States could breed good or happy citizens, and as morally unacceptable the proposition that to lose oneself in the life and welfare of one's society is the highest form of individual self-fulfilment.

Belief in the primacy of human rights over other claims is the first principle that separates pluralist from centralised societies, and Welfare States, mixed economies, 'New Deal' policies, from one-party governments, 'closed' societies, 'five-year plans', and, in general, forms of life built to serve a single goal that transcends the varied goals of differing groups or individuals. Chernyshevsky was more fanatical than most of his followers in the 1870s and 1880s, and believed far more strongly in organisation, but even he neither stopped his ears to the cries for immediate help which he heard upon all sides, nor believed in the need to suppress the wants of individuals who were making desperate efforts to escape destruction, in the interests of even the most sacred and over-mastering purpose. There were times when he was a narrow and unimaginative pedant, but at his worst he was never impatient, or arrogant, or inhumane, and was perpetually reminding his readers and himself that, in their zeal to help, the educators must not end by bullying their would-be beneficiaries; that what 'we' – the rational intellectuals – think good for the peasants may not be what they themselves want or need, and that to ram 'our' remedies down 'their' throats is not permitted. Neither he nor Lavrov, nor even the most ruthlessly Jacobin among the proponents of terror and violence, ever took cover behind the inevitable direction of history as a justification of what would otherwise have been patently unjust or brutal. If violence was the only means to a given end, then there might be circumstances in which it was right to employ it; but this must be justified in each case by the intrinsic moral claim of the end – an increase in happiness, or solidarity, or justice, or peace, or some other universal human value that outweighs the evil of the means – never by the view that it was rational and necessary to march in step with history, ignoring one's scruples and dismissing one's own 'subjective' moral principles because they were necessarily provisional, on the ground that history herself transformed all moral systems and retrospectively justified only those principles which survived and succeeded.

The mood of the populists, particularly in the 1870s, can fairly be described as religious. This group of conspirators or propagand-ists saw itself, and was seen by others, as constituting a dedicated order. The first condition of membership was the sacrifice of one's entire life to the movement, both to the particular group and party, and to the cause of the revolution in general. But the notion of the dictatorship of the party or of its leaders over individual lives – in particular over the beliefs of individual revolutionaries – is not part of this doctrine, and is indeed contrary to its entire spirit. The only censor over the individual's acts is his individual conscience. If one has promised obedience to the leaders of the party, such an oath is sacred, but it extends only to the specific revolutionary objectives of the party and not beyond them, and ends with the completion of whatever specific goals the party exists to promote – in the last resort, the revolution. Once the revolution has been made, each individual is free to act as he thinks fit, since discipline is a temporary means and not an end. The populists did indeed virtually invent the conception of the party as a group of professional conspirators with no private lives, obeying a total discipline – the core of the 'hard' professionals as against mere sympathisers and fellow-travellers; but this sprang from the specific situation that obtained in tsarist Russia, and the necessity and conditions for effective conspiracy, and not from belief in hierarchy as a form of life desirable or even tolerable in itself. Nor did the conspirators justify their acts by appealing to a cosmic process which sanctified their every act, since they believed in freedom of human choice and not in determinism. The later Leninist conception of the revolutionary party and its dictatorship, although historically it owed much to these trained martyrs of an earlier day, sprang from a very different outlook. The young men who poured into the villages during the celebrated summer of 1874, only to meet with non-comprehension, suspicion and often outright hostility on the part of the peasants, would have been profoundly astonished and indignant if they had been told that they were to look upon themselves as the sacred instruments of history, and that their acts were therefore to be judged by a moral code different from that common to other men.

The populist movement was a failure. Socialism 'simply bounces off the Russian masses like peas from a wall', wrote the celebrated terrorist Kravchinsky to his fellow-revolutionary Vera Zasulich in 1878, four years after the original wave of enthusiasm had died down.[1] 'They listen to our people as they do to the priest'[2] – respectfully, without understanding, without any effect upon their actions.

> There is noise in the capitals
> The prophets thunder
> A furious war of words is waged
> But in the depths, in the heart of Russia,
> There all is still, there is ancient peace.[3]

These lines by Nekrasov convey the mood of frustration which followed the failure of the sporadic efforts made by the revolutionary idealists in the late 1860s and early 1870s, peaceful propagandists and isolated terrorists alike – of whom Dostoevsky painted so violent a picture in his novel *The Possessed*. The government caught these men, exiled them, imprisoned them, and by its obstinate unwillingness to promote any measures to alleviate the consequences of an inadequate land reform drove liberal opinion towards sympathy with the revolutionaries. They felt that public opinion was on their side, and finally resorted to organised terrorism. Yet their ends always remained moderate enough. The open letter which they addressed to the new Emperor in 1881 is mild and liberal in tone. 'Terror', said the celebrated revolutionary Vera Figner many years later, 'was intended to create opportunities for developing the faculties of men for service to society.'[4] The society

1   Letter of 24 July 1878, in E. Korol'chuk, 'Iz perepiski S. M. Kravchinskogo', *Krasnyi arkhiv* 19 (1926 No 6), 196.
2   [Untraced.]
3   'V stolitsakh shum [. . .]' (1858), in N. A. Nekrasov, *Polnoe sobranie sochinenii i pisem v pyatnadtsati tomakh* (Leningrad, 1981–2000), ii 46.
4   [This appears to be a reference to a remark Figner made, according to her memoirs, in the speech she delivered to the court at the end of her trial in 1884: 'I consider it most important, most essential, that such conditions should be established as will allow the individual to develop his abilities to the fullest extent, and to devote them wholeheartedly to the good of society.' Vera Figner, *Zapechatlennyi trud* (Moscow, 1921–2), part 1, 320; *Memoirs*

for which violence was to blast the way was to be peaceful, tolerant, decentralised and humane. The principal enemy was still the
State.

The wave of terrorism reached its climax with the assassination
of Alexander II in 1881. The hoped-for revolution did not break
out. The revolutionary organisations were crushed, and the new
Tsar decided upon a policy of extreme repression. In this he was,
on the whole, supported by public opinion, which recoiled before
the assassination of an Emperor who had, after all, emancipated
the peasants, and was said to have been meditating other liberal
measures. The most prominent leaders of the movement were
executed or exiled; lesser figures escaped abroad, and the most
gifted of those who were still free – Plekhanov and Aksel'rod –
gradually moved towards Marxism. They felt embarrassed by
Marx's own concession that Russia could in principle avoid passing through a capitalist stage even without the aid of a Communist
world revolution – a thesis which Engels conceded far more grudg-
ingly and with qualifications – and maintained that Russia had in
fact already entered the capitalist stage. They declared that since
the development of capitalism in Russia was no more avoidable
than it had been in its day in the West, nothing was to be gained
by averting one's face from the 'iron' logic of history, and that for
these reasons, so far from resisting industrialisation, socialists
should encourage it, indeed profit by the fact that it, and it alone,
could breed the army of revolutionaries which would be sufficient
to overthrow the capitalist enemy – an army to be formed out of
the growing city proletariat, organised and disciplined by the very
conditions of its labour.

The vast leap forward in industrial development made by Russia
in the 1890s seemed to support the Marxist thesis. It proved
attractive to revolutionary intellectuals for many reasons: because
it claimed to be founded on a scientific analysis of the laws of
history which no society could hope to evade; because it claimed to
be able to prove that, although, as the pattern of history inexorably
unfolded itself, much violence, misery and injustice were bound

of a Revolutionist (DeKalb, 1991), 165. If this is right, the link to terror is at
most implicit.]

to occur, yet the story would have a happy ending. Hence the conscience of those who felt guilty because they acquiesced in exploitation and poverty, or at any rate because they did not take active – that is, violent – steps to alleviate or prevent them, as populist policy had demanded, felt assuaged by the 'scientific' guarantee that the road, covered though it might be with the corpses of the innocent, led inevitably to the gates of an earthly paradise. According to this view, the expropriators would find themselves expropriated by the sheer logic of human development, although the course of history might be shortened, and the birth-pangs made easier, by conscious organisation, and above all an increase in knowledge (that is, education) on the part of the workers and their leaders. This was particularly welcome to those who, understandably reluctant to continue with useless terrorism which merely led to Siberia or the scaffold, now found doctrinal justification for peaceful study and the life of ideas, which the intellectuals among them found far more congenial than bomb-throwing.

The heroism, the disinterestedness, the personal nobility of the populists were often admitted by their Marxist opponents. They were regarded as worthy forerunners of a truly rational revolutionary party, and Chernyshevsky was sometimes accorded an even higher status and was credited with insights of genius – an empirical and unscientific, but instinctively correct, approach to truths of which only Marx and Engels could provide the demonstration, armed as they were with the instrument of an exact science to which neither Chernyshevsky, nor any other Russian thinker of his day, had yet attained. Marx and Engels grew to be particularly indulgent to the Russians: they were praised for having done wonders for amateurs, remote from the West and using home-made tools. They alone in Europe had, by 1880, created a truly revolutionary situation in their country; nevertheless it was made clear, particularly by Kautsky, that this was no substitute for professional methods and the use of the new machinery provided by scientific socialism. Populism was written off as an amalgam of unorganised moral indignation and Utopian ideas in the muddled heads of self-taught peasants, well-meaning university intellectuals and other social casualties of the confused interim between the end of an obsolescent feudalism and the beginning of the new capitalist phase in a backward country. Marxist historians still tend to describe it as a movement compounded of systematic misinterpretation of economic facts and social realities, noble but useless individual terrorism, and spontaneous or ill-directed peasant risings – the necessary but pathetic beginnings of real revolutionary activity, the prelude to the real play, a scene of naive ideas and frustrated practice destined to be swept away by the new revolutionary, dialectical science heralded by Plekhanov and Lenin.

What were the ends of populism? Violent disputes took place about means and methods, about timing, but not about ultimate purposes. Anarchism, equality, a full life for all, these were universally accepted. It is as if the entire movement – the motley variety of revolutionary types which Franco Venturi describes in his book[1] so well and so lovingly – Jacobins and moderates, terrorists and educators, Lavrovists and Bakuninists, 'troglodytes', 'recalcitrants', 'country folk', members of 'Land and Liberty' and of 'The People's Will', were all dominated by a single myth: that once the monster was slain, the sleeping princess – the Russian peasantry – would awaken without further ado and live happily for ever after.

This is the movement of which Franco Venturi has written the history, the fullest, clearest, best-written and most impartial account of a particular stage of the Russian revolutionary movement in any language. Yet if the movement was a failure, if it was founded on false premises and was so easily extinguished by the tsarist police, has it more than historical interest – that of a narrative of the life and death of a party, of its acts and its ideas? On this question Venturi discreetly, as behoves an objective historian, offers no direct opinion. He tells the story in chronological sequence; he explains what occurs; he describes origins and consequences; he illuminates the relations of various groups of populists to one another, and leaves moral and political speculation to others. His work is not an apologia either for populism or its opponents. He does not praise or condemn, and seeks only to understand. Success in this task plainly needs no further reward.

1   op. cit. (260 above, note 2).

And yet one may, at moments, wonder whether populism should be dismissed quite as easily as it still is today, both by Communist and by bourgeois historians. Were the populists so hopelessly in error? Were Chernyshevsky and Lavrov – and Marx who listened to them – totally deluded?

Was capitalism, in fact, inevitable in Russia? The consequences of accelerated industrialisation prophesied by the neo-populist economists in the 1880s, namely a degree of social and economic misery as great as any undergone in the West during the Industrial Revolution, did occur, both before and, at an increasing tempo, after the October Revolution. Were they avoidable? Some writers on history consider this type of question to be absurd as such. What happened, happened. We are told that if we are not to deny causality in human affairs, we must suppose that what took place can only have done so precisely as it did; to ask what might have happened if the situation had been different is the idle play of the imagination, not worthy of serious historians. Yet this academic question is not without acute contemporary relevance. Some countries, such as, for example, Turkey, India, and some States in the Middle East and Latin America, have adopted a slower tempo of industrialisation and one less likely to bring immediate ruin to backward areas before they can be rehabilitated, and have done so in conscious preference to the forced marches of collectivisation upon which, in our day, the Russians, and after them the Chinese, have embarked. Are these non-Marxist governments inescapably set upon a path to ruin? For it is populist ideas which lie at the base of much of the socialist economic policy pursued by these and other countries today.

When Lenin organised the Bolshevik Revolution in 1917, the technique that he adopted, prima facie at least, resembled those commended by the Russian Jacobins, Tkachev and his followers, who had learnt them from Blanqui or Buonarroti, more than any to be found in the writings of Marx or Engels, at any rate after 1851. It was not, after all, full-grown capitalism that was enthroned in Russia in 1917. Russian capitalism was a still growing force, not yet in power, struggling against the fetters imposed upon it by the monarchy and the bureaucracy, as it had done in eighteenth-century France. But Lenin acted as if the bankers and

industrialists were already in control. He acted and spoke as if
this was so, but his revolution succeeded not so much by taking
over the centres of finance and industry (which history should
already have undermined) but by a seizure of strictly political
power on the part of a determined and trained group of professional revolutionaries, precisely as had been advocated by
Tkachev. If Russian capitalism had reached the stage which,
according to Marxist historical theory, it had to reach before a
proletarian revolution could be successful, the seizure of power
by a determined minority, and a very small one at that – a mere
Putsch – could not, *ex hypothesi*, have retained it long. And this,
indeed, is what Plekhanov said over and over again in his bitter
denunciations of Lenin in 1917: ignoring his argument that much
may be permitted in a backward country provided that the results
were duly saved by orthodox Marxist revolutions successfully
carried out soon after in the industrially more advanced West.

These conditions were not fulfilled; Lenin's hypothesis proved
historically irrelevant; yet the Bolshevik Revolution did not collapse. Could it be that the Marxist theory of history was mistaken?
Or had the Mensheviks misunderstood it, and concealed from
themselves the anti-democratic tendencies which had always been
implicit in it? In which case were their charges against Mikhailovsky and his friends wholly just? By 1917 their own fears of the
Bolshevik dictatorship rested upon the same basis. Moreover, the
results of the October Revolution turned out to be oddly similar to
those which Tkachev's opponents had prophesied that his methods
must inevitably produce: the emergence of an élite, wielding dic-
tatorial power, designed in theory to wither away once the need
for it had gone; but, as the populist democrats had said over and
over again, in practice more likely to grow in aggressiveness and
strength, with a tendency towards self-perpetuation which no
dictatorship seems able to resist.

The populists were convinced that the death of the peasant
commune would mean death, or at any rate a vast setback, to
freedom and equality in Russia; the Left Socialist Revolutionaries,
who were their direct descendants, transformed this into a demand
for a form of decentralised, democratic self-government among the
peasants, which Lenin adopted when he concluded his temporary

alliance with them in October 1917. In due course the Bolsheviks repudiated this programme, and transformed the cells of dedicated revolutionaries – perhaps the most original contribution of populism to revolutionary practice – into the hierarchy of centralised political power which the populists had steadily and fiercely denounced until they were themselves finally, in the form of the Socialist Revolutionary Party, proscribed and annihilated. Communist practice owed much, as Lenin was always ready to admit, to the populist movement; for it borrowed the technique of its rival and adapted it with conspicuous success to serve the precise purpose which it had been invented to resist.

TOLSTOY AND
ENLIGHTENMENT
(1960)

'Two things are always said about Count Tolstoy,' wrote the celebrated Russian critic Mikhailovsky in a forgotten essay published in the mid-1870s, 'that he is an outstandingly good writer of fiction and a bad thinker. This [. . .] has become a sort of axiom needing no demonstration.'[1] This almost universal verdict has reigned, virtually unchallenged, for something like a hundred years; and Mikhailovsky's attempt to question it remained relatively isolated. Tolstoy dismissed his left-wing ally as a routine liberal hack, and expressed surprise that anyone should take an interest in him. This was characteristic, but unjust. The essay, which its author called *The Right Hand and the Left Hand of Lev Tolstoy*, is a brilliant and convincing defence of Tolstoy on both intellectual and moral grounds, directed mainly against the liberals and socialists who saw in the novelist's ethical doctrines, and in particular in his glorification of the peasants and natural instinct, and his constant disparagement of scientific culture, a perverse and sophisticated obscurantism which discredited the liberal cause, and played into the hands of priests and reactionaries. Mikhailovsky rejected this view, and in the course of his long and careful attempt to sift the enlightened grain from the reactionary chaff in Tolstoy's opinions, reached the conclusion that there was an unresolved, and unavowed, conflict in the great novelist's conceptions both of human nature and of the problems facing

1 'Desnitsa i shuitsa L'va Tolstogo' (1875), in N. Mikhailovsky, *Literaturnaya kritika: stat'i o russkoi literature XIX–nachala XX veka* (Leningrad, 1989), 37. [More literally 'The reputation of Count Tolstoy is twofold: as one of a line of outstanding belletrists and as a bad thinker. This reputation has already become a sort of axiom needing no demonstration.']

Russian and Western civilisation. Mikhailovsky maintained that, so far from being a 'bad thinker', Tolstoy was no less acute, clear-eyed and convincing an analyst of ideas than of instincts or characters or actions. In his zeal for his paradoxical thesis – paradoxical certainly at the time at which he wrote it – Mikhailovsky sometimes goes too far; but in substance it seems to me to be right; or at any rate, more right than wrong, and my own remarks are no more than an extended gloss on it.

Tolstoy's opinions are always subjective and can be (as, for example, in his writings on Shakespeare or Dante or Wagner) wildly perverse. But the questions which in his most didactic essays he tries to answer are nearly always cardinal questions of principle, always first-hand, and cut far deeper, in the deliberately simplified and naked form in which he usually presents them, than those of more balanced and 'objective' thinkers. Direct vision always tends to be disturbing. Tolstoy used this gift to the full to destroy both his own peace and that of his readers. It was this habit of asking exaggeratedly simple but fundamental questions, to which he did not himself – at any rate in the 1860s and 1870s – possess the answers, that gave him the reputation of being a 'nihilist'. Yet he certainly had no desire to destroy for the sake of destruction. What he desired, more than anything else in the world, was to know the truth. How annihilating this passion can be is shown by others who have chosen to cut below the limits set by the wisdom of their generation: Machiavelli, Pascal, Rousseau; the author of the Book of Job. Like them, Tolstoy cannot be fitted into any of the public movements of his own, or indeed any other, age. The only company to which Tolstoy belongs is the subversive one of questioners to whom no answer has been, or seems likely to be, given – at least no answer which they or those who understand them will begin to accept.

As for Tolstoy's positive ideas – and they varied less during his long life than has sometimes been represented – they are not at all unique: they have something in common with the French Enlightenment of the eighteenth century; something with those of the twentieth century; little with those of his own times. In Russia he belonged to neither of the great ideological streams which divided educated opinion in that country during his youth. He was not

a radical intellectual, with his eyes turned to the West; nor a
Slavophil, that is to say, a believer in a Christian and nationalist
monarchy. His views cut across these categories. Like the radicals,
he had always condemned political repression, arbitrary violence,
economic exploitation, and all that creates and perpetuates inequality among men. But the rest of the 'Westernising' outlook –
the heart of the ideology of the intelligentsia – the overwhelming
sense of civic responsibility, the belief in natural science as the
door to all truth, in social and political reform, in democracy,
material progress, secularism – this celebrated amalgam Tolstoy
rejected, early in life, out of hand. He believed in individual liberty
and, indeed, in progress too, but in a queer sense of his own.[1] He
looked with contempt on liberals and socialists, and with even
greater hatred on the right-wing parties of his time. His closest
affinity, as has often been remarked, is with Rousseau; he liked
and admired Rousseau's views more than those of any other
modern writer. Like Rousseau, he rejected the doctrine of original
sin, and believed that man was born innocent, and had been
ruined by his own bad institutions; especially by what passed for
education among civilised men. Like Rousseau again, he put the
blame for this process of decadence largely on the intellectuals –
the self-appointed élites of experts, sophisticated coteries remote
from common humanity, self-estranged from natural life. These
men are damned because they have all but lost the most precious
of all human possessions, the capacity with which all men are
born – to see the truth, the immutable, eternal truth which only
charlatans and sophists represent as varying in different circumstances and times and places – the truth which is visible fully only
to the innocent eye of those whose hearts have not been corrupted

---

1   Education for him is 'an activity based on the human need for equality and
the immutable law of the advance of education', which he interprets as the
constant equalisation of knowledge, knowledge which is always growing
because I know what the child does not know; moreover, each generation
knows what the previous generations have thought, whereas they do not
know what future generations will think. The equality is between the teacher
and the taught; this desire for equality on the part of both is itself for him
the spring of progress – progress in the sense of advance in knowledge of
what men are and what they should do. 'O narodnom obrazovanii', T viii
25; 'On the Education of the People', E 85.

– children, peasants, those not blinded by vanity and pride, the simple, the good. Education, as the West understands it, ruins innocence. That is why children resist it bitterly and instinctively; that is why it has to be rammed down their throats, and, like all coercion and violence, maims the victim and at times destroys him beyond redress. Men crave for truth by nature; therefore true education must be of such a kind that children and unsophisticated, ignorant people will absorb it readily and eagerly. But to understand this, and to discover how to apply this knowledge, the educated must put away their intellectual arrogance, and make a new beginning. They must purge their minds of theories, of false, quasi-scientific analogies between the world of men and the world of animals, or of men and inanimate things. Only then will they be able to re-establish a personal relationship with the uneducated – a relationship which only humanity and love can achieve.

In modern times only Rousseau, and perhaps Dickens, seem to him to have seen this. Certainly the people's condition will never be improved until not only the tsarist bureaucracy, but the 'progressists', as Tolstoy called them, the vain and doctrinaire intelligentsia, are prised off the people's necks – the common people's, and the children's too. So long as fanatical theorists bedevil education, little is to be hoped for. Even the old-fashioned village priest – so Tolstoy maintains in one of his early tracts – was less harmful: he knew little and was clumsy, idle and stupid; but he treated his pupils as human beings, not as scientists treat specimens in a laboratory; he did what he could; he was often corrupt, ill-tempered, unjust, but these were human – 'natural' – vices, and therefore their effects, unlike those of machine-made modern instructors, inflicted no permanent injury.

With these ideas, it is not surprising to find that Tolstoy was personally happier among the Slavophil reactionaries. He rejected their ideas; but at least they seemed to him to have some contact with reality – the land, the peasants, traditional ways of life. At least they believed in the primacy of spiritual values and the futility of trying to change men by changing the more superficial sides of their life by political or constitutional reform. But the Slavophils also believed in the Orthodox Church, in the unique historical destiny of the Russian people, the sanctity of history as a divinely ordained process, and therefore the justification of many absurdities because they were native and ancient, and therefore instruments in the divine tactic; they lived by a Christian faith in the great mystical body – at once community and Church – of the generation of the faithful, past, present and yet unborn. Intellectually Tolstoy repudiated this, temperamentally he responded to it all too strongly. He understood well only the nobility and the peasants; and the former better than the latter; he shared many of the instinctive beliefs of his country neighbours; like them he had a natural aversion to all forms of middle-class liberalism: the bourgeoisie scarcely appears in his novels. His attitude to parliamentary democracy, the rights of women, universal suffrage, was not very different from that of Cobbett or Carlyle or Proudhon or D. H. Lawrence. He shared deeply the Slavophil suspicions of all scientific and theoretical generalisations as such, and this created a bridge which made personal relations with the Moscow Slavophils congenial to him. But his intellect was not at one with his instinctive convictions. As a thinker he had profound affinities with the eighteenth-century *philosophes*. Like them he looked upon the patriarchal Russian State and Church, which the Slavophils defended, as organised and hypocritical conspiracies. Like the great thinkers of the Enlightenment he looked for values not in history, nor in the sacred missions of nations or cultures or Churches, but in the individual's own personal experience. Like them, too, he believed in eternal (and not in historically evolving) truths and values, and rejected with both hands the romantic notion of race or nation or culture as creative agents, still more the Hegelian conception of history as the self-realisation of self-perfecting reason incarnated in men or in movements or in institutions (ideas which had deeply influenced his generation) – all his life he looked on this as cloudy metaphysical nonsense.

This clear, cold, uncompromising realism is quite explicit in the notes and diaries and letters of his early life. The reminiscences of those who knew him as a boy or as a student in the University of Kazan reinforce this impression. His character was deeply conservative, with a streak of caprice and irrationality; but his mind remained calm, logical and unswerving; he followed the argument easily and fearlessly to whatever extreme it led him – a typically, and sometimes fatally, Russian combination of qualities. What did not satisfy his critical sense, he rejected. He left the University of Kazan because he decided that the professors were incompetent and dealt with trivial issues. Like Helvétius and his friends in the mid-eighteenth century, Tolstoy denounced theology, history, the teaching of dead languages – the entire classical curriculum – as an accumulation of data and rules that no reasonable man could wish to know. History particularly irritated him as a systematic attempt to answer non-existent questions with all the real issues carefully left out: 'history is like a deaf man replying to questions which nobody puts to him',[1] he announced to a startled fellow-student, while they were both locked in the university detention room for some minor act of insubordination. The first extended statement of his full 'ideological' position belongs to the 1860s: the occasion for it was his decision to compose a treatise on education. All his intellectual strength and all his prejudice went into this attempt.

In 1860, Tolstoy, then thirty-two years old, found himself in one of his periodic moral crises. He had acquired some fame as a writer: *Sevastopol Sketches*, *Childhood*, *Adolescence and Youth*, two or three shorter tales, had been praised by the critics. He was on terms of friendship with some of the most gifted of an exceptionally talented generation of writers in his country – Turgenev, Nekrasov, Goncharov, Panaev, Pisemsky, Fet. His writing struck everyone by its freshness, sharpness, marvellous descriptive power, and the precision and originality of its images. His style was at times criticised as awkward and even barbarous; but he was unquestionably the most promising of the younger prose writers; he had a future; yet his literary friends felt reservations about him. He paid visits to the literary salons, both right- and left-wing (political divisions had always existed and were becoming sharper in Petersburg and Moscow), but he seemed at ease in none of them. He was bold, imaginative, independent. But he was not a man of letters, not fundamentally concerned with problems of literature and writing, still less of writers; he had wandered in from another, less intellectual, more aristocratic and more primi-

1   loc. cit. (43 above, note 2). [Berlin's ascription of this remark to Tolstoy's university days here (but not in 'The Hedgehog and the Fox') appears to derive from its similarity to sentiments recounted by Nazar'ev: see 35 above.]

tive world. He was a well-born dilettante; but that was nothing
new: the poetry of Pushkin and his contemporaries, unequalled in
the history of Russian literature, had been created by amateurs of
genius. It was not his origin but his unconcealed indifference to
the literary life as such – to the habits or problems of professional
writers, editors, publicists – that made his friends among the men
of letters feel uneasy in his presence. This worldly, clever young
officer could be exceedingly agreeable; his love for writing was
genuine and very deep; but at literary gatherings he was contemptuous, formidable and reserved; he did not dream of opening
his heart in a milieu dedicated to intimate, unending self-
revelation. He was inscrutable, disdainful, disconcerting, arrogant, a little frightening. He no longer, it was true, lived the life of
an aristocratic officer. The wild nights on which the young radicals
looked with hatred and contempt as characteristic of the dissipated
habits of the reactionary *jeunesse dorée* no longer amused him.
He had married and settled down, he was in love with his wife,
and became for a time a model (if occasionally exasperating)
husband. But he did not trouble to conceal the fact that he had
far more respect for all forms of real life – whether of the free
Cossacks in the Caucasus, or that of the rich young guards officers
in Moscow with their race-horses and balls and gypsies – than
for the world of books, reviews, critics, professors, political discussions and talk about ideals, opinions and literary values. Moreover, he was opinionated, quarrelsome and at times unexpectedly
savage; with the result that his literary friends treated him with
nervous respect, and, in the end, drew away from him; or perhaps
he abandoned them. Apart from the poet Fet, who was an eccentric
and deeply conservative country squire himself, Tolstoy had no
intimates among the writers of his own generation. His breach
with Turgenev is well known. He was even remoter from the other
littérateurs; he liked Nekrasov better than his poetry; but then
Nekrasov was an editor of genius and admired and encouraged
Tolstoy from his earliest beginnings.

The sense of the contrast between life and literature haunted
Tolstoy. It made him doubt his own vocation as a writer. Like
other young Russians of birth and fortune, he was conscience-
stricken by the appalling condition of the peasants. Mere reflection

or denunciation seemed to him a way of evading action. He must act, he must start with his own estate. Like the eighteenth-century radicals he was convinced that men were born equal and were made unequal by the way in which they were brought up. He established a school for the boys of his village; and, dissatisfied with the educational theories then in vogue in Russia, decided to go abroad to study Western methods in theory and in practice. He derived a great deal from his visits to England, France, Switzerland, Belgium, Germany – including the title of his greatest novel. But his conversations with the most advanced Western authorities on education, and observation of their methods, had convinced him that these methods were at best worthless, at worst harmful, to the children upon whom they were practised. He did not stay long in England and paid little attention to its 'antiquated' schools. In France he found that learning was almost entirely mechanical – by rote. Prepared questions, lists of dates, for example, were answered competently, because they had been learnt by heart. But the same children, when asked for the same facts from some unexpected angle, often produced absurd replies, which showed that their knowledge meant nothing to them. The schoolboy who replied that the murderer of Henri IV of France was Julius Caesar seemed to him typical: the boy neither understood nor took an interest in the facts he had stored up; at most all that was gained was a mechanical memory.

But the true home of theory was Germany. The pages which Tolstoy devotes to describing teaching and teachers in Germany rival and anticipate the celebrated pages in *War and Peace* in which he makes savage fun of admired experts in another field – the German strategists employed by the Russian army – whom he represents as grotesque and pompous dolts.

In *Yasnaya Polyana*, a journal which he had had privately printed in 1861–2, Tolstoy speaks of his educational visits to the West and, by way of example, gives a hair-raising (and exceedingly entertaining) account of the latest methods of teaching the alphabet, used by a specialist trained in one of the most advanced of the German teachers' seminaries.[1] He describes the pedantic,

---

1   'O metodakh obucheniya gramoty' (1862), T viii 137–8; 'On Methods of Teaching Reading', E 280–2.

immensely self-satisfied schoolmaster, as he enters the room, and notes with approval that the children are seated at their desks, crushed and obedient, in total silence, as prescribed by German rules of behaviour. 'He casts a look round the class, and knows already what it is that they ought to understand; he knows this, and he knows what the children's souls are made of, and much else that the seminary has taught him.' He is armed with the latest and most progressive pedagogic volume, called *Das Fischbuch*. It contains pictures of a fish.

'What is this, dear children?' 'A fish,' replies the brightest. 'No.' And he will not rest until some child says that what they see is not a fish, but a book. That is better. 'And what do books contain?' 'Letters,' says the boldest boy. 'No, no,' says the schoolmaster sadly, 'you really *must* think of what you are saying.' By this time the children are beginning to be hopelessly demoralised: they have no notion of what they are meant to say. They have a confused and perfectly correct feeling that the schoolmaster wants them to say something unintelligible – that the fish is not a fish – that whatever it is he wants them to say, is something they will never think of. Their thoughts begin to stray. They wonder (this is very Tolstoyan) why the teacher is wearing spectacles, why he is looking through them instead of taking them off, and so on. The teacher urges them to concentrate, he harries and tortures them until he manages to make them say that what they see is not a fish, but a picture, and then, after more torture, that the picture represents a fish. If that is what he wants them to say, would it not be easier, Tolstoy asks, to make them learn this piece of profound wisdom by heart, instead of tormenting them with the *Fischbuch* method, which so far from causing them to think 'creatively', merely stupefies them?

The genuinely intelligent children know that their answers are always wrong; they cannot tell why; they know only that this is so; while the stupid, who occasionally provide the right answers, do not know why they are praised. All that the German pedagogue is doing is to feed dead human material – or rather living human beings – into a grotesque mechanical contraption invented by fanatical fools who think that this is a way of applying scientific method to the education of men. Tolstoy assures us that his account (of which I have quoted only a short fragment) is not a parody, but a faithful reproduction of what he saw and heard in the advanced schools of Germany and in 'those schools in England that have been fortunate enough to acquire these wonderful [. . .] methods'.

Disillusioned and indignant, Tolstoy returned to his Russian estate and began to teach the village children himself. He built schools, continued to study, reject and denounce current doctrines of education, published periodicals and pamphlets, invented new methods of learning geography, zoology, physics; composed an entire manual of arithmetic of his own, inveighed against all methods of coercion, especially those which consisted of forcing children against their will to memorise facts and dates and figures. In short, he behaved like an original, enlightened, energetic, opinionated, somewhat eccentric eighteenth-century landowner who had become a convert to the doctrines of Rousseau or the abbé Mably. His accounts of his theories and experiments fill two stout volumes in the pre-Revolutionary editions of his collected works. They are still fascinating, if only because they contain some of the best descriptions of village life and especially of children, both comical and lyrical, that even he had ever composed. He wrote them in the 1860s and 1870s when he was at the height of his creative powers. His overriding didactic purpose is easily forgotten in the unrivalled insight into the twisting, criss-crossing pattern of the thoughts and feelings of individual village children, and the marvellous concreteness and imagination with which their talk and behaviour, and physical nature round them, are described. And side by side with this direct vision of human experience, there run the clear, firm dogmas of a fanatically doctrinaire eighteenth-century rationalist – doctrines not fused with the life that he describes, but superimposed upon it, like windows with rigorously symmetrical patterns drawn upon them, unrelated to the world on which they open, and yet achieving a kind of illusory artistic and intellectual unity with it, owing to the unbounded vitality and constructive genius of the writing itself. It is one of the most extraordinary performances in the history of literature.

The enemy is always the same: experts, professionals, men who claim special authority over other men. Universities and professors are a frequent target for attack. There are intimations of this already in the section entitled 'Youth' of his earlier autobiographical novel. There is something eighteenth-century, reminiscent both of Voltaire and of Bentham, about Tolstoy's devastating accounts of the dull and incompetent professors and the desperately bored and obsequious students in Russia in his time. The tone is unusual in the nineteenth century: dry, ironical, didactic, mordant, at once withering and entertaining; the whole based on the contrast between the harmonious simplicity of nature and the self-destructive complications created by the malice or stupidity of men – men from whom the author feels himself detached, whom he affects not to understand, and mocks from a distance.

We are at the earliest beginnings of a theme which grew obsessive in Tolstoy's later life: that the solution to all our perplexities stares us in the face – that the answer is about us everywhere, like the light of day, if only we would not close our eyes or look everywhere but at what is there, staring us in the face, the clear, simple, irresistible truth.

Like Rousseau and Kant and the believers in natural law, Tolstoy was convinced that men have certain basic material and spiritual needs, in all places, at all times. If these needs are fulfilled, they lead harmonious lives, which is the goal of their nature. Moral, aesthetic and other spiritual values are objective and eternal, and man's inner harmony depends upon his correct relationship to these. Moreover, all his life he defended the proposition – which his own novels and sketches do not embody – that human beings are more harmonious in childhood than under the corrupting influences of education in later life; and also that simple people (peasants, Cossacks and so on) have a more 'natural' and correct attitude towards these basic values than civilised men; and that they are free and independent in a sense in which civilised men are not. For (he insists on this over and over again) peasant communities are in a position to supply their own material and spiritual needs out of their own resources, provided that they are not robbed or enslaved by oppressors and exploiters; whereas civilised men need for their survival the forced labour of others – serfs, slaves, the exploited masses, called ironically 'dependants', because their masters depend on *them*. The masters are parasitic upon others: they are degraded not merely by the fact that to enslave and exploit others is a denial of such objective values as justice, equality, human dignity, love – values which men crave to realise because they cannot help this, because they are men – but for the further, and to him even more important, reason that to live on robbed or borrowed goods, and so fail to be self-subsistent, falsifies 'natural' feelings and perceptions, corrodes men morally, and makes them both wicked and miserable. The human ideal is a society of free and equal men, who live and think by the light of what is true and right, and so are not in conflict with each other or themselves. This is a form – a very simple one – of the classical doctrine of natural law, whether in its theological or secular, liberal-anarchist form. To it Tolstoy adhered all his life; as much in his 'secular' period as after his 'conversion'. His early stories express this vividly. The Cossacks Lukashka and Uncle Yeroshka are morally superior, as well as happier and aesthetically more harmonious beings, than Olenin in *The Cossacks*; Olenin knows this; indeed that is the heart of the situation. Pierre in *War and Peace* and Levin in *Anna Karenina* have a sense of this in simple peasants and soldiers; so does Nekhlyudov in *The Morning of a Landowner*. This conviction fills Tolstoy's mind to a greater and greater degree, until it overshadows all other issues in his later works: *Resurrection* and *The Death of Ivan Il'ich* are not intelligible without it.

Tolstoy's critical thought constantly revolves round this central notion – the contrast between nature and artifice, truth and invention. When, for instance, in the 1890s he laid down conditions of excellence in art (in the course of an introduction to a Russian translation of Maupassant's stories), he demanded of all writers, in the first place the possession of sufficient talent; in the second that the subject itself must be morally important; and finally that they must truly love (what was worthy of love) and hate (what was worthy of hate) in what they describe – 'commit' themselves – retain the direct moral vision of childhood, and not maim their natures by practising self-imposed, self-lacerating and always illusory impartiality and detachment – or, still worse, deliberate perversion of 'natural' values. Talent is not given equally to all men; but everyone can, if he tries, discover eternal, unchanging attributes – what is good and what is bad, what is important and what is trivial. Only false – 'made-up' – theories delude men and writers about this, and so distort their lives and creative activity. Tolstoy applies his criterion literally, almost mechanically. Thus Nekrasov, according to him, treated subjects of profound importance, and possessed superb skill as a writer; but his attitude towards his suffering peasants and crushed idealists remained chilly and unreal. Dostoevsky's subjects lack nothing in seriousness, and his concern is profound and genuine; but the first condition is unfulfilled: he is diffuse and repetitive; he does not know how to tell the truth clearly and then to stop. Turgenev, on the other hand, is judged to be both an excellent writer and to stand in a real, morally adequate, relationship to his subjects; but he fails on the second count: the subjects are too circumscribed and trivial – and for this no degree of integrity or skill can compensate. Content determines form, never form content; and if the content is too small or trivial, nothing will save the work of the artist. To hold the opposite of this – to believe in the primacy of form – is to sacrifice truth; to end by producing works that are contrived. There is no harsher word in Tolstoy's entire critical vocabulary than 'made-up', indicating that the writer did not truly experience or imagine, but merely 'composed' – 'made up' – that which he is purporting to describe.

So, too, Tolstoy maintained that Maupassant, whose gifts he admired greatly, betrayed his genius precisely owing to false and vulgar theories of this kind; yet he remained, none the less, a good writer to the degree to which, like Balaam, although he might have meant to curse virtue, he could not help discerning what was good; and this perception attracted his love to it, and forced him against his own will towards the truth. Talent is vision, vision reveals the truth, truth is eternal and objective. To see the truth about nature or about conduct, to see it directly and vividly as only a man of genius (or a simple human being or a child) can see it, and then to deny or tamper with the vision in cold blood, no matter for the sake of what, is monstrous, unnatural; a symptom of a deeply diseased character.

Truth is discoverable: to follow it is to be good, inwardly sound, harmonious. Yet it is clear that our society is not harmonious or composed of internally harmonious individuals. The interests of the educated minority – what Tolstoy calls the professors, the barons and the bankers – are opposed to those of the majority – the peasants, the poor; each side is indifferent to, or mocks, the values of the other. Even those who, like Olenin, Pierre, Nekhlyudov, Levin, realise the spuriousness of the values of the professors, barons and bankers, and the moral decay in which their false education has involved them, even those who are truly contrite cannot, despite Slavophil pretensions, go native and 'merge' with the mass of the common people. Are they too corrupt ever to recover their innocence? Is their case hopeless? Or can it be that civilised men have acquired (or discovered) certain true values of their own, values which barbarians and children may know nothing of, but which they, the civilised, cannot lose or forget, even if, by some impossible means, they could transform themselves into peasants or the free and happy Cossacks of the Don and the Terek? This is one of the central and most tormenting problems in Tolstoy's life, to which he goes back again and again, and to which he returns conflicting answers.

Tolstoy knows that he himself clearly belongs to the minority of barons, bankers, professors. He knows the symptoms of his condition only too well. He cannot, for example, deny his passionate love for the music of Mozart or Chopin or the poetry of Tyutchev or Pushkin, the ripest fruits of civilisation. He needs, he cannot do without, the printed word and all the elaborate paraphernalia of the culture in which such lives are lived and such works of art are created. But what is the use of Pushkin to village boys, when his words are not intelligible to them? What real benefits has the invention of printing brought the peasants? We are told, Tolstoy observes, that books educate societies ('that is, make them more corrupt'),[1] that it was the written word that has promoted the emancipation of the serfs in Russia. Tolstoy denies this: the government would have done the same without books or pamphlets. Pushkin's *Boris Godunov* pleases only him, Tolstoy: but to the peasants it means nothing. The triumphs of civilisation?

---

1   'Vospitanie i obrazovanie' (1862), T viii 216; 'Training and Education', E 296.

The telegraph tells him about his sister's health, or about the prospects of King Otto I of Greece; but what benefits do the masses gain from it? Yet it is they who pay and have always paid for it all; they know this well. When peasants kill doctors in the 'cholera riots' because they regard them as poisoners, what they do is no doubt wrong, but these murders are no accident: the instinct which tells the peasants who their oppressors are is sound, and the doctors belong to that class. When Wanda Landowska played to the villagers of Yasnaya Polyana, the great majority of them remained unresponsive. Yet can it be doubted that it is the simple people who lead the least broken lives, immeasurably superior to the warped and tormented lives of the rich and educated?

The common people, Tolstoy asserts in his early educational tracts, are self-subsistent not only materially but spiritually – folksong, the *Iliad*, the Bible, spring from the people itself, and are therefore intelligible to all men everywhere, as the marvellous poem *Silentium* by Tyutchev, or *Don Giovanni*, or the Ninth Symphony is not. If there is an ideal of man, it lies not in the future, but in the past. Once upon a time there was the Garden of Eden and in it dwelt the uncorrupted human soul as the Bible and Rousseau conceived it, and then came the Fall, corruption, suffering, falsification. It is mere blindness (Tolstoy says over and over again) to believe, as liberals or socialists – the progressives – believe, that the golden age is still before us, that history is the story of improvement, that material advance in natural science or material skills coincides with real moral advance. The truth is the reverse of this.

The child is closer to the ideal harmony than the grown man, and the simple peasant than the torn, 'alienated', morally and spiritually unanchored and self-destructive parasites who form the civilised élite. From this doctrine springs Tolstoy's notable anti-individualism: and in particular his diagnosis of the individual's will as the source of misdirection and perversion of 'natural' human tendencies, and hence the conviction (derived largely from Schopenhauer's doctrine of the will as the source of frustration) that to plan, organise, rely on science, try to create rational patterns of life in accordance with rational theories, is to swim against the stream of nature, to close one's eyes to the saving truth within us, to torture facts to fit artificial schemata, and torture human beings to fit social and economic systems against which their natures cry out. From the same source, too, comes the obverse of this: Tolstoy's faith in an intuitively grasped direction of things as not merely inevitable, but objectively – providentially – good; and therefore belief in the need to submit to it: his quietism.

This is one aspect of his teaching – the most famous, the most central idea of the Tolstoyan movement – and it runs through all his works, imaginative, critical, didactic, from *The Cossacks* and *Family Happiness* to his last religious tracts. This is the doctrine which the liberals and Marxists condemned. It is in this mood that Tolstoy maintains that to imagine that heroic personalities determine events is a piece of colossal megalomania and self-deception; his narrative is designed to show the insignificance of Napoleon or Tsar Alexander, or of the aristocratic and bureau-cratic society in *Anna Karenina*, or of the judges and official persons in *Resurrection*; or again, the emptiness and intellectual impotence of historians and philosophers who try to explain events by employing concepts like 'power', which is attributed to great men, or 'influence' ascribed to writers, orators, preachers – words, abstractions which, in his view, explain nothing, being themselves far more obscure than the facts for which they purport to account. He maintains that we do not begin to understand, and therefore cannot explain or analyse, what it is to wield authority or strength, to influence, to dominate. Explanations that do not explain are, for Tolstoy, a symptom of the disruptive and self-inflated intellect, the faculty that destroys innocence and leads to false ideas and the ruin of human life.

That is the strain, inspired by Rousseau and present in early romanticism, which inspired primitivism in art and in life, not in Russia alone. Tolstoy imagines that he and others can find the path to the truth about how one should live by observing simple people, by the study of the Gospels.

His other strain is the direct opposite of this. Mikhailovsky says, with justice, that Olenin cannot, charmed as he is by the Caucasus and the Cossack idyll, transform himself into a Lukashka, return to the childlike harmony, which in his case has long been broken. Levin knows that if he tried to become a peasant this could only be a grotesque farce, which the peasants would be the first to perceive and deride; he and Pierre and Nikolay Rostov know obscurely that in some sense they have something to give that the peasants have not. Tolstoy tells the educated reader that the peasant 'needs what your life of ten generations uncrushed by hard labour has given you. You had the leisure to search, to think, to suffer – then give him that for whose sake you suffered; he is in need of it; [. . . do not] bury in the earth the talent given you by history.'[1]

Leisure, then, need not be merely destructive. Progress can occur: we can learn from what happened in the past, as those who lived in that past could not. It is true that we live in an unjust order. But this itself creates direct obligations. Those who are members of the civilised élite, cut off as they tragically are from the mass of the people, have the duty to attempt to recreate broken humanity, to stop exploiting them, to give them what they most need – education, knowledge, material help, a capacity for living better lives. Levin in *Anna Karenina*, as Mikhailovsky remarks, takes up where Nikolay Rostov in *War and Peace* left off. They are not quietists, and yet what they do is right. The emancipation of the peasants, in Tolstoy's view, although it did not go far enough, was nevertheless an act of will – goodwill – on the part of the government, and now it is necessary to teach peasants to read and write and grasp the rules of arithmetic, something which they cannot do for themselves; to equip them for the use of freedom. I cannot merge myself with the mass of peasants; but I can at least use the fruit of the unjustly obtained leisure of myself and my ancestors – my education, knowledge, skills – for the benefit of those whose labour made it possible.

This is the talent I may not bury. I must work to promote a just society in accordance with those objective standards which all men, except the hopelessly corrupt, see and accept, whether they

1   'Yasno-polyanskaya shkola za noyabr' i dekabr' mesyatsy [1861]' (1862), T viii 48; 'The Yasnaya Polyana School in the Months of November and December [1861]', E 108. [After the semi-colon Tolstoy writes: 'but like an Egyptian priest you conceal yourself from him in a mysterious mantle and bury in the earth the talent given you by history'.]

live by them or not. The simple see them more clearly, the sophisticated more dimly, but all men can see them if they try; indeed to
be able to see them is part of what it is to be a man. When injustice
is perpetrated, I have an obligation to speak out and act against
it; nor may artists any more than others sit with folded hands.
What makes good writers good is ability to see truth – social and
individual, material and spiritual – and so present it that it cannot
be escaped. Tolstoy holds that Maupassant, for example, is doing
precisely this, despite himself and his aesthetic fallacies. He may,
because he is a corrupt human being, take the side of the bad
against the good, write about a worthless Paris seducer with
greater sympathy than he feels for his victims. But provided that
he tells the truth at a level that is sufficiently profound – and men
of talent cannot avoid doing this – he will face the reader with
fundamental moral questions, whether he means to do this or not,
questions which the reader can neither escape nor answer without
rigorous and painful self-examination.

This, for Tolstoy, opens the path to regeneration, and is the
proper function of art. Vocation – talent – is obedience to an inner
need: to fulfil it is the artist's purpose and his duty. Nothing is
more false than the view of the artist as a purveyor, or a craftsman
whose sole function it is to create a beautiful thing, as Flaubert,
or Renan, or Maupassant[1] maintain. There is only one human
goal, and it is equally binding on all men, landowners, doctors,
barons, professors, bankers, peasants: to tell the truth, and be
guided by it in action, that is, to do good, and persuade others to
do so. That God exists, or that the *Iliad* is beautiful, or that men
have a right to be free and also equal, are all eternal and absolute
truths. Therefore we must persuade men to read the *Iliad* and not
pornographic French novels, and to work for an equal society,
not a theocratic or political hierarchy. Coercion is evil; men have

---

1   Tolstoy is moved to indignation by Maupassant's celebrated dictum (which
     he [slightly mis-]quotes at T xxx 15) that the business of the artist is not to
     entertain, delight, move, astonish, cause his reader to dream, reflect, smile,
     weep or shudder, but '[faire] quelque chose de beau, dans la forme qui
     vous conviendra le mieux, suivant votre tempérament' ('[to make] something
     beautiful, in the form that will suit you best, according to your character').
     Guy de Maupassant, 'Le Roman', preface to *Pierre et Jean* (Paris, 1888); 37
     in the edition by G. Hainsworth (London etc., 1966).

always known this to be true; therefore they must work for a society in which there will be no wars, no prisons, no executions, in any circumstances, for any reason; for a society in which individual freedom exists to the maximum degree. By his own route Tolstoy arrived at a programme of Christian anarchism which had much in common with that of the Russian populists, with whom, but for their doctrinaire socialism, and their belief in science and faith in the methods of terrorism, Tolstoy's attitude had much in common. For what he now appeared to be advocating was a programme of action, not of quietism; this programme underlay the educational reform that he attempted to carry out. He strove to discover, collect, expound eternal truths, awaken the spontaneous interest, the imagination, love, curiosity of children or simple folk; above all to liberate their 'natural' moral, emotional and intellectual forces, which he did not doubt, as Rousseau did not doubt, would achieve harmony within men and between them, provided that we eliminate everything that might maim, cramp and kill them.

This programme – that of making possible the free self-development of all human faculties – rests on one vast assumption: that there exists at least one path of development on which these faculties will neither conflict with each other, nor develop disproportionately – a sure path to complete harmony in which everything fits and is at peace; with the corollary that knowledge of man's nature gained from observation or introspection or moral intuition, or from the study of the lives and writings of the best and wisest men of all ages, can show us this path. This is not the place for considering how far the doctrine is compatible with ancient religious teachings or modern psychology. The point I wish to stress is that it is, above all, a programme of action, a declaration of war against current social values, against the tyranny of States, societies, Churches, against brutality, injustice, stupidity, hypocrisy, weakness, above all against vanity and moral blindness. A man who has fought a good fight in this war will thereby expiate the sin of having been a hedonist and an exploiter, and the son and beneficiary of robbers and oppressors.

This is what Tolstoy believed, preached and practised. His 'conversion' altered his view of what was good and what was evil. It did not weaken his faith in the need for action. His belief in the principles themselves never wavered. The enemy entered by another door: Tolstoy's sense of reality was too inexorable to keep out tormenting doubts about how these principles – no matter how true themselves – should be applied. Even though *I* believe some things to be beautiful or good, and others to be ugly and evil, what right have *I* to bring up others in the light of my convictions, when I know that I cannot help liking Chopin and Maupassant, while these far better men – peasants or children – do not? Have I, who stand at the end of a long period of elaboration – of generations of civilised, unnatural living – have I the right to touch *their* souls?

To seek to influence someone is to engage in a morally suspect enterprise. This is obvious in the case of the crude manipulation of one man by another. But in principle it holds equally of education. All educators seek to shape the minds and lives of the educated towards a given goal, or to resemble a given model. But if we – the sophisticated members of a deeply corrupt society – are ourselves unhappy, inharmonious, gone astray, what can we be doing but trying to change children born healthy into our own sick semblance, to make cripples of them like ourselves? We are what we have become, we cannot help our love of Pushkin's verse, of Chopin's music; we discover that children and peasants find them unintelligible or tedious. What do we do? We persist, we 'educate' them until they too appear to enjoy these works or, at least, see why we enjoy them. What have we done? We find the works of Mozart and Chopin beautiful only because Mozart and Chopin were themselves children of our decadent culture, and therefore their words speak to our diseased minds; but what right have we to infect others, to make them as corrupt as ourselves? We can see the blemishes of other systems. We see all too clearly how the human personality is destroyed by Protestant insistence on obedience, by Catholic stress on emulation, by the appeal to self-interest and the importance of social position or rank on which Russian education, according to Tolstoy, is based. Is it not, then, either monstrous arrogance or a perverse inconsistency to behave as if our own favoured systems of education – something recommended by Pestalozzi, or the Lancaster method, systems which merely reflect their inventors' civilised, and consequently perverted, personalities – are necessarily superior, or less destructive, than what we condemn so readily and justly in the superficial French or the stupid and pompous Germans?

How is this to be avoided? Tolstoy repeats the lessons of Rousseau's *Émile*. Nature: only nature will save us. We must seek ⟵ to understand what is 'natural', spontaneous, uncorrupt, sound, in harmony with itself and other objects in the world, and clear paths for development on these lines; not seek to alter, to force into a mould. We must listen to the dictates of our stifled original nature, not look on it as mere raw stuff upon which to impose our unique personalities and powerful wills. To defy, to be Promethean, to create goals and build worlds in rivalry with what our moral sense knows to be eternal truths, given once and for all to all men, truths in virtue of which they are men and not beasts – that is the monstrous sin of pride, committed by all reformers, all revolutionaries, all men judged great and effective. And no less by government officials, or by country squires who, from liberal convictions or simply caprice or boredom, interfere with the lives of the peasants.[1] Do not teach; learn: that is the sense of Tolstoy's essay, written nearly a hundred years ago, 'Who should learn to write from whom? Should peasants' children learn from us, or should we learn from peasants' children?',[2] and of all the accounts published in the 1860s and 1870s, written with his customary freshness, attention to detail, and unapproachable power of direct perception, in which he gives examples of stories written by the children in his village, and speaks of the awe which he felt while in the presence of the act of pure creation, in which, he assures us, he played no part himself. These stories would only be spoilt by his 'corrections'; they seem to him far more profound than any of the works of Goethe; he explains how deeply ashamed they make him of his own superficiality, vanity, stupidity, narrowness, lack

1   Mikhailovsky maintains that in *Polikushka*, one of Tolstoy's best stories, composed during the period of the educational tracts, he represents the tragic death of the hero as ultimately due to the wilful interference with the lives of her peasants on the part of the well-meaning, but vain and foolish, landowner. His argument is highly convincing.

2   'Komu u kogo uchit'sya pisat', krest'yanskim rebyatam u nas, ili nam u krest'yanskikh rebyat?' (1862), T viii 301–24; 'Should we teach the peasant children to write, or should they teach us?', E 222–47.

of moral and aesthetic sense. If one can help children and peasants, it is only by making it easier for them to advance freely along their own instinctive path. To direct is to spoil. Men are good and need only freedom to realise their goodness.

'Education', writes Tolstoy in 1862, 'is the action of one man on another with a view to causing this other person to acquire certain moral habits. (We say: they have brought him up to be a hypocrite, a robber or a good man. The Spartans brought up brave men, the French bring up one-sided and self-satisfied persons.)'[1] But this is speaking of – and using – human beings as so much raw material that we model; this is what 'bringing up' to be like this or like that means. We are evidently ready to alter the direction spontaneously followed by the souls and wills of others, to deny their independence – in favour of what? Of our own corrupt, false or, at best, uncertain values? But this involves always some degree of moral tyranny. In a wild moment of panic Tolstoy wonders whether the ultimate motive of the educator is not *envy*, for the root of the educator's passion for his task is 'envy of the purity of the child and the desire to make the child like himself, that is, more corrupt'.[2] What has the entire history of education been? All philosophers of education, from Plato to Kant, sought one goal: 'to free education from the oppression of the chains of the historic past'.[3] They want 'to guess at what men need and then build their new schools on what, less or more correctly, they take this to be'.[4] They struck off one yoke only to put another in its place. Certain scholastic philosophers insisted on Greek because that was the language of Aristotle, who knew the truth. But, Tolstoy continues, Luther denied the authority of the Church Fathers and insisted on inculcating the original Hebrew, because he *knew* that that was the language in which God had revealed eternal truths to men. Bacon looked to empirical knowledge of nature, and his theories contradicted those of Aristotle. Rousseau proclaimed his faith in life, life as he conceived it, and not in theories.

But about one thing they were all agreed: that one must liberate

1   op. cit. (286 above, note 1), T viii 215; E 294.
2   ibid. 216; E 296.
3   op. cit. (275 above, note 1), T viii 10; E 71.
4   ibid.

the young from the blind despotism of the old; and each immediately substituted his own fanatical, enslaving dogma in its place. If I am sure that I know the truth and that all else is error, does that alone entitle me to superintend the education of another? Is such certainty enough? Whether or not it disagrees with the certainties of others? By what right do I put a wall round the pupil, exclude all external influences, and try to mould him as I please, into my own or somebody else's image?

The answer to this question, Tolstoy passionately says to the progressives, must be 'Yes' or 'No': 'If it is "Yes", then the Jews' synagogue, the church school, has as much legitimate right to exist as all our universities.'[1] He declares that he sees no moral difference, at least in principle, between the compulsory Latin of the traditional establishments and the compulsory materialism with which the radical professors indoctrinate their captive audiences. There might indeed be something to be said for the things that the liberals delight in denouncing: education at home, for example. For it is surely natural that parents should wish their children to resemble them. Again there is a case for a religious upbringing, for it is natural that believers should want to save all other human beings from what they, at any rate, are certain must be eternal damnation. Similarly the government is entitled to train men, for society cannot survive without some sort of government, and governments cannot exist without some qualified specialists to serve them.

But what is the basis of 'liberal education' in schools and universities, staffed by men who do not even claim to be sure that what they teach is true? Empiricism? The lessons of history? The only lesson that history teaches us is that all previous educational systems have proved to be despotisms founded on falsehoods, and later roundly condemned. Why should the twenty-first century not look back on us in the nineteenth with the same scorn and amusement as that with which we now look on medieval schools and universities? If the history of education is the history merely of tyranny and error, what right have we to carry on this abominable farce? And if we are told that it has always been so, that it is

1   op. cit. (286 above, note 1), T viii 217; E 297.

nothing new, that we cannot help it, and must do our best – is this not like saying that murders have always taken place, so that we might as well go on murdering, even though we have now discovered what it is that makes men murder?

In these circumstances, we should be villains if we did not say at least so much as this: that since, unlike the Pope or Luther or modern positivists, we do not ourselves claim to base our education (or other forms of interference with human beings) on the knowledge of absolute truth, we must at least stop torturing others in the name of what we do not know. All we can know for certain is what men actually want. Let us at least have the courage of our admitted ignorance, of our doubts and uncertainties. At least we can try to discover what others, children or adults, require, by taking off the spectacles of tradition, prejudice, dogma, and making it possible for ourselves to know men as they truly are, by listening to them carefully and sympathetically, and understanding them and their lives and their needs, one by one individually. Let us at least try to provide them with what they ask for, and leave them as free as possible. Give them *Bildung* (for which he produces a Russian equivalent, and points out with pride that there is none in French or English) – that is to say, seek to influence them by precept and by the example of our own lives; but do not apply 'education' to them, which is essentially a method of coercion, and destroys what is most natural and sacred in man – the capacity for knowing and acting for himself in accordance with what he thinks to be true and good – the power and the right of self-direction.

But he cannot let the matter rest there, as many a liberal has tried to do. For the question immediately arises: how are we to contrive to leave the schoolboy and the student free? By being morally neutral? By imparting only factual knowledge, not ethical, or aesthetic, or social or religious doctrine? By placing the 'facts' before the pupil, and letting him form his own conclusions, without seeking to influence him in any direction, for fear that we might infect him with our own diseased outlooks? But is it really possible for such neutral communications to occur between men? Is not every human communication a conscious or unconscious impression of one temperament, attitude to life, scale of values, upon another? Are men ever so thoroughly insulated from each other, that the careful avoidance of more than the minimum degree of social intercourse will leave them unsullied, absolutely free to see truth and falsehood, good and evil, beauty and ugliness, with their own, and only their own, eyes? Is this not an absurd conception of individuals as creatures who can be kept pure from all social influence – absurd in the world even of Tolstoy's middle years – even, that is, without the new knowledge of human beings that we have acquired today, as the result of the labours of psychologists, sociologists, philosophers? We live in a degenerate society: only the pure can rescue us. But who will educate the educators? Who is so pure as to know how, let alone be able, to heal our world or anyone in it?

Between these poles – on one side facts, nature, what there is; on the other duty, justice, what there should be; on one side innocence, on the other education; between the claims of spontaneity and those of obligation, between the injustice of coercing others, and the injustice of leaving them to go their own way, Tolstoy wavered and struggled all his life. And not only he, but all those populists and socialists and idealistic students who in Russia 'went to the people', and could not decide whether they went to teach or to learn, whether the 'good of the people' for which they were ready to sacrifice their lives was what 'the people' in fact desired, or something that only the reformers knew to be good for them, what the 'people' should desire – would desire if only they were as educated and wise as their champions – but, in fact, in their benighted state, often spurned and violently resisted.

These contradictions, and his unswerving recognition of his failure to reconcile or modify them, are, in a sense, what gives their special meaning both to Tolstoy's life and to the morally agonised, didactic pages of his art. He furiously rejected the compromises and alibis of his liberal contemporaries as mere feebleness and evasion. Yet he believed that a final solution to the problems of how to apply the principles of Christ must exist, even though neither he nor anyone else had wholly discovered it. He rejected the very possibility that some of the tendencies and goals of which he speaks might be literally both real and incompatible. Historicism versus moral responsibility; quietism versus the duty to resist evil; teleology or a causal order against the play of chance and irrational force; spiritual harmony, simplicity, the mass of the people on the one hand, and the irresistible attraction of the culture of minorities and its art on the other; the corruption of the civilised portion of society on one side, and its direct duty to raise the masses of the people to its own level on the other; the dynamism and falsifying influence of passionate, simple, one-sided faith, as against the clear-sighted sense of the complex facts and inevitable weakness in action which flows from enlightened scepticism – all these strains are given full play in the thought of Tolstoy. His adhesion to them appears as a series of inconsistencies in his system because it may be that the conflicts exist in fact and lead to collisions in real life.[1] Tolstoy is incapable of suppressing, or falsifying, or explaining away by reference to dialectical or other 'deeper' levels of thought, any truth when it presents itself to him, no matter what this entails, where it leads, how much it destroys of what he most passionately longs to believe. Everyone knows that Tolstoy placed truth highest of all the virtues. Others have said this too, and have celebrated her no less memorably. But Tolstoy is among the few who have truly earned that rare right: for he sacrificed all he had upon her altar – happiness, friendship, love, peace, moral and intellectual certainty, and, in the end, his life. And all she gave him in return was doubt, insecurity, self-contempt and insoluble contradictions.

In this sense, although he would have repudiated this violently, he is a martyr and a hero – perhaps the most richly gifted of all – in the tradition of European enlightenment. This seems a paradox; but then his entire life bears witness to the proposition to the denial of which his last years were dedicated: that the truth is seldom wholly simple or clear, or as obvious as it may sometimes seem to the eye of the common observer.

---

1   Some Marxist critics, notably Lukács, represent these contradictions as the expression in art of the crisis in Russian feudalism and in particular in the condition of the peasants whose predicament Tolstoy is held to reflect. This seems to me an over-optimistic view: the destruction of Tolstoy's world should have made his dilemmas obsolete. The reader can judge for himself whether this is so.

FATHERS AND CHILDREN
(1970)
Turgenev and the Liberal Predicament

You do not, I see, quite understand the Russian public. Its
character is determined by the condition of Russian society,
which contains, imprisoned within it, fresh forces seething and
bursting to break out; but crushed by heavy repression and
unable to escape, they produce gloom, bitter depression, apathy.
Only in literature, in spite of our Tartar censorship, there is still
some life and forward movement. This is why the writer's calling
enjoys such respect among us, why literary success is so easy
here even when there is little talent [. . .] This is why, especially
amongst us, universal attention is paid to every manifestation
of any so-called liberal trend, no matter how poor the writer's
gifts [. . . The public] sees in Russian writers its only leaders,
defenders, and saviours from dark autocracy, Orthodoxy and
the national way of life . . .

Vissarion Belinsky, Letter to Gogol, 15 July 1847[1]

On 9 October 1883 Ivan Turgenev was buried, as he had wished,
in St Petersburg, near the grave of his admired friend, the critic
Vissarion Belinsky. His body was brought from Paris after a brief

---

1   op. cit. (198 above, note 1), 217–18; Matlaw 89. Belinsky's words – *samo-*
derzhavie, pravoslavie i narodnost' – echo the official patriotic formula
invented by a Minister of Education early in the reign of Nicholas I. The last
of these words – *narodnost'* – was evidently intended as the Russian equivalent of *Volkstum*; it was used in this context to contrast the traditional
'folkways' of the common people with the imported, 'artificial' constructions
of 'wiseacres' influenced by Western enlightenment. In practice it connoted
official patriotism as well as such institutions as serfdom, the hierarchy of
estates, and the duty of implicit obedience to the emperor and his government.
Belinsky's letter is a bitter indictment of Gogol for using his genius 'sincerely
or insincerely' (ibid. 217) to serve the cause of obscurantism and reaction. It
was on the charge of reading the letter at a secret meeting of a subversive
group that Dostoevsky was arrested and condemned to death.

ceremony near the Gare du Nord, at which Ernest Renan and
Edmond About delivered appropriate addresses. The burial service
took place in the presence of representatives of the imperial
government, the intelligentsia and workers' organisations, perhaps the first and last occasion on which these groups peacefully
met in Russia. The times were troubled. The wave of terrorist acts
had culminated in the assassination of Alexander II two years
earlier; the ringleaders of the conspiracy had been hanged or
sent to Siberia, but there was still great unrest, especially among
students. The government feared that the funeral procession
might turn into a political demonstration. The press received a
secret circular from the Ministry of the Interior instructing it to
print only official information about the funeral, without disclosing that any such instructions had been received. Neither the
St Petersburg municipality nor the workers' organisations were
permitted to identify themselves in the inscriptions on their
wreaths. A literary gathering at which Tolstoy was to have spoken
about his old friend and rival was cancelled by government order.
A revolutionary leaflet was distributed during the funeral procession, but no official notice of this was taken, and the occasion
seems to have passed off without incident. Yet these precautions,
and the uneasy atmosphere in which the funeral was conducted,
may surprise those who see Turgenev as Henry James or George
Moore or Maurice Baring saw him, and as most of his readers
perhaps see him still: as a writer of beautiful lyrical prose, the
author of nostalgic idylls of country life, the elegiac poet of the
last enchantments of decaying country houses and of their ineffective but irresistibly attractive inhabitants, the incomparable storyteller with a marvellous gift for describing nuances of mood and
feeling, the poetry of nature and of love, gifts which have given
him a place among the foremost writers of his time. In the French
memoirs of the time he appears as *le doux géant*, as his friend
Edmond de Goncourt had called him,[1] the good giant, gentle,
charming, infinitely agreeable, an entrancing talker, known as
'the Siren' to some of his Russian companions, the admired friend

1   Edmond and Jules de Goncourt, *Journal des Goncourt: Mémoires de la vie
     littéraire* (Paris, 1887–96), entry for 23 February 1863.

of Flaubert and Daudet, George Sand and Zola and Maupassant, the most welcome and delightful of all the habitués of the salon of his intimate lifelong companion, the singer Pauline Viardot. Yet the Russian government had some grounds for its fears. They had not welcomed Turgenev's visit to Russia, more particularly his meetings with students, two years before, and had found a way of conveying this to him in unambiguous terms. Audacity was not among his attributes; he cut his visit short and returned to Paris.

The government's nervousness is not surprising, for Turgenev was something more than a psychological observer and an exquisite stylist. Like virtually every major Russian writer of his time, he was, all his life, profoundly and painfully concerned with his country's condition and destiny. His novels constitute the best account of the social and political development of the small, but influential, élite of the liberal and radical Russian youth of his day – of it and of its critics. His books, from the point of view of the authorities in St Petersburg, were by no means safe. Yet, unlike his great contemporaries Tolstoy and Dostoevsky, he was not a preacher and did not wish to thunder at his generation. He was concerned, above all, to enter into, to understand, views, ideals, temperaments, both those which he found sympathetic and those by which he was puzzled or repelled. Turgenev possessed in a highly developed form what Vico called *fantasia*, an ability to enter into beliefs, feelings and attitudes alien and at times acutely antipathetic to his own, a gift which Renan had emphasised in his eulogy;[1] indeed, some of the young Russian revolutionaries freely conceded the accuracy and justice of his portraits of them. During much of his life he was painfully preoccupied with the controversies, moral and political, social and personal, which divided the educated Russians of his day; in particular, the profound and bitter conflicts between Slavophil nationalists and admirers of the West, conservatives and liberals, liberals and radicals, moderates and fanatics, realists and visionaries, above all between old and young. He tried to stand aside and see the scene objectively. He did

1   For the text of the *Discours* delivered on 1 October 1883 see I. Tourguéneff, *Œuvres dernières*, 2nd ed. (Paris, [1885]), 297–302.

not always succeed. But because he was an acute and responsive observer, self-critical and self-effacing both as a man and as a writer, and, above all, because he was not anxious to bind his vision upon the reader, to preach, to convert, he proved a better prophet than the two self-centred, angry literary giants with whom he is usually compared, and discerned the birth of social issues which have grown worldwide since his day. Many years after Turgenev's death the radical novelist Vladimir Korolenko, who declared himself a 'fanatical' admirer, remarked that Turgenev 'irritated [. . .] by touching painfully the most exposed nerves of the live issues of the day'; that he excited passionate love and respect and violent criticism, and was a storm centre, 'yet he knew the pleasures of triumph too; he understood others, and others understood him'.[1] It is on this relatively neglected aspect of Turgenev's writing, which speaks most directly to our own time, that I should like to comment.

I

By temperament Turgenev was not politically minded. Nature, personal relationships, quality of feeling – these are what he understood best, these, and their expression in art. He loved every manifestation of art and of beauty as deeply as anyone has ever done. The conscious use of art for ends extraneous to itself, ideological, didactic or utilitarian, and especially as a deliberate weapon in the class war, as demanded by the radicals of the 1860s, was detestable to him. He was often described as a pure aesthete and a believer in art for art's sake, and was accused of escapism and lack of civic sense, then, as now, regarded in the view of a section of Russian opinion as being a despicable form of irresponsible self-indulgence. Yet these descriptions do not fit him. His writing was not as deeply and passionately committed as that of Dostoevsky after his Siberian exile, or of the later Tolstoy, but it was sufficiently concerned with social analysis to enable both

1   V. G. Korolenko, 'I. A. Goncharov i "molodoe pokolenie" (K 100-letnei godovshchine rozhdeniya)' (1912), *Polnoe sobranie sochinenii* (Petrograd, 1914), ix 324.

the revolutionaries and their critics, especially the liberals among them, to draw ammunition from his novels. The Emperor Alexander II, who had once admired Turgenev's early work, ended by looking upon him as his *bête noire*.

In this respect Turgenev was typical of his time and his class. More sensitive and scrupulous, less obsessed and intolerant than the great tormented moralists of his age, he reacted just as bitterly against the horrors of the Russian autocracy. In a huge and backward country, where the number of educated persons was very small and was divided by a gulf from the vast majority of their fellow men – they could scarcely be described as citizens – living in conditions of unspeakable poverty, oppression and ignorance, a major crisis of public conscience was bound sooner or later to arise. The facts are familiar enough: the Napoleonic wars precipitated Russia into Europe, and thereby, inevitably, into a more direct contact with Western enlightenment than had previously been permitted. Army officers drawn from the land-owning élite were brought into a degree of companionship with their men, lifted as they all were by a common wave of vast patriotic emotion. This for the moment broke through the rigid stratification of Russian society. The salient features of this society included a semi-literate, State-dominated, largely corrupt Church; a small, incompletely Westernised, ill-trained bureaucracy struggling to keep under and hold back an enormous, primitive, half-medieval, socially and economically undeveloped, but vigorous and potentially undisciplined, population straining against its shackles; a widespread sense of inferiority, both social and intellectual, before Western civilisation; a society distorted by arbitrary bullying from above and nauseating conformity and obsequiousness from below, in which men with any degree of independence or originality or character found scarcely any outlet for normal development.

This is enough, perhaps, to account for the genesis, in the first half of the century, of what came to be known as the 'superfluous man',[1] the hero of the new literature of protest, a member of the tiny minority of educated and morally sensitive men, who, unable to find a place in his native land, is driven in upon himself, and

1   [See 172 above, note 1.]

liable to escape either into fantasies and illusions, or into cynicism
or despair, ending, more often than not, in self-destruction or
surrender. Acute shame or furious indignation caused by the
misery and degradation of a system in which human beings – serfs
– were viewed as 'baptised property', together with a sense of
impotence before the rule of injustice, stupidity and corruption,
tended to drive pent-up imagination and moral feeling into the
only channels that the censorship had not completely shut off –
literature and the arts. Hence the notorious fact that in Russia
social and political thinkers turned into poets and novelists, while
creative writers often became publicists. Any protest against institutions, no matter what its origin or purpose, under an absolute
despotism is *eo ipso* a political act. Consequently literature became
the battleground on which the central social and political issues
of life were fought out. Literary or aesthetic questions which in
their birthplace – in Germany or France – were confined to academic or artistic coteries became personal and social problems
that obsessed an entire generation of educated young Russians not
primarily interested in literature or the arts as such. So, for example, the controversy between the supporters of the theory of
pure art and those who believed that it had a social function – a
dispute that preoccupied a relatively small section of French critical opinion during the July Monarchy – in Russia grew into a
major moral and political issue, of progress against reaction, enlightenment versus obscurantism, moral decency, social responsibility and human feeling against autocracy, piety, tradition,
conformity, and obedience to established authority.

  The most passionate and influential voice of his generation was
that of the radical critic Vissarion Belinsky. Poor, consumptive,
ill-born, ill-educated, a man of incorruptible sincerity and great
strength of character, he became the Savonarola of his generation
– a burning moralist who preached the unity of theory and practice, of literature and life. His genius as a critic and his instinctive
insight into the heart of the social and moral problems that
troubled the new radical youth made him its natural leader. His
literary essays were to him and to his readers an unbroken, agonising, unswerving attempt to find the truth about the ends of life,
what to believe and what to do. A man of passionate and un-

divided personality, Belinsky went through violent changes of position, but never without having lived painfully through each of his convictions and having acted upon them with the whole force of his ardent and uncalculating nature until, one by one, they failed him and forced him, again and again, to make a new beginning, a task ended only by his early death. Literature was for him not a *métier*, nor a profession, but the artistic expression of an all-embracing outlook, an ethical and metaphysical doctrine, a view of history and of man's place in the cosmos, a vision that embraced all facts and all values. Belinsky was, first and foremost, a seeker after justice and truth, and it was as much by the example of his profoundly moving life and character as by his precepts that he bound his spell upon the young radicals. Turgenev, whose early efforts as a poet he encouraged, became his devoted and lifelong admirer. The image of Belinsky, particularly after his death, became the very embodiment of the committed man of letters; after him no Russian writer was wholly free from the belief that to write was, first and foremost, to bear witness to the truth: that the writer, of all men, had no right to avert his gaze from the central issues of his day and his society. For an artist – and particularly a writer – to try to detach himself from the deepest concerns of his nation in order to devote himself to the creation of beautiful objects or the pursuit of personal ends was condemned as self-destructive egoism and frivolity; he would only be maimed and impoverished by such betrayal of his chosen calling.

The tormented honesty and integrity of Belinsky's judgements – the tone, even more than the content – penetrated the moral consciousness of his Russian contemporaries, sometimes to be rejected, but never to be forgotten. Turgenev was by nature cautious, judicious, frightened of all extremes, liable at critical moments to take evasive action; his friend the poet Yakov Polonsky many years later described him to a reactionary minister as being 'kind and soft as wax [. . .] feminine [. . .] without character'.[1] Even if this goes too far, it is true that he was highly impressionable and liable to yield to stronger personalities all his life. Belinsky died in

1848, but his invisible presence seemed to haunt Turgenev for the rest of his life. Whenever from weakness, or love of ease, or craving for a quiet life, or sheer amiability of character, Turgenev felt tempted to abandon the struggle for individual liberty or common decency and to come to terms with the enemy, it may well have been the stern and moving image of Belinsky that, like an icon, at all times stood in his way and called him back to the sacred task. A *Sportsman's Sketches* was his first and most lasting tribute to his dying friend and mentor. To its readers this masterpiece seemed, and seems still, a marvellous description of the old and changing rural Russia, of the life of nature and of the lives of peasants, transformed into a pure vision of art. But Turgenev looked on it as his first great assault on the hated institution of serfdom, a cry of indignation designed to burn itself into the consciousness of the ruling class. When, in 1879, he was made an Honorary Doctor of Laws by the University of Oxford in this very place,[1] James Bryce, who presented him, described him as a champion of freedom. This delighted him.

Belinsky was neither the first nor the last to exercise a dominating influence on Turgenev's life; the first, and perhaps the most destructive, was his widowed mother, a strong-willed, hysterical, brutal, bitterly frustrated woman who loved her son, and broke his spirit. She was a savage monster even by the none too exacting standards of humanity of the Russian landowners of those days. As a child Turgenev had witnessed abominable cruelties and humiliations which she inflicted upon her serfs and dependants, and an episode in his story *The Brigadier* is apparently founded on his maternal grandmother's murder of one of her boy serfs: she struck him in a fit of rage; he fell wounded on the ground; irritated by the spectacle she smothered him with a pillow.[2] Memories of

1   The Sheldonian Theatre, Oxford, in which a shortened version of this essay was delivered as a Romanes Lecture on 12 November 1970.
2   Ludwig Pietsch describes this incident as related to him by Turgenev. See 'Vospominaniya Ludviga Picha', in *Inostrannaya kritika o Turgeneve* (St Petersburg, 1884), 147. Pietsch is quoted by Evgeny Solov'ev – *I. S. Turgenev, ego zhizn' i literaturnaya deyatel'nost': biograficheskii ocherk* (Kazan, 1922), 39–40 – who in turn is quoted by J. Mourier, *Ivan Serguéiévitch Tourguéneff à Spasskoé* (St Petersburg–Moscow, 1899), 28. This latter, apparently misreading Solov'ev, has it that the woman in question was Turgenev's mother.

this kind fill his stories, and it took him his entire life to work them out of his system.

It was early experience of scenes of this kind on the part of men brought up at school and university to respect the values of Western civilisation that was largely responsible for the lasting preoccupation with the freedom and dignity of the individual, and for the hatred of the relics of Russian feudalism, that characterised the political position of the entire Russian intelligentsia from its beginnings. The moral confusion was very great. 'Our time longs for convictions, it is tormented by hunger for the truth,' wrote Belinsky in 1842, when Turgenev was twenty-four and had become intimate with him, '[. . .] our age is all questioning, questing, searching, nostalgic longing for the truth . . .'.[1] Thirteen years later Turgenev echoed this: 'There are epochs when literature cannot *merely* be artistic, there are interests higher than poetry.'[2] Three years later Tolstoy, then dedicated to the ideal of pure art, suggested to him the publication of a purely literary and artistic periodical divorced from the squalid political polemics of the day. Turgenev replied that it was not 'lyrical twittering' that the times were calling for, nor 'birds singing on boughs';[3] 'you loathe this political morass; true, it is a dirty, dusty, vulgar business. But there is dirt and dust in the streets, and yet we cannot, after all, do without towns.'[4]

The conventional picture of Turgenev as a pure artist drawn into political strife against his will but remaining fundamentally alien to it, drawn by critics both on the right and on the left (particularly by those whom his political novels irritated), is misleading. His major novels, from the middle 1850s onwards, are deeply concerned with the central social and political questions that troubled the liberals of his generation. His outlook was profoundly and permanently influenced by Belinsky's indignant humanism and in particular by his furious philippics against all

---

1   'Rech' o kritike', B vi 267, 269.
2   Letter to Vasily Botkin, 28 June 1855, P ii 282.
3   Letter to L. N. Tolstoy, 29 January 1858, P iii 188.
4   To Tolstoy, 7 April 1858, P iii 210.

that was dark, corrupt, oppressive, false.[1] Two or three years earlier, at the University of Berlin, he had listened to the Hegelian sermons of the future anarchist agitator Bakunin, who was his fellow student, sat at the feet of the same German philosophical master and, as Belinsky had once done, admired Bakunin's dialectical brilliance. Five years later he met in Moscow and soon became intimate with the radical young publicist Herzen and his friends. He shared their hatred of every form of enslavement, injustice and brutality, but unlike some among them he could not rest comfortably in any doctrine or ideological system. All that was general, abstract, absolute, repelled him: his vision remained delicate, sharp, concrete and incurably realistic. Hegelianism, right-wing and left-wing, which he had imbibed as a student in Berlin, materialism, socialism, positivism, about which his friends ceaselessly argued, populism, collectivism, the Russian village commune idealised by those Russian socialists whom the ignominious collapse of the left in Europe in 1848 had bitterly disappointed and disillusioned – these came to seem mere abstractions to him, substitutes for reality, in which many believed, and a few even tried to live, doctrines which life, with its uneven surface and irregular shapes of real human character and activity, would surely resist and shatter if ever a serious effort were made to translate them into practice. Bakunin was a dear friend and a delightful boon companion, but his fantasies, whether Slavophil or anarchist, left no trace on Turgenev's thought. Herzen was a different matter: he was a sharp, ironical, imaginative thinker, and in their early years they had much in common. Yet Herzen's populist socialism seemed to Turgenev a pathetic fantasy, the dream of a man whose earlier illusions were killed by the failure of the revolution in the West, but who could not live long without faith; with his old ideals, social justice, equality, liberal democracy, impotent before the forces of

1   'Doubts tormented [Belinsky], robbed him of sleep, food, relentlessly gnawed at him, burnt him, he would not let himself sink into forgetfulness, did not know fatigue [. . .] his sincerity affected me too,' he wrote in his reminiscences with characteristic self-deprecating irony and affection, 'his fire communicated itself to me, the importance of the topic absorbed me; but after talking for two to three hours I used to weaken, the frivolity of youth would take its toll, I wanted to rest, I began to think of a walk, of dinner [. . .]'. 'Vospominaniya o Belinskom' (1869), S xiv 28–9.

reaction in the West, he must find himself a new idol to worship: against the golden calf of acquisitive capitalism, he set up 'the sheepskin coat' (to use Turgenev's words)[1] of the Russian peasant.

Turgenev understood and sympathised with his friend's cultural despair. Like Carlyle and Flaubert, like Stendhal and Nietzsche, Ibsen and Wagner, Herzen felt increasingly asphyxiated in a world in which all values had become debased. All that was free and dignified and independent and creative seemed to Herzen to have gone under beneath the wave of bourgeois philistinism, the commercialisation of life by corrupt and vulgar dealers in human commodities and their mean and insolent lackeys who served the huge joint-stock companies called France, England, Germany; even Italy (he wrote), 'the most poetical country in Europe', when the 'fat, bespectacled little bourgeois of genius', Cavour, offered to keep her, could not restrain herself and, deserting both her fanatical lover Mazzini and her Herculean husband Garibaldi, gave herself to him.[2] Was it to this decaying corpse that Russia was to look as the ideal model? The time was surely ripe for some cataclysmic transformation – a barbarian invasion from the East which would clear the air like a healing storm. Against this, Herzen declared, there was only one lightning conductor – the Russian peasant commune, free from the taint of capitalism, from the greed and fear and inhumanity of destructive individualism. Upon this foundation a new society of free, self-governing human beings might yet be built.

Turgenev regarded all this as a violent exaggeration, the dramatisation of private despair. Of course the Germans were pompous and ridiculous; Louis Napoleon and the profiteers of Paris were odious, but the civilisation of the West was not crumbling. It was the greatest achievement of mankind. It was not for Russians, who had nothing comparable to offer, to mock at it or keep it from their gates. He accused Herzen of being a tired and disillusioned man, who after 1849 was looking for a new divinity and had found it in the simple Russian peasant.

> You erect an altar to this new and unknown God because almost
> nothing is known about him, and one can [. . .] pray and believe and

1   Letter to Herzen of 8 October 1862, P v 52.
2   A. I. Herzen, 'Kontsy i nachala', first letter (1847), H xvi 138.

wait. This God does not begin to do what you expect of him; this, you say, is temporary, accidental, injected by outside forces; your God loves and adores that which you hate, hates that which you love; [he] accepts precisely what you reject on his behalf: you avert your eyes, you stop your ears [. . .] Either you must serve the revolution, and European ideals as before. Or, if you now think that there is nothing in all this, you must have the courage to look the devil in *both* eyes, plead guilty to the *whole of Europe* – to its face – and not make an open or implied exception for some coming Russian Messiah

– least of all for the Russian peasant who is, in embryo, the worst conservative of all, and cares nothing for liberal ideas.[1] Turgenev's sober realism never deserted him. He responded to the faintest tremors of Russian life; in particular, to the changes of expression on what he called 'the swiftly altering physiognomy of those who belong to the cultured section of Russian society'.[2] He claimed to do no more than to record what Shakespeare called the 'form and pressure' of the time.[3] He faithfully described them all – the talkers, the idealists, the fighters, the cowards, the reactionaries and the radicals – sometimes, as in *Smoke*, with biting polemical irony, but, as a rule, so scrupulously, with so much understanding for all the overlapping sides of every question, so much unruffled patience, touched only occasionally with undisguised irony or satire (without sparing his own character and views), that he angered almost everyone at some time.

Those who still think of him as an uncommitted artist, raised high above the ideological battle, may be surprised to learn that no one in the entire history of Russian literature, perhaps of literature in general, has been so ferociously and continuously attacked, both from the right and from the left, as Turgenev. Dostoevsky and Tolstoy held far more violent views, but they were formidable figures, treated with nervous respect by most of their bitterest opponents. Turgenev was not in the least formidable; he was amiable, sceptical, too courteous and too self-

1   Letter to Herzen, 8 November 1862, P v 67–8. On this topic see *Pis'ma K. Dm. Kavelina i Iv. S. Turgeneva k A. I. Gertsenu*, ed. M. Dragomanov (Geneva, 1892), letters by Turgenev for 1862–3 (142–80).
2   Introduction to his collected novels (1880), S xii 303.
3   *Hamlet* 3.2.25.

distrustful to frighten anyone. He embodied no clear principles, advocated no doctrine, no panacea for the 'accursed questions',[1] as they came to be called, personal and social. 'He felt and understood the opposite sides of life,' said Henry James of him, '[. . .] Our Anglo-Saxon, Protestant, moralistic conventional standards were far away from him [. . .] half the charm of conversation with him was that one breathed an air in which cant phrases [. . .] simply sounded ridiculous.'[2] In a country in which readers, and especially the young, to this day look to writers for moral direction, he refused to preach. He was aware of the price he would have to pay for such reticence. He knew that the Russian reader wanted to be told what to believe and how to live, expected to be provided with clearly contrasted values, clearly distinguishable heroes and villains. When the author did not provide this, Turgenev wrote, the reader was dissatisfied and blamed the writer, since he found it difficult and irritating to have to make up his own mind, find his own way. And, indeed, it is true that Tolstoy never leaves you in doubt about whom he favours and whom he condemns; Dostoevsky does not conceal what he regards as the path of salvation. Among these great, tormented Laocoöns, Turgenev remained cautious and sceptical; the reader is left in suspense, in a state of doubt: central problems are raised, and for the most part left – it seemed to some a trifle complacently – unanswered.

No society demanded more of its authors than Russia, then or now. Turgenev was accused of vacillation, temporising, infirmity of purpose, of speaking with too many voices. Indeed, this very topic obsessed him. *Rudin, Asya, On the Eve*, the major works of the 1850s, are preoccupied with weakness – the failure of men of generous heart, sincerely held ideals, who remain impotent and give in without a struggle to the forces of stagnation. Rudin, drawn partly from the young Bakunin, partly from himself,[3] is a

1   See 33 above, note 1.

2   For James's view of Turgenev see his two essays in *The Art of Fiction and Other Essays* (Oxford, 1948); this passage is at 100.

3   His critical friend Herzen said that Turgenev created Rudin 'in biblical fashion – after his own image and likeness'. 'Rudin', he added, 'is Turgenev the Second, plus [*naslushavshiisya*] a lot of [. . .] Bakunin's philosophical jargon.' 'Byloe i dumy', part 7, chapter 4 ('M. Bakunin i pol'skoe delo', 1870), H xi 359; 'M. Bakunin and the Cause of Poland', M iii 1357.

man of high ideals, talks well, fascinates his listeners, expresses views which Turgenev could accept and defend. But he is made of paper. When he is faced with a genuine crisis which calls for courage and resolution, he crumples and collapses. His friend Lezhnev defends Rudin's memory: his ideals were noble but he had 'no character, no blood'.[1] In the epilogue (which the author added as an afterthought to a later edition), after aimless wanderings, Rudin dies bravely but uselessly on the barricades of Paris in 1848, something of which his prototype Bakunin was, in Turgenev's view, scarcely capable. But even this was not open to him in his native land; even if Rudin had blood and character, what could he have done in the Russian society of his time? This 'superfluous man', the ancestor of all the sympathetic, futile, ineffective talkers in Russian literature, should he, could he, in the circumstances of his time have declared war upon the odious aristocratic lady and her world, to which he capitulates? The reader is left without guidance. The heroine of *On the Eve*, Elena, who looks for a heroic personality to help her escape from the false existence of her parents and their milieu, finds that even the best and most gifted Russians in her circle lack will-power, cannot act. She follows the fearless Bulgarian conspirator Insarov, who is thinner, drier, less civilised, more wooden than the sculptor Shubin or the historian Bersenev, but, unlike them, is possessed by a single thought – to liberate his country from the Turk, a simple dominant purpose that unites him with the last peasant and the last beggar in his land. Elena goes with him because he alone, in her world, is whole and unbroken, because his ideals are backed by indomitable moral strength.

Turgenev published *On the Eve* in the *Contemporary* (*Sovremennik*), a radical journal then moving steadily and rapidly to the left. The group of men who dominated it were as uncongenial to him as they were to Tolstoy; he thought them dull, narrow doctrinaires, devoid of all understanding of art, enemies of beauty, uninterested in personal relationships (which were everything to him), but they were bold and strong, fanatics who judged everything in the light of a single goal – the liberation of the Russian

1   *Rudin* (1856), chapter 12, S vi 348.

people. They rejected compromise: they were bent on a radical solution. The emancipation of the serfs, which moved Turgenev and all his liberal friends profoundly, was to these men not the beginning of a new era, but a miserable fraud: the peasants were still chained to their landlords by the new economic arrangements. Only the 'peasant's axe', a mass rising of the people in arms, would give it freedom. Dobrolyubov, the literary editor of the magazine, in his review of *On the Eve*, acclaimed the Bulgarian as a positive hero: for he was ready to give his life to drive out the Turk from his country. And we? We Russians, too (he declared), have our Turks – only they are internal: the Court, the gentry, the generals, the officials, the rising bourgeoisie, oppressors and exploiters whose weapons are the ignorance of the masses and brute force. Where are *our* Insarovs? Turgenev speaks of an eve; when will the real day dawn? If it has not dawned yet, this is because the good, the enlightened young men, the Shubins and Bersenevs in Turgenev's novel, are impotent. They are paralysed, and will, for all their fine words, end by adapting themselves to the conventions of the philistine life of their society, because they are too closely connected with the prevailing order by a network of family and institutional and economic relationships which they cannot bring themselves to break entirely. 'If you sit in an empty box', said Dobrolyubov, in the final version of his article, 'and try to upset it with yourself inside it, what a fearful effort you have to make! But if you come at it from outside, one push will topple this box.'[1] Insarov stood outside his box – the box is the Turkish invader. Those who are truly serious must get out of the Russian box, break off every relationship with the entire monstrous structure, and then knock it over from outside. Herzen and Ogarev sit in London and waste their time in exposing isolated cases of injustice, corruption or mismanagement in the Russian Empire; but this, so far from weakening that Empire, may even help it to eliminate such shortcomings and last longer. The real task is to destroy the whole inhuman system. Dobrolyubov's

---

1   This sentence does not occur in the original review of 1860, but was included in the posthumous edition of Dobrolyubov's essays two years later. See 'Kogda zhe pridet nastoyashchii den'?', *Sobranie sochinenii* (Moscow, 1961–4), vi 126.

advice is clear: those who are serious must endeavour to abandon the box – remove themselves from all contact with the Russian State as it is at present, for there is no other means to acquire an Archimedean point, leverage for causing it to collapse. Insarov rightly lets private revenge – the execution of those who tortured and killed his parents – wait until the larger task is accomplished. There must be no waste of energy on piecemeal denunciations, on the rescue of individuals from cruelty or injustice. This is mere liberal fiddling, escape from the radical task. There is nothing common between 'us' and 'them'. 'They', and Turgenev with them, seek reform, accommodation. 'We' want destruction, revolution, new foundations of life; nothing else will destroy the reign of darkness. This, for the radicals, is the clear implication of Turgenev's novel; but he and his friends are evidently too craven to draw it.

Turgenev was upset and, indeed, frightened by this interpretation of his book. He tried to get the review withdrawn. He said that if it appeared he would not know what to do or where to run. Nevertheless he was fascinated by these new men. He loathed the gloomy puritanism of these 'Daniels of the Neva', as they were called by Herzen,[1] who thought them cynical and brutal and could not bear their crude anti-aesthetic utilitarianism, their fanatical rejection of all that he held dear – liberal culture, art, civilised human relationships. But they were young, brave, ready to die in the fight against the common enemy, the reactionaries, the police, the State. Turgenev wished, in spite of everything, to be liked and respected by them. He tried to flirt with Dobrolyubov, and constantly engaged him in conversation. One day, when they met in the offices of the *Contemporary*, Dobrolyubov suddenly said to him, 'Ivan Sergeevich, do not let us go on talking to each other: it bores me,' and walked away to a distant corner of the room. Turgenev did not give up immediately. He was a celebrated charmer; he did his best to find a way to woo the grim young man. It was of no use; when he saw Turgenev approach he stared at the wall or pointedly left the room. 'You can talk to Turgenev if you like,' Dobrolyubov said to his fellow editor Chernyshevsky, who

1   'Lishnie lyudi i zhelcheviki' (1860), H xiv 322.

at this time still looked with favour and admiration to Turgenev, and he added, characteristically, that in his view bad allies were no allies.[1] This is worthy of Lenin; Dobrolyubov had, perhaps, the most Bolshevik temperament of all the early radicals. Turgenev in the 1850s and early 1860s was the most famous writer in Russia, the only Russian writer with a great and growing European reputation. Nobody had ever treated him like this. He was deeply wounded. Nevertheless, he persisted for a while, but in the end, faced with Dobrolyubov's implacable hostility, gave up. There was an open breach. He crossed over to the conservative review edited by Mikhail Katkov, a man regarded by the left wing as their deadliest enemy.

In the meanwhile the political atmosphere grew more stormy. The terrorist Land and Liberty League was created in 1861, the very year of the great Emancipation. Violently worded manifestos calling on the peasants to revolt began to circulate. The radical leaders were charged with conspiracy, were imprisoned or exiled. Fires broke out in the capital and university students were accused of starting them; Turgenev did not come to their defence. The booing and whistling of the radicals, their brutal mockery, seemed to him mere vandalism; their revolutionary aims, dangerous Utopianism. Yet he felt that something new was rising – a vast social mutation of some kind. He declared that he felt it everywhere. He was repelled and at the same time fascinated by it. A new and formidable type of adversary of the regime – and of much that he and his generation of liberals believed in – was coming into existence. Turgenev's curiosity was always stronger than his fears: he wanted, above everything, to understand the new Jacobins. These men were crude, fanatical, hostile, insulting, but they were un-demoralised, self-confident, and, in some narrow but genuine sense, rational and disinterested. He could not bear to turn his back upon them. They seemed to him a new, clear-eyed generation, undeluded by the old romantic myths; above all they

1   N. G. Chernyshevsky's reminiscences quoted in *I. S. Turgenev v vospominani-yakh sovremennikov* (Moscow, 1969), i 356–8. This story was recorded by Chernyshevsky in 1884, many years after the event, at the request of his cousin Pypin, who was collecting material about the radical movement of the 1860s; there is no reason for doubting its accuracy.

were the young, the future of his country lay in their hands; he did not wish to be cut off from anything that seemed to him alive, passionate and disturbing. After all, the evils that they wished to fight were evils; their enemies were, to some degree, his enemies too; these young men were wrong-headed, barbarous, contemptuous of liberals like himself, but they were fighters and martyrs in the battle against despotism. He was intrigued, horrified and dazzled by them. During the whole of the rest of his life he was obsessed by a desire to explain them to himself, and perhaps himself to them.

II

Young Man to Middle-Aged Man: 'You had content but no force.'
Middle-Aged Man to Young Man: 'And you have force but no content.'   From a contemporary conversation[1]

This is the topic of Turgenev's most famous, and politically most interesting, novel, *Fathers and Children*. It was an attempt to give flesh and substance to his image of the new men, whose mysterious, implacable presence, he declared, he felt about him everywhere, and who inspired in him feelings that he found difficult to analyse. 'There was', he wrote many years later to a friend, '– please don't laugh – some sort of *fatum*, something stronger than the author himself, something independent of him. I know one thing: I started with no preconceived idea, no "tendency"; I wrote naively, as if myself astonished at what was emerging.'[2] He said that the central figure of the novel, Bazarov, was mainly modelled on a Russian doctor whom he met in a train in Russia. But Bazarov has some of the characteristics of Belinsky too. Like him, he is the son of a poor army doctor, and he possesses some of Belinsky's brusqueness, his directness, his intolerance, his liability to explode at any sign of hypocrisy, of solemnity, of

1   The original epigraph to *Fathers and Children*, which Turgenev later discarded: S viii 446. See also A. Mazon, *Manuscrits parisiens d'Ivan Tourguénev* (Paris, 1930), 65.
2   Letter to M. E. Saltykov, 15 January 1876, P xi 190–1.

pompous conservative, or evasive liberal, cant. And there is, despite Turgenev's denials, something of the ferocious, militant anti-aestheticism of Dobrolyubov too. The central topic of the novel is the confrontation of the old and young, of liberals and radicals, traditional civilisation and the new, harsh positivism which has no use for anything except what is needed by a rational man. Bazarov, a young medical researcher, is invited by his fellow student and disciple Arkady Kirsanov to stay at his father's house in the country. Nikolay Kirsanov, the father, is a gentle, kindly, modest country gentleman, who adores poetry and nature, and greets his son's brilliant friend with touching courtesy. Also in the house is Nikolay Kirsanov's brother Pavel, a retired army officer, a carefully dressed, vain, pompous, old-fashioned dandy, who had once been a minor lion in the salons of the capital, and is now living out his life in elegant and irritated boredom. Bazarov scents an enemy, and takes deliberate pleasure in describing himself and his allies as 'nihilists', by which he means no more than that he, and those who think like him, reject everything that cannot be established by the rational methods of natural science. Truth alone matters: what cannot be established by observation and experiment is useless or harmful ballast – 'romantic rubbish'[1] – which an intelligent man will ruthlessly eliminate. In this heap of irrational nonsense Bazarov includes all that is impalpable, that cannot be reduced to quantitative measurement – literature and philosophy, the beauty of art and the beauty of nature, tradition and authority, religion and intuition, the uncriticised assumptions of conservatives and liberals, of populists and socialists, of landowners and serfs. He believes in strength, will-power, energy, utility, work, in ruthless criticism of all that exists. He wishes to tear off masks, blow up all revered principles and norms. Only irrefutable facts, only useful knowledge, matter. He clashes almost immediately with the touchy, conventional Pavel Kirsanov: 'At present', he tells him, 'the most useful thing is to deny. So we deny.' 'Everything?' asks Pavel Kirsanov. 'Everything.' 'What? Not only art, poetry ... but even ... too horrible to utter ...' 'Everything.' [...] 'So you destroy everything ... but surely one

1   FC 7, 226.

must build, too?' 'That's not our business . . . First one must clear
the ground.'[1]

The fiery revolutionary agitator Bakunin, who had just then
escaped from Siberia to London, was saying something of this
kind: the entire rotten structure, the corrupt old world, must be
razed to the ground, before something new can be built upon it;
what this is to be is not for us to say; we are revolutionaries, our
business is to demolish. The new men, purified from the infection
of the world of idlers and exploiters, and its bogus values – these
men will know what to do. The German social democrat Eduard
Bernstein once quoted Marx as saying '*Anyone who makes plans
for after the revolution is a reactionary*.'[2]

This went beyond the position of Turgenev's radical critics from
the *Contemporary*: they did have a programme of sorts: they
were democratic populists. But faith in the people seems just as
irrational to Bazarov as the rest of the 'romantic rubbish'.[3] 'Our
peasants', he declares, 'are prepared to rob themselves in order to
drink themselves blind at the inn.'[4] A man's first duty is to develop
his own powers, to be strong and rational, to create a society in
which other rational men can breathe and live and learn. His mild
disciple Arkady suggests to him that it would be ideal if all peasants lived in a pleasant whitewashed hut, like the head man of
their village. 'I have conceived a loathing for this [. . .] peasant,'
Bazarov says, '[. . .] I have to work the skin off my hands for him,
and he won't so much as thank me for it . . . anyway, what do I
need his thanks for? He'll go on living in his whitewashed hut,

1   FC 10, 243.
2   Bernstein reports that this passage occurs in a letter which, according to
    the economist Lujo Brentano (writing in Munich's *Allgemeine Zeitung*
    shortly before Bernstein), Marx wrote to one of his English friends, E. S.
    Beesly: Ed. Bernstein, 'Des forces de la démocratie industrielle: Réponse
    a Mlle Luxemburg', *Mouvement Socialiste* 1899 vol. 2 (July–November),
    1 September, 257–71, at 270. [However, the only article attributed to
    Brentano that fits this description, 'Der soziale Friede und die Wandlungen
    der Sozialdemokratie', *Allgemeine Zeitung* (Munich), 23 April 1899, 1–2,
    has nothing to say about such a letter, which also appears not to have
    survived.]
3   loc. cit. (317 above, note 1).   4   FC 10, 245.

while weeds grow out of me [. . .].'[1] Arkady is shocked by such talk; but it is the voice of the new, hard-boiled, unashamed materialistic egoism. Nevertheless Bazarov is at his ease with peasants; they are not self-conscious with him even if they think him an odd sort of member of the gentry. Bazarov spends his afternoon in dissecting frogs. 'A decent chemist', he tells his shaken host, 'is twenty times more use than any poet.'[2] Arkady, after consulting Bazarov, gently draws a volume of Pushkin out of his father's hands, and slips into them Büchner's *Kraft und Stoff*,[3] the latest popular exposition of materialism. Turgenev describes the older Kirsanov walking in his garden: 'Nikolay Petrovich dropped his head, and passed his hand over his face. "But to reject poetry," he thought again, "not to have a feeling for art, for nature . . ." and he cast about him, as if trying to understand how it was possible not to have a feeling for nature.'[4] All principles, Bazarov declares, are reducible to mere sensations. Arkady asks whether, in that case, honesty is only a sensation. 'You find this hard to swallow?' says Bazarov. 'No, friend, if you have decided to knock everything down, you must knock yourself down, too! . . .'[5] This is the voice of Bakunin and Dobrolyubov: 'one must clear the ground'.[6] The new culture must be founded on real, that is materialist, scientific values: socialism is just as unreal and abstract as any other of the 'isms' imported from abroad. As for the old aesthetic, literary culture, it will crumble before the realists, the new, tough-minded men who can look the brutal truth in the face. 'Aristocracy, liberalism, progress, principles [. . .] what a lot of foreign . . . and useless words. A Russian would not want them as a gift.'[7] Pavel Kirsanov rejects this contemptuously; but his nephew Arkady cannot, in the end, accept it either.

'You aren't made for our harsh, bitter, solitary kind of life [Bazarov tells him], you aren't insolent, you aren't nasty, all you have is the audacity, the impulsiveness of youth, and that is of no use in our

---

1   FC 21, 325.   2   FC 6, 219.

3   Turgenev calls it *Stoff und Kraft*, FC10, 238; cf. letter of 22 April 1862 to K. K. Sluchevsky, P iv 379.

4   FC 11, 249.   5   FC 21, 325.

6   loc. cit. (318 above, note 1).   7   FC 10, 242.

business. Your type, the gentry, cannot get beyond noble humility, noble indignation, and that is nonsense. You won't, for instance, fight, and yet you think yourselves terrific. We want to fight [. . .] Our dust will eat out your eyes, our dirt will spoil your clothes, you haven't risen to our level yet, you still can't help admiring yourselves, you like castigating yourselves, and that bores us. Hand us others – it is them we want to break. You are a good fellow, but, all the same, you are nothing but a soft, beautifully bred, liberal boy [. . .]'[1]

Bazarov, someone once said, is the first Bolshevik; even though he is not a socialist, there is some truth in this. He wants radical change and does not shrink from brute force. The old dandy, Pavel Kirsanov, protests against this:

'Force? There is force in savage Kalmucks and Mongols, too. What do we want it for? Civilisation [. . .] its fruits, are dear to us. And don't tell me they are worthless. The most miserable dauber [. . .] the pianist who taps on the keys in a restaurant [. . .] they are more useful than you are, because they represent civilisation and not brute Mongol force. You imagine that you are progressive; you should be sitting in a Kalmuck wagon!'[2]

In the end, Bazarov, against all his principles, falls in love with a cold, clever, well-born society beauty, is rejected by her, suffers deeply, and not long after dies as a result of an infection caught while dissecting a corpse in a village autopsy. He dies stoically, wondering whether his country had any real need of him and men like him; and his death is bitterly lamented by his old, humble, loving parents. Bazarov falls because he is broken by love and fate, not through failure of will or intellect. 'I conceived him', Turgenev later wrote to a young student, 'as a sombre figure, wild, huge, half-grown out of the soil, powerful, nasty, honest, but doomed to destruction because he still stands only in the gateway to the future.'[3] This brutal, fanatical, dedicated figure, with his unused powers, is represented as an avenger for insulted human

1   FC 26, 380–1.   2   FC 10, 246.
3   Letter to K. K. Sluchevsky, 22 April 1862, P iv 381.

reason; yet, in the end, he is incurably wounded by a love, by a human passion that he suppresses and denies within himself, a crisis by which he is humiliated and humanised. In the end, he is crushed by heartless nature, by what the author calls the cold-eyed goddess Isis,[1] who does not care for good or evil, or art or beauty, still less for man, the creature of an hour; he is not saved either by his egoism or by his altruism, by faith or works, by rational hedonism or puritanical pursuit of duty; he struggles to assert himself; but nature is indifferent; she obeys her own inexorable laws.

Fathers and Children was published in the spring of 1862 and caused the greatest storm among its Russian readers of any novel before or, indeed, since. What was Bazarov? How was he to be taken? Was he a positive or a negative figure? A hero or a devil? He is young, bold, intelligent, strong, he has thrown off the burden of the past, the melancholy impotence of the 'superfluous men' beating vainly against the bars of the prison house of Russian society. The critic Strakhov in his review spoke of him as a character conceived on a heroic scale.[2] Many years later Lunacharsky described him as the first 'positive' hero in Russian literature. Does he then symbolise progress? Freedom? Yet his hatred of art and culture, of the entire world of liberal values, his cynical asides – does the author mean to hold these up for admiration? Even before the novel was published, his editor, Mikhail Katkov, protested to Turgenev. This glorification of nihilism, he complained, was nothing but grovelling at the feet of the young radicals. 'Turgenev', he said to the novelist's friend Annenkov, 'should be ashamed of lowering the flag before a radical', or saluting him as an honourable soldier.[3] Katkov declared that he was not deceived by the author's apparent objectivity: 'Concealed approval can masquerade as horror and repugnance [. . .] This fellow, Bazarov, definitely dominates the others and does not encounter proper resistance', and he

---

1   See the first paragraph of the short story 'Poezdka v poles'e' (1857), S vii 51; 'A Tour in the Forest', in *The Diary of a Superfluous Man and Other Stories*, trans. Constance Garnett (London, 1899), 101–2.

2   *Vremya* 9 ([April] 1862), section 2, 50–84. See also his essays on Turgenev in N. Strakhov, *Kriticheskie stat'i ob I. S. Turgeneve i L. N. Tolstom (1862–85)* (St Petersburg, 1885), which includes this review.

3   op. cit. (315 above, note 1), i 343.

concluded that what Turgenev had done was politically dangerous.[1] Strakhov was more sympathetic. He wrote that Turgenev, with his devotion to timeless truth and beauty, wanted only to describe reality, not to judge it. He too, however, spoke of Bazarov as towering over the other characters, and declared that Turgenev might claim to be drawn to him by an irresistible attraction, but it would be truer to say that he feared him. Katkov echoes this: 'One gets the impression of a kind of embarrassment in the author's attitude to the hero of his story [. . .] It is as if the author didn't like him, felt lost before him, and, more than this, was terrified of him!'[2]

The attack from the left was a good deal more virulent. Dobrolyubov's successor, Antonovich, accused Turgenev in the *Contemporary*[3] of perpetrating a hideous and disgusting caricature of the young. Bazarov was a brutish, cynical sensualist, hankering after wine and women, unconcerned with the fate of the people; his creator, whatever his views in the past, had evidently crossed over to the blackest reactionaries and oppressors. And, indeed, there were conservatives who congratulated Turgenev for exposing the horrors of the new, destructive nihilism, and thereby rendering a public service for which all men of decent feeling must be grateful. But it was the attack from the left that hurt Turgenev most. Seven years later he wrote to a friend that 'mud and filth' had been flung at him by the young. He had been called fool, donkey, reptile, Judas, police agent.[4] And again:

> While some accused me of [. . .] backwardness, black obscurantism,
> and informed me that 'my photographs were being burnt amid

1   ibid. 343–4.
2   Letter to Turgenev, quoted by him in 'Po povodu "Ottsov i detei"' (1868–9),
     S xiv 97–109, at 104, note.
3   See M. A. Antonovich, 'Asmodei nashego vremeni', *Sovremennik* 1862 No
     3, 'Sovremennoe obozrenie', 65–114, and V. G. Bazanov, 'Turgenev i anti-
     nigilisticheskii roman (Bazarov i nigilisty v russkoi literature)', in *Kareliya:
     al'manakh soyuza sovetskikh Karelii*, book 4 (Petrozavodsk, 1939), 160–9.
     Also V. Zelinsky, *Kriticheskie razbory romana I. S. Turgeneva 'Ottsy i deti'*,
     2nd ed. (Moscow, 1907), and V. Tukhomitsky, 'Prototipy Bazarova (Po
     povodu 40-letiya "Ottsov i detei" Turgeneva i 20-letiya smerti ego)', '*K
     pravde': literaturno-publitsisticheskii sbornik* (Moscow, 1904), 227–85.
4   To L. Pietsch, 3 June 1869, P viii 38–9.

contemptuous laughter', yet others indignantly reproached me with kowtowing to the [. . .] young. 'You are crawling at Bazarov's feet!' cried one of my correspondents. 'You are only pretending to condemn him. Actually you scrape and bow to him, you wait obsequiously for the favour of a casual smile!'[1]

At least one of his liberal friends who had read the manuscript of *Fathers and Children* told him to burn it, since it would compromise him for ever with the progressives. Hostile caricatures appeared in the left-wing press, in which Turgenev was represented as pandering to the fathers, with Bazarov as a leering Mephistopheles, mocking his disciple Arkady's love for his father.[2] At best, the author was drawn as a bewildered figure simultaneously attacked by frantic democrats from the left and threatened by armed fathers from the right, as he stood helplessly between them.[3] But the left was not unanimous. The radical critic Pisarev came to Turgenev's aid. He boldly identified himself with

1 'Po povodu "Ottsov i detei"', S xiv 104.

2 [These caricatures (324–6 below), by A. Volkov, engraved by F. Freind, are the first 3 in a series of 43 published under the title 'Ottsy i deti' ('Fathers and Children') in the satirical left-wing weekly magazine *Iskra* ('The Spark'), 1868 Nos 12–20 – these ones in No 12, 7 April 1868, 144–5. The first two (324–5 below) contrast (*left*) the alleged crudity and distortion of Turgenev's portrayal of the eponymous children – giving Bazarov an absurd costume and a Struwwelpeter wig, and painting him with a brush dipped in mud – with (*right*) his flattering depiction of the fathers – pouring water for them to wash in; the third (326 below) shows Bazarov smirking sarcastically as Arkady Kirsanov rushes into his father's arms when he reaches his house (an episode at the beginning of the novel) – an unnatural act, Turgenev is said to believe, in the eyes of a student of natural science.] See M. Klevensky, 'I. S. Turgenev v karikaturakh i parodiyakh', *Golos minuvshego* 1918 Nos 1–3 (January–March), 185–218 [Volkov's three drawings are reproduced at 191–2], and D. D. Minaev's satirical poem 'Ottsy ili deti? Parallel'', in *Dumy i pesni D. D. Minaeva i yumoristicheskie stikhotvoreniya oblichitel'nogo poeta (temnogo cheloveka)* (St Petersburg, 1864), 211–13.

3 e.g. in N. V. Ievlev's 'The children and the fathers are both out of control!' (328 below), *Osa* ('The Wasp', a satirical supplement to the conservative weekly magazine *Yakor'*, 'The Anchor'), 12 June 1863, [4]. [The slogans on the nihilists' banners on the left read, from left to right, 'Yes to the emancipation of suckling baby girls', 'We don't need railways' and 'Cut it down to nothing!!', and the word hovering above the demonstrators is 'children'; the banner on the right reads 'Fathers'.]

Отношенія романиста къ дѣтямъ, истинно-отеческія.
Посмотри, съ какой заботою къ своему герою онъ при-
готовилъ для него и парикъ «Степки-Растрепки», героя
дѣтской повѣсти, и смазные дегтемъ сапоги, совершенно
не нужныя и дурацкой «балахонъ — однимъ словомъ
«кисть художника надъ нимъ играла» вынутая изъ взба-
ламученной грязи....

*The attitude of the novelist to the children is truly paternalistic. See
with what care for his hero he provides him with a 'Stepka-Rastrepka'
wig (S-R is a character in a children's novel [the basis for
Struwwelpeter]), completely unnecessary polished boots, and a
foolish cloak: in a word 'the paintbrush used on him' was dipped
in stirred mud . . . [See 323 above, note 2.]*

Bazarov and his position. Turgenev, Pisarev wrote, might be too
soft or tired to accompany us, the men of the future; but he knows
that true progress is to be found not in men tied to tradition, but
in active, self-emancipated, independent men, free, like Bazarov,
from fantasies, from romantic or religious nonsense. The author
does not bully us, he does not tell us to accept the values of
the 'fathers'. Bazarov is in revolt; he is the prisoner of no theory;
that is his attractive strength; that is what makes for progress and

Лучше поздно чѣмъ никогда.

Пословица.

Отношенія же его къ «Отцамъ» совершенно другія.—
Онъ умываетъ, причесываетъ, старается показать ихъ
бѣленькими, приноситъ имъ и мыло и «духи благородные»
и щеточки и гребеночки и... и многое другое...

Better late than never. Proverb.
*His attitude to the 'fathers', on the other hand, is totally different. – He
washes their faces, brushes their hair, tries to show them looking whiter
than white, brings them soap and 'noble perfume' and little brushes and
little combs ... and many other things ... [See 323 above, note 2.]*

freedom. Turgenev may wish to tell us that we are on a false
path, but in fact he is a kind of Balaam: he has become deeply
attached to the hero of his novel through the very process of
creation, and pins all his hopes to him. 'Nature is a work-
shop, not a temple',[1] and we are workers in it; not melancholy
daydreams, but will, strength, intelligence, realism – these, Pisarev
declares, speaking through Bazarov, these will find the road.

1   FC 9, 236.

Романъ начинается пріѣздомъ нигилиста въ деревню Кирсано-
выхъ. Аркадій Кирсановъ бросается въ объятія отца, а Базаровъ сар-
кастически улыбается, ибо радость при свиданіи отца съ сыномъ, по
мнѣнію автора, для человѣка, занимающагося естественными нау-
ками—неестественна.

The novel begins with the arrival of the nihilist in Kirsanov's village.
Arkady Kirsanov throws himself into his father's arms, but Bazarov
smiles sarcastically, because in the author's opinion the joy of a
meeting between father and son is unnatural for a person studying
natural sciences. [See 323 above, note 2.]

Bazarov, he adds, is what parents today see emerging in their sons
and daughters, sisters in their brothers. They may be frightened by
it, they may be puzzled, but that is where the road to the future lies.[1]

1   D. I. Pisarev, 'Bazarov', *Russkoe slovo*, 1862 No 3, 'Russkaya literatura',
     1–54, *Polnoe sobranie sochinenii* (St Petersburg, 1900–7), ii 379–428; and

Turgenev's familiar friend, Annenkov, to whom he submitted all his novels for criticism before he published them, saw Bazarov as a Mongol, a Genghis Khan, a wild beast symptomatic of the savage condition of Russia, only 'thinly concealed by books from the Leipzig Fair'.[1] Was Turgenev aiming to become the leader of a political movement? 'The author himself [. . .] does not know how to take him,' he wrote, 'as a fruitful force for the future, or as a disgusting boil on the body of a hollow civilisation, to be removed as rapidly as possible.'[2] Yet he cannot be both, 'he is a Janus with two faces, each party will see only what it wants to see or can understand.'[3]

Katkov, in an unsigned review in his own journal (in which the novel had appeared), went a good deal further. After mocking the confusion on the left as a result of being unexpectedly faced with its own image in nihilism, which pleased some and horrified others,

---

'Realisty' (1864), ibid. iv 1–146. It is perhaps worth noting for the benefit of those interested in the history of Russian radical ideas that it was the controversy about the character of Bazarov that probably influenced Chernyshevsky in creating the character of Rakhmetov in his famous didactic novel *What Is To Be Done?*, published in the following year; but the view that Rakhmetov is not merely 'the answer' to Bazarov, but a 'positive' version of Turgenev's hero (e.g. in a recent introduction to one of the English translations of the novel) is without foundation. Pisarev's self-identification with Bazarov marks the line of divergence between the rational egoism and potential élitism of the 'nihilists' of *Russkoe slovo* with their neo-Jacobin allies of the 1860s – culminating in Tkachev and Nechaev – and the altruistic and genuinely egalitarian socialism of *Sovremennik* and the populists of the 1870s, with their acuter sense of civic duty, whom Turgenev later attempted to describe, not always successfully, in *Virgin Soil* (1877) – see on this Joseph Frank, 'N. G. Chernyshevsky: A Russian Utopia', *Southern Review* [Baton Rouge] 3 No 1 (January 1967), 68–84. This emerges most clearly in the famous controversy between Tkachev and Lavrov in the 1870s. Bazarov's historical importance is considerable, not because he is the original but because he is one of the antitheses of Rakhmetov; and this despite the story, which, according to at least one source, Turgenev did not deny, that the same individual may have served as the 'model' for both. To this extent the indignant attacks by Antonovich and later by Shelgunov, however intemperate or valueless as criticism, were not without foundation.

1   Letter to Turgenev, 26 September 1861, quoted in V. A. Arkhipov, 'K tvor-cheskoi istorii romana I. S. Turgeneva "Ottsy i deti"', *Russkaya literatura* 1958 No 1, 132–62, at 148.

2   ibid. 147.   3   ibid.

The children and fathers are both out of control! [See 323 above, note 3.]

he reproaches the author for being altogether too anxious not to
be unjust to Bazarov, and consequently for representing him
always in the best possible light. There is such a thing, he says, as
being too fair: this leads to its own brand of distortion of the
truth. Bazarov is represented as being brutally candid: that is good,
very good; he believes in telling the whole truth, however upsetting
to the poor, gentle Kirsanovs, father and son, with no respect
for persons or circumstances: admirable; he attacks art, riches,
luxurious living: yes, but in the name of what? Of science and
knowledge? But, Katkov declares, this is simply not true. Bazarov's
purpose is not the discovery of scientific truth, else he would not
peddle cheap popular tracts – Büchner and the rest – which are
not science at all, but journalism, materialist propaganda. Bazarov
(he goes on to say) is not a scientist; this species scarcely exists in
Russia in our time. Bazarov and his fellow nihilists are merely
preachers: they denounce phrases, rhetoric, inflated language
– Bazarov tells Arkady not to talk so 'beautifully' – but only in
order to substitute for this their own political propaganda;
they offer not hard scientific facts, in which they are not inter-

ested, with which, indeed, they are not acquainted, but slogans, diatribes, radical cant. Bazarov's dissection of frogs is not genuine pursuit of the truth, it is only an occasion for rejecting civilised and traditional values which Pavel Kirsanov, who in a better-ordered society – say England – would have done useful work, rightly defends. Bazarov and his friends will discover nothing; they are not researchers; they are mere ranters, men who declaim in the name of a science which they do not trouble to master; in the end they are no better than the ignorant, benighted Russian priesthood from whose ranks they mostly spring, and far more dangerous.[1]

Herzen, as always, was both penetrating and amusing. 'Turgenev was more of an artist in his novel than people think, and for this reason lost his way, and, in my opinion, did very well. He wanted to go to one room, but ended up in another and a better one.'[2] The author clearly started by wanting to do something for the fathers, but they turned out to be such nonentities that he 'became carried away by Bazarov's very extremism; with the result that instead of flogging the son, he whipped the fathers'.[3] Herzen may well be right: it may be that, although Turgenev does not admit this, Bazarov, whom the author began as a hostile portrait, came to fascinate his creator to such a degree that, like Shylock, he turns into a figure more human and a great deal more complex than the design of the work had originally allowed for, and so at once transforms and perhaps distorts it. Nature sometimes imitates art: Bazarov affected the young as Werther, in the previous century, influenced them, like Schiller's *The Robbers*, like Byron's Laras and Giaours and Childe Harolds in their day. Yet these new men, Herzen added in a later essay, are so dogmatic, doctrinaire, jargon-ridden as to exhibit the least attractive aspect of the Russian character, the policeman's – the martinet's – side of it, the brutal bureaucratic jackboot; they want to break the yoke of the old despotism, but only in order to replace it with one of their

1   'Roman Turgeneva i ego kritiki', *Russkii vestnik*, May 1862, 393–426, and 'O nashem nigilizme: po povodu romana Turgeneva', ibid. July 1862, 402–26.
2   'Eshche raz Bazarov' (1868), H xx/1 339.
3   ibid.

own. The 'generation of the '40s', his own and Turgenev's, may have been fatuous and weak, but does it follow that their successors – the brutally rude, loveless, cynical, philistine young men of the 1860s, who sneer and mock and push and jostle and don't apologise[1] – are necessarily superior beings? What new principles, what new constructive answers have they provided? Destruction is destruction. It is not creation.

In the violent babel of voices aroused by the novel, at least five attitudes can be distinguished.[2] There was the angry right wing which thought that Bazarov represented the apotheosis of the new nihilists, and sprang from Turgenev's unworthy desire to flatter and be accepted by the young. There were those who congratulated him on successfully exposing barbarism and subversion. There were those who denounced him for his wicked travesty of the radicals, for providing reactionaries with ammunition and playing into the hands of the police; by them he was called renegade and traitor. Still others, like Dmitry Pisarev, proudly nailed Bazarov's colours to their mast and expressed gratitude to Turgenev for his honesty and sympathy with all that was most living and fearless in the growing party of the future. Finally there were some who detected that the author himself was not wholly sure of what he wanted to do, that his attitude was genuinely ambivalent, that he was an artist and not a pamphleteer, that he told the truth as he saw it, without a clear partisan purpose.

This controversy continued in full strength after Turgenev's death. It says something for the vitality of his creation that the debate did not die even in the following century, neither before nor after the Russian Revolution. Indeed, as lately as ten years ago[3] the battle was still raging amongst Soviet critics. Was Turgenev for us or against us? Was he a Hamlet blinded by the pessimism of his declining class, or did he, like Balzac or Tolstoy, see beyond it? Is Bazarov a forerunner of the politically committed, militant Soviet intellectual, or a malicious caricature of

---

1   loc. cit. (118 above, note 2).
2   For a full analysis of the immediate reaction to the novel see 'Z' (E. F. Zarin), 'Ne v brov', a v glaz', *Biblioteka dlya chteniya* 170 (1862), 'Sovremennaya letopis'', April, 21–55, May, 137–86.
3   [Written in 1970.]

the fathers of Russian Communism? The debate is not over yet.[1]
Turgenev was upset and bewildered by the reception of his
book. Before sending it to the printer, he had taken his usual
precaution of seeking endless advice. He read the manuscript
to friends in Paris, he altered, he modified, he tried to please everyone. The figure of Bazarov suffered several transformations in
successive drafts, up and down the moral scale as this or that
friend or consultant reported his impressions. The attack from the

1   The literature, mostly polemical, is very extensive. Among the most represen-
    tative essays may be listed: V. V. Vorovsky's celebrated 'Bazarov i Sanin: Dva
    nigilizma', in *Literaturnyi raspad: kriticheskii sbornik*, book 2 (St Petersburg
    1909), 144–65 (published under the pseudonym 'P. Orlovsky'); V. P. Kin,
    'Gamletizm i nigilizm v tvorchestve Turgeneva', *Literatura i marksizm* 1929
    No 6, 71–116; L. V. Pumpyansky, ' "Ottsy i deti": istoriko-literaturnyi
    ocherk', in I. S. Turgenev, *Sochineniya* (Moscow/Leningrad, 1929–30), vi
    167–86; I. Ippolit, 'Lenin o Turgeneve', *Literaturnyi kritik* 1933 No 6, 33–
    44; I. I. Veksler, *I. S. Turgenev i politicheskaya bor'ba shestidesyatykh godov*
    (Leningrad, 1934); V. A. Arkhipov, op. cit. (327 above, note 1; G. A. Byaly,
    'V. Arkhipov protiv I. Turgeneva', *Novy mir* 1958 No 8, 255–9; A. I. Batyuto,
    'K voprosy o zamylse "Ottsov i detei" ', in *I. S. Turgenev (1818–1883–1958):
    stat'i i materialy* (Orel, 1960), 77–95; P. G. Pustovoit, *Roman I. S. Turgeneva
    'Ottsy i deti' i ideinaya bor'ba 60-kh godov XIX veka* (Moscow, 1960);
    N. Chernov, 'Ob odnom znakomstve I. S. Turgeneva', *Voprosy literatury* 1961
    No 8, 188–93; William Egerton, 'I. S. Turgenev i spornyi vopros o yakush-
    kinykh', *Russkaya literatura* 1967 No 1, 149–54. This represents a mere
    sample of the continuing controversy, in which Lenin's scathing reference to
    the similarity of Turgenev's views to those of German right-wing social
    democrats is constantly quoted both for and against the conception of
    Bazarov as a prototype of Bolshevik activists. There is an even more extensive
    mass of writing on the question of whether, and how far, Katkov managed
    to persuade Turgenev to amend his text in a 'moderate' direction by darkening
    Bazarov's image. That Turgenev did alter his text as a result of Katkov's
    pleading is certain; he may, however, have restored some, at any rate, of the
    original language when the novel was published as a book. On this see
    N. M. Gut'yar, *Ivan Sergeevich Turgenev* (Yurev, 1907), 385–7, and V. Baza-
    nov, *Iz literaturnoi polemiki 60kh godov* (Petrozavodsk, 1941), 46–8. But
    see also A. Batyuto, 'Parizhskaya rukopis' romana I. S. Turgeneva "Ottsy i
    deti" ', *Russkaya literatura* 1961 No 4, 57–78. Turgenev's relations with
    Katkov deteriorated rapidly; Turgenev came to look on him as a vicious
    reactionary and refused his proffered hand at a banquet in honour of Pushkin
    in 1880; one of his favourite habits was to refer to the gout which tormented
    him as Katkovitis (*katkovka*): see letter to M. M. Stasyulevich, 23 May 1877,
    P xii/1 160. The list of 'corrections' in the text for which Katkov is held
    responsible is ritually reproduced in virtually every Soviet study of Turgenev's
    works.

left inflicted wounds which festered for the rest of his life. Years later he wrote, 'I am told that I am on the side of the "fathers" – [...] I, who, in the person of Pavel Kirsanov, actually sinned against artistic truth, went too far, exaggerated his defects to the point of travesty, and made him ridiculous!'[1] As for Bazarov, he was 'honest, truthful, a democrat to his fingertips'.[2] Many years later, Turgenev told the anarchist Kropotkin that he loved Bazarov 'very, very much [...] I will show you my diaries – you will see how I wept when I ended the book with Bazarov's death.'[3] 'Tell me honestly,' he wrote to one of his most caustic critics, the satirist Saltykov (who complained that the word 'nihilist' was used by reactionaries to damn anyone they did not like), 'how could anybody be offended by being compared to Bazarov? Do you not yourself realise that he is the most sympathetic of all my characters?'[4] As for 'nihilism', that, perhaps, was a mistake.

> I am ready to admit [...] that I had no right to give our reactionary scum the opportunity to seize on a name, a catchword; the writer in me should have brought the sacrifice to the citizen – I admit the justice of my rejection by the young and of all the gibes hurled at me ... The issue was more important than artistic truth, and I ought to have foreseen this.[5]

He claimed that he shared almost all Bazarov's views, all save those on art.[6] A lady of his acquaintance had told him that he was neither for the fathers, nor for the children, but was a nihilist himself; he thought she might be right.[7] Herzen had said that there had been something of Bazarov in them all, in himself, in Belinsky, in Bakunin, in all those who in the 1840s denounced the Russian kingdom of darkness in the name of the West and science and civilisation.[8] Turgenev did not deny this either. He did, no doubt,

1   'Po povodu "Ottsov i detei" ', S xiv 102.
2   Letter to K. K. Sluchevsky, 26 April 1862, P iv 379.
3   op. cit. (315 above, note 1), i 441.
4   Letter to M. E. Saltykov, 15 January 1876, P xi 191.
5   ibid.
6   'Po povodu "Ottsov i detei" ', S xiv 100, 102.
7   ibid. 103.
8   'Eshche raz Bazarov', H xx/1 335–50.

adopt a different tone in writing to different correspondents. When radical Russian students in Heidelberg demanded clarification of his own position, he told them that

> if the reader does not love Bazarov, as he is – coarse, heartless, ruthlessly dry and brusque [. . .] the fault is mine; I have not succeeded in my task. But to 'dip him in syrup' (to use his own expression) – that I was not prepared to do [. . .] I did not wish to buy popularity by this sort of concession. Better lose a battle (and I think I have lost this one), than win it by a trick.[1]

Yet to his friend the poet Fet, a conservative landowner, he wrote that he did not himself know if he loved Bazarov or hated him. Did he mean to praise or denigrate him? He did not know.[2] And this is echoed eight years later: 'My personal feelings [towards Bazarov] were confused (God only knows whether I loved him or hated him!).'[3] To the liberal Madame Filosofova he wrote, 'Bazarov is my beloved child; on his account I quarrelled with Katkov [. . .] Bazarov, that intelligent, heroic man – a caricature?!?' This he describes as 'a senseless charge'.[4]

He found the scorn of the young unjust beyond endurance. He wrote that in the summer of 1862 'despicable generals praised me, the young insulted me'.[5] The socialist leader Lavrov reports that he bitterly complained to him of the injustice of the radicals' change of attitude towards him.[6] Turgenev returns to this in one of his late *Poems in Prose*: 'Honest souls turn away from him in disgust. Honest faces grow red with indignation at the mention of his name.'[7] This was not mere wounded *amour propre*. He suffered from a genuine sense of having got himself into a politically false

1   Letter to K. K. Sluchevsky, 26 April 1862, P iv 381.

2   Letter of 18 April 1862, P iv 371.

3   Letter to I. P. Borisov, 4 January 1869, P viii 152.

4   Letter of 30 August 1874, P x 281.

5   Letter to Marko Vovchok (Mme Markovich), 27 August 1862, P v 41.

6   P. Lavrov, 'I. S. Turgenev i razvitie russkogo obshchestva', *Vestnik Narodnoi voli* 1884 No 2, 69–149, at 119.

7   From Turgenev's prose poem of February 1858, ' "Uslyshish' sud gluptsa . . ." ', S xiii 151, quoted by Lavrov, loc. cit. (previous note). Turgenev's title (' "You will hear the verdict of the fool . . ." ') is a quotation from Pushkin's poem *Poetu* (1830), line 3.

position. All his life he wished to march with the progressives, with the party of liberty and protest. But, in the end, he could not bring himself to accept their brutal contempt for art, civilised behaviour, for everything that he held dear in European culture. He hated their dogmatism, their arrogance, their destructiveness, their appalling ignorance of life. He went abroad, lived in Germany and France, and returned to Russia only on flying visits. In the West he was universally praised and admired. But in the end it was to Russians that he wished to speak. Although his popularity with the Russian public in the 1860s, and at all times, was very great, it was the radicals he most of all wanted to please. They were hostile or unresponsive.

His next novel, *Smoke*, which he began immediately after the publication of *Fathers and Children*, was a characteristic attempt to staunch his wounds, to settle his account with all his opponents. It was published five years later, in 1867, and contained a biting satire directed at both camps: at the pompous, stupid, reactionary generals and bureaucrats, and at the foolish, shallow, irresponsible left-wing talkers, equally remote from reality, equally incapable of remedying the ills of Russia. This provoked further onslaughts on him. This time he was not surprised. 'They are all attacking me, Reds and Whites, from above and below, and from the sides, especially from the sides.'[1] The Polish rebellion of 1863 and, three years later, Karakozov's attempt to assassinate the Emperor produced great waves of patriotic feeling even within the ranks of the liberal Russian intelligentsia. Turgenev was written off by the Russian critics, of both the right and the left, as a disappointed man, an expatriate who no longer knew his country from the distance of Baden-Baden and Paris. Dostoevsky denounced him as a renegade Russian and advised him to procure a telescope which might enable him to see Russia a little better.[2]

In the 1870s he began nervously, in constant fear of being insulted and humiliated, to rebuild his relations with the left wing. To his astonishment and relief, he was well received in Russian

1   Letter to Herzen, 4 June 1867, P vi 260.
2   See Dostoevsky's letter to the poet A. N. Maikov of 16 August 1867, D xv/2 173–82, quoted in N. M. Gut'yar, op. cit. (331 above, note 1), 337–40: see 339.

revolutionary circles in Paris and London; his intelligence, his goodwill, his undiminished hatred for tsardom, his transparent honesty and fair-mindedness, his warm sympathy with individual revolutionaries, his great charm, had its effect on their leaders. Moreover, he showed courage, the courage of a naturally timorous man determined to overcome his terrors: he supported subversive publications with secret gifts of money, he took risks in openly meeting proscribed terrorists shadowed by the police in Paris or London; this melted their resistance. In 1877 he published *Virgin Soil* (which he intended as a continuation of *Fathers and Children*) in a final attempt to explain himself to the indignant young.

> The younger generation [he wrote in the following year] have, so far, been represented in our literature either as a gang of cheats and crooks [. . .] or [. . .] elevated into an ideal, which again is wrong, and, what is more, harmful. I decided to find the middle way, to come closer to the truth – to take young people, for the most part good and honest, and show that, in spite of their honesty, their cause is so devoid of truth and life that it can only end in a total fiasco. How far I have succeeded is not for me to say [. . .] But they must feel my sympathy [. . .] if not for their goals, at least for their personalities.[1]

The hero of *Virgin Soil*, Nezhdanov, a failed revolutionary, ends by committing suicide. He does so largely because his origins and character make him incapable of adapting himself to the harsh discipline of a revolutionary organisation, or to the slow and solid work of the true hero of the novel, the practical reformer Solomin, whose quietly ruthless labours within his own democratically organised factory will create a more just social order. Nezhdanov is too civilised, too sensitive, too weak, above all too complex, to fit into an austere, monastic new order: he thrashes about painfully, but, in the end, fails because he cannot '*simplify*' himself;[2] nor – and this (as Irving Howe has pointed out)[3] is the central

---

1   Letter to M. M. Stasyulevich, 3 January 1876, P xii/1 43–4.
2   *Virgin Soil* (1877), chapter 37, S xii 288.
3   See the excellent essay 'Turgenev: The Politics of Hesitation' in his *Politics and the Novel* (London, 1961), 137–8.

point – could Turgenev. To his friend Yakov Polonsky he wrote:
'If I was beaten with sticks for *Fathers and Children*, for *Virgin
Soil* they will beat me with staves, from both sides, as usual.'[1]
Three years later Katkov's newspaper again denounced him for
performing clownish somersaults to please the young.[2] As always,
he replied at once: he had not, he said, altered his views by an
iota during the last forty years. 'I am, and have always been, a
"gradualist", an old-fashioned liberal in the English dynastic
sense, a man expecting reform *only from above*. I oppose revolution in principle [...] I should regard it as unworthy of [our
youth] and myself, to represent myself in any other light.'[3]

By the late 1870s his shortcomings had been forgiven by the
left. His moments of weakness, his constant attempts to justify
himself before the Russian authorities, his disavowals of relations
with the exiles in London or Paris – all these sins seem to have
been all but forgotten.[4] His charm, his sympathy for the persons
and convictions of individual revolutionaries, his truthfulness as
a writer won much goodwill among the exiles, even though they
harboured no illusions about the extreme moderation of his views
and his inveterate habit of taking cover when the battle became

---

1   Letter of 11 November 1876, P xi 351.
2   See B. M. Markevich (under the pseudonym 'Inogorodny Obyvatel''), 'S
    beregov Nevy XIII', *Moskovskie vedomosti*, 9 December 1879, 5–6.
3   Letter to *Vestnik Evropy*, 2 January 1880, S xv 185.
4   In 1863 he was summoned back from Paris to be interrogated by a Senatorial
    Commission in St Petersburg about his relations with Herzen and Bakunin.
    How could he have plotted with these men, he protested, he who was a
    lifelong monarchist, a butt of bitter onslaughts by the 'Reds' (H xviii 35)?
    After *Fathers and Children*, he assured the Senators, his relations with Herzen,
    which had never been very close, had been severed (P v 394). There was an
    element of truth in this. But it was not perhaps surprising that Herzen (who
    had not forgotten Turgenev's refusal to sign his and Ogarev's manifesto
    criticising the shortcomings of the Act of Emancipation of the serfs) should,
    characteristically, have referred to a 'white-haired Magdalen of the male sex'
    (H xviii 35) who could not sleep at night for thinking that the Emperor might
    not have heard of her repentance. Turgenev and Herzen saw each other again
    in later years, but never again on the same intimate terms. In 1879 Turgenev
    similarly hastened to deny all connection with Lavrov and his fellow revolu-
    tionaries. Lavrov, too, forgave him. For Turgenev's relations with Lavrov
    and other revolutionary émigrés see P. L. Lavrov, op. cit. (333 above, note
    6), and Michel Delines [M. O. Ashkinazy], 'Tourguéneff et les nihilistes', in
    Tourguéneff inconnu (Paris, [1888]), 53–75.

too hot. He went on telling the radicals that they were mistaken. When the old has lost authority and the new works badly, what is needed is something that he spoke of in *Smoke*: 'active patience [. . .] not without some ingenuity, at times cunning'.[1] When the crisis is upon us, when, in his telling phrase, 'the incompetent come up against the unscrupulous',[2] what is wanted is practical good sense, not the absurd, nostalgic idyll of Herzen and the populists, with their blind, idolatrous adoration of the peasant, who is the worst reactionary of the lot. He said over and over again that he loathed revolution, violence, barbarism. He believed in slow progress, made only by minorities, if only they do not destroy each other. As for socialism, it was a fantasy. It is characteristic of Russians, says his hero and mouthpiece, Potugin, in *Smoke*, 'to pick up an old, worn-out shoe which long, long ago fell from the foot of a Saint-Simon or a Fourier, and, placing it reverently on one's head, to treat it as a sacred object'.[3] As for equality, to the revolutionary Lopatin he said, 'We are not, all of us, really going to walk about in identical yellow tunics *à la* Saint-Simon, all buttoned at the back?'[4] Still, they were the young, the party of freedom and generosity, the party of the have-nots, of those in pain or at least in distress; he would not refuse them his sympathy, his help, his love, even while all the time looking over his shoulder guiltily at his right-wing friends to whom he tried again and again to minimise his unceasing flirtation with the left. On his visits to Moscow or St Petersburg he tried to arrange meetings with groups of radical students. Sometimes the conversations went well; at other times, particularly when he tried to charm them with his reminiscences of the 1840s, they tended to become bored, contemptuous and resentful. Even when they liked or admired him, he felt that a gulf divided them, divided those who wanted to destroy the old world, root and branch, from those who, like him, wished to save it, because in a new world,

---

1   *Smoke* (1867), chapter 27, S ix 318.
2   ibid.   3   ibid., chapter 14, S ix 234.
4   See German Lopatin's reminiscences in M. K. Kleman and N. K. Piksanova (eds), *I. S. Turgenev v vospominaniyakh revolyutsionerov-semidesyatnikov* (Moscow/Leningrad, 1930), 124.

created by fanaticism and violence, there might be too little worth living for.

It was his irony, his tolerant scepticism, his lack of passion, his 'velvet touch', above all his determination to avoid too definite a social or political commitment that, in the end, alienated both sides. Tolstoy and Dostoevsky, despite their open opposition to 'the progressives', embodied unshakeable principles and remained proud and self-confident, and so did not become targets for those who threw stones at Turgenev. His very gifts, his power of minute and careful observation, his fascination with the varieties of character and situation as such, his detachment, his inveterate habit of doing justice to the full complexity and diversity of goals, attitudes, beliefs – these seemed to them morally self-indulgent and politically irresponsible. Like Montesquieu, he was accused by the radicals of too much description, too little criticism. Beyond all Russian writers, Turgenev possessed what Strakhov described as his poetic and truthful genius – a capacity for rendering the very multiplicity of interpenetrating human perspectives that shade imperceptibly into each other, nuances of character and behaviour, motives and attitudes, undistorted by moral passion. The defence of civilisation by the spoilt but intelligent Pavel Kirsanov is not a caricature, and carries a kind of conviction, while the defence of what are apparently the very same values by the worthless Panshin in *A Nest of Gentlefolk* does not, and is not meant to do so; Lavretsky's Slavophil feeling is moving and sympathetic; the populism of both the radicals and the conservatives in *Smoke* is – and is intended to be – repulsive. This clear, finely discriminating, slightly ironical vision, wholly dissimilar from the obsessed genius of Dostoevsky or Tolstoy, irritated all those who craved for primary colours, for certainty, who looked to writers for moral guidance and found none in Turgenev's scrupulous, honest but – as it seemed to them – somewhat complacent ambivalence. He seemed to enjoy his very doubts: he would not cut too deep. Both his great rivals found this increasingly intolerable. Dostoevsky, who began as an enthusiastic admirer, came to look on him as a smiling, shallow, cosmopolitan poseur, a cold-hearted traitor to Russia. Tolstoy thought him a gifted and truthful writer but a moral weakling, and hopelessly blind to the deepest and most agonising spiritual problems of mankind. To Herzen he was an amiable old friend, a gifted artist and a feeble ally, a reed that bent too easily before every storm, an inveterate compromiser.

Turgenev could never bear his wounds in silence. He complained, he apologised, he protested. He knew that he was accused of lack of depth or seriousness or courage. The reception of *Fathers and Children* continued to prey upon him. 'Seventeen years have passed since the appearance of *Fathers and Children*,' he wrote in 1880, 'yet [. . .] the attitude of the critics [. . .] has not become stabilised. Only last year, I happened to read in a journal apropos Bazarov that I am nothing but "a bashi-bazouk[1] who beats to death men wounded by others".'[2] His sympathies, he insisted again and again, were with the victims, never the oppressors – with peasants, students, artists, women, civilised minorities, not the big battalions. How could his critics be so blind? As for Bazarov, there was, of course, a great deal wrong with him, but he was a better man than his detractors; it was easy enough to depict radicals as men with rough exteriors and hearts of gold; 'the trick is to make Bazarov a wild wolf, and still manage to justify him [. . .]'.[3]

The one step Turgenev refused to take was to seek an alibi in the doctrine of art for art's sake. He did not say, as he might easily have done, 'I am an artist, not a pamphleteer; I write fiction, which must not be judged by social or political criteria; my opinions are my private affair; you don't drag Scott or Dickens or Stendhal or even Flaubert before your ideological tribunals – why don't you leave me alone?' He never seeks to deny the social responsibility of the writer; the doctrine of social commitment was instilled into him once and for all by his adored friend Belinsky, and from it he never wholly departed. This social concern colours even his most lyrical writing, and it was this that broke through the reserve of the revolutionaries he met abroad. These men knew perfectly well that Turgenev was genuinely at his ease only with old friends of his own class, men who held views that could not conceivably be described as radical – with civilised liberals or country squires with whom he went duck-shooting whenever he could. Nevertheless,

1 A barbarous Turkish mercenary.
2 Introduction to his collected novels, S xii 307–8.
3 Letter to Herzen, 28 April 1862, P iv 383.

the revolutionaries liked him because he liked them, because
he sympathised with their indignation: 'I know I am only a stick
they use to beat the government with, but' (at this point, according
to the exiled revolutionary Lopatin, who reports this conversation, he made an appropriate gesture) 'let them do it, I am only
too glad.'[1] Above all, they felt drawn to him because he was
responsive to them as individuals and did not treat them simply
as representatives of parties or outlooks. This was, in a sense,
paradoxical, for it was precisely individual social or moral characteristics that, in theory, these men tried to ignore; they believed in
objective analysis, in judging men sociologically, in terms of the
role that, whatever their conscious motives, they played (whether
as individuals or as members of a social class) in promoting or
obstructing desirable human ends – scientific knowledge, or the
emancipation of women, or economic progress, or the revolution.
   This was the very attitude that Turgenev recoiled from; it was
what he feared in Bazarov and the revolutionaries of *Virgin Soil*.
Turgenev, and liberals generally, saw tendencies, political attitudes,
as functions of human beings, not human beings as functions of
social tendencies.[2] Acts, ideas, art, literature were expressions of
individuals, not of objective forces of which the actors or thinkers
were merely the embodiments. The reduction of men to the function
of being primarily carriers or agents of impersonal forces was as
deeply repellent to Turgenev as it had been to Herzen or, in his later
phases, to his revered friend Belinsky. To be treated with so much
sympathy and understanding, and indeed affection, as human
beings and not primarily as spokesmen for ideologies, was a rare
enough experience, a kind of luxury, for Russian revolutionary
exiles abroad. This alone goes some way to account for the fact
that men like Stepnyak, Lopatin, Lavrov and Kropotkin responded
warmly to so understanding, and, moreover, so delightful and so
richly gifted, a man as Turgenev. He gave them secret subsidies but
made no intellectual concessions. He believed – this was his 'old-
fashioned' liberalism in the 'English dynastic [he meant consti-

1   G. Lopatin, op. cit. (337 above, note 4), 126.
2   For this excellent formulation of the distinction between liberals and radicals
     see R. W. Mathewson, *The Positive Hero in Russian Literature* (New York,
     1958), 122.

tutional] sense'[1] – that only education, only gradual methods, 'industry, patience, self-sacrifice, without glitter, without noise',[2] homoeopathic injections of science and culture, could improve the lives of men. He shook and shivered under the ceaseless criticisms to which he had exposed himself, but, in his own apologetic way, refused to 'simplify' himself. He went on believing – perhaps this was a relic of his Hegelian youth – that no issue was closed for ever, that every thesis must be weighed against its antithesis, that systems and absolutes of every kind – social and political no less than religious – were a form of dangerous idolatry;[3] above all, one must never go to war unless and until all that one believes in is at stake and there is literally no other way out. Some of the fanatical young men responded with genuine regard and, at times, profound admiration. A young radical wrote in 1883: 'Turgenev is dead. If Shchedrin[4] should die too, then one might as well go down to the grave alive! For us, everywhere, these men replaced parliament, meetings, life, liberty!'[5] A hunted member of a terrorist organisation, in a tribute illegally published on the day of Turgenev's funeral, wrote: 'A gentleman by birth, an aristocrat by upbringing and character, a gradualist by conviction, Turgenev, perhaps without knowing it himself, [...] sympathised with, and even served, the Russian revolution.'[6] The special police precautions at Turgenev's funeral were clearly not wholly superfluous.

1   loc. cit. (336 above, note 3). See also the letters to Stasyulevich (335 above, note 1), and to Herzen of 25 November 1862, P v 72–3, and F. Volkhovsky's article 'Ivan S. Tourguenev', *Free Russia* 9 No 4 (1 April 1898), 26–9 – a review of *Tourguéneff and His French Circle*, ed. E. Halperine-Kaminsky, trans. Ethel M. Arnold (London, 1898).

2   Letter to A. P. Filosofova, 23 September 1874, P x 295.

3   See the letters to Countess Lambert in 1864 (3 September, P v 278), and to the writer M. A. Milyutina in 1875 (6 March, P xi 31), quoted with much other relevant material in V. N. Gorbacheva, *Molodye gody Turgeneva (po neizdannym materialam)* (Kazan, 1926): letters at 36.

4   The satirist Saltykov-Shchedrin.

5   'Turgenev v materialakh perlyustratsii III otdeleniya i departamenta politsii: II. Otkliki na smert' Turgeneva, 3. Vypiska iz pis'ma Ya. Lure iz Peterburga ot 8 Sentyabrya 1883 g. k studentu universiteta Fishelyu Tolkachevskomu v Kiev', *Literaturnoe nasledstvo* 76 (1967), *I. S. Turgenev: novye materialy i issledovaniya*, 332.

6   The author of the pamphlet – which is quoted in K. I. Bonetsky (ed.), *Turgenev v russkoi kritike* (Moscow, 1953), 401 – was P. F. Yakubovich.

III

It is time that Saturns ceased dining off their children; time, too,
that children stopped devouring their parents like the natives of
Kamchatka.   Alexander Herzen[1]

Critical turning-points in history tend to occur, we are told, when
a form of life and its institutions are increasingly felt to cramp and
obstruct the most vigorous productive forces alive in a society –
economic or social, artistic or intellectual – and it has not enough
strength to resist them. Against such a social order, men and
groups of very different tempers and classes and conditions unite.
There is an upheaval – a revolution – which, at times, achieves a
limited success. It reaches a point at which some of the demands
or interests of its original promoters are satisfied to an extent
which makes further fighting on their part unprofitable. They
stop, or struggle uncertainly. The alliance disintegrates. The most
passionate and single-minded, especially among those whose purposes or ideals are furthest from fulfilment, wish to press on. To
stop half-way seems to them a betrayal. The sated groups, or the
less visionary, or those who fear that the old yoke may be followed
by an even more oppressive one, tend to hang back. They find
themselves assailed on two sides. The conservatives look on them
as, at best, knock-kneed supporters, at worst as deserters and
traitors. The radicals look on them as pusillanimous allies, more
often as diversionists and renegades.

Men of this sort need a good deal of courage to resist magnetisa-
tion by either polar force and to urge moderation in a disturbed
situation. Among them are those who see, and cannot help seeing,
many sides of a case, as well as those who perceive that a humane
cause promoted by means that are too ruthless is in danger of
turning into its opposite, liberty into oppression in the name of
liberty, equality into a new, self-perpetuating oligarchy to defend
equality, justice into crushing of all forms of nonconformity, love
of men into hatred of those who oppose brutal methods of achiev-

ing it. The middle ground is a notoriously exposed, dangerous and ungrateful position. The complex position of those who, in the thick of the fight, wish to continue to speak to both sides is often interpreted as softness, trimming, opportunism, cowardice. Yet this description, which may apply to some men, was not true of Erasmus; it was not true of Montaigne; it was not true of Spinoza when he agreed to talk to the French invader of Holland; it was not true of the best representatives of the Gironde, or of some among the defeated liberals in 1848, or of stout-hearted members of the European left who did not side with the Paris Commune in 1871. It was not weakness or cowardice that prevented the Mensheviks from joining Lenin in 1917, or the unhappy German socialists from turning Communist in 1932.

The ambivalence of such moderates, who are not prepared to break their principles or betray the cause in which they believe, has become a common feature of political life after the last war. This stems, in part, from the historic position of nineteenth-century liberals, for whom the enemy had hitherto always been on the right – monarchists, clericals, aristocratic supporters of political or economic oligarchies, men whose rule promoted, or was indifferent to, poverty, ignorance, injustice and the exploitation and degradation of men. The natural inclination of liberals has been, and still is, towards the left, the party of generosity and humanity, towards anything that destroys barriers between men. Even after the inevitable split they tend to be deeply reluctant to believe that there can be real enemies on the left. They may feel morally outraged by the resort to brutal violence by some of their allies; they protest that such methods will distort or destroy the common goal. The Girondins were driven into this position in 1792; liberals like Heine or Lamartine in 1848; Mazzini, and a good many socialists, of whom Louis Blanc was the most representative, were repelled by the methods of the Paris Commune of 1871. These crises passed. Breaches were healed. Ordinary political warfare was resumed. The hopes of the moderates began to revive. The desperate dilemmas in which they found themselves could be viewed as being due to moments of sudden aberration which could not last. But in Russia, from the 1860s until the Revolution of 1917, this uneasy feeling, made more painful by periods of repression and horror, became a chronic condition – a long, unceasing malaise of the entire enlightened section of society. The dilemma of the liberals became insoluble. They wished to destroy the regime which seemed to them wholly evil. They believed in reason, secularism, the rights of the individual, freedom of speech, of association, of opinion, the liberty of groups and races and nations, greater social and economic equality, above all in the rule of justice. They admired the selfless dedication, the purity of motive, the martyrdom of those, no matter how extremist, who offered their lives for the violent overthrow of the status quo. But they feared that the losses entailed by terrorist or Jacobin methods might be irreparable, and greater than any possible gains; they were horrified by the fanaticism and barbarism of the extreme left, by its contempt for the only culture that they knew, by its blind faith in what seemed to them Utopian fantasies, whether anarchist or populist or Marxist.

These Russians believed in European civilisation as converts believe in a newly acquired faith. They could not bring themselves to contemplate, still less to sanction, the destruction of much that seemed to them of infinite value for themselves and for all men in the past, even the tsarist past. Caught between two armies, denounced by both, they repeated their mild and rational words without much genuine hope of being heard by either side. They remained obstinately reformist and non-revolutionary. Many suffered from complex forms of guilt: they sympathised more deeply with the goals upon their left; but, spurned by the radicals, they tended to question, like the self-critical, open-minded human beings that they were, the validity of their own positions; they doubted, they wondered, they felt tempted, from time to time, to jettison their enlightened principles and find peace by conversion to a revolutionary faith, above all by submission to the domination of the zealots. To stretch themselves upon a comfortable bed of dogma would, after all, save them from being plagued by their own uncertainties, from the terrible suspicion that the simple solutions of the extreme left might, in the end, be as irrational and as repressive as the nationalism, or élitism, or mysticism of the right. Moreover, despite all its shortcomings the left still seemed to them to stand for a more human faith than the frozen, bureau-

cratic, heartless right, if only because it was always better to be
with the persecuted than with the persecutors. But there was one
conviction which they never abandoned: they knew that evil means
destroyed good ends. They knew that to extinguish existing liberties, civilised habits, rational behaviour, to abolish them today,
in the belief that, like a phoenix, they would arise in a purer and
more glorious form tomorrow, was to fall into a terrible snare and
delusion. Herzen told his old friend the anarchist Bakunin in
1869 that to order the intellect to stop because its fruits might be
misused by the enemy, to arrest science, invention, the progress of
reason, until men were made pure by the fires of a total revolution
– until 'we are free' – was nothing but a self-destructive fallacy.

> One cannot stop intelligence [Herzen wrote in his last and magnifi-
> cent essay], because the majority lacks understanding, while the
> minority makes evil use of it [. . .] Wild cries to close books, abandon
> science, and go to some senseless battle of destruction – that is the
> most violent and harmful kind of demagoguery. It will be followed
> by the eruption of the most savage passions [. . .] No! Great revol-
> utions are not achieved by the unleashing of evil passions [. . .] I do
> not believe in the seriousness of men who prefer crude force and
> destruction to development and arriving at settlements [. . .][1]

And then, in an insufficiently remembered phrase, 'One must open
men's eyes, not tear them out.'[2] Bakunin had declared that one
must first clear the ground: then we shall see. That savoured to
Herzen of the dark ages of barbarism. In this he spoke for his
entire generation in Russia. This is what Turgenev, too, felt and
wrote during the last twenty years of his life. He declared that he
was a European; Western culture was the only culture that he
knew; this was the banner under which he had marched as a young
man: it was his banner still.[3] His spokesman is Potugin in Smoke,
when he says: 'I am devoted to Europe, or to be more precise [. . .]
to civilisation [. . .] this word [. . .] is pure and holy, while all the
other words, "nationality", for example, or – yes, or "glory",

1   'K staromu tovarishchu', fourth letter, H xx/2 592–3.
2   ibid. 593.
3   Letter to Herzen of 25 November 1862, P v 73.

smell of blood . . .'.[1] His condemnation of political mysticism and
irrationalism, populist and Slavophil, conservative or anarchist,
remained absolute.

But short of this, these 'men of the '40s' were less sure: to
support the left in its excesses went against the civilised grain; but
to go against it, or even to remain indifferent to its fate, to abandon
it to the forces of reaction, seemed even more unthinkable. The
moderates hoped, against all evidence, that the ferocious anti-
intellectualism, which, liberals in Russia told Turgenev, was
spreading like an infectious disease among the young, the contempt for painting, music, books, the mounting political terrorism, were passing excesses due to immaturity, lack of education;
they were results of a long frustration; they would disappear once
the pressures that had generated them were removed. Consequently they explained away the violent language and the violent
acts of the extreme left, and continued to support the uneasy
alliance.

This painful conflict, which became the permanent predicament
of the Russian liberals for half a century, has now grown worldwide. We must be clear: it is not the Bazarovs who are the champions of the rebellion today. In a sense, the Bazarovs have won.
The victorious advance of quantitative methods, belief in the
organisation of human lives by technological management, reliance on nothing but calculation of utilitarian consequences in
evaluating policies that affect vast numbers of human beings, this
is Bazarov, not the Kirsanovs. The triumphs of the calm moral
arithmetic of cost-effectiveness which liberates decent men from
qualms, because they no longer think of the entities to which they
apply their scientific computations as actual human beings who
live the lives and suffer the deaths of concrete individuals – this,
today, is rather more typical of the Establishment than of the
opposition. The suspicion of all that is qualitative, imprecise,
unanalysable, yet precious to men, and its relegation to Bazarov's
obsolete, intuitive, pre-scientific rubbish heap, has, by a strange
paradox, stirred both the anti-rationalist right and the irrationalist
left to an equally vehement opposition to the technocratic estab-

1   *Smoke*, chapter 5, S ix 173.

lishment in the middle. From their opposed standpoints the
extreme left and the extreme right see such efforts to rationalise
social life as a terrible threat to what both sides regard as the
deepest human values. If Turgenev were living at this hour, the
young radicals whom he would wish to describe, and perhaps to
please, are those who wish to rescue men from the reign of those
very 'sophisters, oeconomists, and calculators'[1] whose coming
Burke lamented – those who ignore or despise what men are and
what they live by. The new insurgents of our time favour – so far
as they can bring themselves to be at all coherent – something like
a vague species of the old, natural law. They want to build a
society in which men treat one another as human beings with
unique claims to self-expression, however undisciplined and wild,
not as producing or consuming units in a centralised, worldwide,
self-propelling social mechanism. Bazarov's progeny has won, and
it is the descendants of the defeated, despised 'superfluous men',
of the Rudins and Kirsanovs and Nezhdanovs, of Chekhov's
muddled, pathetic students and cynical, broken doctors, who are
today preparing to man the revolutionary barricades. Yet the
similarity with Turgenev's predicament does hold: the modern
rebels believe, as Bazarov and Pisarev and Bakunin believed, that
the first requirement is the clean sweep, the total destruction of
the present system; the rest is not their business. The future must
look after itself. Better anarchy than prison; there is nothing in
between. This violent cry meets with a similar response in the
breasts of our contemporary Shubins and Kirsanovs and Potugins,
the small, hesitant, self-critical, not always very brave, band of
men who occupy a position somewhere to the left of centre, and
are morally repelled both by the hard faces to their right and the
hysteria and mindless violence and demagoguery on their left.
Like the men of the '40s, for whom Turgenev spoke, they are at
once horrified and fascinated. They are shocked by the violent
irrationalism of the dervishes on the left, yet they are not prepared
to reject wholesale the position of those who claim to represent
the young and the disinherited, the indignant champions of the

1   Edmund Burke, *Reflections on the Revolution in France* (1790), in *The
    Writings and Speeches of Edmund Burke*, ed. Paul Langford (Oxford,
    1981–   ), vol. 8, *The French Revolution*, ed. L. G. Mitchell (1989), 127.

poor and the socially deprived or repressed. This is the notoriously unsatisfactory, at times agonising, position of the modern heirs of the liberal tradition.

'I understand the reasons for the anger which my book provoked in a certain party,' wrote Turgenev just over a hundred years ago. 'A shadow has fallen upon my name [. . .] But is this really of the slightest importance? Who, in twenty or thirty years' time, will remember all these storms in a teacup, or indeed my name, with or without a shadow?'[1] Turgenev's name still lies under a shadow in his native land. His artistic reputation is not in question; it is as a social thinker that he is still today the subject of a continuing dispute. The situation that he diagnosed in novel after novel, the painful predicament of the believers in liberal Western values, a predicament once thought peculiarly Russian, is today familiar everywhere. So, too, is his own oscillating, uncertain position, his horror of reactionaries, his fear of the barbarous radicals, mingled with a passionate anxiety to be understood and approved of by the ardent young. Still more familiar is his inability, despite his greater sympathy for the party of protest, to cross over unreservedly to either side in the conflict of ideas, classes and, above all, generations. The figure of the well-meaning, troubled, self-questioning liberal, witness to the complex truth, which, as a literary type, Turgenev virtually created in his own image, has today become universal. These are the men who, when the battle grows too hot, tend either to stop their ears to the terrible din, or attempt to promote armistices, save lives, avert chaos.

As for the storm in a teacup of which Turgenev spoke, so far from being forgotten, it blows over the entire world today. If the inner life, the ideas, the moral predicament of men matter at all in explaining the course of human history, then Turgenev's novels, especially *Fathers and Children*, quite apart from their literary qualities, are as basic a document for the understanding of the Russian past and of our present as the plays of Aristophanes for the understanding of classical Athens, or Cicero's letters, or novels by Dickens or George Eliot, for the understanding of Rome and Victorian England.

1   'Po povodu "Ottsov i detei"', S xiv 105–6.

Turgenev may have loved Bazarov; he certainly trembled before him. He understood, and to a degree sympathised with, the case presented by the new Jacobins, but he could not bear to think of what their feet would trample. 'We have the same credulity', he wrote in the mid-1860s, 'and the same cruelty; the same hunger for blood, gold, filth, [. . .] the same meaningless suffering in the name of [. . .] the same nonsense as that which Aristophanes mocked at two thousand years ago.'[1] And art? And beauty? 'Yes, these are powerful words [. . .] The *Venus of Milo* is perhaps less open to question than Roman Law or the principles of 1789'[2] – yet she, too, and the works of Goethe and Beethoven would perish. Cold-eyed Isis – as he calls nature – 'has no cause for haste. Soon or late, she will have the upper hand [. . .] She knows nothing of art or liberty, as she does not know the good.'[3] But why must men hurry so zealously to help her with her work of turning all to dust? Education, only education, can retard this painful process, for our civilisation is far from exhausted yet.

Civilisation, humane culture, meant more to the Russians, late-comers to Hegel's feast of the spirit, than to the blasé natives of the West. Turgenev clung to it more passionately, was more conscious of its precariousness, than even his friends Flaubert and Renan. But, unlike them, he discerned behind the philistine bourgeoisie a far more furious opponent – the young iconoclasts bent on the total annihilation of his world in the certainty that a new and more just world would emerge. He understood the best among these Robespierres, as Tolstoy, or even Dostoevsky, did not. He rejected their methods, he thought their goals naive and grotesque, but his hand would not rise against them if this meant giving aid and comfort to the generals and the bureaucrats. He offered no clear way out: only gradualism and education, only reason. Chekhov once said that a writer's business was not to provide solutions, only to describe a situation so truthfully, do such justice to all sides of the question, that the reader could no longer evade it. The doubts Turgenev raised have not been stilled.

1   From *Dovol'no*, an address read by him in 1864, which was later caricatured by Dostoevsky in *The Possessed*. See S ix 118–19.
2   ibid. 119.
3   ibid. 120. For cold-eyed Isis see 321 above, note 1.

The dilemma of morally sensitive, honest, and intellectually responsible men at a time of acute polarisation of opinion has, since
his time, grown acute and worldwide. The predicament of what,
for him, was only the 'educated section' of a country then scarcely
regarded as fully European has come to be that of men in every
class of society in our day. He recognised it in its earlier beginnings,
and described it with incomparable sharpness of vision, poetry
and truth.

APPENDIX

As an illustration of the political atmosphere in Russia in the
1870s and 1880s, especially with regard to the mounting wave of
political terrorism, the account that follows of a conversation with
Dostoevsky by the famous editor A. S. Suvorin may be of interest.
Both Suvorin and Dostoevsky were loyal supporters of the autocracy and were looked upon by liberals, not without reason, as
strong and irredeemable reactionaries. Suvorin's periodical, *New
Times* (*Novoe vremya*), was the best-edited and most powerful
extreme right-wing journal published in Russia towards the end
of the nineteenth and the beginning of the twentieth century.
Suvorin's political position gives particular point to this entry in
his diary.

On the day of the attempt by Mlodetsky[1] on Loris-Melikov I was
with F. M. Dostoevsky.
  He lived in a shabby little apartment. I found him sitting by a
small round table in the drawing-room, he was rolling cigarettes;
his face was like that of someone who had just emerged from a
Russian bath, from a shelf on which he had been steaming himself
[. . .] I probably did not manage to conceal my surprise, because he
gave me a look and, after greeting me, said, 'I have just had an
attack; I am glad, very glad, to see you', and went on rolling his
cigarettes. Neither he nor I yet knew anything about the attempted

1   Ippolit Mlodetsky made his attempt on the life of the head of the government
     on 20 February 1880, some weeks after the failure of Khalturin's attempt to
     kill the Tsar. He was hanged two days later.

assassination. But our conversation presently turned to political crimes in general, and a [recent] explosion in the Winter Palace in particular. In the course of talking about this, Dostoevsky commented on the odd attitude of the public to these crimes. Society seemed to sympathise with them, or, it might be truer to say, was not too clear about how to look upon them. 'Imagine', he said, 'that you and I are standing by the window of Daziaro's shop and looking at the pictures. A man is standing near us, and pretending to look too. He seems to be waiting for something, and keeps looking round. Suddenly another man comes up to him hurriedly and says, "The Winter Palace will be blown up very soon. I've set the machine." We hear this. You must imagine that we hear it – that these people are so excited that they pay no attention to their surroundings or how far their voices carry. How would we act? Would we go to the Winter Palace to warn them about the explosion, would we go to the police, or get the corner constable to arrest these men? Would you do this?'

'No, I would not.'

'Nor would I. Why not? After all, it is dreadful; it is a crime. We might have forestalled it.[1] This is what I had been thinking about before you came in, while I was rolling my cigarettes. I went over all the reasons that might have made me do this. Weighty, solid reasons. Then I considered the reasons that would have stopped me from doing it. They are absolutely trivial. Simply fear of being thought an informer. I imagined how I might come, the kind of look I might get from them, how I might be interrogated, perhaps confronted with someone, be offered a reward, or, maybe, suspected of complicity. The newspapers might say that "Dostoevsky identified the criminals." Is this my affair? It is the job of the police. This is what they have to do, what they are paid for. The liberals would never forgive me. They would torment me, drive me to despair. Is this normal? Everything is abnormal in our society; that is how these things happen, and, when they do, nobody knows how to act – not only in the most difficult situations, but even in the simplest. I might write about this. I could say a great deal that might be good and bad both for society and for the government; yet this cannot be

1   The Russian word can also mean 'give warning'.

done. About the most important things we are not allowed to talk.'
He talked a great deal on this theme, and talked with inspired
feeling. He added that he would write a novel, the hero of which
would be Alesha Karamazov. He wanted to take him through a
monastery and make him a revolutionary; he would then commit a
political crime; he would be executed. He would search for the
truth, and in the course of this quest would naturally become a
revolutionary [. . .][1]

1   *Dnevnik A. S. Suvorina*, ed. Mikh. Krichevsky (Moscow/Petrograd, 1923),
    15–16. This entry for 1887 is the first in the diary of Dostoevsky's (and
    Chekhov's) friend and publisher. The editor of this text, which he calls a
    'fragment', mentions (ibid. 379) a passage in the novel in which Ivan Kara-
    mazov speaks to his saintly brother Alesha about the case of the general who
    set his dogs to hound a peasant boy to death before the eyes of his mother;
    he asks Alesha whether he would want the general to be killed for this.
    Alesha, after a tormented silence, says that he would. 'Bravo,' says Ivan.

Glossary of names

Jason Ferrell

This glossary is not intended to be exhaustive. Its main purpose is to identify and contextualise the more important Russian personalities referred to by Berlin in this volume, with the addition of Joseph de Maistre, a key figure in 'The Hedgehog and the Fox'. A number of the entries are taken, with minor adjustments, from Helen Rappaport's exemplary glossary in Berlin's The Soviet Mind *(see xvi above), which provided the model for this one. Thanks are due to her both for her own entries and for her helpful comments on the new ones.*

Aksakovs, pre-eminent family of Slavophil writers, ideologists and literary critics. Sergey Timofeevich (1791–1859) was a bureaucrat, writer and theatre critic, famous for his fictionalised autobiographical work *Semeinaya khronika* (*Family Chronicle*, 1856), about life on the family estate in the Russian borderlands. His eldest son Konstantin Sergeevich (1817–60) became radicalised at the University of Moscow, where he was a devotee of the philosophy of Hegel, and a friend of Bakunin, Herzen and Belinsky (qq.v.). He later abandoned Hegelianism to become an outspoken Slavophil. His younger brother Ivan Sergeevich (1823–86) studied law in St Petersburg (1838–42) and edited a succession of radical journals. After the death of Konstantin, Sergey assumed his leadership of the Slavophils, publishing increasingly extremist, nationalistic essays in journals such as *Den'* (Day) and *Moskva* (Moscow), and inciting Russia's war of 1877–8 against the Turks.

Alexander II (1818–81), son of Tsar Nicholas I, Tsar of Russia 1855–81. His reign comprised a reformist period (1855–66) and a reactionary period (1866–81). During the former, some of the restrictive measures of Nicholas I were relaxed, creating the hope that Alexander might make the absolute monarchy constitutional. Serfdom was officially abolished, trial by jury instituted, and limited forms of local government tried out. But the reforms encouraged progressives and populists to engage in activities considered threatening (such as the spontaneous movement 'Going to the People' of 1874, when over 2,000 students went to the countryside to live among the serfs and try to educate them). Revolutionaries were also emboldened, and various groups, such as 'The People's Vengeance', arose with the explicit aim of over-throwing the government by force. In the face of these pressures, as well as an assassination attempt in 1866, Alexander halted his programme of liberalisation. After other unsuccessful attempts, he was assassinated in 1881.

Annenkov, Pavel Vasil'evich (*c.*1812–87), writer, critic and memoirist, best known for his vivid reminiscences of his contemporaries Herzen and Belinsky, Turgenev and Bakunin (qq.v.). During the 1840s Annenkov travelled in Europe, where he developed close friendships with Gogol (then living in Italy) and Marx. Returning to Russia and literary scholarship, he edited the first, seven-volume, collection of Pushkin's works, published in 1855; he also wrote several notable studies on Pushkin, including *A. S. Pushkin v Aleksandrovskuyu epokhu, 1799–1826* (*A. S. Pushkin in the Age of Alexander*, 1874). He is now, however, mainly remembered for his vivid memoir of Russian intellec-tual life in the 1830s and 1840s, *Zamechatel'noe desyatiletie* (*A Remarkable Decade*, 1880), of which Berlin was a great admirer, and from which he took the title of his 1954 Northcliffe Lectures, included in this volume.

Annensky, Innokenty Fedorovich (1856–1909), poet, literary critic and translator. A classical scholar, Annensky taught Greek and Latin. He translated Euripides (published 1907–21), as well as French and Ger-man poetry. His poetic œuvre was inspired by the French rather than the Russian symbolist movement (he rejected the latter as too mystical), and inspired Acmeist poets such as Anna Akhmatova and Nikolay Gumilev. His major verse collections were *Tikhie pesni* (*Quiet Songs*, 1904) and *Kiparisovyi larets* (*The Cyprus Chest*, 1910); he also pro-duced two volumes of literary criticism, *Knigi otrazhenii* (*Books of Reflections*, 1906 and 1909).

Bakunin, Mikhail Aleksandrovich (1814–76), anarchist born into a noble family. Passing up a potentially prestigious military career, Bakunin became interested in German philosophy after encountering the works of Fichte and Hegel. Continuing his studies in Germany and then France, he investigated the work of more revolutionary thinkers, eventually meeting Marx. The two strong personalities became rivals, developing competing ideologies. Eventually, Bakunin's differences with Marx led to his expulsion from the International Workingmen's Association. Unlike Marx, however, Bakunin was an activist, participating in many of the revolutionary upheavals that convulsed Europe in the mid-nineteenth century. Among his more significant works are *Dieu et l'État* (*God and the State*, 1882), a posthumous extract from a work which condemns religion and government authority, and *Gosudarstvennost' i anarkhiya* (*Statism and Anarchy*, 1873), a longer work that seeks to interpret the outcome of the Franco-Prussian War. Bakunin is best known for his insistence that revolution cannot occur without a passionate commitment to destruction, which led others to characterise him as a nihilist. His ideas influenced Russian radicals of the later nineteenth century, and inspired revolutionaries such as Nechaev (q.v.) to adopt terrorist tactics. After participating in minor rebellions in Lyons (1870) and Bologna (1874), he died in Switzerland.

Baratynsky, Evgeny Abramovich (1800–44), poet. A product of tsarist military school, Baratynsky served in the imperial army, while also pursuing his literary interests as a member of the Free Society of Amateurs of Russian Literature. A contemporary and admirer of Pushkin (q.v.), he was one of the so-called Pushkin Pleiad of poets, producing narrative works such as *Eda* (1824), based on the six years he spent in Finland (1820–6), and *Bal* (*The Ball*, 1825–8), in which he satirised Moscow high society. His later poetry, notably *Poslednyaya smert'* (*The Last Death*, 1827) and *Osen'* (*Autumn*, 1836–7), became increasingly pessimistic and reflective. After falling into obscurity for fifty years, Baratynsky's work was enthusiastically rediscovered by Anna Akhmatova and her generation in the 1900s.

Belinsky, Vissarion Grigor'evich (1811–48), literary critic, philosopher and political thinker. Belinsky was a central figure in radical debating circles at Moscow University from 1829, where he was a friend of Herzen (q.v.), but was expelled for his radicalism. He joined the journal *Teleskop* (the *Telescope*) as a literary critic in 1833. After this was closed down in 1836 he eked out a living from tutoring and journalism and worked as literary critic of the journal *Otechestvennye zapiski* (*Notes of the Fatherland*, 1839–46). He finally made his mark at Nekrasov's (q.v.) journal *Sovremennik* (the *Contemporary*), but by now was severely weakened by years of living in abject poverty and by the onset of consumption, which killed him two years later. Despite his early death, Belinsky's legacy in Russia was, and remains, considerable, and marked the rise of a new breed of lower-class, non-aristocratic intellectuals, the *raznochinets*.

Benediktov, Vladimir Grigor'evich (1807–73), poet, official in the Ministry of Finance. Benediktov's writing was popular in the 1830s, subsequently falling out of favour. His poetry was known for its ornamentation and rhetorical excess, which eventually drew censure from Belinsky (q.v.) and other critics, for whom literature and poetry should not simply be aesthetically pleasing, but should serve a social purpose.

Blok, Aleksandr Aleksandrovich (1880–1921), revered symbolist poet of the Revolutionary era, best known for his narrative poem *Dvenadtsat'* (*The Twelve*, 1918), a vivid depiction of the turmoil of the October Revolution. Blok studied philology at the University of St Petersburg and published his first collection of poetry, *Stikhi o prekrasnoi dame* (*Verses on a Beautiful Lady*), in 1904. His dreams of a new moral and political world order inspired by the Revolution soon faded away, although on the strength of *Dvenadtsat'* he remained an officially sanctioned poet throughout the Soviet era. In the last years of his life, he sank into a deep melancholia, writing little and dying in poverty. Berlin translated his 'The Collapse of Humanism' in *Oxford Outlook* 11 (1931), 89–112, and discusses him in 'A Sense of Impending Doom' (1935; original title 'Literature and the Crisis'), *The Times Literary Supplement*, 27 July 2001, 11–12.

Botkin, Vasily Petrovich (1811–69), literary and art critic. A man of means, Botkin was acquainted with many leading figures of the nineteenth century. As a young man he espoused liberal ideals influenced by philosophers such as Fichte, Hegel and Schelling. Among his best-known works are *Pis'ma ob Ispanii* (*Letters on Spain*, 1847–51; his impressions of a visit there) and *Stikhotvoreniya A. A. Fet* (*The Poetry of A. A. Fet*, 1857; Fet [q.v.] was his brother-in-law). After the 1848 revolutions, Botkin gradually became more conservative, and, in opposition to literary critics such as Belinsky (q.v., with whom he had a well-known exchange of letters), he became a proponent of the ideal of 'art for art's sake'.

Bulgarin, Faddey Venediktovich (1789–1859), novelist and journalist. Known for an adventurous life (including stints as a mercenary and a police informer), Bulgarin was one of the most highly regarded writers of the 1830s. His *Ivan Vyzhigin* (1829) brought him both commercial and critical success, and was followed by two novels dealing with significant historical events, *Dmitrii samozvanets* (*Dmitry the Pre-*

tender, 1830) and *Mazepa* (1833–4). Unfortunately Bulgarin's acid journalism eventually antagonised his contemporaries, and Pushkin (q.v.) wrote a series of savage satires that effectively destroyed his literary reputation.

Catherine II (1729–96), Empress of Russia 1762–96, known as Catherine the Great. The early period of her rule is associated with the Enlightenment: Catherine pursued a vigorous programme aimed at cultivating the arts and sciences. Her initial efforts met with success: European scholars of rank came to visit her Court, and Russian intellectuals were allowed to travel abroad. A climate of intellectual openness pervaded the country, and political reform was expected to follow. Catherine partially encouraged such expectations, seeking to cultivate an image of herself as the embodiment of Enlightenment ideals. She convened a 'Grand Commission' drawn from every level of society, ostensibly intended as a consultative council. But her willingness to institute major reforms was limited: her participation in the partitioning of Poland, her aggressive campaigns to extend Russia's borders, and her strong response to Pugachev's (q.v.) rebellion were acts more befitting a despot than an enlightened ruler. When the French Revolution began in 1789, Catherine's infatuation with the Enlightenment ended, as the tension between the democratic ideals of that movement and the autocratic basis of her regime became clear.

Chaadaev, Petr Yakovlevich (1794–1856), philosopher. Chaadaev prompted the Slavophil–Westerner debate among Russian intellectuals with his series of *Lettres philosophiques*, written between 1827 and 1831. He was born into the landowning gentry and served in the imperial army during the Napoleonic Wars, afterwards travelling in Europe. When one of his letters, containing an outspoken critique of Russia's cultural and intellectual backwardness, was published in the journal *Teleskop* (the *Telescope*) in 1836, the journal was closed down, and Chaadaev, declared mad, was placed under house arrest. Although public discussion of his ideas was strictly forbidden, Chaadaev remained an inspirational figure to many of his generation.

Chekhov, Anton Pavlovich (1860–1904), short-story writer, playwright and physician. Regarded as one of the greatest short-story writers, Chekhov is known for his delicate style and humane tone. Overcoming a bleak childhood and an abusive father, he studied medicine at Moscow University. He began writing to pay for his studies, and as his stories gained in popularity he began to concentrate more and more upon his literary work. His early stories are characterised by their humour and mild satire, while his later works are known for their introspection and psychological depth. He eventually began to experiment with longer stories, and some of his finer tales followed, including 'Duel' ('The Duel', 1891), 'Palata No 6' ('Ward No 6', 1892), 'Zhena' ('The Wife', 1892) and 'Rasskaz neizvestnogo cheloveka' ('Story of an Unknown Man', 1893). Among his best-known plays are *Tri sestry* (*Three Sisters*, 1901) and *Vishnevyi sad* (*The Cherry Orchard*, 1903).

Chernyshevsky, Nikolay Gavrilovich (1828–89), journalist, literary critic, novelist and radical activist. Educated for the priesthood, Chernyshevsky lost his early religious faith while studying history and philology at St Petersburg University. After joining the staff of *Sovremennik* (the *Contemporary*), the leading literary journal, he inherited Belinsky's (q.v.) mantle, and established himself as the foremost critic of the day. He was influenced by the Enlightenment, accepting its basic arguments for the application of science to society. His *Antropologicheskii printsip v filosofii* (*The Anthropological Principle in Philosophy*, 1860) contains the fullest statement of his philosophical beliefs, rooted in the concept of 'rational egoism'. According to this idea, individual behaviour is primarily self-regarding, and society's institutions should be constructed accordingly. His influential novel *Chto delat'?* (*What Is To Be Done?*, 1863), written in prison, is an attempt to portray rational egoism through the story of young revolutionaries. It established Chernyshevsky's reputation as a radical democrat, and proved to be his last major work, for he was subsequently sent to Siberia, where illness and the strains of exile effectively ended his writing.

Chicherin, Boris Nikolaevich (1828–1903), historian, philosopher and jurist. A university teacher who served briefly as the mayor of Moscow, Chicherin was a liberal with conservative tendencies. Author of the voluminous *Istoriya politicheskikh uchenii* (*A History of Political Doctrines*, 1869–1902), Chicherin was a respected academic who made significant contributions to the fields of metaphysics, logic and the philosophy of law. A proponent of social reform, he envisaged a State that combined liberal rights, a vigorous judiciary and free-market economics with a strong monarchy. Unusually, his convictions were matched by his actions: he resigned his university chair in protest against government policy, and was forced to step down as mayor because of a political dispute with the Tsar. The highly abstract nature of his writings, couched in the arcane language of Hegel's 'Absolute', has adversely affected his reputation.

Danilevsky, Nikolay Yakovlevich (1822–85), historian, scientist, philosopher. An ichthyologist by training, Danilevsky was a leading reactionary theorist of the late nineteenth century. Best known for his work *Rossiya i Evropa* (*Russia and Europe*, 1869), he argued that cultures were incommensurable and that progress was to be measured in terms relative to a given society. Distinguishing ten types of civilisation, he believed that each had a centre of gravity uniquely its own, and that attempts to measure one civilisation against the accomplishments of another were misguided. He proposed an eleventh type of civilisation – a 'Slavic historico-cultural' type – whose political form was monarchical, and whose economy was based on the village commune, which was to serve as a bulwark against the advent of a revolutionary proletariat. Danilevsky's ideas were blatantly nationalistic: his main intention was to show that Russia was not inferior to Europe. Consequently, his work was used by conservatives against both liberals and radicals, who were criticised for judging Russian culture by European standards.

Derzhavin, Gavrila Romanovich (1743–1816), outstanding eighteenth-century lyric poet, an important precursor of Pushkin. Born to impoverished nobility, Derzhavin served in the army and in 1777 entered the civil service. The publication of his *Oda k Felitse* (*Ode to Felitsa*, 1793), a thinly disguised paean to Catherine the Great (q.v.), followed by several others in the same mode, won him official approval, and appointment as her secretary in 1791. He also served Alexander I as Minister of Justice, retiring in 1803. He was a master of the classical ode, and his most famous works, such as 'Na smert' knyaza Meshcherskogo' ('On the Death of Prince Meshchersky', 1779) and 'Vodopad' ('The Waterfall', 1791–4), despite their moralising and didactic tone, also celebrate the power of nature in vivid imagery.

Dobrolyubov, Nikolay Aleksandrovich (1836–61), journalist and literary critic. A lapsed seminarian, Dobrolyubov was one of the younger literary critics associated with Chernyshevsky (q.v.), and was known for his acerbic temperament and pointed critiques. Less concerned with the aesthetic merits of a text, Dobrolyubov demanded that fiction reflect reality. His 'real criticism' was meant to be an antidote to the impotence of preceding generations, whose writers were thought incapable of instigating social change. By insisting that writers portray social oppression realistically, Dobrolyubov hoped to prompt the younger generation to act. His best-known essay, 'Chto takoe oblomovshchina?' ('What is Oblomovism?', 1859), is one of the pivotal works of nineteenth-century Russian literature. In it he suggests that the generation of 'the '40s' was composed of 'superfluous men', which ignited a fierce debate. His career was cut short when he succumbed to tuberculosis.

Dostoevsky, Fedor Mikhailovich (1821–81), novelist, short-story writer and journalist; often considered, with his contemporary Tolstoy, one of the greatest Russian writers. Born to a father who claimed nobility through legal, as opposed to hereditary, title, and a devoutly religious mother, Dostoevsky established his reputation with *Bednye lyudi* (*Poor Folk*, 1846), a novel known for its social commentary. His strongly progressive opinions drew him to the Petrashevsky (q.v.) Circle; when he read in public a letter by Belinsky (q.v.) banned by the authorities he was exiled to Siberia for eight years. During his imprisonment – the basis for the novel *Zapiski iz mertvogo doma* (*Notes from the House of the Dead*, 1860–2) – he had a religious awakening which shaped his later literary output. His best-known later works, such as *Brat'ya Karamazovy* (*The Brothers Karamazov*, 1880), were heavily influenced by his idiosyncratic vision of Orthodoxy, incorporating themes of human frailty and suffering, redemption and transfiguration. Some, such as *Prestuplenie i nakazanie* (*Crime and Punishment*, 1866) and *Besy* (*The Possessed*, 1872), also contain strongly critical portraits of political radicals.

Eikhenbaum, Boris Mikhailovich (1886–1959), Soviet academician, literary historian and formalist critic. He lectured in philology at Leningrad University from 1918 until his retirement in 1949, publishing studies such as *Melodiki russkogo liricheskogo stikha* (*The Melodics of Russian Lyric Verse*, 1923), and writing extensively on Tolstoy, of whose collected works (1928–64; 'T' in this volume) he was one of the editors. He is famous for having condemned the poetry of Anna Akhmatova in a review article of 1923, labelling her 'half nun, half harlot', and so fuelling what would be the long-standing Soviet antipathy to her work.

Fet, Afanasy Afanas'evich (1820–92), poet and translator, friend of Tolstoy and Turgenev (qq.v.). Fet studied at Moscow University and began publishing his verse in the 1840s, while serving in the imperial army. He was a conservative and an aesthete, and his work was attacked by radical intellectuals in the 1860s. He published nothing between 1863 and 1883, when he finally brought out several volumes of verse, collectively entitled *Vechernie ogni* (*Evening Lights*). His later poetry, which was metaphysical in tone, was a precursor of the symbolist movement

in Russian poetry at the end of the century. An admirer of Schopenhauer, Fet translated his *Die Welt aus Wille und Vorstellung* (*The
World as Will and Representation*, 1819, 1844) into Russian in 1881;
he also translated Latin poets such as Ovid, Catullus and Vergil.

Figner, Vera Nikolaevna (1852–1942), radical and revolutionary terrorist. Known for her *Zapechatlennyi trud* (*Memoirs of a Revolutionist*,
1921–2), Figner was a member of various radical groups that actively
sought to overthrow the government in the latter half of the nineteenth
century. At first a member of 'Land and Liberty', she went on to help
found the more revolutionary group 'The People's Will', serving on its
Executive Committee and helping to coordinate the distribution of
revolutionary propaganda in an attempt to ignite a general uprising.
When this proved futile, the Committee turned to more violent means.
After several abortive attempts, Figner helped plan the assassination of
Alexander II (q.v.) in 1881. The authorities responded with a sweeping
crackdown, and were able to capture the majority of the Committee's
members. Figner escaped the initial wave of arrests and attempted to
reorganise the group. Eventually she was caught, imprisoned for twenty
years, and then expelled from the country. She returned to Russia
during the Revolution and settled in Moscow, where she wrote her
memoirs.

Fonvizin, Denis Ivanovich (1744–92), playwright, journalist and writer.
Fonvizin is best known for two plays, *Brigadir* (*The Brigadier*, 1768–9)
and *Nedorosl'* (*The Minor*, 1782), in which he gently mocks Russian
infatuation with French culture, as well as highlighting those aspects
of Russian culture that he thought equally valuable. He was one of the
earliest Russian writers to point to the potentially subversive force of
literature: both plays criticise contemporary practices before reaffirm-
ing traditional beliefs. His works frequently emphasise the importance
of virtue, and are regarded as characteristic of the 'Russian Enlightenment'. Fonvizin made several trips to Europe, starting in 1777, before
suffering a stroke on his way home in 1785. He suffered paralysis and,
though he continued to write short pieces, he was unable to complete
his confessions.

Gogol, Nikolay Vasil'evich (1809–52), writer, novelist and playwright.
One of the most influential figures in Russian literature, the Ukrainian
Gogol was best known for his comic stories, which portray the mun-
dane and the absurd. Moving to St Petersburg at the age of nineteen, he
hoped to pursue a literary career. His initial efforts were unsuccessful:

though his early work was critically acclaimed, it did not resonate with the general public. Stories such as 'Nevskii Prospekt' ('Nevsky Prospect', 1835), 'Zapiski sumasshedshego' ('Diary of a Madman', 1835) and 'Nos' ('The Nose', 1836) were clearly innovative, but their black humour, hyper-realism and dark irony made them unlike anything else written at the time. Things changed in 1836 with the production of Gogol's play *Revizor* (*The Government Inspector*), a comedy of errors revolving around a set of corrupt provincial officials who mistake a petty bureaucrat for a government inspector. From now on Gogol's reputation was established, and he was considered a writer comparable to Pushkin (q.v.). Of Gogol's later works, the two most significant are his novel *Mertvye dushi* (*Dead Souls*) and the short story 'Shinel'' ('The Overcoat'), both published in 1842. The latter was particularly influential, as it was taken to be a commentary on the wretched conditions of urban life. Although Gogol himself expressed conservative views, his writings were greatly admired by liberals and socialists, who took his work as an indictment of Russian autocracy. This admiration gave way to dismay with the appearance of *Vybrannye mesta iz perepiski s druz'yami* (*Selected Passages from Correspondence with Friends*, 1847), in which Gogol unambiguously asserted his support for the Tsar and the Orthodox Church. Belinsky (q.v.) responded with his 'Letter to Gogol' of 1847, an impassioned defence of progressive values which was circulated privately, and is regarded as a watershed moment in Russian intellectual history. Gogol died a few years afterwards, following weeks of fasting brought on by an episode of religious inspiration.

Goncharov, Ivan Aleksandrovich (1812–91), novelist. Born into the gentry and employed in government service, Goncharov is one of the earliest writers in the realist tradition. By contrast with writers such as Pushkin and Lermontov (qq.v.), he intentionally avoided an ornate literary style, in order to avoid the sentimentalism often associated with romanticism. His novels confront idealistic dreamers with a reality indifferent to their aspirations. His best-known work, *Oblomov* (1859), inspired Dobrolyubov (q.v.) to coin the term 'Oblomovism'. The novel's eponymous protagonist is a member of the gentry whose most characteristic trait is his lethargy. Unable to overcome his inertia, Oblomov wastes away. Taken as the paradigmatic instance of the 'superfluous man', Oblomov represents the politically and socially impotent aristocrats of the early nineteenth century. Similarly, 'Oblomovism' refers to the moral and spiritual paralysis that undercuts the desire to act, and was taken to characterise the generation of the

1840s. Goncharov's other novels treat similar themes, but none had as profound an effect upon social discourse.

Gorky, Maxim (pseudonym of Aleksey Maksimovich Peshkov) (1868–1936), Soviet writer, journalist and dramatist from peasant stock. His early life was extremely impoverished, as reflected in his masterpiece, the autobiographical trilogy *Detstvo, V lyudyakh* and *Moi universitety* (*My Childhood*, 1915; *In the World*, 1916; *My Universities*, 1922) and his most successful play, *Na dne* (*The Lower Depths*, 1902). Originally highly critical of the Bolshevik stranglehold on political life after the Revolution, his controversial newspaper *Novaya zhizn'* (*New Life*) was repressed by the Bolsheviks in 1918. In 1924 he went to live in Italy, where he became much fêted. With a combination of flattery and material inducements, Stalin lured him back to the Soviet Union in 1928 to take the ideological lead in establishing uniformity in Soviet writing under socialist realism. As chairman, from 1934, of the newly established Union of Soviet Writers, he was heaped with honours, but subservience to Stalin brought with it inevitable entrapment and ultimate isolation.

Griboedov, Aleksandr Sergeevich (1795–1829), lyric poet and playwright, whose only enduring play, *Gore ot uma* (*Woe from Wit*, 1822–4), remains a standard in the Russian repertoire. After studying law and science at Moscow University, Griboedov served in the army and became a civil servant at the Ministry of Foreign Affairs. Although he wrote and adapted other plays, his reputation largely rests on *Gore ot uma* (often titled *Chatsky* in translation, after its hero), which was rejected by the tsarist censor and not published in full till 1861. In 1825, during Russia's war with Persia, Griboedov was sent to the Caucasus on official business. After negotiating the peace settlement, he was appointed ambassador to Tehran, where he was murdered by rioters soon after his arrival.

Herzen, Alexander (Aleksandr Ivanovich Gertsen) (1812–70), revolutionary thinker, journalist and writer, around whom gravitated many of the great minds of his generation. The illegitimate son of a wealthy nobleman, Herzen was educated at Moscow University. His involvement in radical circles led to arrest in 1834 and exile until 1840. Back in Moscow, he became a close associate of Belinsky (q.v.), but left Russia in 1847 for Paris, where he witnessed the 1848 revolution. In 1852 he moved to London, his inherited wealth enabling him to set up a Russian press and publish the influential newspaper *Kolokol* (the

Bell, 1857–67), through which he campaigned vigorously for political reform in Russia, especially the emancipation of the serfs (achieved in 1861). Herzen's seminal political essays, collected as *S togo berega* (*From the Other Shore*, 1847–50; published in English in 1956 – 'F' in this volume – with an introduction by Berlin), are the best-known portion of a considerable body of political and philosophical debate conducted by letter and in the radical press with his many émigré contemporaries. He remembered many of these friends, as well as his family, with great eloquence and affection in his masterpiece 'Byloe i dumy' ('My Past and Thoughts', 1852–68), to the 1968 English edition of which Berlin also wrote an introduction. Berlin's introductions to Herzen's works are reprinted, respectively, in his collections *The Power of Ideas* and *Against the Current* (see above, xv and xi, note 2).

Ivanov, Vyacheslav Ivanovich (1866–1945), émigré historian and symbolist poet. Ivanov studied ancient history and classical philosophy in Moscow, Berlin and Paris, after which he spent time in the Middle East. His first collections of poetry, *Kormchie zvezdy* (*Lodestars*, 1903) and *Prozrachnost'* (*Transparency*, 1904), were published in Europe. Back in Russia in 1905 he published a series of mystical religious essays, as well as a notable discourse on Russian culture, *Perepiska iz dvukh uglov* (*Correspondence between Two Corners*, 1920). After teaching Greek in Baku (1920–4) he left Russia for Italy, where he converted to Roman Catholicism and taught at the University of Pavia (1926–34) and the Papal Institute for Eastern Studies (1934–43). Although he spent the remainder of his life in Italy, his work was published in Paris.

Khemnitser, Ivan Ivanovich (1745–84), satirist and fabulist. A popular writer of modest reputation, Khemnitser is known for his fables. His writings exhibited a concern for social problems, but he counselled reconciliation with circumstances rather than social transformation. Unlike some of his contemporaries, he avoided satirising individuals; instead he used allegories and fanciful imagery to ridicule institutions and social structures. His works include 'Na khudykh sudei' ('On Bad Judges') and 'Oda na pod'iachikh' ('Ode to Clerks'), both published posthumously in *Baiki i skazki I. I. Khemnitsera v trekh chastiakh* (*Fables and Tales of I. I. Khemnitser in Three Parts*, 1799).

Kol'tsov, Aleksey Vasil'evich (1809–42), poet. A member of the Stankevich (q.v.) Circle and close friend of Belinsky (q.v.), Kol'tsov was known for his poetry and folk songs. Forced by his father to discontinue his studies at the age of twelve, Kol'tsov was not highly educated. But his work was well regarded, as it was taken to represent the authentic experiences of the peasantry. His expressive verse idealised agrarian existence as well as displaying its difficulties, and served as a counterpoint to the presumed artificiality of urban life. His work helped usher in a concern for pastoral themes, and contributed to the idealisation of rural living.

Koshelev, Aleksandr Ivanovich (1806–83), writer and statesman. An original member of the Society of Wisdom Lovers, Koshelev was a conservative liberal who helped found the short-lived journal *Mnemosyne* (in classical mythology Mnemosyne is the goddess of memory, mother of the Muses). Both the Society and the journal were heavily influenced by German romanticism, according to which art is the organic union of the world and the individual. From this perspective, the artist forges new creations rather than merely depicting reality. Such ideas distinguished the Society from the Decembrists, many of whom were influenced by the French *philosophes*, and paved the way for Russian Hegelianism. The Society was also a predecessor of the Slavophil movement, since some of its members (including Koshelev) believed that the moral regeneration of Russia required the preservation of the village commune and a strong landed aristocracy.

Kravchinsky, Sergey Mikhailovich (1851–95), author, activist and terrorist. Known by his pseudonym, 'Stepnyak' ('son of the Steppe'), Kravchinsky was a radical who murdered the head of the secret police with a dagger in the streets of St Petersburg. Well educated, he spent time as a young man travelling in Europe, where he worked with various revolutionary groups. Returning home, he joined 'Land and Liberty', a populist organisation which sought to rouse the people through direct action and propaganda. When its efforts met with only limited success, some of its members (including Kravchinsky) resorted to violence, and assassination attempts were made on the lives of prominent public figures. Kravchinsky fled to England, where he spent the remainder of his life writing books and essays about his revolutionary experiences, including the widely popular *La Russia sotterranea* (*Underground Russia*, 1881, originally published in Italian).

Kropotkin, Petr Alekseevich (1842–1921), geographer and anarchist communist. Born into an aristocratic family, Kropotkin had the opportunity to pursue a prestigious military career, but his exposure to progressive ideas led him to opt for service in Siberia, where his geographical work gained him a scholarly reputation, and membership of the Russian Geographical Society. After a trip to Europe he abandoned his scholarly pursuits in favour of a more politically active life. He joined an underground revolutionary group, the Chaikovsky Circle, and was imprisoned in 1874. He escaped two years later, was forced to live in exile, and fled to Europe. He wrote prolifically during this time and, despite clashing with local authorities, was a popular lecturer (he twice toured North America, and was even offered a chair in geography at Cambridge). His main ideas concern the innate sociability of man, which expresses itself in a capacity for compassionate activity that he termed 'mutual aid'. He strongly criticised State institutions (which he thought corrupted this natural tendency by their reliance upon coercion) as well as capitalism, which for him provided the economic foundations of State domination. More controversially, he advocated 'propaganda by the deed', which was interpreted as a thinly veiled reference to revolutionary terrorism. After the Revolution he returned to Russia, where he died shortly afterwards, strongly critical of the Bolsheviks and Lenin.

Krylov, Ivan Andreevich (1769–1844), fabulist, playwright and author. Like Khemnitser (q.v.), Krylov is known for his fables. Although he initially wrote satirical short stories and composed a handful of plays, he eventually turned to fables as a more effective means of expression. Inspired by La Fontaine, his fables delineate the shortcomings both of society and of individuals. Conservative in tone, the fables tend gently to chide those who are impatient with the status quo, but also show the need for social reform. His work was widely appreciated not only for the directness of the fables, but also for its timeliness and the simplicity of his often colloquial writing style.

Lavrov, Petr Lavrovich (1823–1900), editor, historian, political theorist and sociologist. Born into the nobility, Lavrov rose to the rank of colonel in the army and taught mathematics at different institutes. He was court-martialled in 1866 for his association with radicals, whose assassination attempt upon Alexander II (q.v.) led to a sweeping crackdown. Exiled to the province of Vologda, he wrote his most influential work, *Istoricheskie pis'ma* (*Historical Letters*, 1870), which argued that history is rooted in the development of critical reason. In 1870 he fled to Europe, where he participated in the Paris Commune, joined the International Workingmen's Association, and eventually became friends with Marx and Engels. He published the revolutionary journal *Vpered!* (*Forward!*) from 1873 to 1876, and publicly contested

Nechaev's (q.v.) claim that all means were permitted to overthrow the government. His time abroad somewhat distanced him from actual conditions in Russia, and he persisted in arguing that the peasantry could serve as the source of radical change, even after the failures of the movement 'Going to the People' of 1874. An intellectual luminary for populist revolutionaries, he was a member of 'The People's Will', whose journal he edited. He eventually turned his attention to sociology, and composed several studies of intellectual history, including a well-known work on the Paris Commune.

Leont'ev, Konstantin Nikolaevich (1831–1891), author, diplomat, literary critic, philosopher and playwright. One of the most original thinkers of the nineteenth century, Leont'ev was a staunch conservative who extolled autocracy and sharply criticised both the Westerners and the Slavophils for their reliance on European ideas. He regarded Europe as a decadent civilisation, and argued that Russia should cleave to her Byzantine heritage. He articulated a theory of cultural development and decay that was influenced by Danilevsky (q.v.), and provided an 'aesthetic' defence of aristocracy that anticipated Nietzsche's views. He argued that liberalism encouraged crass materialism, while democracy ignored the natural inequality of humanity. His political ideals blended monarchy and Orthodoxy, and demanded absolute subjugation of the individual to authority. Strongly nationalistic, he urged an aggressive foreign policy in the hope of restoring the Byzantine Empire. After a brief stint in the consular service, he underwent a religious awakening that eventually led him to cloister himself in a monastery, where he remained until he died. His best-known work is *Vizantism i slavyanstvo* (*Byzantinism and Slavdom*, 1875).

Lermontov, Mikhail Yur'evich (1814–41), novelist, poet, playwright and soldier; a leading Russian romantic whose writings are characterised by their lyricism and introspection. Among his best-known works are 'Smert' poeta' ('The Death of a Poet', 1837), commemorating Pushkin (q.v., considered Russia's greatest poet), and *Geroi nashego vremeni* (*A Hero of Our Time*, 1840), a novel recounting the exploits of a brooding military officer serving in the Caucasus. Although circulated only in handwritten copies, 'The Death of a Poet' outraged the Russian authorities because of its suggestion that Pushkin's death in a duel was the responsibility of a jealous aristocrat. Lermontov was arrested and sent as a soldier to the Caucasus, where his experiences provided the material for *Geroi nashego vremeni*, which expresses the frustration and anguish of the Russian élites who could find no outlet for their talents after the Decembrist Revolt – a theme later taken up by Tolstoy, Dostoevsky, Turgenev (qq.v.) and others. Lermontov was known for his daring on the battlefield as well as for his arrogance and difficult temperament. Like Pushkin, he died young in a duel, the victim of a childhood acquaintance who had finally had enough of his ridicule.

Leskov, Nikolay Semenovich (1831–95), short-story writer, famous for his use of traditional fables and folklore. Leskov grew up on a country estate and lacked any formal education, taking up journalism in the 1860s. As a traditionalist, wary of political reform, he attacked radicalism in novels such as *Na nozhakh* (*At Daggers Drawn*, 1870–1). But such works remained little read, his fame resting on his gifts as a storyteller of great popular appeal, in tales such as *Ledi Makbet mtsenskogo uezda* (*Lady Macbeth of Mtsensk*, 1865) – the basis for Shostakovich's 1934 opera – and *Ocharovannyi strannik* (*The Enchanted Wanderer*, 1873). In later life Leskov became an adherent of the religious and ethical ideas of Tolstoy (q.v.), and his work took on an increasingly moralistic tone.

Lomonosov, Mikhail Vasil'evich (1711–65), literary critic, philosopher, playwright, poet, scientist and translator. Born into the peasantry, Lomonosov became the leading figure of the Russian Enlightenment. Given the opportunity to study at the Academy of Sciences in St Petersburg, he quickly distinguished himself as a specially gifted student, and was sent to Germany to further his education. At the University of Marburg he studied not only science but also classical philosophy and German literature. On his return to Petersburg he worked as a university teacher of chemistry before helping to found Moscow University. His interests were wide-ranging: his work on glass manufacture changed the way mosaics were made; he proposed an international academy to develop scientific means of navigation; he championed surveys of Siberia to determine its natural resources; he propounded a theory concerning the density of the atmosphere of the planet Venus; and he experimented with electricity. His greatest literary achievement was his work on Russian grammar, which clarified the use of vernacular Russian and provided the foundation for the advent of popular literature.

Lunacharsky, Anatoly Vasil'evich (1875–1933), Soviet dramatist and literary critic, a visionary figure in early Soviet culture. As a young political activist in the 1890s Lunacharsky suffered arrest and exile, becoming the leader of the Russian revolutionaries living in Paris.

Returning to St Petersburg in 1905 to edit the Social Democrat newspaper *Novaya zhizn'* (*New Life*), he worked as a literary critic. Having been a Bolshevik organiser in Petrograd during the 1917 Revolution, he was given a key appointment in the new government as People's Commissar for Culture and Education (1917–29). During this period he initiated educational reforms and programmes in adult literacy under Lenin's New Economic Policy. Lunacharsky's encouragement of diversity in the Soviet arts soon came under suspicion; although he kept away from party politics, in 1933 Stalin removed him from office and sent him away to an ambassadorship in Spain. Lunacharsky died in Paris en route to his new post.

Maistre, Joseph Marie, comte de (1753–1821), diplomat, lawyer and philosopher. A key figure in the transmission of anti-revolutionary ideas to Russia, Maistre was a Savoyard lawyer who served as the King of Sardinia's envoy to Alexander I. Adamantly opposed to the French Revolution, Maistre wrote several works which attempted to undermine its philosophical foundations. In opposition to the Enlightenment's assumption of the necessity of progress, and to its faith in reason, Maistre asserted the constancy of sin and the frailty of human rationality. He argued that man's fallen state necessitated the imposition of order, which could be achieved only through the institutions of Church and State. Without religion and autocracy, men would be consumed by violence. His ideas not only challenged the political ideals of the Enlightenment, but also denied their scientific basis. He was briefly influential among the Russian nobility, until Napoleon's campaigns led to a reaction against the French. Among his best-known works are *Considérations sur la France* (*Considerations on France*, 1796), *Les Soirées de Saint-Pétersbourg* (*St Petersburg Dialogues*, 1821) and *Examen de la philosophie de Bacon* (*An Examination of the Philosophy of Bacon*, 1836).

Mikhailovsky, Nikolay Konstantinovich (1842–1904), editor, journalist, literary critic and sociologist. A leading theorist of populism, Mikhailovsky established his reputation with the article 'Chto takoe progress?' ('What is Progress?', 1869–70), in which he argued that, as society becomes more complex, individual development regresses. It followed that earlier societies allowed for the greatest cultivation of individual personality, since individuals were not required to specialise in one activity, as industrial labour required. His arguments were used by populists to justify their vision of an agrarian socialism centred upon the peasant commune, viewed as a better alternative to capitalist production. Because Mikhailovsky argued against the conventional Marxist interpretation of economic development, which regarded capitalism as a necessary stage in the advent of communism, socialists such as Lenin and Plekhanov (q.v.) rejected his position. Nevertheless, he exerted a profound influence on radical democrats, many of whom were first introduced by his essays to the ideas of Comte, Spencer, Mill and Proudhon.

Nadezhdin, Nikolay Ivanovich (1804–56), editor, ethnographer, literary critic and university teacher. Expelled from his seminary, Nadezhdin became one of the more significant literary critics before Belinsky (q.v.). After a degree at Moscow University (where he wrote a dissertation on German philosophy in Latin), he worked briefly as a university teacher of fine arts and archaeology. His literary reputation is based on his claim that art expresses divine truths, which led to his belief that poetry has a normative dimension. He was especially critical of Russian romantic poets, whose work, for him, lacked a proper moral depth. He is best known for publishing Chaadaev's (q.v.) *Lettres philosophiques* (*Philosophical Letters*, 1836) in the journal *Teleskop* (the *Telescope*), an act which led to his brief exile to Siberia. There he became interested in ethnography, and after his return eventually became the chairman of the ethnographic division of the Russian Geographic Society.

Nechaev, Sergey Gennadievich (1847–82), founder of the revolutionary organisation 'The People's Vengeance'. Highly charismatic but fanatical in his radicalism, Nechaev associated with revolutionary figures such as Bakunin (q.v.), who thought highly of the younger man. Nechaev's historical significance is twofold: he is credited with composing 'Katekhizis revolyutsionera' ('Catechism of a Revolutionary', 1869); and he was involved in the murder of Ivan Ivanov, who attempted to leave the group in 1869, whereupon he was beaten up, shot and strangled. The 'Catechism' was a manifesto for revolutionary violence that justified the use of any means to overthrow the government, while Ivanov's murder produced a popular backlash against radicalism that briefly slowed revolutionary pressures upon the State, and gave the government the pretext for a vigorous crackdown on all dissidents. Dostoevsky (q.v.) used this as the inspiration for his novel *The Possessed* (1872). Eventually captured in Switzerland, Nechaev was turned over to the Russian authorities, and died in prison.

Nekrasov, Nikolay Alekseevich (1821–78), poet and publisher, a patron of writers and critics, notably Turgenev, Tolstoy and Belinsky (qq.v.). Though a member of the gentry, Nekrasov had to write hack poetry and vaudevilles to pay for his university studies in St Petersburg, as his father refused to support him. He purchased the journal *Sovremennik* (the *Contemporary*) in 1846, and fought the tsarist censorship to keep it running until it was finally closed in 1866. He then acquired *Otechestvennye zapiski* (*Notes of the Fatherland*) in 1868, which he co-edited with Saltykov (q.v.). Nekrasov's most popular verse, such as 'Vlas' (1854) and the narrative poem *Moroz krasny-nos* (*Frost the Red-Nosed*, 1863), is drawn from Russian folklore. His long satirical poem *Komu na Rusi zhit' khorosho?* (*Who Can Be Happy in Russia?*, 1873–6) celebrates the virtues of the Russian peasantry.

Nicholas I (1796–1855), third son of Tsar Paul I, Tsar of Russia 1825–55. Nicholas assumed the crown after Alexander I died unexpectedly and Constantine I refused the throne. During the initial confusion as to who would become tsar, Nicholas was forced to suppress the Decembrist Revolt mounted by members of the aristocracy and military who wanted to overthrow the monarchy. This determined the tone of Nicholas's reign, and he suspended the period of political experimentation begun by Peter the Great and continued by Catherine the Great (qq.v.). Fearful of further unrest, Nicholas instituted a series of measures aimed at curbing dissent and controlling political debate. These curbs applied even to informal discussion-groups such as the Petrashevsky (q.v.) Circle, whose existence was considered threatening as it involved a 'conspiracy of ideas'. Although he successfully limited criticisms of his rule and halted further social reforms, his actions unintentionally pushed many moderates towards radicalism, and thereby indirectly contributed to the revolutionary fervour of the late nineteenth century.

Odoevsky, Prince Vladimir Fedorovich (c.1803–69), poet, philosopher, educator and critic. An admirer of Schelling, Odoevsky led the Moscow-based philosophical group the Society of Wisdom Lovers (1823–4). From 1826 he lived in St Petersburg, where he became a civil servant involved in public education and culture, as director of the Rumyantsev Museum and assistant director of the city's public library. An ardent Slavophil, Odoevsky criticised Western influence on Russian culture in his philosophical conversations *Russkie nochi* (*Russian Nights*, 1844). His short stories and fantastical tales, such as 'God 4338' ('The Year 4338', not published in full until 1926), frequently reflected his interest in mysticism and scientific progress.

Ogarev, Nikolay Platonovich (1813–77), editor, journalist and poet. A close friend of Herzen (q.v.), Ogarev was the co-editor of *Polyarnaya zvezda* (the *Polar Star*) and *Kolokol* (the *Bell*). As youths, the two took an oath to complete the work begun by the Decembrists, and as university students they attempted to do this by establishing a discussion group that debated philosophical and aesthetic matters. However, because such discussions often involved political issues, the group was broken up by the authorities, who sent both men into exile. Eventually granted his freedom, Ogarev emigrated to England, where he continued his collaboration with Herzen. Although he was a notable poet, his biggest influence was exercised through his work as an editor, and he encouraged Russia's nascent socialist movement by publishing the writings of men such as Bakunin and Nechaev (qq.v.).

Orlov, Prince Aleksey Fedorovich (1786–1861), general. A close confidant of Nicholas I (q.v.), Orlov was one of the military leaders who remained loyal to the Tsar during the Decembrist revolt, helping to ensure its failure. He is famous for signing the Treaty of Unkiar Skelessi in 1833, which forged a military alliance between Russia and the Ottoman Empire, and for serving as the head of the infamous Third Section. A secret department whose mission was to prevent sedition, the Third Section served as a political police force which censored the press and conducted surveillance operations against those who were suspected of subversive activities. Orlov was eventually ennobled for his services by Alexander II (q.v.), who also appointed him president of the advisory Council of State, and to oversee a committee on the emancipation of the serfs (which Orlov opposed).

Panaev, Ivan Ivanovich (1812–62), editor, journalist and novelist, nephew of V. I. Panaev (q.v.). Though not a major literary figure, Panaev helped Nekrasov (q.v.) turn *Sovremennik* (the *Contemporary*) into a profitable journal. He is best known for his 'physiological sketches', a genre that exhibited the details of daily life by briefly portraying the activities of ordinary individuals (usually petty bureaucrats). Such sketches were typically used to display the grim circumstances of urban life. His novel *L'vy v provintsii* (*Provincial Lions*, 1852), notable for its treatment of women's emancipation, was a modest success.

Panaev, Vladimir Ivanovich (1792–1859), uncle of I. I. Panaev (q.v.), minor author known for his idylls. Influenced by Vergil and other classical writers, Panaev composed highly sentimental pastorals. He sought to illustrate the beauty of rustic living by displaying the simplicity of manners and innocence of attitude that he believed character-ised an agrarian existence. His idylls had little to do with Russia, relying strongly on ancient Greek and Roman themes, settings and subjects. However, his writings were tinged with a slightly critical edge, implying that Russia had become insensitive to the imaginative impulse that underlies poetic creativity. His endeavours earned him the nickname 'the Russian Gessner', after the Swiss poet Salomon Gessner.

Peter I (1672–1725), Tsar of Russia 1682–1725, known as Peter the Great. Having travelled throughout Europe as a young man, Peter returned to Russia and introduced a series of sweeping reforms that were meant to modernise the nation. His main concern was to trans-form the army and the civil service, and to this end he instituted a 'Table of Ranks'. According to the Table, nobility entailed the obligation to serve, and military service became mandatory for all nobles. This integrated the interests of the nobility with those of the State, and undermined the power of hereditary nobles. Peter also founded St Petersburg (which became the new seat of government), and engaged in wars with the Ottoman Empire and Sweden in an attempt to turn Russia into a maritime power. Ultimately, the controversial nature of his innovations split the nobility into those who wanted further reforms and those who wanted a return to the 'old ways' – a division that foreshadowed many of the debates of the nineteenth century.

Petrashevsky, Mikhail Vasil'evich (1821–66), lawyer and translator. An interpreter and translator for the Ministry of Foreign Affairs, Petra-shevsky's reputation stems from his hosting weekly meetings that eventually led to a confrontation with the authorities. He was a voracious reader who was able to use his job to amass a large personal library, and he and his friends originally met informally on Fridays to discuss topics of personal interest. Given the repressive atmosphere of the time, in which public discussion had been severely restricted by Nicholas I (q.v.), the Petrashevsky Circle quickly grew in size, as it provided one of the few outlets for philosophical debate. Public figures such as Dostoevsky and Pleshcheev (qq.v.) started to attend meetings, which became more overtly political. Eventually Nicholas ordered Petrashev-sky's arrest, and the authorities rounded up the most active members of the group. After a trial involving extensive hearings – as recorded in *Delo petrashevtsev* (*The Petrashevsky Affair*, 1937–51) – a mock execution was staged, in which Petrashevsky and other members were lined up before a firing squad. A last-minute reprieve was then read, whereupon the most prominent figures of the group were exiled to Siberia.

Pisarev, Dmitry Ivanovich (1840–68), journalist and literary critic. Along with Chernyshevsky and Dobrolyubov (qq.v.), Pisarev was one of the leading literary critics after Belinsky. A self-proclaimed nihilist, he insisted that literature be judged not by its aesthetic qualities, but by its truthfulness. Praising Turgenev's (q.v.) portrait of Bazarov in *Ottsy i deti* (*Fathers and Children*, 1862), he held that science provided the correct standard for ascertaining truth, and dismissed the historical philosophy associated with Hegel and his followers as speculative. This set him at odds with many socialists and radicals, who accused him of being too materialistic. Undaunted by the charge, he produced a body of work notable for its clarity of argument and its rigorous analysis. Among his more influential essays were 'Bazarov' (1862), 'Razrushenie estetiki' ('The Abolition of Aesthetics', 1865) and 'Pushkin i Belinskii' ('Pushkin and Belinsky', 1865). His career was cut short when he drowned while bathing in the Baltic Sea.

Plekhanov, Georgy Valentinovich (1856–1918), revolutionary and lead-ing Marxist thinker. Plekhanov's political activities began in the popu-list movement of the 1870s, but he soon rejected the terrorism of the extremists and left Russia in 1880. He lived in exile in Geneva until 1917, founding a political group based on German Marxism in 1883. In 1898 this group would be renamed the Russian Social Democratic Workers' Party. A close colleague of Lenin's, Plekhanov edited the Marxist newspaper *Iskra* (the *Spark*) with him from 1900, but in 1903 their association ended with the split in the RSDWP between the Bolsheviks, led by Lenin, and the Mensheviks, led by Plekhanov. He returned briefly to Russia in 1917, but, being opposed to the Revolu-tion, left soon after for Finland. Although he never held political power, and was profoundly disillusioned by the new Bolshevik hege-mony in Russia, he is still revered for contributing a massive body of theory – in twenty-six volumes – to European Marxism that remains an inspiration to Marxist thinkers worldwide. An essay on him by Berlin appears in *The Power of Ideas* (see xv above).

Pleshcheev, Aleksey Nikolaevich (1825–93), journalist, literary critic, poet, playwright and translator. A close friend of Dostoevesky (q.v.), Pleshcheev was known for his religiously infused poetry and short stories. An aristocrat with socialist leanings, he was exiled to Siberia for his involvement in the Petrashevsky (q.v.) Circle. Eventually par-doned, he returned to Moscow and resumed his literary career. Though fairly conventional, his works were well received by his contempor-aries, who appreciated his concern for ordinary individuals. He was especially praised for portraying 'active' characters, which critics like Dobrolyubov (q.v.) contrasted favourably with the image of the 'superfluous man'.

Pobedonostsev, Konstantin Petrovich (1827–1907), adviser to the tsar, lawyer, university teacher, and procurator-general of the Orthodox Church. Son of a priest, Pobedonostsev taught law at Moscow University and wrote a three-volume text on civil law. He was appointed tutor to Alexander III, and became one of Alexander's closest advisors when he assumed the throne. A radical conservative, he urged Alexander to avoid concessions to reformers, on the grounds that this would only encourage revolutionary violence. He is credited with being the intellectual architect of Alexander's manifesto of 1881, which reiterated the absolute sovereignty of the tsar. Known as highly critical but unimaginative, he later distilled his ideas in *Moskovskii sbornik* (*Moscow Collection*, 1896, translated as *Reflections of a Russian Statesman*), in which he argued that contemporary society was threatened by a moral degeneration that could be redressed only through the institutions of the Church and State. Like many conservatives, he believed Western ideals were inappropriate for Russia, whose large size and dispersed population required a centralised autocracy.

Pogodin, Mikhail Petrovich (1800–75), historian, journalist, university teacher and editor. A teacher at Moscow University, Pogodin was a conservative historian who provided a strongly nationalistic reading of Russia's past. Influenced by German philosophers such as Schelling and Schlegel, he belonged to a group of scholars known as the 'romantic nationalists', who idealised Russian history, claiming that the simplicity of the peasantry and their agrarian way of life had insulated the nation from revolution. They further argued that since Russia had avoided the moral degeneracy that afflicted Europe, she could serve as the source of the moral regeneration of humanity. Pogodin popularised these ideas in his lectures, which were published in collected form in the multi-volume *Issledovaniya, zamechaniya i lektsii o russkoi istorii* (*Studies, Remarks and Lectures about Russian History*, 1846–56).

Polevoy, Nikolay Alekseevich (1796–1846), author, historian, journalist and literary critic. Son of a Siberian merchant, Polevoy was one of the first successful non-aristocratic writers. With his brother, he ran the progressive journal *Moskovskii telegraf* (the *Moscow Telegraph*), which was suspended when he published a highly critical review of a popular conservative play. He was primarily known for his *Istoriya*

russkogo naroda (*The History of the Russian People*, 1829–33), which
was his response to Karamzin's *Istoriya gosudarstva rossiiskogo* (*The
History of the Russian State*, 1818–29). Like most of his contemporaries, he was influenced by German romanticism, and believed
that there are laws of historical development that govern societies.
However, contrary to Karamzin, he believed that these laws applied
directly to peoples rather than to institutions. Pushkin (q.v.) parodied
Polevoy's ideas in *Istoriya sela Goryukhino* (*The History of the Village
of Goryukhino*, 1837).

Pugachev, Emel'yan Ivanovich (*c.*1740–75), rebel. A Cossack who had
served in the Russian military, Pugachev led a major peasant rebellion
against Catherine II (q.v.) in 1773. Claiming to be Catherine's husband
Peter III (who had died under questionable circumstances), he fomented
an insurrection which lasted for some two years, during which he was
able to conquer a great expanse of territory stretching from the Ural
mountains to the Volga river. Catherine dispatched troops to put down
the rebellion, but their initial efforts failed. Eventually the rebels were
defeated and Pugachev was publicly executed, but not before he had
acquired a legendary reputation. He inspired later revolutionaries, who
regarded his challenge to authority as comparable to their own. Pushkin
(q.v.) was particularly fascinated by Pugachev: he wrote a history of
the rebellion, and also used it for the basis of his novel *Kapitanskaya
dochka* (*The Captain's Daughter*, 1836).

Pushkin, Aleksandr Sergeevich (1799–1837), poet, playwright and novelist. Russia's national poet, Pushkin was the foremost writer of his
generation. Though born into the gentry, he was among the first to write
extensively in the vernacular and to incorporate the daily existence of
ordinary individuals into his work. Although his political sympathies
became more conservative as he grew older, his writings exhibit progressive tendencies that strongly inspired later liberals, and provided the
foundation for modern Russian literature. His poems are known for their
lyricism and elegance, and his prose for its clarity of expression. 'Russia's
Shakespeare', Pushkin is best known for his narrative poems, including
the 'novel in verse' *Evgenii Onegin* (*Eugene Onegin*, 1825–32), for
which he invented his own verse form, the 'Onegin stanza'. Among
his other works are *Boris Godunov* (1825), *Poltava* (1829), *Povesti
pokoinogo Ivana Petrovicha Belkina* (*The Tales of Ivan Petrovich
Belkin*, 1830), *Mednyi vsadnik* (*The Bronze Horseman*, 1833), *Piko-
vaya dama* (*The Queen of Spades*, 1833), *Istoriya Pugacheva* (*The
History of Pugachev*, 1834) and *Kapitanskaya dochka* (*The Captain's

Daughter, 1836). He was fatally wounded in a duel with Georges d'Anthès, fought over the latter's relationship with Pushkin's wife.

Ryleev, Kondraty Fedorovich (1795–1826), poet and friend of Pushkin (q.v.), leader of the Decembrist Revolt of 1825. A romantic poet, Ryleev celebrated civic pride in his revolutionary lyrics, satirised the autocracy in his so-called 'agitational songs', and in epic verse recounted the glorious martyrdom of past historical heroes, for example the Ukrainian nationalist Mazepa in his poem *Voinarovskii* (1824–5). From 1823 to 1825 he edited the journal *Polyarnaya zvezda* (the *Polar Star*). Prominent in the Northern Society (a group of republicans who plotted the overthrow of the imperial family), he was one of the five ringleaders of the abortive Decembrist Revolt, after which he was arrested and hanged in 1826.

Saltykov, Mikhail Evgrafovich (he also used the pseudonym N. Shchedrin, and is usually referred to as Saltykov-Shchedrin) (1826–89), novelist and satirist. Saltykov entered the tsarist civil service in 1844. Some early short stories critical of the regime led to his exile in Vyatka, although he remained a civil servant, returning to Moscow in 1855. Here he co-edited the journals *Sovremennik* (the *Contemporary*) and *Otechestvennye zapiski* (*Notes of the Fatherland*) with Nekrasov (q.v.), leaving the civil service in 1868. His satirical sketches, published from the 1850s, were the forerunners of one of his finest works, *Istoriya odnogo goroda* (*The History of a Town*, 1869–70), and of his bitter attack on the decaying Russian gentry, *Gospoda Golovlevy* (*The Golovlev Family*, 1876–80).

Samarin, Yury Fedorovich (1819–76), Slavophil philosopher, essayist and civil servant. From the 1850s Samarin contributed to the Slavophil journal *Russkaya beseda* (*Russian Colloquy*), collaborating with Konstantin Aksakov (q.v.) and other leading figures. In his capacity as a civil servant he worked on Alexander II's Great Reforms of the 1860s, drafting the declaration under which the serfs were emancipated in 1861. He died in Berlin.

Speransky, Mikhail Mikhailovich (1772–1839), statesman. Son of an impoverished priest, Speransky was one of Russia's most prominent liberals. Known for his intelligence, he quickly rose through the ranks of the civil service to become an advisor to Alexander I, who consulted closely with him. Given permission to reform the State civil service, Speransky drafted a constitutional framework that would have introduced the equivalent of a parliament. He planned gradually to transform the tsarist autocracy into a European-style constitutional monarchy. An initial success was the establishment of the State Council, an advisory body on legislation. But Court intrigues undermined his relationship with Alexander, when conservatives claimed that he privately disparaged the Tsar, and called into question his ties to France, against whom Russia was preparing to go to war. Dismissed from Court service, he briefly served as governor-general of Siberia, before eventually being given a post on the State Council. In his later years he was appointed by Nicholas I (q.v.) to codify the legal code.

Stankevich, Nikolay Vladimirovich (1813–40), philosopher and poet. Though not a major literary figure in his own right, Stankevich played a pivotal role in the development of Russian philosophy. As the leader of an informal discussion group at Moscow University, he provided a forum for the individuals who would eventually shape nineteenth-century Russian thought. Herzen, Granovsky, Bakunin and Katkov (qq.v.) – among others – were all participants in the Stankevich Circle, which served as the model for similar groups that arose later, e.g. Petrashevsky's (q.v.). Deeply interested in German romanticism, he travelled to Europe, where he studied Hegelian philosophy in Berlin. But he had contracted tuberculosis, and succumbed to the disease while abroad.

Strakhov, Nikolay Nikolaevich (1828–96), literary critic and philosopher. Trained in zoology, Strakhov was one of the foremost theorists of the *pochvenniki* ('men of the soil'). Influenced by Hegel, he believed that the world had a spiritual unity that gave meaning to human existence. He argued that the denial of such meaning was symptomatic of nihilism and its mechanistic conception of reason. The only way to combat the atomistic tendencies of nihilism was to acknowledge the 'organic' aspects of existence associated with religion and the nation, which he saw as situated in 'the soil'. A friend of Dostoevsky and Tolstoy (qq.v.), he influenced the conservative tendencies of their later works.

Tkachev, Petr Nikitich (1844–86), journalist and radical. An acquaintance of Nechaev's (q.v.), Tkachev was one of the more influential Russian writers of the late nineteenth century. His main contribution to radical thought was the idea that the peasantry, too lethargic to act on its own, needed to be prompted by a cadre of dedicated revolutionaries. This placed him in opposition to Bakunin and Kropotkin (qq.v.), both of whom believed the revolution would be a spontaneous occurrence. He also disputed Marx's view of history, claiming that Russia did not need to pass through all the phases of economic development in order to achieve communism. This led to a celebrated exchange with Engels, who took the contrary view. Ultimately Tkachev's ideas influenced Lenin, who, having encountered his essays while exiled in Geneva, argued a similar case in *Gosudarstvo i revolyutsiya* (*State and Revolution*, 1917).

Tolstoy, Count Lev Nikolaevich (1828–1910), author. Tolstoy is one of the greatest Russian writers. His literary career began with *Detstvo* (*Childhood*, 1854), written while he was in the army. After retiring from military service in 1856 he devoted his full attention to writing, and published a variety of short stories and articles, as well as *Sevastopolskie rasskazy* (*Sevastopol Sketches*, 1855–6), *Kazaki* (*The Cossacks*, 1863) and *Voina i mir* (*War and Peace*, 1865–9). The latter work – an epic chronicle of the Franco-Russian War – was met with great acclaim, and established his reputation as an author without peer. After a brief respite he wrote *Anna Karenina* (1875–7), a tragic love story that was also a critical and popular success. However, while composing it he suffered from periodic bouts of depression, and eventually he became so distressed that he contemplated suicide. At this point he experienced a spiritual awakening – the subject of *Ispoved'* (*Confession*, 1882) – which marked a new period in his life. Henceforward his writings were overtly religious and philosophical, and show a preoccupation with mortality and morality. Among his best-known later works are *Smert' Ivana Il'icha* (*The Death of Ivan Il'ich*, 1886), *Kreitserova sonata* (*The Kreutzer Sonata*, 1889), *Tsarstvo Bozh'e vnutri vas* (*The Kingdom of God Is within You*, 1894), *Khozyain i rabotnik* (*Master and Man*, 1895), *Chto takoe iskusstvo?* (*What Is Art?*, 1897) and *Voskresenie* (*Resurrection*, 1899). Although banned in Russia, *Tsarstvo Bozh'e vnutri vas* proved especially influential, since it led to a correspondence with Gandhi in which Tolstoy clarified his ideas about non-violence.

Tredyakovsky, Vasily Kirilovich (1703–69), essayist, poet, playwright and university teacher. A contemporary of Lomonosov (q.v.), Tredyakovsky was a respected scholar who taught at the Academy of Sciences. Educated at the University of Paris, where he studied linguistics, philosophy and mathematics, he is known for his translations of Tallemant's *Voyage à l'isle d'amour* (*Voyage to the Isle of Love*, 1730) and Fénelon's *Les Aventures de Télémaque* (*The Adventures of Telemachus*, 1766), as well as for the highly theoretical *Novyi i kratkii* *sposob k slozheniyu rossiiskikh stikhov* (*A New and Brief Method for Composing Russian Verse*, 1735). His historical significance derives primarily from the latter work, which pushed poetry towards a form of versification more suitable to the Russian language.

Trotsky, Leon (pseudonym of Lev Davidovich Bronstein) (1879–1940), international revolutionary and political theorist, born in the Ukraine into a family of Russified Jews. Trotsky abandoned his studies for revolutionary activities (1897–8), which resulted in the first of his many imprisonments. In exiled revolutionary circles in London he sided with the Mensheviks against Lenin, and operated as a political free-wheeler back in Russia in 1905, leading strikes and demonstrations and becoming an outstanding public speaker. In prison again in 1905, he worked feverishly on his theory of 'permanent revolution', and was at the centre of activities during the 1917 Revolution. He was appointed to the important post of Commissar for War (1918–25) and founded the Red Army, becoming notorious for his use of brutal coercive measures during the ensuing Civil War. He failed to seize power after Lenin's death in 1924, and Stalin rapidly marginalised him. Exiled to Central Asia, he was deported in 1928. He spent the remainder of his life pouring out invective against Stalin in a succession of political works. He found refuge in Mexico City in 1936, where an agent of the NKVD finally assassinated him.

Turgenev, Ivan Sergeevich (1818–83), novelist, short-story writer and poet. Son of an aristocrat, Turgenev was a leading literary figure, known for his realism and lyricism. His writings embody the liberal aspirations which defined the Westerners. He established his reputation with *Zapiski okhotnika* (*A Sportsman's Sketches*, 1852), a provocative account of rural life which portrayed the hardships of serfdom (and has been compared with *Uncle Tom's Cabin*). He followed it with *Rudin* (1856), *Dvoryanskoe gnezdo* (*A Nest of Gentlefolk*, 1859) and *Nakanune* (*On the Eve*, 1860), each of which was critically acclaimed and consolidated his reputation. His best-known work was *Ottsy i deti* (*Fathers and Children*, 1862), a novel about the intergenerational tensions between the 'fathers of the '40s' and the 'sons of the '60s'. Unlike his earlier novels, however, *Ottsy i deti* proved deeply controversial, since liberals, conservatives and radicals all found reasons to condemn it. Turgenev's account of the moral dilemmas facing Russia indicted each party in some way, which proved inflammatory. He attempted to respond to his critics – notably in *Dym* (*Smoke*, 1867) and *Nov'* (*Virgin Soil*, 1877) – but without much success, as his reputation had been damaged by the perceived insults of *Ottsy i deti*. After this he spent his time in Europe (where he continued his lifelong relationship with the mezzo-soprano Pauline García-Viardot), and eventually died in France.

Tyutchev, Fedor Ivanovich (1803–73), outstanding nature poet, ranked with Pushkin and Lermontov (qq.v.). Born into the nobility, Tyutchev became a diplomat in 1822 and was posted to Germany and then Italy, living abroad until 1844. He corresponded with Heine, whose poetry he translated, while much of his own verse, inspired by Schelling's *Naturphilosophie*, was published anonymously in *Sovremennik* (the *Contemporary*) during 1836–7 under the rubric 'Poems Sent from Germany'. Returning to Russia, he worked as an official censor and finally published work under his own name in 1854, having been discovered by Nekrasov (q.v.). His nature- and love-lyrics gave way in later life to more political verse which expressed his pan-Slavist sentiments. Interest in his work fell into decline until he was redis-covered by Russian symbolist poets at the end of the nineteenth century.

Venevitinov, Dmitry Vladimirovich (1805–27), literary critic, philo-sopher and poet. A founder of the Society of Wisdom Lovers, Veneviti-nov was one of the earliest proponents of Russian romanticism. Influenced by German philosophers such as Schelling and Fichte, he believed that art is a divinely inspired vehicle for the expression of truth. Among his best-known works are 'Poet' ('The Poet', 1826), 'Poet i drug' ('The Poet and His Friend', 1827) and 'Elegiya' ('Elegy', 1826–7). His literary output was brief – comprising around 40 poems – as his life was cut short by influenza.

Vorovsky, Vatslav Vatslavovich (1871–1923), literary critic and journ-alist, leading Bolshevik writer on the editorial board of the Party newspaper *Vpered* (*Forward*). A close associate of Lenin, after the Revolution Vorovsky served in Stockholm as one of the first Russian envoys to the West. In 1922 he was a delegate at the International Economic Conference. He was assassinated in Lausanne by the Russian-born Swiss Maurice Conradi while attending an international confer-ence on the Turkish question. Vorovsky published several books, including *Russkaya intelligentsiya i russkaya literatura* (*The Russian Intelligentsia and Russian Literature*, 1923).

Vyazemsky, Prince Petr Andreevich (1792–1878), civil servant, literary critic, poet, soldier and translator. An ardent liberal who served briefly as the head of the Censorship (1856–8), Vyazemsky was acquainted with many of the leading literary figures of the early nineteenth century, including Karamzin (his brother-in-law), Pushkin, Baratynsky and Gogol (qq.v.). A stern polemicist, he frequently engaged in heated literary debates, and was known for his criticisms of conservatives as well as radicals. Among his best-known works is his biography of Fonvizin (q.v., 1848); and his notebooks and letters have provided valuable information on the intellectual climate of the early nineteenth century.

Zasulich, Vera Ivanovna (1849–1919), editor, revolutionary and translator. One of three daughters of an impoverished noble, Zasulich achieved notoriety for trying to assassinate the governor-general of St Petersburg in 1878. Her attempt was prompted by an incident in which a young prisoner failed to remove his hat before the governor-general, who then ordered that the youth be flogged. Acquitted at her trial, she subsequently fled to Europe, where she helped found the group the Emancipation of Labour, the first Russian-Marxist organisation. During this time, she also helped edit two journals, *Iskra* (the *Spark*) and *Zarya* (*Dawn*), wrote articles, and translated some of Marx's works into Russian. She eventually returned to Russia after the revolution of 1905 and settled in Petersburg. Her revolutionary fervour having abated, she condemned the October Revolution of 1917 as a perversion of Marxism.

Zhukovsky, Vasily Andreevich (1783–1852), poet and translator, whose poetry was influenced by English and German pre-romantic literature. In 1808 Zhukovsky became editor of the literary journal *Vestnik Evropy* (*Messenger of Europe*). His appointment as tutor to the future Alexander II (q.v.) in 1825 allowed him the opportunity quietly to inject a liberal element at Court, and he frequently offered his protection to writers, including Pushkin (q.v.), when they were in dispute with the authorities. After his retirement from Court in 1839, he settled in Germany, where he became a notable translator of Goethe and Schiller. He also translated the English poets Gray, Southey and Byron; his translation of Homer's *Odyssey* was a lifetime's labour of love. A melancholy preoccupation with the supernatural and the gothic in his work, which comprised mainly meditative elegies, reflected his own growing interest in mysticism.

Concordance to the first edition

The aim of this concordance is to enable readers to find references to the original 1978 page-numbering of Russian Thinkers *easily in the present volume. The first column lists the pages of the first edition, the second column specifies on which page of the present edition the opening words of the original page are to be found (square brackets in this column indicating a change between editions), and the third column gives those opening words.*

1978 edition	This edition	1978 page begins
xiii	xxiii	Do not look for solutions
xiv	xxiv	the belief, deeply
xv	[xxv]	He has argued that the great
xvi	xxvi	price that must be paid
xvii	xxvii	sensitive among them
xviii	[xxviii]	concealed or justified
xix	xxix	when only a consistent
xx	[xxx]	the intellectual and moral
xxi	[xxxi]	nihilism was a passionate
xxii	xxxii	when liberals and radicals
xxiii	[xxxiii]	his intelligence and sense
xxiv	[xxxv]	example is at all costs
1	1	The year 1848
2	2	the possibility of even
3	3	echoed thirteen years
4	4	The extreme contradictions
5	5	or in religion
6	6	become increasingly
7	7	Its beliefs and principles
8	8	revolutionary art
9	10	*from a Correspondence*

1978 edition	This edition	1978 page begins
10	11	[reinforce]ments were sent
11	12	popular feeling
12	13	in the history of Russia
13	14	[ignor]ance of each
14	15	[bitter]ness about the
15	16	admirer of the Roman
16	17	Baron Korf
17	18	temperament and
18	20	– meant business
19	21	mood of profound
20	22	greater detail by
21	23	personal disillusionment
22	24	A queer combination
23	25	hedgehogs; Herodotus
24	26	other writer. Is he
25	27	primarily as a novelist
26	28	but a lot of mystical
27	30	E. J. Simmons, not
28	31	sage – dogmatic, perverse
29	32	Tolstoy's interest in
30	33	beginning to the end
31	34	But side by side
32	35	natural science, and
33	36	the elements which
34	38	he is mortally
35	39	'lost' on the battlefield
36	40	talking, writing
37	41	superlative skill
38	42	them so well
39	[43]	. . . the new history
40	44	importance of their own
41	45	other exactly similar
42	46	They are ordinary
43	48	the corrupt and somewhat
44	49	*War and Peace* are devoted
45	50	how things happen
46	51	Patiently and mildly
47	52	historical truth and falsehood
48	[53]	be, if the vision was to be
49	54	very penetrating
50	55	has always made his

1978 edition	This edition	1978 page begins
51	57	If we may recall once
52	58	employing for this
53	59	have shown,[1] not as much
54	60	upon Tolstoy of his
55	61	tradition of the Russian
56	62	Tolstoy, there was at least
57	63	battles appear to those
58	64	writing are closer to
59	66	which all the French
60	67	or 'free' personal
61	68	aurait fait chanter
62	70	vous tirez, je tire . . .
63	71	Indeed, Tolstoy's accounts
64	72	have applauded. Both speak
65	73	still be on the path
66	74	declares it to be
67	75	quarter of the nineteenth
68	77	But there is a larger
69	78	as well as to spiritual
70	79	not, but this is so not
71	80	[under]standing: understanding of
72	81	conceived categories or
73	82	Tolstoy, consist in his
74	83	in which the progress
75	85	'scientism'. Their purpose
76	86	[con]ceivable at all: some
77	87	This is remarkably close
78	88	[uncon]vincing. Maistre sighs
79	89	[dis]tinguish what is isolable
80	90	awareness of the 'deep
81	91	Tolstoy began with a
82	93	'Human life is a great
83	94	genius, whose autobiography
84	95	folly. Accurate knowledge of
85	96	bits of matter; they were souls
86	97	some mystical, some going
87	98	solve the problems of
88	99	arguments which Herzen
89	101	neighbours – the French turn

1978 edition	*This edition*	*1978 page begins*
90	102	Since these abstractions
91	103	history is a tale told by
92	104	Then there are those who
93	105	to try their strength
94	106	for the sake of some
95	107	And most people do not
96	108	French radicals in 1848]
97	110	better, and can suppress
98	111	I, too, I am sorry
99	112	Such passages as these
100	113	change, as advocated by
101	114	their own time and are
102	115	of Serno-Solovievich, and
103	117	freedom of individuals
104	118	is open to the abolition
105	119	enough. He feared mobs
106	120	and in words. More than any
107	121	not too blind or too wicked
108	123	unintelligible notion of being
109	124	arise spontaneously like the
110	125	convictions'.[1] That is Bakunin's
111	126	an outlook and a temperament
112	127	terms like 'liberty' or
113	128	with his gusto and his logic
114	130	My title – 'A Remarkable
115	131	'A Remarkable Decade' is a
116	132	content, to an even higher
117	133	The concept of intelligentsia
118	134	vast majority of the inhabitants
119	135	There were other factors
120	136	than they could ever have been
121	137	life of all there is
122	138	liberal reform and every attempt
123	140	eastern and the western Churches
124	141	of a Renaissance tradition

1978 edition	This edition	1978 page begins
125	142	would be seized upon with
126	143	recoil from them
127	144	some great western liberator
128	146	The French writers of the
129	147	to the worship of some
130	148	committed to the belief
131	149	idealism, believed with moral
132	150	caricature – but nevertheless it
133	151	its immediate and its accidental
134	153	The sort of society which
135	154	– and a little guiltily –
136	155	All – or nearly all
137	156	without some grasp of the fact
138	157	vision. He saw the universe
139	158	churches, you would for ever
140	159	activity of the imagination
141	160	[respons]ible for the characteristically
142	161	He taught that a proper
143	162	did not disturb the deeper
144	164	could, however cryptically
145	165	coldly, clearly, and ironically
146	166	Bakunin. In Moscow he enjoyed
147	167	acclaimed by his friends
148	168	of both men and things
149	169	unimpressive, his prose style
150	170	In 1856, Ivan Aksakov
151	171	as tutor in a country house
152	172	are. Sometimes comical
153	173	gifted and formidable
154	174	notices, and reviews in
155	175	finally broke in himself
156	177	to a kind of moral frenzy
157	178	crooked; which leads them to
158	179	become), you had to distinguish
159	180	did discover and over-praise

1978 edition	*This edition*	*1978 page begins*
160	181	this embarrassing and spoke
161	183	Do not worry about the
162	184	work in assigning their due
163	185	changed his spiritual domicile
164	186	returned full of German
165	187	Belinsky at the beginning
166	189	literature, and killed our own . . .
167	190	to reality and that you do not
168	191	the name of an abstract ideal
169	192	and awkward manner, and then
170	193	And in his letters there are
171	195	from the spell of a half-
172	196	It is this mystical vision
173	197	[reac]tion, defender of a Tartar way
174	198	The central issue of Russian
175	199	and humble origin, but he rose
176	200	terms – without surrendering
177	202	excessive brutality upon the
178	203	squires. But in due course
179	204	temper; it was connected with
180	205	they are forced to emigrate
181	206	by the social and psychological
182	207	citizen are one; and whether
183	208	evasions. This search for
184	210	erratic because he took pride
185	211	poets, the novelists, the critics
186	212	Alexander Herzen is
187	213	embittered his life, and
188	214	kinds of sources, from
189	215	him all his life. Driven by it
190	216	also perpetual alertness
191	217	[intelli]gible. In all that Herzen
192	218	be true solutions to real
193	219	This ideal of detachment
194	221	Blanc, the French socialist

1978 edition	This edition	1978 page begins
195	222	being a mere means to the
196	223	at all. But nature is not so
197	224	This is Herzen's central
198	225	responsibility from his own
199	227	He is terrified of the oppressors
200	228	of Figaros, but of Figaros
201	229	himself and not be utterly
202	230	Herzen wrote novels, but
203	231	of Hamlet and the morality
204	232	slightly grotesque émigré
205	233	This kind of sweeping
206	235	revolutionaries had attacked
207	236	for, the victory of the
208	237	intellectual, for violent
209	238	or any political doctrine
210	240	Russian populism is the name
211	241	phase of economic
212	242	sprang naturally from
213	243	loathing of the rigidly
214	244	Thus they accepted, in broad
215	245	autocracy, men who would
216	246	[revolu]tionaries had come
217	248	Russian populists were agreed
218	249	persecuted religious
219	250	radical wing of the
220	251	means divert educated men
221	252	a corrupt and detested
222	253	just and free society lay
223	254	and most agonising problem
224	255	contrasted 'realism' with
225	257	theoretical generalisations, or
226	258	the peasant commune and
227	259	Chernyshevsky had evolved
228	260	Chernyshevsky believed in the
229	261	and that the maximisation
230	262	preached that there must be
231	264	unacceptable the proposition
232	265	party or of its leaders over

1978 edition	*This edition*	*1978 page begins*
233	266	These lines by Nekrasov convey
234	267	The vast leap forward
235	268	heads of self-taught peasants
236	270	bourgeois historians. Were the
237	271	Russian capitalism had
238	273	'Two things are always
239	274	and cut far deeper, in the
240	275	He looked with contempt on
241	276	'prised off the people's necks'
242	277	Like them, too, he believed
243	278	prose writers; he had a future
244	279	The sense of the contrast
245	281	as prescribed by German rules
246	282	continued to study, reject and
247	283	himself detached, whom he
248	284	vividly. The Cossacks Lukashka
249	285	[con]trived. There is no harsher word
250	286	the ripest fruits of civilisation
251	287	From this doctrine springs
252	288	with justice, that Olenin cannot
253	290	writers good is ability to see
254	291	attempted to carry out
255	292	educators seek to shape the minds
256	293	with the lives of the peasants.[1]
257	294	schools on what, less or more
258	295	with the same scorn and
259	296	thoroughly insulated from each
260	298	corruption of the civilised
261	299	You do not, I see
262	299	Vissarion Belinsky. His body
263	301	this to him in unambiguous
264	302	respect and violent criticism

1978 edition	This edition	1978 page begins
265	303	owning élite were brought into
266	304	issue, of progress against reaction
267	305	of his Russian contemporaries
268	307	pillow.[1] Memories of this kind
269	307	novels, from the middle 1850s
270	308	not live long without faith
271	310	and wait. This God does not
272	311	panacea for the 'accursed questions'
273	312	wanderings, Rudin dies bravely
274	313	are *our* Insarovs?
275	314	appeared he would not know
276	315	with conspiracy, were imprisoned
277	316	was', he wrote many years later
278	317	facts, only useful knowledge
279	319	more use than any poet
280	320	miserable dauber . . .
281	321	his hatred of art and culture
282	322	left that hurt Turgenev most
283	325	these will find the road
284	327	Yet he cannot be both
285	329	was more of an artist in his novel
286	330	police; by them he was called
287	331	Turgenev was upset and
288	332	and I ought to have foreseen
289	[333]	indignation at the mere mention
290	334	and humiliated, to rebuild his
291	336	for 'performing clownish somersaults
292	[337]	ingenuity'. When the crisis
293	338	and diversity of goals

1978 edition	This edition	1978 page begins
294	339	His sympathies, he insisted
295	340	This was the very attitude
296	341	genuine regard and, at times
297	342	and traitors. The radicals look on
298	343	repelled by the methods of the Paris
299	344	irrational and as repressive as the
300	346	and irrationalism, populist and
301	347	despise what men are and what
302	348	peculiarly Russian, is today
303	349	But why must men hurry so
304	350	twentieth century. Suvorin's
305	351	thought an informer. I imagined

Index

Douglas Matthews

Asterisked persons appear in the glossary of names